W9-BHX-511

GED® Test
FOR
DUMMIES®
A Wiley Brand

3rd Edition

by Murray Shukyn, BA,
Dale E. Shuttleworth, PhD,
and Achim K. Krull, BA, MAT

**GED® Test For Dummies®, 3rd Edition**

Published by: **John Wiley & Sons, Inc.,** 111 River Street, Hoboken, NJ 07030-5774, www.wiley.com

Copyright © 2015 by John Wiley & Sons, Inc., Hoboken, New Jersey

Published simultaneously in Canada

For general information on our other products and services, please contact our Customer Care Department within the U.S. at 877-762-2974, outside the U.S. at 317-572-3993, or fax 317-572-4002. For technical support, please visit www.wiley.com/techsupport.

Wiley publishes in a variety of print and electronic formats and by print-on-demand. Some material included with standard print versions of this book may not be included in e-books or in print-on-demand. If this book refers to media such as a CD or DVD that is not included in the version you purchased, you may download this material at http://booksupport.wiley.com. For more information about Wiley products, visit www.wiley.com.

Library of Congress Control Number: 2014935517

ISBN 978-1-118-67807-7 (pbk); ISBN 978-1-118-67819-0 (ebk); ISBN 978-1-118-67816-9 (ebk)

Manufactured in the United States of America

10  9  8  7  6  5  4  3  2  1

# Contents at a Glance

# Table of Contents

# Introduction

Perhaps you've applied for a job and have been refused an application because you don't have a high-school diploma or a General Educational Development (GED) diploma. Or maybe you were up for a promotion at work, but when your boss found out that you didn't finish high school, he said you weren't eligible for the new job. Maybe you've always wanted to go to college but couldn't even apply because the college of your choice requires a high-school diploma or equivalent (the GED diploma) for admission. Or perhaps your kids are just about to graduate from high school, and you're motivated to finish, too. Perhaps you just want to set a good example for them.

Whatever your reasons for wanting to earn a high-school diploma — whether we've mentioned them here or not — this book is for you. It helps you to prepare for the new computerized GED test — which, if you pass, offers you the equivalent of a high-school diploma without attending all the classes.

## About This Book

If you want a high-school diploma, you can always go back and finish high school the old-fashioned way. Of course, it may take you a few years, and you may have to quit your job to do it. Plus, you'd have to sit in a class with teenagers for six or so hours a day (and probably be treated like one, too). You could also try night school, but at one or two courses a year, that could take forever.

For most people, that situation doesn't sound too appealing. *GED Test For Dummies*, 3rd Edition, presents a different solution: Earn a high-school diploma and do so in the shortest time possible, without ever having to share a classroom with other people. If you don't mind preparing yourself for a series of challenging test sections that determine whether you've mastered key skills, you can get a GED diploma that's the equivalent of a high-school education — and you can do so in much less than four years.

If taking the GED test to earn your diploma sounds like a great idea to you, this book is a necessary study tool. It's a fun-filled and friendly instruction manual for succeeding on the new, all-computerized GED test. Use this book as your first stop. It isn't a subject-matter preparation book — that is, it doesn't take you through the basics of math and then progress into algebra, geometry, and so on. It does, however, prepare you for the GED test by giving you detailed information about each section, two full-length practice tests for each section (and access to more practice questions online), and plenty of easy-to-understand answers and explanations for the test questions. After taking the practice tests and going through the answers and explanations, you can determine which subject areas you need to work on.

Just as important, we walk you through how the GED test has changed. Although people needing special accommodations may still have access to the old paper-and-pencil test format, for most, it's now offered only on a computer. Having basic computer knowledge is much more important. Some of the question formats have changed as well, so knowing how to use the computer mouse and keyboard to solve them is also important.

# Foolish Assumptions

When we wrote this book, we made a few assumptions about you, dear reader. Here's who we think you are:

- ✔ You're serious about earning a high-school diploma or GED endorsement for existing qualifications as quickly as you can.

- ✔ You've made earning a high-school diploma and an endorsement a priority in your life because you want to advance in the workplace or move on to college.

- ✔ You're willing to give up some activities so you have the time to prepare, always keeping in mind your other responsibilities, too.

- ✔ You meet your state's requirements regarding age, residency, and the length of time since leaving school that make you eligible to take the GED test. (Double-check with your local GED test administrator to find out your state's requirements.)

- ✔ You have sufficient English language skills to handle the test.

- ✔ You want a fun and friendly guide that helps you achieve your goal.

If any of these descriptions sounds like you, welcome aboard. We've prepared an enjoyable tour of the GED test.

# Icons Used in This Book

Icons — little pictures you see in the margins of this book — highlight bits of text that you want to pay special attention to. Here's what each one means:

Whenever we want to tell you a special trick or technique that can help you succeed on the GED test, we mark it with this icon. Keep an eye out for this guy.

This icon points out information you want to burn into your brain. Think of the text with this icon as the sort of stuff you'd tear out and put on a bulletin board or your refrigerator.

Take this icon seriously! Although the world won't end if you don't heed the advice next to this icon, the warnings are important to your success in preparing to take the GED test.

We use this icon to flag example questions that are much like what you can expect on the actual GED test. So if you just want to get familiar with the types of questions on the test, this icon is your guide.

# Beyond the Book

In addition to the book content, you can find valuable free material online. We provide you with a Cheat Sheet that addresses things you need to know and consider when getting ready for the GED test. You can access this material at `www.dummies.com/cheatsheet/gedtest`.

We also include additional articles at `www.dummies.com/extras/gedtest`. There you can read about how to prepare for test day and how to be a winner in this challenge.

But wait, there's more!

In addition to the two complete practice exams contained in this book, your book purchase also comes with a free one-year subscription to additional practice questions that appear online. Create your own question sets and view personalized reports that show what you need to study most.

To gain access to the online practice, all you have to do is register. Just follow these simple steps:

1. **Find your PIN access code.**

   - **Print book users:** If you purchased a hard copy of this book, turn to the front cover of this book to find your access code.

   - **E-book users:** If you purchased this book as an e-book, you can get your access code by registering your e-book at `www.dummies.com/go/getaccess`. Go to this website, find your book and click it, and answer the security question to verify your purchase. Then you'll receive an e-mail with your access code.

2. **Go to `learn.dummies.com` and click Already have an Access Code?**

3. **Enter your access code and click Next.**

4. **Follow the instructions to create an account and establish your personal login information.**

That's all there is to it! You can come back to the online program again and again — simply log in with the username and password you chose during your initial login. No need to use the access code a second time. If you have trouble with the access code or can't find it, contact Wiley Product Technical Support at 877-762-2974 or `http://support.wiley.com`. Your registration is good for one year from the day you activate your access code. After that time frame has passed, you can renew your registration for a fee. The website gives you all the important details about how to do so.

For even *more* test practice, you can get a 20 percent discount on your purchase of GED Ready™ vouchers — the official practice test for the GED® test. To get your access to GED Ready™, go to `www.gedmarketplace.com/wiley` and follow the instructions provided.

# Where to Go from Here

Some people like to read books from beginning to end. Others prefer to read only the specific information they need to know now. Chapter 1 starts off with an overview of the GED test and how to register for the exam. For those less comfortable with computers, Chapter 2 provides a lot more detail about the computerized GED test and what computer basics you need to know. If you want an overview of the different types of questions and how you can prepare for those subjects, check out Chapter 3. Chapter 4 gives you plenty of hands-on material to help you leading up to and the morning of test day, including what to do right before the test starts.

The chapters in Parts II, III, IV, and V go into detail about each of the test sections, starting with Reasoning through Language Arts, then Social Studies, Science, and finally Mathematical Reasoning. In each of those parts, you can find an introduction to the specific test section, along with question types and solving strategies, and some preliminary practice questions.

When you're ready to dive into full-length practice tests that mimic the real GED test, check out Parts VI and VII and then check your answers with the detailed answer explanations we provide for each test section (but be sure to wait until *after* you take the practice test to look at the answers!).

Also, don't forget to visit this book's website for bonus content and extra practice. Go to www.dummies.com and search for this book's title.

# Part I
# Getting Started with the GED Test

# In this part . . .

✔ Discover how the GED test and its various sections are organized and what to expect on the test. Get familiar with each test section's specific focus and manner of dealing with the content.

✔ Explore the format of the computerized GED test, including how the questions are presented and how you're expected to answer them.

✔ Prepare for the actual test day, and find out what you should or shouldn't do on the day(s) before, the day of, and during the exam.

# Chapter 1

# Taking a Quick Glance at the GED Test

The GED test offers high-school dropouts, people who leave school early, and people who were educated outside the United States an opportunity to earn the equivalent of an American high-school diploma without the need for full-time attendance in either day or night school. The GED test is a recognized standard that makes securing a job or college placement easier.

The 2014 GED test has been completely revamped to bring it in line with current Grade 12 standards in the United States. It now meets the College and Career Readiness Standards for Adult Education. The GED test also covers the Common Core Standards, used by 46 states. These standards are based on the actual expectations stated by employers and postsecondary institutions.

The GED test measures whether you understand what high-school seniors across the country have studied before they graduate. Employers need better-educated employees. In addition, some colleges may be uncertain of the quality of foreign credentials. The GED diploma provides those assurances. When you pass the GED test, you earn a high-school equivalency diploma. That can open many doors for you — perhaps doors that you don't even know exist at this point.

You may wonder why you should even bother taking the GED test and getting your GED diploma. People with high-school diplomas earn more and spend less time unemployed than people without. Some 59 percent of people with a high-school diploma or GED were employed full-time or part-time, compared to only 49 percent without a high-school diploma. Incomes were about 30 percent higher for high-school (or GED) graduates than people without high-school diplomas.

Ready to get started? This chapter gives you the basics of the GED test: how the test is now administered, what the test sections look like, how to schedule the test, including whether you're eligible, and how the scores are calculated (so you know what you need to pass).

## What to Expect: The New Testing Format

A computer now administers the GED test. That means that all the questions appear on a computer screen, and you enter all your answers into a computer. You read, calculate, evaluate, analyze, and write everything on the computer. Even for work like rough math calculations or draft essay writing, you don't use paper. Instead, the test centers provide you with an erasable tablet. If you know how to use a computer and are comfortable with a keyboard and a mouse, you're ahead of the game. If not, practice your keyboarding. Also, practice reading from a computer screen because reading from a screen is very different from reading printed materials. At the very least, you need to get more comfortable with computers, even if that means taking a short course at a local learning emporium. In the case of the GED test, the more familiar you are with computers, the more comfortable you'll feel taking the computerized test.

Under certain circumstances, as a special accommodation, the sections are available in booklet format. Check with the GED Testing Service to see what exceptions are acceptable.

The computer-based GED test allows for speedy detailed feedback on your performance. When you pass (yes, we said *when* and not *if,* because we believe in you), the GED Testing Service provides both a diploma and a detailed transcript of your scores, similar to what high-school graduates receive. They're now available online at www.gedtestingservice. com within a day of completing the test. You can then send your transcript and diploma to an employer or college. Doing so allows employers and colleges access to a detailed outline of your scores, achievement, and demonstrated skills and abilities. This outline is also a useful tool for you to review your progress. It highlights those areas where you did well and areas where you need further work. If you want to (or have to) retake the test, these results will provide a detailed guide to what you should work on to improve your scores. Requests for additional copies of transcripts are handled online and also are available within a day.

# Reviewing the Test Sections

The GED test includes the following four sections (also referred to as tests), each of which you can take separately:

- Reasoning through Language Arts
- Social Studies
- Science
- Mathematical Reasoning

You can take each of the four test sections separately, at different times, and in any order you want. This is one of the benefits of doing the test by computer. Because everyone is working individually on the various test sections rather than as a group exam, the computer-based test eliminates the need for the whole group of test-takers to work in tandem. For example, you may be working on the Mathematical Reasoning test, while your neighbor is working on the Social Studies test. Just don't look around at all your neighbors to verify this because proctors may think you're doing more than satisfying your curiosity.

The following sections offer a closer look into what the test sections cover and what you can expect.

Because the computerized GED test is new and still evolving as we write this book, be sure to check out the latest and greatest about the GED test at www.gedtestingservice.com.

## Reasoning through Language Arts test

The Reasoning through Language Arts (RLA) test is one long test that covers all the literacy components of the GED test. You have 150 minutes overall. However, the test is divided into three sections: first, you have 35 minutes on all content in question-and-answer format, then 45 minutes for the Extended Response (essay), followed by a 10-minute break, and then another 60 minutes for more general test items. Remember that the time for the Extended Response can't be used to work on the other questions in the test, nor can you use leftover time from the other sections on the Extended Response.

Here's what you can expect on the RLA test:

- The literacy component asks you to correct text, respond to writings, and generally demonstrate a critical understanding of various passages. This includes demonstrating a command of proper grammar, punctuation, and spelling.

- The Extended Response item, also known as "the essay," examines your skills in organizing your thoughts and writing clearly. Your response will be based on one or two source text selections, drawing key elements from that material to prepare your essay.

  The essay is evaluated both on your interpretation of the source texts and the quality of your writing. You type on the computer, using a tool that resembles a word processor. It has neither a spell-checker nor a grammar-checker. How well you use spelling and grammar as you write is also part of your evaluation. You'll have an erasable tablet on which to prepare a draft before writing the final document.

- The scores from both components will be combined into one single score for the RLA test.

The question-answer part of this test consists mainly of various types of multiple-choice questions (also called items) and the occasional fill-in-the-blank question. Most items will be in the traditional multiple-choice format with four answer choices, but you'll also see drag-and-drop and drop-down menu items. For details on the different question types, see Chapters 2 and 3.

These items are based on source texts, which are materials presented to you for your response. Some of this source material is nonfiction, from science and social studies content as well as from the workplace. Only 25 percent is based on literature. Here's a breakdown of the materials:

- **Workplace materials:** These include work-related letters, memos, and instructions that you may see on the job.

- **U.S. founding documents and documents that present part of the Great American Conversation:** These may include extracts from the Bill of Rights, the Constitution, and other historical documents. They also may include opinion pieces of relevant issues in American history and civics.

- **Informational works:** These include documents that present information (often dry and boring information), such as the instructional manual that tells you how to set the clock on your DVD player. They also include materials that you may find in history, social studies, or science books.

- **Literature:** Extracts from novels, plays, and similar materials.

You find a variety of problems in the RLA test, including the following:

- **Correction:** In these items, you're asked to correct sentences presented to you.

- **Revision:** In these items, you're presented with a sentence that has a word or phrase underlined. If the sentence needs a correction, one of the answer choices will be better than the words or phrase underlined. If no correction is needed, either one of the answer choices will be the same as the underlined portion or one of the choices will be something like "no correction needed."

- **Construction shift:** In these types of problems, you have to correct a sentence by altering the sentence structure. The original sentence may not be completely wrong, but it can be improved with a little editing. In these cases, the question presents you with optional rewording or allows you to change the sentence order in a paragraph.

✔ **Text analysis:** These problems require you to read a passage and respond in some manner. It may be an analysis of the content, a critique of the style, review for biases or other influences, or responses to something in the content.

See Chapters 3, 5, 6 and 7 for the lowdown on the RLA test and Chapters 17 and 25 for two practice Reasoning through Language Arts tests, with answers and explanations in Chapters 18 and 26. Check out Chapter 2 for the format of the items as they appear on the computer.

## Social Studies test

The Social Studies test is scheduled for 90 minutes. Sixty-five minutes are allocated for the multiple-choice and fill-in-the-blank questions, whereas the Extended Response item (an essay) is allowed 25 minutes. Here's a breakdown of what you'll see on this test:

✔ **Multiple-choice and fill-in-the-blank questions:** The source text and data for these question types varies. About half of the questions are based on one source item, such as a graph or text, with one question. Other items have a single source item, such as a graph or text, as the basis for several questions. In either case, you'll need to analyze and evaluate the content presented to you as part of the question. The test items evaluate your ability to answer questions, using reasoning and analysis skills. The information for the source materials comes from primary and secondary sources, both text and visual. That means you need to be able to "read" charts, tables, maps, and graphs as well as standard text materials.

✔ **Extended Response:** This part of the Social Studies test requires similar skills and works much like the RLA Extended Response (refer to the previous section on Reasoning through Language Arts). You're presented with one or two source texts, and your assignment is to evaluate the source text. You need to consider the quality of the argument(s) presented and then write an essay responding to and evaluating the opinions or information presented.

The content of the Social Studies test is drawn from these four basic areas:

✔ **Civics and government:** The largest part (about 50 percent of the test) focuses on civics and government. The civics and government items examine the development of democracy, from ancient times to modern days. Other topics include how civilizations change over time and respond to crises.

✔ **American history:** American history makes up 20 percent of the test. It covers all topics from the pilgrims and early settlement to the Revolution, Civil War, World Wars I and II, Vietnam War, and current history — all of which involve the United States in one way or another.

✔ **Economics:** Economics make up about 15 percent of the test. The economics portion examines basic theories, such as supply and demand, the role of government policies in the economy, and macro- and microeconomic theory.

✔ **Geography and the world:** This area also makes up 15 percent of the test. The areas with which you need to become familiar are very topical: sustainability and environmental issues, population issues, and rural and urban settlement. Other topics include cultural diversity and migration and those issues that are of universal and not national concern.

# Science test

The Science test is scheduled for 90 minutes. Our advice for the Science test is very similar to the Reasoning through Language Arts test. Most importantly, read as much as you can, especially science material. Whenever you don't understand a word or concept, look it up in a dictionary or online. The items in the Science test assume a high-school level of science vocabulary.

You don't have to be a nuclear physicist to answer the questions, but you should be familiar with the vocabulary normally understood by someone completing high school. If you work at improving your scientific vocabulary, you should have little trouble with the Science test. (*Note:* That same advice applies to all the GED test's sections. Improve your vocabulary in each subject, and you'll perform better.)

The Science test concentrates on two main themes:

- ✔ Human health and living systems
- ✔ Energy and related systems

In addition, the content of the problems focus on one of the following areas:

- ✔ **Physical science:** About 40 percent of the test focuses on physics and chemistry, including topics such as conservation, transformation, and flow of energy; work, motion, and forces; and chemical properties and reactions related to living systems.

- ✔ **Life science:** Another 40 percent of the Science test deals with life science, including biology and, more specifically, human body and health, relationship between life functions and energy intake, ecosystems, structure and function of life, and molecular basis for heredity and evolution.

- ✔ **Earth and space science:** This area makes up the remaining 20 percent of this test and includes astronomy — interaction between Earth's systems and living things, Earth and its system components and interactions, and structure and organization of the cosmos.

Go ahead and type in one of the three areas of content into your favorite search engine to find material to read. You'll find links to articles and material from all different levels. Filter your choices by the level you want and need — for example, use keywords such as "scientific theories," "scientific discoveries," "scientific method," "human health," "living systems," "energy," "the universe," "organisms," and "geochemical systems" — and don't get discouraged if you can't understand technical material that one scientist wrote that only about three other scientists in the world can understand.

Items in the Science test are in multiple-choice, fill-in-the-blank, hot-spot, and drop-down format. (See the sections on Reasoning through Language Arts and Mathematical Reasoning for descriptions of these types of items.) In addition, the Science test includes two Short Answer items that are basically short essays to be completed in about ten minutes based on a stimulus and a response to a prompt.

# Mathematical Reasoning test

The Mathematical Reasoning (Math) test checks your mathematics that you'd normally know by the end of high school. Because this new test is designed to prepare you for both postsecondary education and employment, it has an emphasis on both workplace-related mathematics and academic mathematics. About 45 percent of the test is about quantitative problem solving, and the rest is about algebra.

The Math test consists of different question formats to be completed in 115 minutes. Because the GED test is now administered on the computer, the questions (or items) take advantage of the power of the computer. Check out Chapters 2 and 3 for more information and a sneak peek of what the items look like.

Here are the types of items that you'll encounter in the Math test:

- **Multiple-choice:** Most of the items in the Math test are multiple-choice because this type of question is still one of the most used formats for standardized tests.

- **Drop-down:** This type of question is a form of multiple-choice in that you get a series of possible answers, one of which is correct. The only difference is that you see all the options at once within the text where it's to be used. For an example, see Chapters 2 and 3.

- **Fill-in-the-blank and hot-spot:** In these types of items, you have to provide an answer. The fill-in-the-blank items are straightforward: You're asked for a very specific answer, either a number or one or two words, and you type the answer into the space provided. Hot-spot items use an embedded sensor within an image on the computer screen. You use the mouse to move data to that spot or plot data on a graphic. The secret of doing well on these questions is still to read them carefully and answer what is asked from the information given. These types of problems don't have any tricks, except the ones you may play on yourself by reading information into them that isn't there.

Some items may be stand-alone with only one question for each problem, or stimulus. Others may have multiple items based on a single stimulus. Each stimulus, no matter how many items are based on it, may be text, graphs, tables, or other representation of numbers, geometrical, or algebraic materials. Practice reading mathematical materials and become familiar with the vocabulary of mathematics.

# It's a Date: Scheduling the Test

To take the GED test, you schedule it based on the available testing dates. Each state or local testing center sets its own schedule for the GED test, which means that your state decides how and when you can take each section of the test. It also determines how often you can retake a failed section. Because a computer now administers the test, you can schedule an individual appointment. Your test starts when you start and ends when your allotted time is completed. The test centers are small computer labs, often containing no more than 15 seats, and actual testing facilities are located in many communities in your state.

You book your appointment through the GED Testing Service (www.gedtestingservice. com). Your local GED test administrator can give you all the information you need about scheduling the test. In addition, local school districts and community colleges can provide information about local test centers in your area.

Sending a specific question or request to www.gedtestingservice.com may come with a charge for the service. To save money, you're better off asking a person at your local testing center. That way, you don't have to pay for the privilege of asking a question, and your answer will be based on rules and conditions specific to your area.

The following sections answer some questions you may have before you schedule your test date, including whether you're even eligible to take the test, when you can take the test, and how to sign up to take the test.

## Determining whether you're eligible

Before you schedule your test, make sure you meet the requirements to take the GED test. You're eligible to apply to take the GED test only if

- ✔ **You're not currently enrolled in a high school.** If you're currently enrolled in a high school, you're expected to complete your diploma there. The purpose of the GED test is to give people who aren't in high school a chance to get an equivalent high-school diploma.

- ✔ **You're not a high-school graduate.** If you're a high-school graduate, you should have a diploma, which means you don't need to take the GED test. However, you can use the GED to upgrade or update your skills and to prove that you're ready for further education and training.

- ✔ **You meet state requirements regarding age, residency, and the length of time since leaving high school.** Check with your local GED test administrator to determine your state's requirements concerning these criteria. Residency requirements are an issue, because you may have to take the test in a different jurisdiction, depending on how long you've lived at your present address.

## Knowing when you can take the test

You can take the GED test when you're eligible and prepared. You can then apply to take the GED test as soon as you want. Just contact your local testing center or www. gedtestingservice.com for a test schedule. Pick a day (or days) that works for you.

Taking all four sections of the GED test together takes about seven hours. However, the test is now designed so that you can take each section when you're ready. In most areas, you can take the test sections one at a time, in the evening or on weekends, depending on the individual testing center. If you pass one test section, that section of the GED test is considered done, no matter how you do on the other sections. If you fail one section, you can retake that section of the test at any time. How the test is administered varies from state to state, so check with www.gedtestingservice.com or your local high-school guidance office.

Because the test starts when you're ready and finishes when you have used up the allocated time, you can take it alone and don't have to depend on other people. For you, that means you may be able to find locations that offer the testing in evenings or weekends as well as during regular business hours. Even better, because you don't have to take the test with a group, you may be able to set an individual starting time that suits you.

If circumstances dictate that you must take the paper version of the test, you'll probably have to forgo the flexibility afforded by the computer. Check well in advance to see what the rules are for you.

You can also apply to take the test if you're not prepared, but if you do that, you don't stand a very good chance of passing. If you do need to retake any section of the test, use your time before your next test date to get ready. You can retake the test only three times, and, in most jurisdictions, taking the test costs money (check with your local testing center to find out specifics for your area). To save time and money, prepare before you schedule the test. Refer to the later section "Knowing what to do if you score poorly on one or more tests" for details.

## Are special accommodations available?

If you need to complete the test on paper or have a disability that makes it impossible for you to use the computer, your needs can be accommodated. However, other specifics apply: Your choice of times and testing locations may be much more restricted, but times to complete a test may be extended. Remember also that if accommodation is required, the GED testing centers will ask for documentation of the nature of the accommodation required.

The GED testing centers make every effort to ensure that all qualified people have access to the tests. If you have a disability, you may not be able to register for the tests and take them the same week, but, with some advanced planning, you can probably take the tests when you're ready. Here's what you need to do:

✔ Check with your local testing center or check out www.gedtestingservice.com/testers/accommodations-for-disability.

✔ Contact the GED Testing Service or your local GED test center and explain your disability.

✔ Request any forms that you have to fill out for your special circumstances.

✔ Ensure that you have a recent diagnosis by a physician or other qualified professional.

✔ Complete all the proper forms and submit them with medical or professional diagnosis.

✔ Start planning early so that you're able to take the tests when you're ready.

Note that, regardless of your disability, you still have to be able to handle the mental and emotional demands of the test.

The GED Testing Service in Washington, D.C., defines specific disabilities, such as the following, for which it may make special accommodations, provided the disability severely limits your ability to perform essential skills required to pass the GED test:

✔ Medical disabilities, such as cerebral palsy, epilepsy, or blindness

✔ Psychological disabilities, such as schizophrenia, major depression, attention deficit disorder, or Tourette's syndrome

✔ Specific learning disabilities, including perceptual handicaps, brain injury, minimal brain dysfunction, dyslexia, and developmental aphasia

## Signing up

When you're actually ready to sign up for the test, follow these steps:

1. **Contact your local GED test administrator or go to** www.gedtestingservice.com **to make sure you're eligible.**

   Refer to the earlier section "Determining whether you're eligible" for some help.

2. **Ask the office for an application (if needed) or an appointment.**

3. **Complete the application (if needed).**

4. **Return the application to the proper office, with payment, if necessary.**

   The fees vary state by state, so contact your local administrator or testing site to find out what you have to pay to take the tests. In some states, if you fall into a low-income bracket, you may be eligible for financial assistance.

*Note:* You can also do all of this online, including submitting the payment, either with your computer, tablet, or smartphone. Go to www.gedtestingservice.com to start the process.

Never send cash by mail to pay for the GED test. Most local administrators have payment rules and don't accept cash.

## Working with unusual circumstances

If you feel that you may have a special circumstance that prevents you from taking the GED test at a pre-set schedule, contact the GED test administrator in your area. If, for example, the test is going to be held on your sabbath, the testing center may make special arrangements for you.

When applying for special circumstances, keep the following guidelines in mind:

- ✔ Document everything in your appeal for special consideration.

- ✔ Contact the GED test administrator in your area as early as you can.

- ✔ Be patient. Special arrangements can't be made overnight. The administrator often has to wait for a group with similar issues to gather so he can make arrangements for the entire group.

- ✔ Ask questions. Accommodations can be made if you ask. For example, special allowances include extended time for various disabilities, large print and Braille for visual impairments, and age (for those individuals older than 60 who feel they may have a learning disability).

# Taking the GED Test When English Is Your Second Language

The good news is that English doesn't have to be your first language for you to take the GED test. The GED test is offered in English, Spanish, and French. If you want to take the test in Spanish or French, contact your local GED test administrator so you can apply.

If English, Spanish, or French isn't your first language, you must decide whether you can read and write English as well as or better than 40 percent of high-school graduates because you may be required to pass an English as a Second Language (ESL) placement test. If you write and read English well, prepare for and take the test (either in English or in Spanish or French). If you don't read or write English well, take additional classes to improve your language skills until you think you're ready. An English Language Proficiency Test (ELPT) is also available for people who completed their education in other countries. For more information about the language component of the GED test, check out www.gedtestingservice.com/testers/special-test-editions.

In many ways, the GED test is like the Test of English as a Foreign Language (TOEFL) comprehension test. If you've completed the TOEFL test with good grades, you're likely ready to take the GED test. If you haven't taken the TOEFL test, enroll in a GED test-preparation course to see whether you have difficulty understanding the subjects and skills assessed on the test. GED test courses provide you with some insight into your comprehension ability with a teacher to discuss your skills and struggles.

## Websites that can help you plan to take the GED test

The Internet is a helpful and sometimes scary place. Some websites are there to help you in your GED test preparation, while others just want to sell you something. You have to know how to separate the good from the bad. Here are a couple of essential ones (most are accessible through `www.gedtestingservice.com`):

✔ `adulted.about.com/od/getting yourged/a/stateged.htm` is a website that links to the GED test eligibility requirements and testing locations in your state.

✔ `usaeducation.info/Tests/GED/ International-students.aspx` is a site that explains GED test eligibility for foreign students.

If you're curious and want to see what's out there, type in "GED test" into any search engine and relax while you try to read about 22 million results, ranging from the helpful to the helpless. We suggest leaving this last activity until after you've passed the tests. As useful as the Internet can be, it still provides the opportunity to waste vast amounts of time. And right now, you need to spend your time preparing for the test — and leave the rest for after you get your diploma.

# Figuring Out What You Have to Score to Pass the GED Test

To pass, you need to score a minimum of 150 on each section of the test, and you must pass each section of the test to earn your GED diploma. If you achieve a passing score, congratulate yourself: You've scored better than at least 40 percent of today's high-school graduates, and you're now a graduate of the largest virtual school in the country. And if your marks are in the honors range, you're ready for college or career training.

Be aware that some colleges require scores higher than the minimum passing score. If you plan to apply to postsecondary schools or some other form of continuing education, check with their admissions office for the minimum admission score requirements.

The following sections address a few more points you may want to know about how the GED test is scored and what you can do if you score poorly on some or all of the test sections.

## Identifying how scores are determined

Correct answers may be worth one, two, or more points, depending on the item and the level of difficulty. The Extended Response (also known as the essay) is scored separately. However, the Extended Response is only part of the Reasoning through Language Arts and Social Studies tests. On each test section, you must accumulate a minimum of 150 points.

The computerized GED test is new and still evolving as we write this book. For the most up-to-date details on the scoring for each section of the GED test, check out `www.ged testingservice.com`.

Because you don't lose points for incorrect answers, make sure you answer all the items on each test. After all, a guessed answer can get you a point. Leaving an answer blank, on the other hand, gives you only a zero. Refer to Chapter 4 for some hints to help you narrow down your choices.

## Knowing what to do if you score poorly on one or more tests

If you discover that your score is less than 150 on any test section, start planning to retake the test(s) — and make sure you leave plenty of time for additional studying and preparing.

As soon as possible after seeing your results, contact your local GED test administrator to find out the rules for retaking the failed section of the test. Some states may ask that you wait a certain amount of time and/or limit the number of attempts each year. Some may ask that you attend a preparation course and show that you've completed it before you can take the GED test again. Some may charge you an additional fee. However, you need to retake only those sections of the test that you failed. Any sections you pass are completed and count toward your diploma. Furthermore, the detailed evaluation of your results will help you discover areas of weakness that need more work before redoing any section of the test.

One advantage of taking the GED test on a computer is that you can receive, within a day, detailed feedback on how you did, which includes some specific recommendations of what you need to do to improve your scores.

No matter what score you receive on your first round of the section, don't be afraid to retake any section that you didn't pass. After you've taken it once, you know what you need to work on, and you know exactly what to expect on test day. Just take a deep breath, and get ready to prepare some more before you take your next test.

# Chapter 2

# Examining the Ins and Outs of the New Computerized GED Test

* * * * * * * * * * * * * * * * * * * * * * * * * * * * * * * * * * * * * * * *

## In This Chapter

▶ Getting familiar with the keyboard and mouse for the computerized GED test

▶ Checking out the specific types of questions as they appear on the new GED test

* * * * * * * * * * * * * * * * * * * * * * * * * * * * * * * * * * * * * * * *

The new GED test is offered only on a computer, which means that the test format looks quite different from the old paper version. No longer do you have to fill in little circles or use a pencil or scratchpad. Now everything is paperless, even the scratchpad of previous years has been upgraded to an erasable tablet. Now you enter all your answers into the computer. You use the keyboard to type your essay or the mouse to click on your answer choice.

This chapter provides what you need to know for using the computer to take the GED test and explains the different formats of questions on the GED test. We even throw in a few sample questions to ensure that you understand this important information. Demonstrating how to take a test on a computer with a printed book isn't easy, but this chapter includes several screenshots of question formats and other images you need to understand to be successful. All you have to do is read and digest it. We can't promise you a banquet of information, but this chapter is at least a satisfying meal to help you prepare for the next big step on your road to the future.

## Familiarizing Yourself with the Computer

When taking the computerized GED test, you have two important tools to allow you to answer questions: the keyboard and the mouse. The following sections examine each of them in greater depth and explain exactly how you use them to complete the GED test. Make sure you understand the mechanics and use of the keyboard and mouse beforehand so you don't end up wasting valuable time trying to figure all of this stuff out on test day when you should be answering the questions.

Because bundling the book with a computer would make it very expensive, we developed a different way for you to interact with the GED test questions in this book. We present items in a format somewhat similar to the computer screen for that type of question's format, and you mark your choice directly in the book. Then, you get to check your answer and read the answer explanation. Make sure you read the explanations even if you got the answer right because they provide additional information that may help with other questions. That type of presentation may not be the most technologically savvy, but it does prepare you for the types of questions you'll encounter in the various sections of the GED test. For the practice tests in Parts VI and VII, we provide an answer sheet for you to mark your answer, and we give you the correct answer and detailed explanations for each test in a separate chapter.

## Typing on the keyboard

You need to have at least some familiarity with a computer's keyboard. If you constantly make typing errors or aren't familiar with the keyboard, you may be in trouble. The good news is that you don't have to be a keyboarding whiz. In fact, the behind-the-scenes GED people have shown through their research that even people with minimal keyboarding skills still have adequate time to complete the test.

On the GED test, you'll use the keyboard to type your answers in the essay (Extended Response) segments in the Reasoning through Language Arts and the Social Studies tests and in the Short Answer segment of the Science test. Although you may be familiar with typing by using one or two fingers on your smartphone or tablet, with the screen often predicting and suggesting words that you need with correctly spelled words, the word processor on the GED test for the Extended Response and Short Answer items has a bare minimum of features. It accepts keyboard entries, cuts, pastes, and copies, but no more. It doesn't have a grammar-checker or a spell-checker, so be careful with your keyboarding because spelling and grammatical errors are just that — errors.

The GED test uses the standard English keyboard (see Figure 2-1), so if you're not familiar with it, take time to acquaint yourself with it before you take the GED test. If you're used to other language keyboards, the English keyboard has some letters and punctuation in different places. Before test day, practice using the English keyboard so that the differences in the keyboard don't throw you off the day of the test. You won't have time to figure out the keyboard while the clock is ticking.

**Figure 2-1:**
An example standard English keyboard.

©John Wiley & Sons, Inc.

To complete the test in the required time, you should have

(A)  comfortable running shoes

(B)  minimal keyboarding skills

(C)  really strong thumbs

(D)  lots of coffee at your desk

Choice (B) is the correct answer. In preliminary testing, the GED test-makers and bigwigs found that test-takers with minimal keyboarding skills were able to complete the test in the time allotted. That doesn't mean that working on your keyboarding skills is a waste of time. The better these skills are, the faster you can type in answers, and the more time you'll have for the difficult questions.

You may want to wear comfortable running shoes, as Choice (A) suggests, but that in itself won't help you finish the test in the allotted time, although it may make you more comfortable sitting for all those hours. Choice (C) would be useful if you submitted your answers by texting, but on the computerized GED test, you have to use a traditional keyboard, which requires the use of your fingers and knowing which keys are where. Choice (D) may present you with a new set of problems. Computers and liquids don't go well together, and in most cases, the test centers don't let you take liquids into the test room.

You don't need to become a perfect typist, but you should at least be comfortable pecking away with a couple of fingers. If you want to improve your typing skills, search online in your favorite search engine with the keywords "free typing tutor." Any number of free programs can teach you basic typing skills. (Just know that some software may be free to try for a short period of time or may be loaded with ads.)

When looking at the keyboard, you have to remember that

(A) all keyboards are the same

(B) keyboards from different countries have some letters in different locations

(C) you should always use the space bar with your little finger

(D) touch typists don't have to worry about where the keys are located

Choice (B) is correct. Keyboards from different countries have letters and punctuation in different locations and could present problems to touch typists who have memorized the location of each letter so they don't have to look at the keyboard. Choices (A), (C), and (D) are wrong.

## Clicking and dragging with the mouse

Most questions on the GED test require no more than the ability to use the mouse to point to a selection for your answer and then click on that item, which is very basic. If you're unfamiliar with computers, take time to become familiar with the mouse, including the clickable buttons and the scroll wheel. If the mouse has a scroll wheel, you can use it to move up or down through text or images. When you hold down the left button on the mouse, it highlights text as you drag the cursor across the screen, or you can "drag and drop" items on the screen, like you do when playing Solitaire on the computer.

On the GED test, you'll use the mouse to answer the four main question types: multiple-choice, fill-in-the-blank, drop-down menu, and drag and drop. You'll use both the mouse and the keyboard to answer Extended Responses and Short Answers (the essays). Refer to Chapter 1 for more basics about these types of problems. Here, we simply explain how to use your computer to solve them.

On the new series of GED tests, you indicate your choice of answer by

(A) using a pencil

(B) tapping the screen

(C) clicking the mouse

(D) yelling it out

The correct answer is Choice (C). For most questions, the mouse is your best friend because you use it to indicate the correct answer. The present test computers don't have a touch screen. Tapping on them will only leave fingerprints, so Choice (B) is wrong. If you're going to use a pencil to indicate your answer (Choice [A]), you're taking the wrong version of the GED test or you'll look silly trying to mark on the computer screen with a pencil. If you chose Choice (D), you'll, at a minimum, be ejected from the test site for being a nuisance and a possible cheater.

Fill-in-the-blanks are another type of question you'll encounter on the GED test. They're simply statements with a blank box in the text somewhere. To complete the sentence, you need to enter a word(s), name, or number. The statement will be preceded by directions setting up the text, so you'll know what is expected. Here's an example.

## Getting more help with your computer skills

Some websites offer free training on basic computer skills, but you need a computer to use them. Your local library should have free computer access if you don't have your own. Many libraries and community agencies offer free computer classes that are worth checking out. If you're a bit computer savvy, type "basic computer skills training + free" into a search engine and follow the links until you find one that suits you. Be aware that free or limited-time trial software can be full of advertising.

Take your time at home or in the library developing your skills and working through the practice tests. Test day isn't the time to figure out how to use the computer.

Try this question:

A good place to get help using a computer is

(A) your local school

(B) the Internet

(C) libraries

(D) all of the above

The correct answer is Choice (D). Any place that offers instruction in using a computer is a good place to go for help.

*Type the appropriate word in the box.*

The fill-in-the-blank question simply consists of a statement and a sentence with a [     ] into which you type the appropriate text.

The correct answer is *box*.

You must type the precise word or number required. Spelling mistakes, misplaced decimals, and even wrong capitalization count as errors.

# Recognizing What the Questions Look Like on the Computer Screen

As you take the computerized GED test, you'll encounter four main types of problems to solve: multiple-choice, fill-in-the-blank, drop-down menu, and drag and drop. You may also have to deal with hot-spot questions and Short Answers, depending on the test section. The hot spot is simply an area on the screen that reacts when you roll the mouse pointer over it. It appears mainly on the Mathematical Reasoning and Science tests, where it allows you to work with graphs or charts.

The following sections show you what the different questions look like on the screen in the different test sections and explain how to answer these questions.

## Reasoning through Language Arts test

The Reasoning through Language Arts (RLA) test puts several skills to work, including reading and comprehension, grammar and spelling, and writing skills. Most of the content for answering literature and comprehension questions is in the source text itself, but for grammar and spelling, you need to know the answers from your studying.

### Multiple-choice questions

Like in all the four test sections, the multiple-choice question is the most popular. The basic multiple-choice question, as shown in Figure 2-2, looks very similar to what you may expect. It's presented in split-screen form, with the source text on the left and the question and answer choices on the right. You read the question and the source text first and then answer the question. If the source text extends beyond one screen, you use the scroll bar on the right side of the left screen. When you're ready to answer, use the mouse to click on the appropriate answer, and then click on Next to continue.

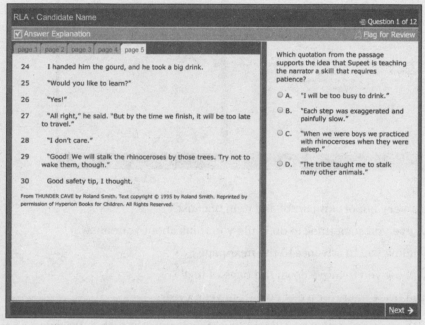

**Figure 2-2:** An example of a standard multiple-choice question.

© 2014 GED Testing Service LLC

If a scroll bar accompanies the source text on the left side of the screen, some of the text isn't visible unless you scroll down. If that scroll bar is on the answer side, some of the answer choices may not be visible without scrolling. This is important to remember because you may miss some important text when trying to answer the item.

The scroll bar in some questions will help you

(A) find scrolls

(B) move around the screen

(C) go on to the next question

(D) recognize that more text is above or below what is currently on the screen

Choice (D) is correct. The scroll bar is simply a visual reminder that the text is longer than what's shown on the screen. It doesn't help you do anything else — not move around the screen, go to the next question, or find scrolls.

Sometimes the source text consists of several screen pages (see Figure 2-3). The tabs at the top of the page are your clue. They actually look like tabs on file folders. Each one opens a different page in the source text when you click on the tab. Remember that you must read all the text to be able to answer the question. Notice, too, that the question side of the screen doesn't change as you go through the tabs. Otherwise, it works the same way: read, decide on an answer, click on the matching choice, and then click on Next to continue.

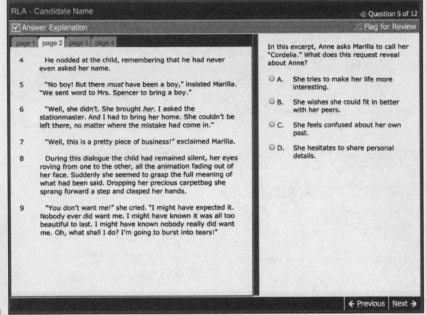

**Figure 2-3:**
An example of a multiple-choice question with tabs.

Tabs are a very important part of any item because

(A)  they give you something to do while you think about your answer

(B)  they allow you to advance to the next page

(C)  they allow you to move down the page of text

(D)  it's the trade name for a diet cola from yesteryear

Choice (B) is the correct answer. If you have to advance through a passage, the tabs give you the mechanism to do so. If you choose not to use the tabs, you'll be able to read only one page of the passage. Because the answer to the item is dependent on all the presented material, it puts you at a major disadvantage.

Most of the items on the test will be some form of multiple-choice, presented in a manner as the preceding two examples.

### Drag-and-drop questions

The RLA test also uses other question formats suited to computer testing. The drag-and-drop question (see Figure 2-4) is one variation. The source text, an excerpt from *Anne of Green Gables*, is on the left side of the screen.

This question covers more than one page, accessible via the tabs at the top of the screen. On the answer side, the scroll bar indicates that the content continues on, and you must scroll down to see it all (see Figure 2-5). When you scroll down, you can see the content you missed on the initial screen.

After you finish reading the content under all four tabs, drag the choices on the right into the boxes. You click on the item, and without letting go of the mouse button, you drag the item up to the correct box. Let go of the mouse, and the item drops into the box. If you've moved it properly, it will stay where you dropped it.

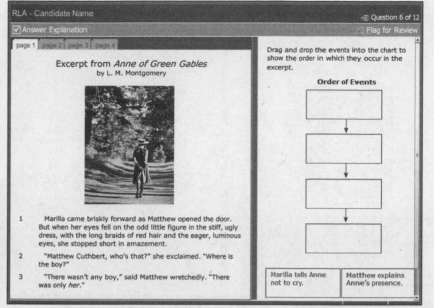

**Figure 2-4:**
An example of a drag-and-drop question using boxes.

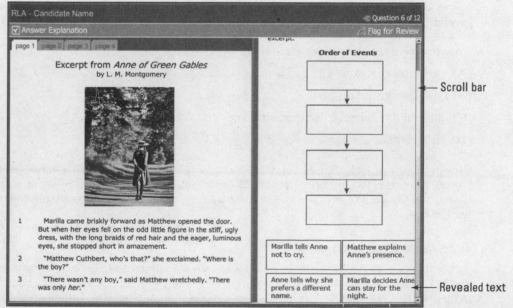

**Figure 2-5:**
Use the scroll bar to scroll down.

Figure 2-6 shows another sample drag-and-drop problem. This question uses the same four-page source text and asks you to select characteristics that apply to Anne. The key is that you can select only three of the five listed words. That isn't stated in the question but is obvious from the drag-and-drop targets, which include only three spaces. You have to read the text carefully to find the correct choices. When you decide which words apply, drag each word to one of the drop targets and leave it there. Click on Next to continue.

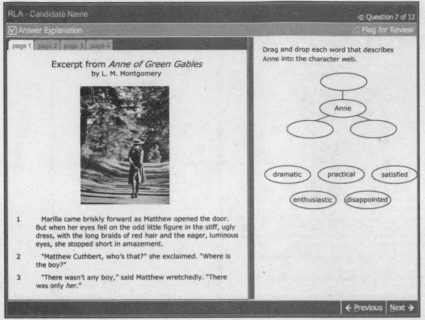

**Figure 2-6:** Another drag-and-drop example.

In this book, you clearly can't drag and drop on the practice tests, so for questions in this format, you indicate your answer on the answer sheet.

Answering a drag-and-drop question on the computer requires you to

(A) move the computer desk to a new location

(B) type directly into a box

(C) click on and move an answer choice

(D) play yet another game of Scrabble

Choice (C) is correct. Choice (A) refers more to rearranging furniture and not taking a test. Choice (B) refers to the directions for fill-in-the-blank, Extended Response, or Short Answer items, and Choice (D) is a prescription for wasting time that could be better spent preparing for the test.

### Drop-down menu questions

You'll also encounter other more technologically enhanced questions. One type asks you to correct, edit, or generally improve samples of writing. In Figure 2-7, the source text contains drop-down menus. In one line of the text, you see a blank space and the word *Select . . .* with an arrow next to it. When you click on that line, a number of variations appear. You pick the best choice as your answer. Figure 2-8 shows what you see when you click on the Select line.

From the context of the letter in the item, you have to select the sentence that fits best and shows both correct grammar and correct spelling. Move the mouse to the proper choice and let go. The corrected wording will appear in the space. You can now read the entire text to review and decide whether you indeed selected the appropriate choice. Figure 2-9 is a close-up of one item where the drop-down menu asks you to choose only a single correct word.

For the purposes of this book, the drop-down menu questions look a lot like multiple-choice questions. We include a list of answer choices for you to choose from, labeled with A, B, C, and D. Just know that on the computerized GED test, you'll have to click on Select to view the answer choices.

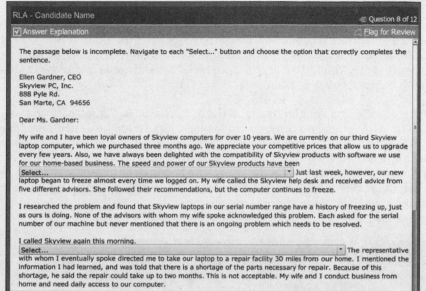

**Figure 2-7:**
An example of a drop-down menu question.

© 2014 GED Testing Service LLC

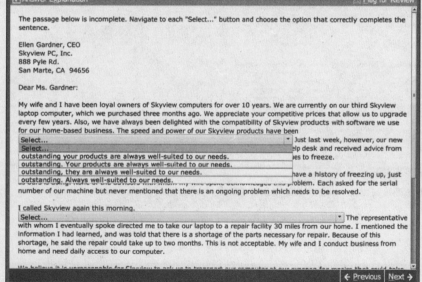

**Figure 2-8:**
Click on Select and a variety of answer choices appear in that line.

© 2014 GED Testing Service LLC

We would like to give Skyview the opportunity to remedy this situation. We firmly believe that Skyview needs to stand behind its products. If our laptop has a problem which makes it unusable, Skyview should immediately replace it with one that works, with as little inconvenience to Select... ▾ as possible.

Select...
We look forward to hearing from you about how | it | to resolve this issue.
us
Sincerely yours, | him
both
James Hendricks

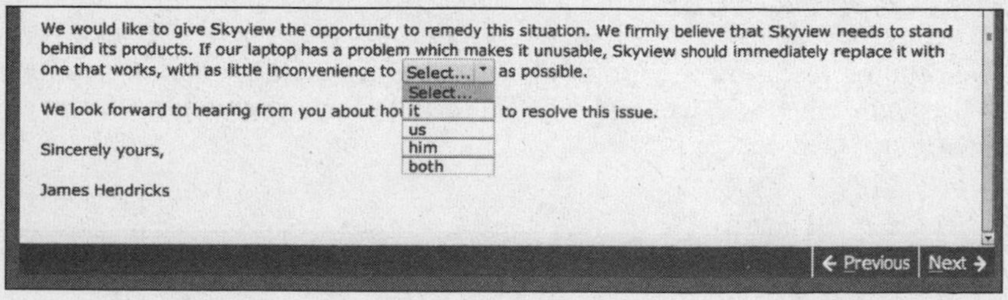

**Figure 2-9:**
Another example of a drop-down menu question.

© 2014 GED Testing Service LLC

### The Extended Response

In the Extended Response of the RLA test, you get 45 minutes to write an essay. Figure 2-10 shows an example. Note that the source material is longer than one screen. The tabs on the top of the left side indicate that this text is spread out over four pages. Be sure to read all four pages with care. You'll have an erasable tablet to take notes and write drafts of your essay. Use it to make notes as you read.

The answer window is a very limited mini word processor. In Figure 2-10, you can see that it allows you only to cut, paste, copy, do, and undo. It doesn't have either a grammar-checker or a spell-checker. Your brain, with its experience and knowledge, supplies those. To copy, cut, paste, or save, you move the mouse cursor to the area of the screen with the symbols for performing these tasks, and then you click on a mouse button to activate the feature (or you can use the standard keyboard shortcuts for cut and paste). You use this feature primarily if you want to quote something in your essay.

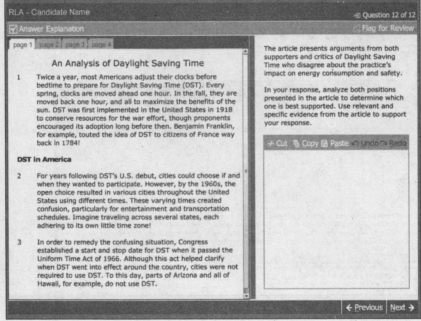

**Figure 2-10:**
A sample
Reasoning
through
Language
Arts
Extended
Response.

© 2014 GED Testing Service LLC

TIP

Take a stab at writing a full-length essay in the practice tests in Chapters 17 and 25. Time the test so you're taking it under the same conditions as the real GED test.

## Social Studies test

In the Social Studies test, you encounter all the same types of questions as you do in the Reasoning through Language Arts test. The following sections give you a brief guide to the kinds of questions to expect.

### Multiple-choice questions

Most questions on the Social Studies test are a variation of multiple-choice questions. You're probably most familiar with this simplest version (see Figure 2-11).

To answer this question, you click on the correct choice, and then click on Next to continue. (To answer this type of question in the book, you simply mark your choice of answer on an answer sheet.)

You'll also find the multiple-choice and other items presented as a split-screen, as in Figure 2-12. In this example, the text exceeds one page but only by a little. A scroll bar on the text side lets you scroll down to see the entire item.

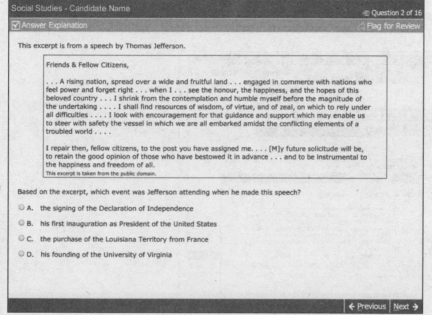

**Figure 2-11:** An example of a Social Studies multiple-choice question.

© 2014 GED Testing Service LLC

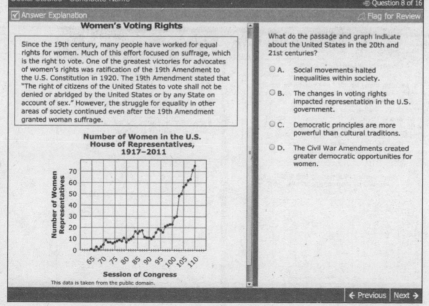

**Figure 2-12:** A Social Studies multiple-choice question with a scroll bar.

© 2014 GED Testing Service LLC

### Other types of Social Studies questions

The other questions on the Social Studies test are just like the ones we discuss earlier in this chapter. They include questions with source text (the materials you need to read to answer the question) spread over several pages (as in Figure 2-13). The tabs on the top left of the screen indicate more pages of text. Each page is one tab.

You'll also encounter fill-in-the-blank questions (as in Figure 2-14). On this type of item, you use the material presented in the passage to fill in the box. As in other subject areas, you need a specific word or number for the blank. You must be accurate; spelling mistakes are scored as an error. In this book, you write the answer on the answer sheet.

**Figure 2-13:**
An example of a multi-page Social Studies question with source text.

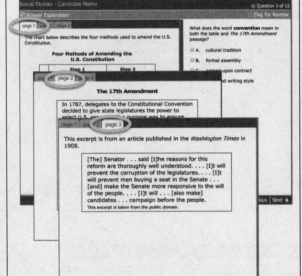

© 2014 GED Testing Service LLC

**Figure 2-14:**
A fill-in-the-blank example question.

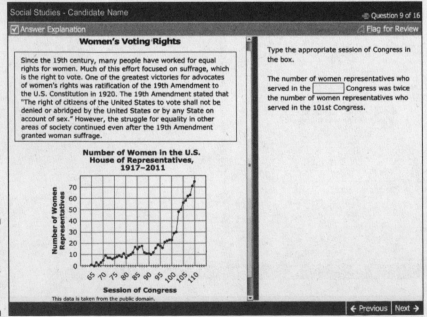

© 2014 GED Testing Service LLC

Another type of problem is the drag and drop. You solve it the same way as the drag-and-drop problem on the Reasoning through Language Arts test (refer to the earlier section "Drag-and-drop questions" for more information). Figure 2-15 is an example of a Social Studies drag-and-drop question.

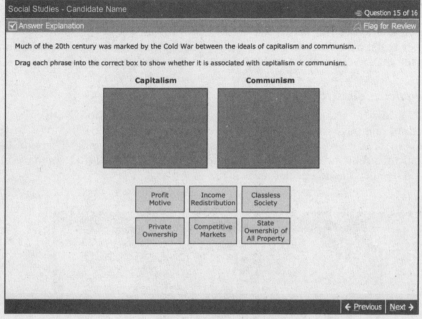

**Figure 2-15:** An example of a Social Studies drag-and-drop question.

## *The Extended Response*

The Social Studies Extended Response item also uses a format similar to that in the Reasoning through Language Arts test. This item gives you several screen pages of source text and a window in which to write your answer. See Figure 2-16 for an example of a Social Studies Extended Response.

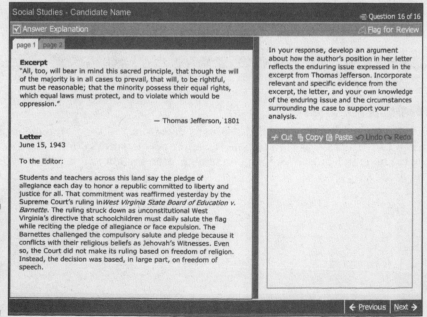

**Figure 2-16:** A sample Social Studies Extended Response.

In this book, you can simply write your response on paper and ask one or two friends to grade it. If you're taking a GED test-preparation course, the instructor may grade it for you. For information on the Social Studies test, see Chapters 3, 8, 9, and 10.

## Science test

When you take the Science test, you have to answer a variety of the same types of questions in the other tests, all in 90 minutes. The following sections focus on the slight differences you may see on the computer screen in the different types of questions.

### Multiple-choice questions

Figure 2-17 shows an example of a multiple-choice Science question. Notice that the passage is longer than one page on the computer screen. Tabs on the side can move the text up and down. Moving it down reveals the other possible answers. Always be aware of the screen size limitation and advance pages or scroll up or down to ensure that you have all the information you need to make a decision.

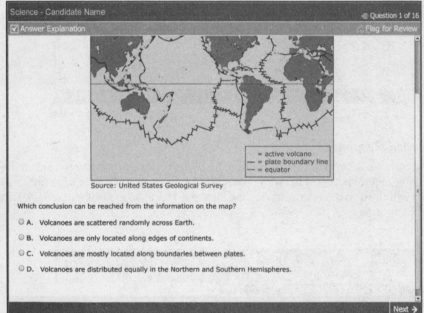

**Figure 2-17:** A sample Science multiple-choice question.

© 2014 GED Testing Service LLC

### Fill-in-the-blank questions

Figure 2-18 shows an example of a fill-in-the-blank question. You see a statement or question followed by a box. You're expected to type the appropriate word(s) or number(s) into that box. In the example in Figure 2-18, the percent sign after each box indicates that you need to enter a number.

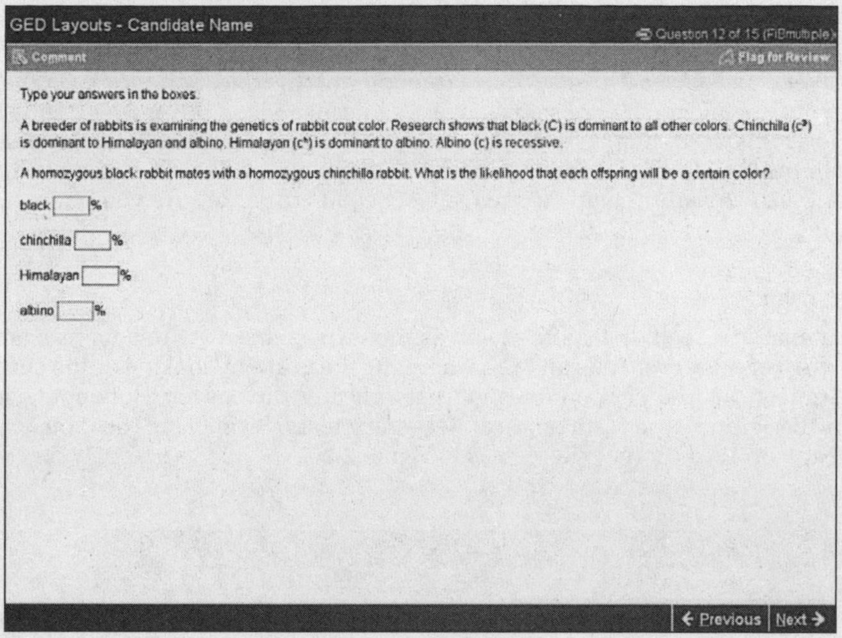

GED Layouts - Candidate Name

Question 12 of 15 (FIBmultiple)

Comment

Flag for Review

Type your answers in the boxes.

A breeder of rabbits is examining the genetics of rabbit coat color. Research shows that black (C) is dominant to all other colors. Chinchilla (c³) is dominant to Himalayan and albino. Himalayan (cʰ) is dominant to albino. Albino (c) is recessive.

A homozygous black rabbit mates with a homozygous chinchilla rabbit. What is the likelihood that each offspring will be a certain color?

black ☐ %

chinchilla ☐ %

Himalayan ☐ %

albino ☐ %

← Previous | Next →

**Figure 2-18:**
A sample Science fill-in-the-blank question.

© 2014 GED Testing Service LLC

## Drop-down menu questions

Questions involving a drop-down menu (see Figure 2-19) are similar to drop-down menu items in the other sections of the GED test. They're just a variation of the multiple-choice questions. You use the mouse to expand the choices and then again to select the correct one. (In the book, you mark your answer on the answer sheet.)

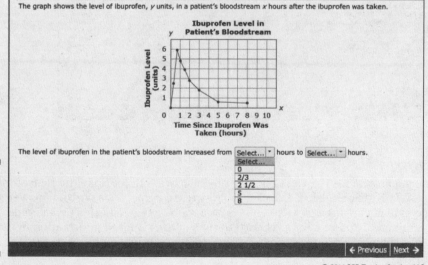

**Figure 2-19:**
An example of a drop-down menu question.

© 2014 GED Testing Service LLC

### Drag-and-drop questions

The general format of these types of questions is similar throughout all the sections of the GED test (refer to Figures 2-4 and 2-15 for examples of this question type). On the computer, you'll see spaces and a list of possible answers to use in filling the spaces. Using the mouse, you can drag the word, numbers, or phrases to their appropriate location to create an answer. (In the book practice tests, write the answers on the answer sheet provided. Always check your answers after completing each test section to make sure you understand the material.)

### Hot-spot items

On the computer screen, hot spots are areas that, when clicked with a mouse, are recognized as correct answers. You can't tell where the areas are by looking at the screen; you have to figure it out and click on the spot that indicates the answer. Hot-spot formats appear in the Science and Mathematical Reasoning tests. By clicking the mouse, you can draw a graph on the computer screen as in Figure 2-20.

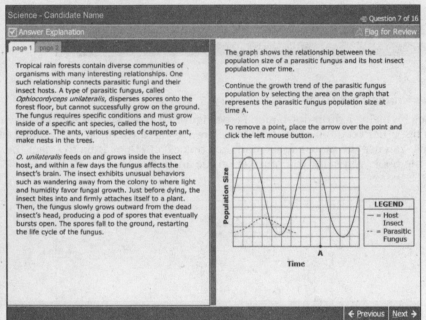

**Figure 2-20:** An example of a hot spot.

© 2014 GED Testing Service LLC

### Short Answer

This item requires more than just clicking on an answer choice. Like the Reasoning through Language Arts and Social Studies Extended Response items, it's a written answer; the only difference is that you have to write only a paragraph or two, and this task should take only about ten minutes. You use the keyboard to type in the required information in the boxes. Figure 2-21 shows an example of a Short Answer item on the computerized test.

## Mathematical Reasoning test

The computerized GED test looks different on-screen than it does in this book. Here are some of the specific test formats you'll encounter in the Mathematical Reasoning (Math) test.

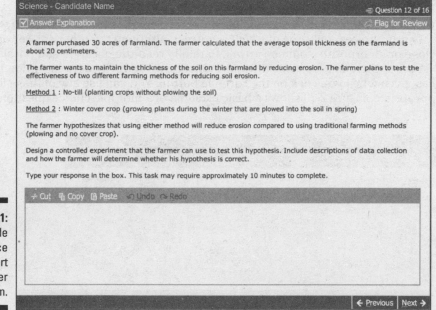

**Figure 2-21:**
A sample
Science
Short
Answer
item.

© 2014 GED Testing Service LLC

## Calculator

The Math test provides a calculator for you to use on all but the first five questions of the test (if you don't see the calculator tab on the screen, then you have to do the math in your head). When you need the calculator, simply click on the Calculator link, and the calculator appears. See Figure 2-22. Find out more about the calculator on the GED test at `www.gedtestingservice.com/testers/calculator`.

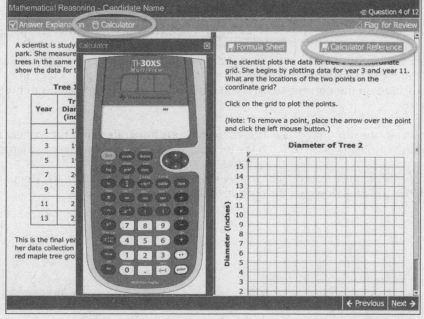

**Figure 2-22:**
The comput-
erized GED
Math test
has a cal-
culator that
you can use
on-screen.

© 2014 GED Testing Service LLC

### Multiple-choice questions

Most of the items in the Math test are multiple-choice. The question presents you with four possible answer choices, only one of which is correct, although the other answer options may be close or incorporate common errors. Carefully read the question and possible answers. Answer the question using the information provided. The only exception is the list of formulas given when you click on the Formula button. You can use any of these formulas where appropriate. Figure 2-23 shows a basic example of a multiple-choice question.

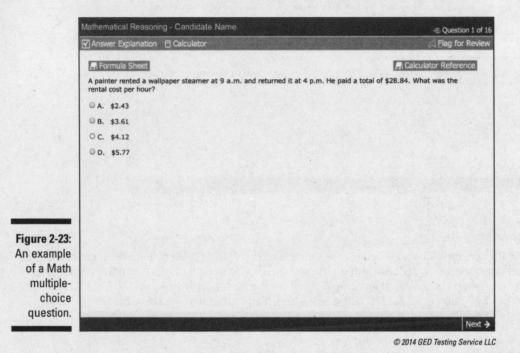

**Figure 2-23:** An example of a Math multiple-choice question.

© 2014 GED Testing Service LLC

On the computer, you use the mouse to select the answer. (In practice tests in this book, you mark your answer on an answer sheet. Always check your answer with the explanation.)

Sometimes multiple-choice questions appear in a split-screen with the question on the left-hand side and the possible answers on the right-hand side (see Figure 2-24). In either case, after you decide on the correct answer, you click on the appropriate answer choice with your mouse.

This particular question has some interesting buttons integrated into the format: a button to call up the calculator, one to fetch the formula sheet, and one for the calculator reference.

Some passages or questions may be longer than the space provided in the item. Look for the scroll bar to scroll down to the bottom of the item.

Mathematical Reasoning - Candidate Name

Question 10 of 16

Answer Explanation Calculator Flag for Review

A scientist is studying red maple tree growth in a state park. She measured the trunk diameters of a sample of trees in the same month every other year. The tables show the data for two of the trees.

**Tree 1**

| Year | Trunk Diameter (inches) |
|---|---|
| 1 | 18.6 |
| 3 | 19.2 |
| 5 | 19.8 |
| 7 | 20.4 |
| 9 | 21.0 |
| 11 | 21.6 |
| 13 | 22.2 |

**Tree 2**

| Year | Trunk Diameter (inches) |
|---|---|
| 1 | 11.4 |
| 3 | 12.0 |
| 5 | 12.6 |
| 7 | 13.2 |
| 9 | 13.8 |
| 11 | 14.4 |
| 13 | 15.0 |

This is the final year in which she will collect data. When her data collection is complete, she will predict future red maple tree growth.

Formula Sheet Calculator Reference

In year 13, the scientist will put tree wrap around tree 1 to protect it from the winter snow. The height of the tree wrap needs to be 45 inches.

Tree Wrap

45 inches

The wrap is priced by the square foot. To the nearest square foot, how many square feet of wrap does she need?

A. 22

B. 44

C. 121

D. 261

Previous Next

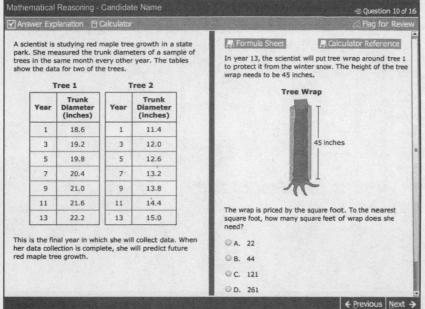

**Figure 2-24:** A split-screen multiple-choice question.



### *Fill-in-the-blank questions*

These questions require that you type a numeric answer or an equation in a box provided, using the keyboard. Check out Figure 2-25. You may have to use the symbols on the keyboard or click on the Symbol tab for additional symbols that you may need (see Figure 2-26).

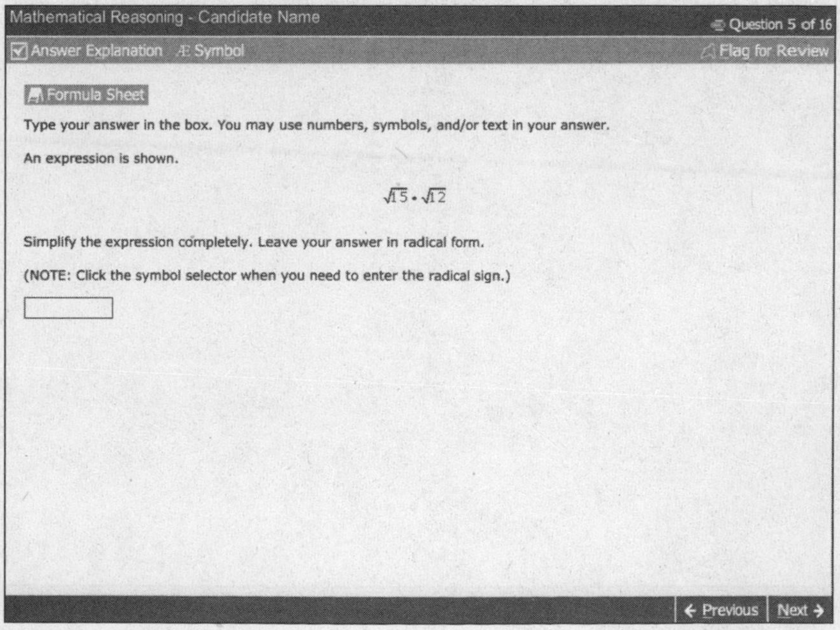

Mathematical Reasoning - Candidate Name

Question 5 of 16

Answer Explanation Symbol Flag for Review

Formula Sheet

Type your answer in the box. You may use numbers, symbols, and/or text in your answer.

An expression is shown.

$$\sqrt{15} \cdot \sqrt{12}$$

Simplify the expression completely. Leave your answer in radical form.

(NOTE: Click the symbol selector when you need to enter the radical sign.)

Previous Next

**Figure 2-25:** An example of a fill-in-the-blank question on the Math test.

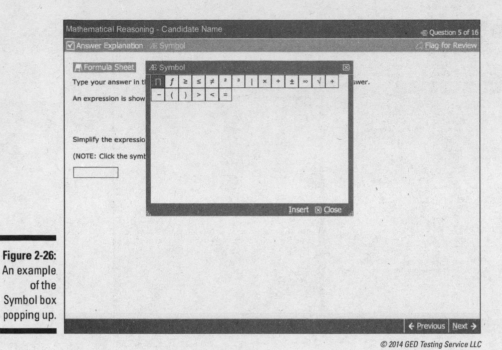

**Figure 2-26:**
An example
of the
Symbol box
popping up.

After reading the item carefully, you use the keyboard to type your answer in the box. If you want to return to the item later on, either to complete the question or double-check your answer, you can use the Flag For Review option.

### Other types of questions

The Mathematical Reasoning test also has drop-down menu, drag-and-drop, and hot-spot questions just like the other three sections of the test. (Refer to those earlier sections for examples of what the questions look like on the computer screen.)

# Chapter 3

# The GED Test's Four Sections and You

*I*t's time to start your preparation for the GED test with a look at what to expect on the four sections that comprise the GED exam — Reasoning through Language Arts, Social Studies, Science, and Mathematical Reasoning. You can take them all at once in one really long and tough day or individually whenever you feel sufficiently prepared. ***Remember:*** You don't have to do all the test sections on the same day. And after you pass a test section, you're finished with that section forever. You'll earn your GED diploma whenever you've completed and passed all four test sections. In this chapter, we break down what you can expect on each section and help you prepare for answering the different question types. See Chapter 2 for examples of all the different question types and how they appear both on the computerized GED test and in the practice tests in this book.

## Examining the Reasoning through Language Arts Test

We break the Reasoning through Language Arts (RLA) test into two parts for easier study. One part deals with reading skills; the other deals with writing. On the actual RLA test, these two skill sets are combined into one section.

In this section, we offer some example questions for each part of the RLA test, which show you how the questions work and what's expected of you to answer them. You first answer a series of shorter items, mainly multiple-choice. However, you'll also see items in the form of fill-in-the-blanks, drag-and-drop, and drop-down menus. In each case, you need to look for the answer in the text presented to you. To find the answer, you may simply have to refer to the text, or you may have to draw conclusions from what you've read and choose the best answer from either the four choices presented or from your understanding of the passage. And, finally, in the writing portion, you have sentence correction and the Extended Response (the essay).

### The reading section

On this part of the RLA test, you're given text to read, followed by a set of questions about that text, designed to test your ability to read and comprehend. Some items will simply ask about content; other items will require analysis. The information you need to answer will be right in the text you read. Some items will ask you to draw conclusions based on the information in the text, which are the "why" or "how do you know" questions.

Here are two bits of collective wisdom: First, before taking the RLA test, read, read, and read some more. And, secondly, when taking the RLA test, read carefully; the answer is in the text. The best guarantee that you'll do well on this section is to become a fluent and analytical reader. Read editorials, analyze how the writers make their point, and provide supportive evidence of their points. Read newspaper stories to extract the bare-bones key points that make the story. Read and think about how the writer creates a mood, image, or point of view. Although you don't have to master any specific content before taking the reading portion of the RLA test, the more you read, the better-equipped you'll be to deal with this.

We go into detail about the types of questions to expect on the RLA test and how to answer them in the following sections.

### Multiple-choice questions

Most of the items on the RLA test are some form of a multiple-choice problem, where you choose from four answers. (Refer to Chapter 2 for how multiple-choice questions appear in this test section on the computer screen when you're taking the actual GED test.)

Multiple-choice items give you the correct answer but make it harder by adding three wrong answers. So when you see this item on the GED test, read the question first and then the text, looking for related material. Go back to the answer choices and eliminate the obviously wrong ones as you progress. Eventually, you'll be left with one or two choices from which to pick your answer.

Pick the most correct, most complete answer from the choices offered. You may find, based on your previous knowledge, that none of the choices is complete. However, you need to go with the materials in the text, so use the answer choice closest to what's in the text.

The best advice for completing the reading portion of the RLA test is

(A) read, read, and read some more

(B) memorize every poem ever written by Shakespeare

(C) read the short versions of any famous books you can find

(D) none of the above

The correct answer is Choice (A). You don't have to know any specific content for this test, but you need to be able to read quickly and accurately and understand what you've read. The only way to do that is to practice and practice and practice some more.

Here are a couple of examples of multiple-choice questions like you'll see on the GED test.

> People have a natural metabolic "set point" that is predetermined at birth and influences just how slim or heavy they will be. That is why it is difficult for the obese to lose weight beyond a particular point and for the slim to gain and retain weight for long. Some studies now suggest that the chemicals in clothing and upholstery flame-retardants interfere with that set point when they are absorbed into the body. This may affect a child in the womb and even after birth, which is one reason some jurisdictions are banning flame-retardants from children's clothing. California is even considering banning them from upholstery, another common application.

Why are chemicals in upholstery potentially harmful?

(A) They can cause retardation.

(B) They interfere with the natural metabolic set point.

(C) California is considering banning them.

(D) None of the above

The correct answer is Choice (B), which is clearly stated in the text. Choice (A) may be true, but it isn't supported by the text, so if you went with that choice, you probably misread the text. Choice (C) is irrelevant to the question, and choice (D) is wrong. Other reasons to place a ban on flame-retardants should be considered, but you're not asked about them, so stick with the options offered.

Why is anyone concerned about the metabolic set point?

(A) The set point determines how much people will weigh. Anything that interferes with that is dangerous.

(B) Most people want to be slim.

(C) People don't want chemicals in their bodies.

(D) People are against the misuse of chemicals in the environment.

The correct answer is Choice (A). The text states that these chemicals interfere with the set point, and that is dangerous, causing obesity or drastic underweight. Choices (B), (C), and (D) are all possibly true but aren't supported by the text.

### Drag-and-drop questions

The RLA test also uses the drag-and-drop question type. This item requires you to drag and drop information from one location on the screen to another. Usually, the purpose is for you to reorder something from least important to most, to place events into a sequence, or simply to select a series of items or choices that apply to the question. For example, you may be asked to pick two or three words that describe a person or event in the text, from a choice of four or five options. Doing so is relatively simple: You just click on the item to move with your mouse, and then, while holding down the mouse button, you drag the item to the new location. When you reach the new location, let go of the mouse button and drop the item. If you've moved it properly, it will stay where you dropped it. Check out Chapter 2 to see how a drag-and-drop question looks on the computerized GED test.

To prepare for the drag-and-drop items on the GED test, practice critical reading. When you're reading editorials and articles, try to pull out key points and look for biases or unsupported conclusions.

Answering a drag-and-drop item requires you to

(A) do some heavy lifting

(B) type directions into a box

(C) click on and move a choice of an answer

(D) play a lot of Solitaire

Choice (C) is correct. Choice (A) refers more to a job in the real world and not taking a test. Choice (B) applies to the directions for fill-in-the-blank or Extended Response items. Choice (D) is one way to waste time that could be better spent preparing for the test. Although playing Solitaire on your computer is a good way to practice using the mouse, this answer choice doesn't answer the specific question based on the material in this section.

Here are a couple types of drag-and-drop problems that you may encounter on the GED test.

Bradley was determined to get the job. Although he wanted to go to the movies with Keesha, he also needed to work, and the job interview looked promising. He loved his job at the mill, but it was not enough to provide him with the income he needed. Of course, the hours were great, but the hourly rate was not. He could have left early, gone to the interview, and still had his date with Keesha, but that would have created problems with his boss at the mill. Bradley made the only choice he could. He finished his day at the mill and then went to the job interview. Keesha waited by the phone but never heard from him.

Put the names and phrases in order of importance to Bradley in the boxes with the most important on top and the least important at the bottom.

(A) Keesha

(B) job at the mill

(C) job interview

(D) a raise

Based on the text, the best order is Choice (D), *a raise;* Choice (C), *job interview;* Choice (B), *job at the mill;* and then Choice (A), *Keesha.*

Which one of these terms best applies to Bradley? Indicate your answer in the box.

(A) friendly

(B) good boyfriend

(C) hardworking

(D) determined

The correct answer is *determined.* The text states that "Bradley was determined to get the job." He left his girlfriend in the lurch, not even leaving his regular work early to keep his date with Keesha, so he is certainly not the best of boyfriends. He may be friendly and hard-working, but the overwhelming point is determination.

In the RLA practice tests in Chapters 17 and 25, when you see an item in this format, you see the content of the boxes as words or phrases preceded by capital letters. You can then enter the letters into boxes on the answer sheet to indicate your choices.

### Fill-in-the-blank questions

You're likely familiar with the fill-in-the-blank question type. It requires you to find one word or number in the source text that answers a question and then type (or write) that word or number in a space. On the GED test, the blank that you need to fill in looks like an empty box. Just click in that box and type in your answer. For the fill-in-the-blank items in this book, you can write your answer directly in the box or on the answer sheet for the practice tests. Refer to the source text in the previous section to answer this question.

Bradley's girlfriend is named [          ].

There is nothing fancy about fill-in-the-blank items; they simply require good reading skills.

## The writing section

The writing part of the RLA test evaluates your ability to use correct spelling and grammar to write clearly and succinctly. It tests your ability in various ways. Some questions ask you to select the correct alternative to a misspelled or grammatically incorrect sentence. Others ask you to provide a better wording for a sentence or select the best choice of words for some text. The text will vary from business letters to extracts from novels. They can be based on instruction manuals for an MP3 player, a newspaper story, or a contract.

To study and prepare for these types of questions, try the following tips:

- ✔ Review your spelling and grammar skills.

- ✔ Use the local library to find high-school grammar texts or look for free grammar and spelling quizzes online. Some online quizzes correct your answers immediately, giving you excellent feedback on what you know and what needs improvement. For a good review of grammar, check out www.grammar-monster.com.

- ✔ After you take the practice tests in Chapters 17 and 25, you may see some areas where you need to improve. Fortunately for you, the *For Dummies* series has just the thing for you: *English Grammar For Dummies,* 2nd Edition, by Geraldine Woods (Wiley). As you work on your grammar and writing skills, periodically redo the practice tests to see how much you have improved.

### Question types

Most of the questions in the writing section are multiple-choice items, but you'll also see some fill-in-the-blanks and drag-and-drop items (see "The reading section" for an overview of these question types). This section includes one other question type: the drop-down menu. In these questions, you select the correct alternative from a number of choices. Like multiple-choice, the drop-down menu usually includes four options (sometimes you'll see as few as three).

The drop-down menu items consist of a sentence with a box on the line containing a down arrow and the word *select.* When you click on Select, several alternative word or sentence choices appear. You click on the best choice, and the sentence appears with your selection. *Note:* In this book, you won't see a drop-down menu but just a list of answer choices. See Chapter 2 for details on this question format.

When we got there, we discovered ☐ car was missing.

(A) their

(B) they're

(C) there

The correct answer is Choice (A), *their.* These words are *homonyms* — words that sound alike but have different meanings. Choice (A), *their,* shows possession, as in "their book"; Choice (B), *they're* is a contraction of *they are;* and Choice (C), *there,* is a location in space or time.

> Dear Mr. Jones
>
> (1) We would like to thank you for you're kind words. (2) As a manufacturer, we try to produce the best possible goods for consumers. (3) The keyboard's we produce do not often receive the recognition your review gives us, and it is much appreciated.

Sentence 1: **We would like to thank you for you're kind words.**

What changes should be made to Sentence 1?

(A) change *would* to *wood*

(B) capitalize *thank you*

(C) change *you're* to *your*

(D) all of the above

The correct answer is Choice (C). It refers to the misuse of *you're,* a contraction of *you are,* when *your,* as in ownership or possession, is appropriate. Choice (A) is another example of homonyms, but the correct word, *would,* is used in the sentence so no change is needed there. Choice (B) is wrong in suggesting a capitalization in the middle of the sentence.

Sentence 2: **As a manufacturer, we try to produce the best possible goods for consumers.**

What corrections need to be made in Sentence 2?

(A) change *manufacturer* to *manufactures*

(B) change *produce* to *produse*

(C) delete the comma after *manufacturer*

(D) none of the above

In this case, the answer is Choice (D), *none of the above.* No error occurs in the sentence. Although often the *all of the above* or *none of the above* answer choices are thrown in to fool you, don't fall into the trap of ignoring the option. Sometimes it does apply.

Sentence 3: **The keyboard's we produce do not often receive the recognition your review gives us, and it is much appreciated.**

What changes need to be made in Sentence 3?

(A) change *keyboard's* to *keyboards*

(B) change *receive* to *recieve*

(C) change *appreciated* to *appreciation*

(D) capitalize *keyboard's*

The correct answer is Choice (A). When you present the plural of *keyboard,* it's *keyboards,* without the apostrophe. Choice (B) is an attempt to lead you into error: The spelling change suggests that you use *recieve,* a common spelling error.

The other questions will be the same as for the reading section. The big difference for this section is that you can study for this section by checking out lists of commonly misspelled words, reviewing grammar and punctuation rules, and getting familiar with homonyms and their proper use.

## The Extended Response

After you finish the first part of the RLA test (the 35-minute question-and-answer section), you start on the Extended Response — where you write an essay by analyzing arguments presented in one or two pieces of sample text. You get 45 minutes to work through this part of the RLA test, and you can't tack on extra time from the previous section. So if you find that you have time left on the first part, go back and review some of the questions where you had difficulties before starting the Extended Response. And remember, after the Extended Response, you have a ten-minute break and then another hour of more mainly multiple-choice type items.

For the Extended Response item, you must write a proper essay, with a clear thesis statement, a proper introduction, followed by four or six paragraphs of supporting argument, and a concluding paragraph. You'll have an erasable tablet on which to make rough notes, and if you need more, you can get additional tablets. You won't use or have access to paper, pencils, or dictionaries. When you complete your rough draft of your essay, you write it into a window on the computer that functions like a basic word processor. The word processor doesn't have a grammar- or spell-checker. You're expected to know how to write properly.

The topic you're given to write on is based on given source material, usually consisting of two documents with different or opposing opinions. You're expected to analyze the source material and write an appropriate analytical response. You must show that you can read and understand the source material, do a critical analysis, and prepare a reasoned response based on content drawn from that source text.

In your essay, you analyze both positions and then give your opinion or explain your viewpoint. Remember to back up your points with specific facts from the source material. When you write this essay, make sure it's a series of interconnected paragraphs on a single topic. Not only should the entire essay begin with an introduction and end with a conclusion, but also each paragraph should have an introductory sentence and a concluding sentence.

Write only on the assigned topic. To make sure you understand what the topic is about, read it several times. Essays written off topic don't receive scores. If you don't get sufficient points on the Extended Response, you likely won't accumulate enough marks on the other portions of the RLA test to pass.

Your essay is evaluated on the following points:

- ✔ Your argument is based specifically on the given source material.

- ✔ You correctly use the evidence from the source material to support your argument.

- ✔ You use valid arguments and separate the supported claims in the material from the unsupported or false claims.

- ✔ Your flow of ideas is logical and well organized.

- ✔ You correctly and appropriately use style, structure, vocabulary, and grammar.

Consider this example of an Extended Response item:

> "I will give up my muscle car when the world runs out of oil, not before. . . ."

> "We need to find alternatives to gasoline-powered vehicles. Climate change is a real threat, and burning fossil fuels contributes to that problem. . . ."

These two opinions are the beginnings of an editorial, taking obviously different positions.

In this example, you start by determining which argument you see as stronger. Then, you make a list of information that may go into your essay to back up your argument. Trim out any information that doesn't pertain to the topic. If one side or the other uses unsubstantiated opinions as evidence, you can use that to argue that it's a weaker argument.

When you start writing your essay, start with a good, strong introductory sentence that will catch a reader's attention. When you're satisfied with your introductory sentence, review your list of information. Follow that introductory sentence with a couple of sentences outlining, without explanation, your key points. Now turn each key point into a paragraph, paying attention to the flow between paragraphs to show that one relates to the previous one. When you have all these paragraphs, it's time for a conclusion. The easiest way to write a good conclusion is to restate your evidence briefly and state that this indeed proves your point. Don't just rewrite your information, but summarize it in a memorable way. This may be difficult the first time, but with practice, it can become second nature.

If you have time, you can test how well your essay works and stays on topic. Read the introduction, the first and last sentence of every paragraph, and then the conclusion. They should all have the same basic points and flow together nicely. If something seems out of place, you need to go back and review.

To prepare for this part of the test, in the months leading up to your test date, read newspapers and news magazines, especially opinion pieces. Analyze how arguments are presented and how the writers try to form and sway your opinion. Examine how well they present their data and how they use relevant and irrelevant data to persuade the reader. Doing so can give you practice in critical reading and in developing your opinions and viewpoints based on others' writings.

# Handling the Social Studies Test

For the Social Studies test, you also have to answer a variety of items. You have 65 minutes to complete the question-answer portion and 25 minutes to write the Extended Response (essay) item. The items use the same format as the RLA test items: multiple-choice questions, fill-in-the-blanks, and drag-and-drop items (see the earlier sections on Reasoning through Language Arts for details). These questions deal with the following subject areas:

- ✔ Civics and government (50 percent)
- ✔ American history (20 percent)
- ✔ Economics (15 percent)
- ✔ Geography and the world (15 percent)

The items in this test are based on written texts (source texts) and visual materials — pictures, charts, tables, graphs, photographs, political cartoons, diagrams, or maps. These textual and visual materials come from a variety of sources, such as government documents, academic texts, work-related documents, and atlases.

You can do only a limited amount of studying for this test. The information to answer each item is in the text or graphic that comes with the question. You need to analyze the material and draw conclusions based on what's presented. However, you can prepare by reading books that offer you a basic outline of American history and learn about how government functions. Read the newspapers to follow current events and the business section for economics. You don't need to go into great depth or memorize pages of dates and names, but you should have an idea of the general flow of history. You also need to know how your governments — from federal to local — work.

A second skill you need to master for this test is reading and extracting information from maps, charts, and tables. On the Social Studies test, you may see a map with different shadings and you have to determine what the shadings mean and what the difference is between a light gray area on the map and the dark gray. They're not just decoration. If you look carefully at all the text and boxes with information on the map or chart, you'll see that everything has a meaning. So get an atlas, and practice reading maps.

The other types of questions and the Extended Response on the Social Studies test are just like the items that we discuss in the Reasoning through Language Arts section in this chapter and in Chapter 2. The only difference on the Extended Response is that you can write a shorter essay, but then you also have less time to do so. However, in the Social Studies Extended Response, some general knowledge of American history is expected.

You may see the following types of problems on the Social Studies test.

*The following question is based on this table.*

| Type of Religion | Date Started (Approximate) | Sacred Texts |
| --- | --- | --- |
| Buddhism | 500 BC | None |
| Christianity | 33 AD | Bible (Old Testament and New Testament) |
| Hinduism | 4000 BC | Vedas; Upanishads |
| Islam | 600 AD | Qur'an; Hadith |
| Judaism | 2000 BC | Hebrew Bible; Talmud |

According to the table, Hinduism

(A) started in 600 AD

(B) uses the Qur'an as one of its sacred texts

(C) is the oldest religion

(D) has no known sacred texts

The correct answer is Choice (C). The table shows that Hinduism is the oldest of the five religions listed because it began around 4000 BC.

*The following question is based on this excerpt from the diary of Christopher Columbus.*

Monday, 6 August. The rudder of the caravel Pinta became loose, being broken or unshipped. It was believed that this happened by the contrivance of Gomez Rascon and Christopher Quintero, who were on board the caravel, because they disliked the voyage. The Admiral says he had found them in an unfavorable disposition before setting out. He was in much anxiety at not being able to afford any assistance in this case, but says that it somewhat quieted his apprehensions to know that Martin Alonzo Pinzon, Captain of the Pinta, was a man of courage and capacity. Made progress, day and night, of twenty-nine leagues.

Why would Rascon and Quintero have loosened the rudder?

(A) They were trying to repair the rudder.

(B) The Admiral found them in an unfavorable disposition.

(C) The captain was very competent.

(D) They did not want to be on the voyage.

The correct answer is Choice (D). This answer is the only one supported by the text. The others may be related to statements in the passage, but they don't answer the question.

*The following question is based on this graph.*

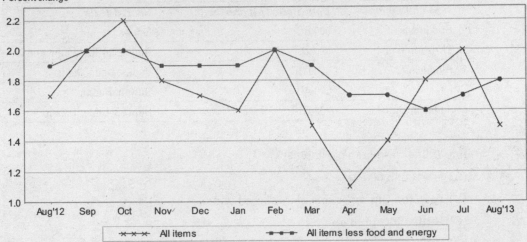

Chart 2. 12-month percent change in CPI for All Urban Consumers (CPI-U), not seasonally adjusted, Aug. 2012 - Aug. 2013

What effect do energy and food prices have on inflation?

(A) They level out the range of change over time.

(B) They amplify the range of change over time.

(C) They increase the rate of inflation.

(D) They have no effect.

The correct answer is Choice (B). The inclusion of food and energy prices makes the graph values swing much wider. The combined graph line shows much wider variation. Hence, food and energy prices amplify inflation.

*The following question asks you to fill in the blank based on the previous graph.*

The range of inflation for "all items" shown on the graph is [          ]%.

The correct answer is 1.1. The highest value for inflation on the *All items* line is 2.2% for October. The lowest value, in April, is about 1.1%. Therefore, the range is approximately 1.1%.

# Knowing How to Grapple the Science Test

When you take the Science test, you have to answer the same variety of question formats, including multiple-choice, fill-in-the-blank, drop-down menu, drag and drop, hot spot, and Short Answer, all in 90 minutes. The questions deal with the following topics:

- ✔ Life science (40 percent)
- ✔ Physical science, including chemistry and physics (40 percent)
- ✔ Earth and space science (20 percent)

Most of the information you need to answer the items on the Science test is given to you in the passages and other excerpts. To get a perfect score, though, you're expected to have picked up a basic knowledge of science. However, even if you correctly answer only the questions based entirely on the information presented, you should get a score high enough to pass.

Although you're not expected to be an expert on the various topics in the Science test, you are expected to understand the words. To accomplish this, read as widely as you can in science books. If you run across words you don't understand, write them down with a definition or explanation. Doing so will provide a vocabulary list for you to review before the test.

You must read and understand the passages in the Science test to be able to select the best choice for an answer. Practice reading quickly and accurately. Because you have a time limit, practice skimming passages to look for key words. The less time you spend on the passages, the more time you'll have to answer the item, and the more time you'll have at the end of the test to review your answers and attempt questions that you found difficult the first time you read them. Attempt to answer every question. You may get a mark for your answer if you try it but you can't get a mark for an item you've left out.

The Science test also includes Short Answer items in which you respond to a passage or passages in a coherent logical way. *Remember:* You're expected to write a response that might be expected of someone ready for employment or college, not a public school student or someone preparing for a doctoral thesis. You should be able to include material from the passage and some from your general knowledge. Because the simplified word processor on the test has limitations, check your spelling and grammar carefully. In science, make sure that if you use a word from your reading, it's spelled correctly and used correctly. Above all, don't panic. If you've prepared, you'll do fine. See Chapter 2 for an example Short Answer item.

Here are some sample problems similar to those that may be in the Science test.

*The following questions are based on this excerpt from a press release.*

A key feature of the Delta 4's operation is the use of a common booster core, or CBC, a rocket stage that measures some 150 feet long and 16 feet wide. By combining one or more CBCs with various upper stages or strap-on solid rocket boosters, the Delta 4 can handle an extreme range of satellite applications for military, civilian, and commercial customers.

The CBC in this context is a

(A) Canadian Broadcasting Corporation

(B) common booster core

(C) cooperative boosters corps

(D) common ballistic cavalier

The correct answer is Choice (B). After all, it's the only answer choice mentioned in the passage. Skimming the passage would give you an idea of where to look for a fuller explanation of the abbreviation.

How can the Delta 4 handle a wide range of applications?

(A) developing a Delta 5

(B) continuing research

(C) using the CBC as the base of a rocket ship

(D) creating a common core booster

The correct answer is Choice (C). The passage says that "By combining one or more CBCs with various upper stages or strap-on solid rocket boosters . . . ," so Choice (C) comes closest to answering the question.

# Conquering the Mathematical Reasoning Test

The Mathematical Reasoning test covers the following four major areas:

- ✔ Algebra, equations, and patterns
- ✔ Data analysis, statistics, and probability
- ✔ Measurement and geometry
- ✔ Number operations

More specifically, about 45 percent of the questions focus on quantitative problem solving and the other about 55 percent focuses on algebraic problem solving.

The Mathematical Reasoning (Math) test has many of the same types of problems as the other sections (multiple-choice, fill-in-the-blank, and so on). Check out Chapter 2 for how these questions look on the computerized test.

Mathematics is mathematics. That may sound simple, but it isn't. To succeed on the Math test, you should have a good grasp of the basic operations: addition, subtraction, multiplication, and division. You should be able to perform these operations quickly and accurately and, in the case of simple numbers, perform them mentally. The more automatic and accurate your responses are, the less time you'll need for each item, and the greater your chances are of finishing the test on time with a few minutes to spare to check any items you may have skipped or answers you want to double-check.

The other skill you should try to master is reading quickly and accurately. Most of the items are written in English prose and you're expected to know how to answer the item from the passage presented. Try to increase your reading speed and test yourself for accuracy. If you are a slow reader, type "speed reading" in any Internet search engine to get some hints. You can check for accuracy by writing down what you think you read without looking at the passage and seeing how close you can come to it. More important than knowing whether you can recall each and every word is knowing how accurate you are so that you can compensate for issues before the test.

Consider the following items (one traditional multiple-choice question and two questions that use different formats that you'll encounter on the computer) that are similar to what you may see on the Math test.

A right-angle triangle has a hypotenuse of 5 feet and one side that is 36 inches long. What is the length of the other side in feet?

(A) 3 ft

(B) 48 ft

(C) 6 ft

(D) 4 ft

The correct answer is Choice (D). The tricky part to this question is that you need to know that you have to apply the Pythagorean theorem to solve this problem. Using the Pythagorean theorem (a formula that's given to you on the formula page of the test), you know that $a^2 + b^2 = c^2$, where $c$ is the hypotenuse and $a$ and $b$ are either of the other two sides. Because you know the hypotenuse and one side, turn the equation around so that it reads $a^2 = c^2 - b^2$.

You can recall the page of formulas on the computer when needed. But keep in mind that the fewer times you need to call it up, the more time you have to answer questions.

To get $c^2$, you square the hypotenuse: (5)(5)= 25.

The other side is given in inches — to convert inches to feet, divide by 12: 36/12 = 3. To get $b^2$, square this side: (3)(3) = 9.

Now solve the equation for $a$: $a^2 = 25 - 9$ or $a^2 = 16$. Take the square root of both sides, and you get $a = 4$.

The Math test presents real-life situations in the items. So if you find yourself answering 37 feet to a question about the height of a room or $3.00 for an annual salary, recheck your answer because you're probably wrong.

*The following question asks you to fill in the blank.*

Barb is counting the number of boxes in a warehouse. In the first storage area, she finds 24 boxes. The second area contains 30 boxes. The third area contains 28 boxes. If the warehouse has 6 storage areas where it stores boxes and the areas have an average of 28 boxes, the total number of boxes in the last three areas is [ ].

The correct answer is 86. If the warehouse has 6 storage areas and it has an average of 28 boxes in each, it has (6)(28) = 168 boxes in the warehouse. The first three areas have 24 + 30 + 28 = 82 boxes in them. The last three areas must have 168 – 82 = 86 boxes in them.

A rectangle has one corner on the origin. The base goes from the origin to the point (3, 0). The right side goes from (3, 0) to (3, 4). Place the missing point on the graph.

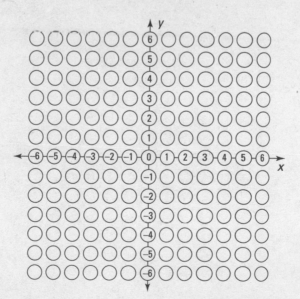

The correct answer is to put Point B at (0, 4). Because you're using a book and not a computer, you just write your answer on the answer sheet. If you draw the three points given on the graph, you see that a fourth point at (0, 4) creates the rectangle. Draw the point as shown on the graph.

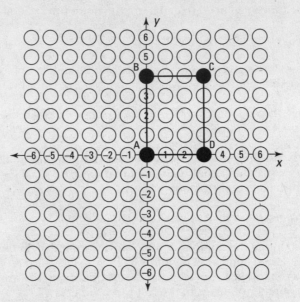

# Chapter 4

# Succeeding on the GED Test

**In This Chapter**

▶ Getting ready in the weeks and the night before and the day of the test

▶ Relying on practice tests

▶ Figuring out what to expect on test day

▶ Nailing down important test-taking strategies

▶ Staying calm and relaxed while you take the test

**Y**ou may never have taken a standardized test before. Or if you have, you may wake up sweating in the middle of the night from nightmares about your past experiences. Whether you've experienced the joys or sorrows of standardized tests, to succeed on the GED test, you must know how to perform well on this type of test, which consists mostly of multiple-choice questions.

The good news is, you've come to the right spot to find out more about this type of test. This chapter explains some important pointers on how to prepare on the days and nights before the test, what to do on the morning of the test, and what to do during the test to be successful. You also discover some important test-taking strategies to help you feel confident.

## Leading Up to Test Time

Doing well on the GED test involves more than walking into the test site and answering the questions. You need to be prepared for the challenges in the test. To ensure that you're ready to tackle the test head-on, make sure you do the following leading up to the test:

✔ **Get enough sleep.** We're sorry if we sound like your parents, but it's true — you shouldn't take tests when you're approaching exhaustion. Plan your time so you can get a good night's sleep for several days before the test and avoid excess caffeine. If you prepare ahead of time, you'll be ready, and sleep will come easier.

✔ **Eat a good breakfast.** A healthy breakfast fuels your mind and body. You have to spend several hours taking the test, and you definitely don't want to falter during that time. Eat some protein, such as eggs, bacon, or sausage with toast for breakfast. Avoid sugars (donuts, jelly, fruit) because they can cause you to tire easily. You don't want your empty stomach fighting with your full brain.

✔ **Take some deep breaths.** During your trip to the testing site, prepare yourself mentally for the test. Clear your head of all distractions, practice deep breathing, and imagine yourself acing the test. Don't panic.

✔ **Start at the beginning, not the end.** Remember that the day of the test is the end of a long journey of preparation and not the beginning. It takes time to build mental muscles.

✔ **Be on time.** Make sure you know what time the test begins and the exact location of your test site. Arrive early. If necessary, take a practice run to make sure you have enough time to get from your home or workplace to the testing center. You don't need the added pressure of worrying about whether you can make it to the test on time. In fact, this added pressure can create industrial-strength panic in the calmest of people.

Traffic congestion happens. No one can plan for it, but you can leave extra time to make sure it doesn't ruin your day. Plan your route and practice it. Then leave extra time in case a meteor crashes into the street and the crowd that gathers around it stalls your progress. Even though the GED test is now administered on a computer and not everyone has to start at the same time, test centers are open only for certain hours, and if they close before you finish, you won't get any sympathy. Check the times the test center is open. Examiners won't show you a lot of consideration if you show up too late to complete the test or tests because you didn't check the times. They have even less sympathy if you show up on the wrong date.

# Using Practice Tests to Your Advantage

Taking practice GED tests is important for a few reasons, including the following:

✔ **They give you an indication of how well you know the material.** One or two tests won't give you a definite answer, because you need to do four or five tests to cover all possible topics, but they do give you an indication of where you stand.

✔ **They confirm whether you know how to use the computer to answer the questions.** Until you try, you simply won't know for sure.

✔ **They familiarize you with the test format.** You can read about test questions, but you can't actually understand them until you've worked through several.

✔ **They can ease your stress.** A successful run-through on a practice test allows you to feel more comfortable and confident in your own abilities to take the GED test successfully and alleviate your overall anxiety.

You can find a practice test of each section in Parts VI and VII. The practice tests are an important part of any preparation program. They're the feedback mechanism that you may normally get from a private tutor. As long as you check your answers after the practice test and read the answer explanations, you can benefit from taking practice tests. If possible, take as many practice tests as you can before taking the actual GED test. You can find more practice tests at www.gedtestingservice.com/educators/freepracticetest and a few more sample questions at www.gedtestingservice.com/testers/sample-questions. Use your favorite Internet search engine to find more examples of practice tests online. The GED Testing Service also offers GED Ready tests that you can purchase through authorized outlets.

# Finding Out What to Take to the GED Test

The GED test may be the most important exam you ever take. Treat it seriously and come prepared. Make sure you bring the following items with you on test day:

✔ **You:** The most important thing to bring to the GED test is obviously you. If you enroll to take the test, you have to show up; otherwise, you'll receive a big fat zero and lose your testing fee. If something unfortunate happens after you enroll, contact the test center and explain your situation to the test administrators. They may reschedule the test without an additional charge.

✔ **Correct identification:** Before test officials let you into the room to take the test, they want to make sure you're you. Bring the approved photo ID — your state GED office can tell you what's an approved form of photo ID. Have your ID in a place where you can reach it easily. And when asked to identify yourself, don't pull out a mirror and say, "Yep, that's me."

✔ **Fees you still owe:** The same people don't run all test centers. With some, you may have to pay in advance, when booking the test. If so, bring your receipt to avoid any misunderstandings. Others may allow you to pay at the door. If so, find out whether you can use cash, check, or credit card. The amount of the GED test registration fee also varies from state to state. (Check with your local administrator to confirm when and where the fee has to be paid and how to pay it.) If you don't pay the fee, you can't take the exam.

If needed, you may be able to get financial assistance to help with the testing fees. Further, if you do the test one section at a time, which we recommend, you can probably pay for each test section separately. Check with your state or local education authorities.

✔ **Registration confirmation:** The registration confirmation is your proof that you did register. If you're taking the test in an area where everybody knows you and everything you do, you may not need the confirmation, but we suggest you take it anyway. It's light and doesn't take up much room in your pocket.

✔ **Other miscellaneous items:** In the instructions you receive after you register for the test, you get a list of what you need to bring with you. Besides yourself and the items we list previously, other items you want to bring or wear include the following:

- **Comfortable clothes and shoes:** When you're taking the test, you want to be as relaxed as possible. Uncomfortable clothes and shoes may distract you from doing your best. You're taking the GED test, not modeling the most recent fashions.

- **A bottle of water or some coffee:** Check with the administrators whether drinks are allowed beforehand. Computers and liquids don't mix, so they may not allow you to take drinks in with you. Mints and gum may be an alternative, but consider taking them in a transparent plastic bag so that no one can question whether you're carrying written material into the test.

- **Reading glasses:** If you need glasses to read a computer monitor, don't forget to bring them to the test. Bring a spare pair, if you have one. You can't do the test if you can't read the screen.

The rules about what enters the testing room are strict. Don't take any chances. If something isn't on the list of acceptable items and isn't normal clothing, leave it at home. Laptops, cellphones, and other electronic devices will most likely be banned from the testing area. Leave them at home or locked in your car. The last place on earth to discuss whether you can bring something into the test site is at the door on test day. If you have questions, contact the test center in advance. Check out www.gedtestingservice.com to start the registration process and find a list of sites close to your home with their addresses and phone numbers. You can also call 800-62-MYGED to ask your questions to real people.

Whatever you do, be sure not to bring the following with you to the GED testing center:

✔ Books

✔ Calculator (one is provided for you on-screen — see Chapter 2)

✔ Notes or scratch paper

✔ MP3 players or tablets

✔ Cellphone (leave it at home or in your car)

✔ Anything valuable, like a laptop computer that you don't feel comfortable leaving outside the room while you take the test

# Making Sure You're Comfortable before the Test Begins

You usually take the GED test in an examination room with at least one official (sometimes called a *proctor* or *examiner*) who's in charge of the test. (Some locations have smaller test centers that have space for no more than 15 test-takers at a time.) In either case, the test is the same.

As soon as you sit down to take the GED test, take a few moments before the test actually starts to relax and get comfortable. You're going to be in the chair for quite some time, so hunker down. Keep these few tips in mind before you begin:

✔ **Make sure that the screen is at a comfortable height and adjust your chair to a height that suits you.** Unlike a pencil-and-paper test, you'll be working with a monitor and keyboard. Although you can shift the keyboard around and maybe change the angle of the monitor, generally you're stuck in that position for the duration of the test. If you need to make any adjustments, make them before you start. You want to feel as physically comfortable as possible.

✔ **Find out whether you can have something to drink at your computer station.** You may depend on that second cup of coffee to keep you upright and thinking. Even a bottle of water may make your life easier.

✔ **Go to the bathroom before you start.** This may sound like a silly suggestion, but it all goes to being comfortable. You don't need distractions. Even if bathroom breaks are permitted during the test, you don't want to take away time from the test.

The proctor reads the test instructions to you and lets you log into the computer to start the test. Listen carefully to these instructions so you know how much time you have to take the test as well as any other important information. Only the Reasoning through Language Arts test has a ten-minute break built into the time. The other tests are 90 minutes (or 115 minutes for the Mathematical Reasoning test) without a break. (Refer to the next section for details of the timing of each test.)

# Discovering Important Test-Taking Strategies

You can increase your score by mastering a few smart test-taking strategies. To help you do so, we give you some tips in these sections on how to

✔ Plan your time.

✔ Determine the question type.

✔ Figure out how to answer the different types of questions.

✔ Guess intelligently.

✔ Review your work.

# Watching the clock: Using your time wisely

When you start the computerized version of the GED test, you may feel pressed for time and have the urge to rush through the questions. We strongly advise that you don't. You have sufficient time to do the test at a reasonable pace. You have only a certain amount of time for each section in the GED exam, so time management is an important part of succeeding on the test. You need to plan ahead and use your time wisely.

You must complete each section in one sitting, except for the Reasoning through Language Arts test. There, you get a ten-minute break after the Extended Response (also known as the essay).

During the test, the computer keeps you constantly aware of the time with a clock in the upper right-hand corner. Pay attention to the clock. When the test begins, check that time, and be sure to monitor how much time you have left as you work your way through the test. Table 4-1 shows you how much time you have for each test section.

| Table 4-1 | Time for Each GED Test Section |
| --- | --- |
| *Test Section* | *Time Limit (in Minutes)* |
| Reasoning through Language Arts | 95 (split into two sections of 35 min and 60 min) |
| Reasoning through Language Arts, Extended Response | 45 |
| Social Studies | 90 |
| Science | 90 |
| Mathematical Reasoning | 115 |

As you start, quickly scroll through the test and find out how many questions you have to answer. Quickly divide the time by the number of questions. Doing so can give you a rough idea of how much time to spend on each question. For example, on the Mathematical Reasoning test, suppose that you see you have 50 questions to answer. You have 115 minutes to complete the test. Divide the time by the number of questions to find out how much time you have for each item: 115/50 = 2.3 minutes or 2 minutes and 18 seconds per item. As you progress, repeat the calculation to see how you're doing. Remember, too, that you can do questions in any order, except for the Extended Response items. Do the easiest questions first. If you get stuck on a question, leave it and come back to it later, if you have time. Keeping to that schedule and answering as many questions as possible are essential.

As you can see from Table 4-1, if you don't monitor the time for each question, you won't have time to answer all the questions on the test. Keep in mind the following general time-management tips to help you complete each exam on time:

✔ **Measure the time you have to answer each question without spending more time on timing than answering.** Group questions together; for example, use the information in Table 4-1 to calculate how much time you have for each item on each test. Multiply the answer by 5 to give you a time slot for any five test items. Then try to make sure that you answer each group of five items within the time you've calculated. Doing so helps you complete all the questions and leaves you several minutes for review.

✔ **Keep calm and don't panic.** The time you spend panicking could be better spent answering questions.

✔ **Practice using the sample tests in this book.** The more you practice timed sample test questions, the easier managing a timed test becomes. You can get used to doing something in a limited amount of time if you practice. Refer to the earlier section, "Using Practice Tests to Your Advantage" for more information.

When time is up, immediately stop and breathe a sigh of relief. When the test ends, the examiner will give you a log-off procedure. Listen for instructions on what to do or where to go next.

## Evaluating the different questions

Although you don't have to know too much about how the test questions, or items, were developed to answer them correctly, you do need some understanding of how they're constructed. Knowing the types of items you're dealing with can make answering them easier — and you'll face fewer surprises.

To evaluate the types of questions that you have to answer, keep these tips in mind:

✔ **As soon as the computer signals that the test is running, start by skimming the questions.** Don't spend a lot of time doing so — just enough to spot the questions you absolutely know and the ones you know you'll need more time to answer.

✔ **Rely on the Previous and Next buttons on the bottom of the screen to scroll through the questions.** After you finish skimming, answer all the questions you know first; that way, you leave yourself much more time for the difficult questions. Check out the later section "Addressing and answering questions" for tips on how to answer questions.

✔ **Answer the easiest ones first.** You don't have to answer questions in order. Nobody except you will ever know, or care, in which order you answer the questions, so do the easiest questions first. You'll be able to answer them fastest, leaving more time for the other, harder, questions.

Knowing the question type can shape the way you think about the answer. Some questions ask you to analyze a passage or extract from a document, which means the information you need is in the source text. Others ask you to infer from the passage, which means that not all of the information is in the passage. Although none of the tests are labeled with the following titles, the GED test questions assess your skills in these areas.

### Analysis

*Analysis* questions require you to break down information and look at how the information bits are related to one another. Analyzing information in this way is part of reasoning and requires you to

✔ **Separate facts from opinions.** Unless the text you're reading gives evidence or "proof" to support statements, treat them as opinion.

✔ **Realize that when an assumption isn't stated that it may not necessarily be true.** Assumptions stated in the passage or question help you find the best answer.

✔ **Identify a cause-and-effect relationship.** For example, you have to eat an ice-cream cone quickly in hot weather. The cause is the hot weather and the effect is that the ice cream melts quickly.

✔ **Infer.** You may be asked to reach a conclusion based on evidence presented in the question. *Inferring* is a fancy way of saying that you'll reach a conclusion. In the preceding example, you can infer that you should stay in an air-conditioned space to eat your ice cream or eat it very quickly.

> ✔ **Compare.** If you consider the similarities between ideas or objects, you're *comparing* them. For example, the world is like a basketball because both are round.
>
> ✔ **Contrast.** If you consider the differences between ideas or objects, you're *contrasting* them. For example, the world isn't like a basketball because it's so much larger and has an irregular surface.

Relating to other people in social situations exposes most people to these skills. For example, in most sports-related conversations between friends (or rivals), you quickly figure out how to separate fact from opinion and how to infer, compare, contrast, and identify cause-and-effect relationships. In other social situations, you come to realize when an assumption isn't stated. For example, you likely assume that your best friend or significant other is going to join you for a late coffee the night before an important test, but, in reality, your friend may be planning to go to bed early. Unstated assumptions you make can get you into trouble, both in life and on the GED test.

### Application

*Application* questions require you to use the information presented to you in one situation to help you in a different situation. You've been applying information left and right for most of your life, but you probably don't realize it. For example, when you use the information from the morning newspaper to make a point in an argument in the afternoon, you use your application skills.

### Comprehension

A *comprehension* question asks whether you understand written material. The GED test-makers expect you to be able to state the info on the test in your own words, develop a summary of the ideas presented, discuss the implications of those ideas, and draw conclusions from those implications. You need to develop these comprehension skills to understand what the questions are asking you and to answer the questions quickly and accurately.

The best way to increase your comprehension is to read extensively and to ask another person to ask you questions about what you read. You can also use commercial books that specifically help you with your comprehension by presenting you with written material and asking you questions about it. One of those books is in your hands. All the other *For Dummies* test-preparation books as well as *AP English Literature & Composition For Dummies,* by Geraldine Woods (Wiley), have reading comprehension as a major focus, too. Feel free to check out these books to improve your comprehension if you still have difficulty after using this book.

### Synthesis

*Synthesis* questions require you to take apart blocks of information presented to you and put the pieces back together to form a hypothesis, theory, or story. Doing so gives you a new understanding or twist on the information that you didn't have before. Have you ever discussed something that happened, giving it your own twist and explanation to create a brand new narrative? If so, you've already put your synthesis skills to use.

### Evaluation

Any time someone presents you with information or opinion, you judge it to make sure it rings true in your mind. This *evaluation* helps you make decisions about the information presented before you decide to use it. If the clerk behind the ice-cream counter suggests that you get a raspberry cone rather than the flavor you wanted because everyone knows that raspberry melts slower than all the other flavors, you may be a bit suspicious. If you notice that the clerk also has four containers of raspberry ice cream and only one of each other flavor, you may evaluate his comment as biased or even incorrect.

### Cognitive skills

Mental skills that you use to get knowledge are called *cognitive skills* and include reasoning, perception, and intuition. They're particularly important in reading for understanding, which is what you're asked to do on the GED test. You can increase your knowledge and comprehension by reading books, researching on the web, or watching documentaries. After you read or watch something new, discuss it with others to make sure you understand it and can use the information in conversation.

## Addressing and answering questions

When you start the test, you want to have a game plan in place for how to answer the questions. Keep the following tips in mind to help you address each question:

- **Whenever you read a question, ask yourself, "What am I being asked?"** Doing so helps you stay focused on what you need to find out to answer the question. You may even want to decide quickly what skills are required to answer the question (see the preceding section for more on these skills). Then try to answer it.

- **Try to eliminate some answers.** Even if you don't really know the answer, guessing can help. When you're offered four answer choices, some will be obviously wrong. Eliminate those choices, and you have already improved your odds of guessing a correct answer.

- **Don't overthink.** Because all the questions are straightforward, don't look for hidden or sneaky questions. The questions ask for an answer based on the information given. If you don't have enough information to answer the question, one of the answer choices will say so.

- **Find the best answer and quickly verify that it answers the question.** If it does, click on that choice, and move on. If it doesn't, leave it and come back to it after you answer all the other questions, if you have time. *Remember:* You need to pick the *most* correct answer from the choices offered. It may not be the perfect answer, but it is what is required.

## Guess for success: Using intelligent guessing

The multiple-choice questions, regardless of the on-screen format, provide you with four possible answers. You get between one and three points for every correct answer. Nothing is subtracted for incorrect answers. That means you can guess on the items you don't know for sure without fear that you'll lose points. Make educated guesses by eliminating as many obviously wrong choices as possible and choosing from just one or two remaining choices.

When the question gives you four possible answers and you randomly choose one, you have a 25 percent chance of guessing the correct answer without even reading the question. Of course, we don't recommend using this method during the test.

If you know that one of the answers is definitely wrong, you now have just three answers to choose from and have a 33 percent chance (1 in 3) of choosing the correct answer. If you know that two of the answers are wrong, you leave yourself only two possible answers to choose from, giving you a 50 percent (1 in 2) chance of guessing right — much better than 25 percent! Removing two or three choices you know are wrong makes choosing the correct answer much easier.

If you don't know the answer to a particular question, try to spot the wrong choices by following these tips:

✔ **Make sure your answer really answers the question at hand.** Wrong choices usually don't answer the question — that is, they may sound good, but they answer a different question than the one the test asks.

✔ **When two answers seem very close, consider both answers carefully because they both can't be right — but they both *can* be wrong.** Some answer choices may be very close, and all seem correct, but there's a fine line between completely correct and nearly correct. Be careful. These answer choices are sometimes given to see whether you really understand the material.

✔ **Look for opposite answers in the hopes that you can eliminate one.** If two answers contradict each other, both can't be right, but both can be wrong.

✔ **Trust your instincts.** Some wrong choices may just strike you as wrong when you first read them. If you spend time preparing for these exams, you probably know more than you think.

## Leaving time for review

Having a few minutes at the end of a test to check your work is a great way to set your mind at ease. These few minutes give you a chance to look at any questions that may be troubling. If you've chosen an answer for every question, enjoy the last few minutes before time is called — without any panic. Keep the following tips in mind as you review your answers:

✔ **After you know how much time you have per item, try to answer each item in a little less than that time.** The extra seconds you don't use the first time through the test add up to time at the end of the test for review. Some questions require more thought and decision making than others. Use your extra seconds to answer those questions.

✔ **Don't try to change a lot of answers at the last minute.** Second-guessing yourself can lead to trouble. Often, second-guessing leads you to changing correct answers to incorrect ones. If you have prepared well and worked numerous sample questions, then you're likely to get the correct answers the first time. Ignoring all your preparation and knowledge to play a hunch isn't a good idea, either at the race track or on a test.

✔ **On tests where you're required to write essays, use any extra time to reread and review your final essay.** You may have written a good essay, but you always need to check for typos and grammar mistakes. The essay is evaluated both for style, content, and proper English. That includes spelling and grammar.

# Keeping Your Head in the Game

To succeed in taking the GED test, you need to be prepared. In addition to studying the content and skills needed for the four test sections, you also want to be mentally prepared. Although you may be nervous, you can't let your nerves get the best of you. Stay calm and take a deep breath. Here are a few pointers to help you stay focused on the task at hand:

✔ **Take time to relax.** Passing the GED test is an important milestone in life. Make sure you leave a bit of time to relax, both while you prepare for the test sections and just before you take them. Relaxing has a place in preparing as long as it doesn't become your main activity.

✔ **Make sure you know the rules of the room before you begin.** If you have questions about using the bathroom during the test or what to do if you finish early, ask the proctor before you begin. If you don't want to ask these questions in public, call the GED office in your area before test day, and ask your questions over the telephone. For general GED questions, call 800-62-MYGED or check out www.gedtestingservice.com. This site has many pages, but the FAQ page is always a good place to start.

✔ **Keep your eyes on your monitor.** Everybody knows not to look at other people's work during the test, but, to be on the safe side, don't stretch, roll your eyes, or do anything else that may be mistaken for looking at another test. Most of the tests will be different on the various computers, so looking around is futile, but doing so can get you into a lot of trouble.

✔ **Stay calm.** Your nerves can use up a lot of energy needed for the test. Concentrate on the job at hand. You can always be nervous or panicky some other time.

Because taking standardized tests probably isn't a usual situation for you, you may feel nervous. This is perfectly normal. Just try to focus on answering one question at a time, and push any other thoughts to the back of your mind. Sometimes taking a few deep breaths can clear your mind; just don't spend a lot of time focusing on your breath. After all, your main job is to pass the GED test.

# Part II

# Minding Your Ps and Qs: The Reasoning through Language Arts Test

## Five Tested Tips for Preparing for the RLA Test

✔ **Read, read, and read some more.** You want to be able to absorb material quickly and accurately. Practice with different types of reading materials, from newspaper articles and novels to textbooks and instruction manuals.

✔ **Learn to discriminate between accurate and false arguments.** Authors of opinion pieces use wording to make their points stronger and more persuasive. Techniques like repetition, appeals to emotions, reams of statistical data, and comparisons all help persuade an audience.

✔ **Review lists of common spelling errors.** Practice spelling these words correctly and using them in your everyday writing. You'll do better if you recognize common mistakes in text and can eliminate it from your own writing.

✔ **Brush up your grammar skills.** Grammar is an important part of the Reasoning through Language Arts test. If you're weak in this area, find a basic grammar book, such as *English Grammar For Dummies*, by Geraldine Woods (Wiley), a used high-school English book, or even an online grammar tutor, such as English Grammar 101 (www.englishgrammar101.com).

✔ **Practice your computer and keyboarding skills.** This test is given on a computer, and you'll be using a modified word processor. No matter what anyone else tells you, the better and more accurate your keyboarding skills are, the faster you can get your ideas on the screen during the Extended Response. The time you save in keyboarding gives you more time for editing your writing, so you end up with a better essay and thus a better mark.

Reading quickly and accurately are important to passing the GED test; for more tips, go to www.dummies. com/extras/gedtest.

## In this part . . .

✔ Find out everything you ever wanted to know about the Reasoning through Language Arts test, including what types of materials you're expected to read and answer questions about, how the test and questions are formatted, and what the Extended Response item is like.

✔ Discover some strategies to help you do your best on this test and put them to practice on some sample test questions.

# Chapter 5

# Preparing for the Reasoning through Language Arts Test

**In This Chapter**

▶ Getting familiar with the writing and grammar component of the RLA test

▶ Developing your reading and comprehension skills

▶ Preparing to write an essay

▶ Discovering tactics to help you succeed

The Reasoning through Language Arts (RLA) test evaluates your skills in comprehending and applying concepts in grammar and writing. (*Grammar* is the basic structure of language — you know: subjects, verbs, sentences, fragments, punctuation, and all that.) Most of what you're tested on (both in writing and grammar) is stuff you've picked up over the years, either in school or just by speaking, reading, and observing, but, to help you prepare better for this test, we give you some more skill-building tips in this chapter.

The RLA test is divided into three sections. You start off with a 35-minute question-and-answer section that focuses on writing and reading comprehension, and then you spend 45 minutes writing an Extended Response (the essay). After a 10-minute break, you finish with a 60-minute question-and-answer section that presents more questions on reading and writing. The length of the two question-and-answer sections may vary slightly, but the overall time is always 150 minutes, including the 10-minute break.

In this chapter, we provide all you need to know to prepare for the RLA test and its different components. From reading everything you can, to practicing your writing, grammar, and spelling, to improving your reading comprehension and speed, this chapter equips you with what you need so you can walk into the testing center on test day armed and ready to ace the test.

## Grasping What's on the Grammar and Writing Component

Although the GED doesn't label question sets with the words *writing* or *grammar,* the concepts are worked into almost everything on the test. To pass this component of the RLA test, you need to demonstrate that you have a command of the conventions of standard English. You need to know the appropriate vocabulary to use and avoid slang. Texting shortcuts may save you time while communicating with your friends, but they're not acceptable in formal writing. You need to be able to spell, identify incorrect grammar, and eliminate basic errors, including such common errors as run-on sentences or sentence fragments.

To help you succeed, we provide insightful information in the following sections about what skills this part of the test covers, what you can do to brush up on those skills, and the general question format for this component. With this information in hand, you can be confident in your ability to tackle any type of grammar or writing question on test day.

## *Looking at the skills the grammar and writing component covers*

The grammar and writing component of the RLA test evaluates you on the following types of skills related to grammar. Note that unlike the other GED test sections, this component of the RLA test expects that you *know* or at least *are familiar with* the rules of grammar. Just looking at the passages provided won't do you much good if you don't understand the basics of these rules already.

- **Mechanics:** You don't have to become a professional grammarian to pass this test, but you should know or review basic grammar. Check out *English Grammar For Dummies,* 2nd Edition, by Geraldine Woods (Wiley), to review what you should know or may have forgotten. The mechanics of writing include the following:

  - **Capitalization:** You have to recognize which words should start with a capital letter and which words don't. All sentences start with a capital letter but so do titles, like *Miss, President,* and *Senator,* when they're followed by a person's name. Names of cities, states, and countries are also capitalized.

  - **Punctuation:** This area of writing mechanics includes everyone's personal favorite: commas. (Actually, most people hate commas because they aren't sure how to use them, but the basic rules are simple.) The more you read, the better you get at punctuation. If you're reading and don't understand why punctuation is or isn't used, check with your grammar guidebook or the Internet.

    A general rule: Don't use a comma unless the next group of words is a complete sentence. For example: "As agonizing as it was to leave her friends, college was what she wanted." *College was what she wanted* is a complete sentence and can stand alone, so using a comma here is correct.

  - **Spelling:** You don't have to spot a lot of misspelled words, but you do have to know how to spell contractions and possessives and understand the different spellings of *homonyms* — words that sound the same but have different spellings and meanings, like *their* and *there.*

  - **Contractions:** This area of writing mechanics has nothing to do with those painful moments before childbirth! Instead, *contractions* are formed when the English language shortens a word by leaving out a letter or a sound. For example, when you say or write *can't,* you're using a shortened form of *cannot.* In this example, *can't* is the contraction.

    The important thing to remember about contractions is that the *apostrophe* (that's a single quotation mark) takes the place of the letter or letters that are left out.

  - **Possessives:** Do you know people who are possessive? They're all about ownership, right? So is the grammar form of possessives. *Possessives* are words that show ownership or possession, usually by adding an apostrophe to a person's or object's name. If Marcia owns a car, that car is *Marcia's* car. The word *Marcia's* is a possessive. Make sure you know the difference between singular and plural possessives. For example: "The girl's coat is torn." (*Girl* and *coat* are singular, so the apostrophe goes before the *s.*) "The girls' coats are torn." (*Girls* and coats are plural, so the apostrophe goes after the *s.*) When working with plural possessives, form the plural first and then add the apostrophe.

- **Organization:** On the test, you're asked to correct passages by changing the order of sentences or leaving out certain sentences when they don't fit. You have to work with passages to turn them into logical, organized paragraphs. You may be asked to work with paragraphs to form a better composition by changing them around, editing them by improving or adding topic sentences, or making sure that all the sentences are about the same topic. The important thing to remember is that the questions all offer you a choice of answers. That means you have only a limited number of options for making the passages better. Read the questions carefully, and you should have no problems.

✔ **Sentence structure:** Every language has rules about the order in which words should appear in a sentence. You get a chance to improve sentences through your understanding of what makes a good sentence. Extensive reading before the test can give you a good idea of how good sentences are structured and put together. The advice here is read, read, and read some more.

✔ **Usage:** This broad category covers a lot of topics. Grammar has a wide variety of rules, and these questions test your knowledge and understanding. Subjects and verbs must agree. Verbs have tenses that must be consistent. Pronouns must refer back to nouns properly. If the last three sentences sound like Greek to you, make sure you review grammatical usage rules. It also covers vocabulary and acceptable standard English usage. People have become very comfortable with short forms used in texting, but "LOL" or "C U L8R" aren't acceptable in standard writing.

Having a firm grasp of these writing mechanics can help you get a more accurate picture of the types of questions you'll encounter on this part of the test.

## Understanding the format of the grammar and writing component

The grammar and writing component consist of a set of questions, mainly multiple-choice but also drag-and-drop or other technologically enhanced question formats and the occasional fill-in-the-blank question. One type of question asks you to read, revise, and edit documents that may include how-to info, informational texts, and workplace materials. Don't worry — almost all of the questions are some form of multiple-choice, which means you don't have to come up with the answers all on your own. And the best part: Practicing for this component helps you understand the grammar and other language skills needed for the Extended Response. It even carries over to the other GED test sections.

To answer the questions in this part of the RLA test, read the information presented to you carefully. Reading the questions before reading the entire text is often helpful because then you know what to look for. And because you're dealing with grammar, as you read each passage, you can ask yourself, "Can I correct this passage? If so, how?"

# Rocking the Reading Comprehension Component

You may not understand why the GED tests your knowledge of literature comprehension. However, in today's society, being able to comprehend, analyze, and apply something you've read is the strongest predictor of career and college readiness and an important skill set to have. In the following sections, we explore the four aspects of good reading skills: comprehension, application, analysis, and synthesis.

## Looking at the skills the reading component covers

The questions on the RLA reading portion of the test focus on the following skills, which you're expected to be able to use as you read both fiction and nonfiction passages:

✔ **Comprehension:** Questions that test your *comprehension* skills assess your ability to read a source of information, understand what you've read, and restate the information in your own words. If you understand the passage, you can rephrase what you read without losing the meaning of the passage. You can also create a summary of the main ideas presented in the passage and explain the ideas and implications of the passage.

- ✔ **Application:** Questions that test your *application* skills assess your ability to use the information you read in the passage in a new situation, such as when you're answering questions. Application-focused questions are most like real life because they often ask you to apply what you read in the passage to a real-life situation. Being able to read and understand a users' manual in order to use the product it came with is a perfect example of using your application skills in real life.

- ✔ **Analysis:** Questions that test your *analysis* skills assess your ability to draw conclusions, understand consequences, and make inferences after reading the passage. To answer these questions successfully, you have to make sure your conclusions are based solely on the written text in the passage and not on outside knowledge or the book you read last week. Questions that focus on your ability to analyze what you read try to find out whether you appreciate the way the passage was written and see the cause-and-effect relationships within it. They also expect you to know when a conclusion is being stated and analyze what it means in the context of the passage.

- ✔ **Synthesis:** Questions that test your *synthesis* skills assess your ability to take information in one form and in one location and put it together in another context. Here, you get a chance to make connections between different parts of the passage and compare and contrast them. You may be asked to talk about the tone, point of view, style, or purpose of a passage — and saying that the purpose of a passage is to confuse and confound test-takers isn't the answer.

Some reading-comprehension questions on the test may ask you to use information in the source text passages combined with information from the text in the questions to answer them. So make sure you read everything that appears on-screen — you never know where an answer may come from.

## *Understanding the format of the reading component*

The RLA reading comprehension section measures your ability to understand and interpret fiction and nonfiction passages. It's plain and simple — no tricks involved. You don't have to do any math to figure out the answers to the questions. You just have to read, understand, and use the material presented to you to answer the corresponding questions.

The passages in this test are similar to the works a high-school student would come across in English class. To help you feel more comfortable with the RLA reading comprehension, we're here to give you a better idea of what this test looks like on paper.

Most source texts (the reading passages) are presented on the left side of a split screen, with the question on the right. A source text or passage will be between 450 and 900 words. The passages in this test may come from workplace (on-the-job) materials or from academic reading materials. Seventy-five percent of the source text will be from informational texts — nonfiction documents. The remaining 25 percent is based on literary texts, including plays, poetry, short stories, and novels. With each source text, you have to answer four to eight questions.

Text passages are text passages. Although the next section describes what types of passages appear on the RLA test to help you prepare, don't worry so much about what type of passage you're reading. Instead, spend your time understanding what information the passage presents to you.

# Identifying the types of passages and how to prepare for them

To help you get comfortable with answering the questions on the reading comprehension portion of the RLA test, you want to have a good idea of what these types of questions look like. The good news is that in this section, we focus on the two main types of passages you'll see: literary and nonfiction. We also give you some practical advice you can use as you prepare for this portion of the test.

## Literary passages

The RLA reading component may include passages from the following literary texts (and plenty of questions to go with them):

✔ **Drama:** *Drama* (that is, a play) tells a story, using the words and actions of the characters. The description of the place and costumes are in the stage directions or in the head of the director. As you read passages from drama, try to imagine the dramatic scene and see the characters and their actions in your head. Doing so makes drama easier to understand.

Stage directions are usually printed in italics, *like this*. Even though you're not acting in the play, pay attention to the stage directions. They may provide valuable information you need to answer the questions that follow the passage.

✔ **Prose fiction:** *Prose fiction* refers to novels and short stories. As you may already know, *fiction* is writing that comes straight from the mind of the author (in other words, it's made up; it's not about something that really happened). The only way to become familiar with prose fiction is to read as much fiction as you can. After you read a book, try to talk about it with other people who have read the book.

## Nonfiction passages

Nonfiction passages may come from many different sources. Here's a list of some of the kinds of passages you may see, and of course, answer questions about:

✔ **Critical reviews of visual and performing arts:** These prose passages are reviews written by people who have enough knowledge of the visual or performing arts to be critical of them. You can find examples of good critical reviews in the library, in some daily papers, and on the Internet. Type in "critical review" into your favorite search engine, and you'll get more critical reviews than you have time to read.

To prepare for this part of the test, try to read critical reviews of books, movies, restaurants, and the like as often as you can. The next time you go to a movie, watch television, or go to a play, write your own critical review (what you thought of the piece of work). Put some factual material into your review and make suggestions for improvement. Compare what the real critics have to say with your own feelings about the movie, television show, or play. Do you agree with their opinions?

✔ **Nonfiction prose:** *Nonfiction prose* is prose that covers a lot of ground — and all the ground is real. Nonfiction prose is material that the author doesn't create in his or her own mind — it's based on fact or reality. In fact, this book is classified as nonfiction prose, and so are the newspaper articles you read every day. The next time you read the newspaper or a magazine, tell yourself, "I'm reading nonfiction prose." Just don't say it out loud in a coffee shop or in your break room at work — or people may start to look at you in strange ways.

✔ **Workplace and community documents:** You run across these types of passages in the job- and community-related areas of life. The following are some examples:

   • **Corporate statements:** Companies and organizations issue rules for employee behavior, rules for hiring and firing, goals for the corporation, even statements about corporate rules on environmental stewardship. These tell the world what the company intends to accomplish and what the basic rules of behavior within the company are. The goal statement for your study group may be as follows: "We're all going to pass the GED test on our first attempt."

- **Historic documents, founding documents, legal documents:** These could include extracts from the Constitution or other founding documents, extracts from treaties, or legal documents. The founding and historical documents are obviously older materials, with a somewhat different writing style from what you may see in a modern legal document. Other documents may include leases, purchase contracts, and bank statements. If you aren't familiar with these kinds of documents, collect some examples from banks or libraries and review them. Have a look at the terms in your lease, mortgage, or credit card statement. If you can explain these types of documents to a friend, you understand them.

- **Letters:** You certainly know what a *letter* is: a written communication between two people. It's not very often that you get to read other people's letters without getting into trouble — here's your chance.

- **Manuals:** Every time you invest in a major purchase, you get a users' manual that tells you how to use the item. Some manuals are short and straightforward; others are so long and complicated that the manufacturers put them on CD-ROMs to save printing costs.

Regardless of what type of passage the questions in the reading component are based on, you have two challenges. The first is grammar. Grammar doesn't change with the type of passage, so, although you should be familiar with the various types of passages, you need to be most familiar with the rules of grammar so you can use them to improve the passages. The second is reading skills. You need to answer questions, using the four skills outlined in the earlier section "Looking at the skills the reading component covers": comprehension, application, analysis, and synthesis.

# Examining the Extended Response Item

In spite of its name, the Extended Response doesn't consist of a real research essay so much as a series of related paragraphs. You aren't expected to produce a book-length opus complete with documented research. Rather, you're expected to write a coherent series of interrelated paragraphs on a given topic and use the rules of grammar and correct spelling. Part of that essay will be an analysis of materials presented to you, and part will be preparation of logical argument. Examiners look for an essay that's well organized and sticks to the topic given.

In the following sections, we show you what you need to know about the Extended Response and give you some tools for writing a successful essay.

## Looking at the skills the Extended Response covers

The evaluation of your essay focuses on three major criteria or skills. By having a clear understanding of the main skills covered in this part of the test, you can ensure that you address all of them when writing your essay — that will translate into success in terms of your essay score. The GED Testing Service defines the three essay criteria you need to address as follows:

✔ **Creation of argument and use of evidence:** This criterion refers to how well you answer the topic, including whether the focus of the response shifts as you write. Stay on topic.

✔ **Development and organizational structure:** This criterion refers to whether you show the reader through your essay that you have a clear idea about what you're writing and that you're able to establish a definable plan for writing the essay. The evaluation expects that you'll present your arguments in a logical sequence and back those arguments with specific supporting evidence from the source text. Remember, you must use specific detail from the source texts; you can elaborate, but your answer must be based on the source text.

✔ **Clarity and command of standard English conventions:** This criterion refers to your ability to appropriately use what the GED Testing Service calls "on-demand, draft writing." That includes the application of the basic rules of grammar, such as sentence structure, mechanics, usage, and so forth. It's also looking for stylistic features, such as transitional phrases, varied sentence structure, and appropriate word choices.

The evaluation grades your essay on a three-point scale. You receive 2, 1, or 0 points, depending on your success in each of these three categories. You can check out a guide for teachers on the RLA Extended Response at `www.gedtestingservice.com/uploads/files/949aa6a0418791c4f3b962a4cd0c92f4.pdf`. Here, you can see a sample essay prompt and breakdown of how it's evaluated. It includes a very detailed look at the criteria and what the evaluators look for in an essay that receives a passing score.

Read the sections on what constitutes a passing score very carefully. If you don't pass the essay, you probably won't accumulate a high enough score on the other sections to pass the RLA test, and that means you'll have to retake the entire test.

## Understanding the Extended Response format

This 45-minute part of the Reasoning through Language Arts (RLA) test has only one item: a prompt on which you have to write a short essay (usually 600 to 800 words).

For this part of the test, you're given one topic and a few instructions. Your task is to write an essay of three or more paragraphs on that topic. Remember that you can't write about another topic or a similar topic — if you do, you'll receive zero points for your essay, and you'll have to retake the entire RLA test.

The focus for the evaluation of this part of the GED test is on your reading comprehension, analysis and organization, and writing skills.

The test presents you with one or two passages of argumentation. That means the writer(s) takes a position on an issue. You must examine the positions, determine which is the stronger and best defended, and write an essay explaining why you made that choice. You have to do that regardless of how you feel about the issue. The point is to analyze and show that you understand the strategies used to defend positions.

As part of that process, you must analyze the arguments for logical consistency, illogical conclusions, and false reasoning. This is where your critical analysis skills come into play. Does Point A from the author really make sense? Is it valid and backed by facts?

Finally, you must write your answer in a clear, concise, and well-organized response. The evaluation examines how well you write, including the following aspects:

✔ Your style

✔ Varied sentence structure and vocabulary

✔ Use of transitional sentences

✔ Appropriate vocabulary

✔ Correct spelling and grammar, including word usage and punctuation

You have an erasable tablet for rough notes, points, and draft organization. Use it. The computer screen has a window that offers a mini-word processor with some basic functions, such as cut and paste and undo and redo. However, it doesn't offer a spell-checker or grammar-checker.

# Preparing to succeed on the Extended Response

The Extended Response essay requires some very specific skills, ranging from grammar and proper language usage to comprehension and analysis skills. If you've ever had an argument about who has the best team or which employer is better, you already know how to assess arguments and respond. Now you need to hone those skills. As you prepare for the RLA Extended Response, do the following:

- ✔ **Read, read, and read some more.** Just like for the other parts of the RLA test (and most other tests on the GED), reading is important. Reading exposes you to well-crafted sentences, which can help you improve your own writing. Reading also expands your horizons and provides you with little bits of information you can work into your essay.

  As you read, make an outline of the paragraphs or chapters you read to see how the material ties together. Try rewriting some of the paragraphs from your outline, and compare what you write to the original. Yours may not be ready for prime time, but this little exercise gives you practice in writing organized, cohesive sentences and paragraphs, which can go a long way in this part of the test.

- ✔ **Practice editing your own work.** After the test starts, the only person able to edit your essay is you. If that thought scares you, practice editing your own work now. Take a writing workshop, or get help from someone who knows how to edit. Practice writing a lot of essays, and don't forget to review and edit them as soon as you're done writing.

- ✔ **Review how to plan an essay.** Few people can sit down, write a final draft of an essay the first time around, and receive a satisfactory grade. Instead, you have to plan what you're going to write. The best way to start is to jot down everything you know about a topic without worrying about the order. From there, you can organize your thoughts into groups. Check out Chapter 6 for more help on planning your essay.

- ✔ **Practice writing on a topic (and not going off topic!).** Your essay must relate to the given topic as closely as possible. If the test asks you to write about your personal goals, and you write about a hockey game you once played in, you can kiss your good score on this part of the test goodbye.

  To help you practice staying on topic, read the newspaper and write a letter to the editor or a response to a columnist. Because you're responding to a very narrow topic that appeared in a particular newspaper article, you have to do so clearly and concisely — if you ever want to see it in print. (You can also practice staying on topic by picking a newspaper article's title and writing a short essay about it. Then read the actual story and see how yours compares.)

- ✔ **Think about, and use, appropriate examples.** You're dealing with information presented in the source text. You'll find information in the source text for and against the position you are to argue. When you take a position, you need to use materials from the source text to support your position. Use that information. Look for flaws in the logic. You can find good examples of such arguments in the editorial section of a newspaper or in blogs. Look at how the writers develop their arguments, use logic to support their positions, and perhaps use false logic or flawed reasoning to persuade the readers.

- ✔ **Practice general writing.** If writing connected paragraphs isn't one of your fortes, practice doing so! Write long e-mails. Write long letters. Write to your member of Congress. Write to your friends. Write articles for community newspapers. Write short stories. Write anything you want — whatever you do, just keep writing.

✔ **Write practice essays.** Check out practice tests in Chapters 17 and 25 for some essay prompts (in actual test format). Write essays based on the topics given, and then ask a knowledgeable friend or former teacher to grade them for you. You can also read a couple of sample essays based on the same topics you're given in Chapters 18 and 26. You may want to take a preparation class in which you're assigned practice topics to write about, too. When you think you're finished practicing, practice some more.

# Preparing for the RLA Test with Tactics That Work

The RLA test requires a number of skills, from knowing proper spelling, usage, and punctuation to reading quickly and accurately. You can master all of these skills with practice. The following sections give some advice on how to do that.

## Developing skills to read well

To succeed on the RLA test, you can prepare in advance by reviewing rules of grammar, punctuation, and spelling and by familiarizing yourself with the format and subject matter of the test. Here are some of the best ways you can prepare:

✔ **Read as often as you can.** This strategy is the best one and is by far the simplest, because reading exposes you to correct grammar. What you read makes a difference. Reading catalogs may increase your product knowledge and improve your research skills, but reading literature is preferable because it introduces you to so many rules of grammar. Reading fiction exposes you to interesting words and sentences. It shows you how paragraphs tie into one another and how each paragraph has a topic and generally sticks to it. Reading historical fiction can give you some insight into what led up to today and can also help you with the Social Studies test (see Chapters 8 through 10 for more on the Social Studies test).

You should also read nonfiction — from instructions to business letters, from press releases to history books and historical documents. Nonfiction is generally written at a higher reading level than fiction and uses a very formal style, the kind expected of you when you write an essay for the Extended Response item. Older documents can be a special problem, because the writing style is very different from what's common today. Getting familiar with such documents will help you to better results and even help with your Social Studies test.

Read everything you can get your hands on — even cereal boxes — and identify what kind of reading you're doing. Ask yourself questions about your reading and see how much of it you can remember.

✔ **Develop your reading speed.** Reading is wonderful, but reading quickly is even better — it gets you through the test with time to spare. Check out *Speed Reading For Dummies,* by Richard Sutz with Peter Weverka (Wiley), or do a quick Internet search to find plenty of material that can help you read faster. Whatever method you use, try to improve your reading rate without hurting your overall reading comprehension.

✔ **Master the rules of basic grammar.** On this test, you don't have to define a gerund and give an example of one, but you do have to know about verb tenses, subject-verb agreement, pronoun-antecedent agreement, possessives, and the like. As your knowledge of grammar and punctuation improves, have a bit of fun by correcting what you read in small-town newspapers and low-budget novels — both sometimes have poor editing.

✔ **Practice grammar and proper English in everyday speaking.** As you review the rules of grammar, practice them every day as you talk to your friends, family, and coworkers. Although correct grammar usually "sounds" right to your ears, sometimes it doesn't because you and the people you talk to have become used to using incorrect grammar. If you see a rule that seems different from the way you talk, put it on a flashcard and practice it as you go through your day. Before long, you'll train your ears so that correct grammar sounds right.

Correcting other people's grammar out loud doesn't make you popular, but correcting it in your head can help you succeed on this test. Also, listen for and avoid slang or regional expressions. *Y'all* may be a great favorite in the South but wouldn't work well on a college application.

✔ **Understand punctuation.** Know how to use commas, semicolons, colons, and other forms of punctuation. To find out more about punctuation and when and why to use its different forms, check out a grammatical reference book like *English Grammar For Dummies,* 2nd Edition, by Geraldine Woods (Wiley).

✔ **Practice writing.** Write as much and as often as you can, and then review it for errors. Look for and correct mistakes in punctuation, grammar, and spelling. If you can't find any, ask someone who knows grammar and punctuation for help.

✔ **Keep a journal or blog.** Journals and blogs are just notebooks (physical or virtual) in which you write a bit about your life every day. They both provide good practice for personal writing. Blogging or responding to blogs gives you practice in public writing because others see what you write. Whether you use a personal journal or a public blog, though, keep in mind that the writing is the important part. If public writing encourages you to write more and more often, do it. If not, consider the private writing of a journal or diary.

✔ **Improve your spelling.** As you practice writing, keep a good dictionary at hand. If you're not sure of the spelling of any word, look it up. We hear you. How do you look up the spelling of a word if you can't spell it? Try sounding out the word phonetically and look in an online dictionary. Type in the word and select the word that looks familiar and correct. If that doesn't work, ask someone for help. Add the word to a spelling list and practice spelling those words. In addition, get a list of common *homonyms* — words that sound the same but are spelled differently and have different definitions — and review them every day. (You need to know, for example, the difference between *their, there,* and *they're* and *to, two,* and *too.*) Many dictionaries contain a list of homonyms.

✔ **Keep in mind that these questions are some form of multiple-choice.** Among the various answer choices, the test questions generally give you the correct answer. Of course, they also tell you three other answers that are incorrect, but all you have to do is find the correct one! As you practice speaking and writing, you tune your ears so the correct answer sounds right, which, believe it or not, makes finding the correct answer easier on the test.

✔ **Take practice tests.** Take as many practice tests as you can. Be strict about time limitations, and check your answers after you're finished. Don't move on until you know and understand the correct answer. (Check out Chapter 7 for some preliminary practice questions and Chapters 17 and 25 for two full-length sample tests.) The time you spend taking and reviewing these practice tests is well worth it.

## *Navigating text to comprehend*

After you know what to read to prepare for this test, you need to focus on how to read. You can't easily skim the type of prose that appears on the test. You need to read each question and passage completely to find the right answer. Here are some tactics that will help you do just that:

- ✔ **Read carefully.** When you read, read carefully. If reading novels, plays, or historical documents is unfamiliar to you, read these items even more carefully. The more carefully you read any material, the easier it'll be for you to get the right answers on the test.

- ✔ **Ask questions.** Ask yourself questions about what you just read. Could you take a newspaper column and reduce the content to four bulleted points and still summarize the column accurately? Do you understand the main ideas well enough to explain them to a stranger (Note that we don't advise going up to strangers to explain things to them in person. Pretend you're going to explain it to a stranger and do all the talking in your head. If you want to explain what you read to someone in person, ask your friends and family to lend you an ear — or two.)

  Ask for help if you don't understand something you read. You may want to form a study group and work with other people. If you're taking a test-preparation course, ask the instructor for help when you need it. If you have family, friends, or coworkers who can help, ask them.

- ✔ **Use a dictionary.** Not many people understand every word they read, so use a dictionary. Looking up unfamiliar words increases your vocabulary, which, in turn, makes passages on the Reasoning through Language Arts test easier to understand. If you have a thesaurus, use it, too. Often knowing a synonym for the word you don't know is helpful. Plus, it improves your Scrabble game.

- ✔ **Use new words.** A new word doesn't usually become part of your vocabulary until you put it to use in your everyday language. When you come across a new word, make sure you know its meaning and try to use it in a sentence. Then try to work it into conversation for a day or two. After a while, this challenge can make each day more exciting. If you don't know what you don't know, you can find lists of important words online, such as "the 100 most commonly misspelled or misunderstood words" or "words important to pass the SAT." These can be a good start to increasing your vocabulary.

- ✔ **Practice.** Take the Reasoning through Language Arts practice tests in Chapters 17 and 25. Do the questions and check your answers. Look at the detailed answer explanations that we provide in Chapters 18 and 26. Don't move on to the next answer until you understand the preceding one. If you want more practice tests, look for additional test-prep books at your local bookstore or library. You can also find some abbreviated tests on the Internet. Type in "GED test questions" or "GED test questions + free" into your favorite search engine and check out some of the results. The GED Testing Service also offers free sample tests; check it out at `www.gedtestingservice.com/educators/freepracticetest`.

  Take as many practice tests as you can. Stick to the time limits, and keep the testing situation as realistic as possible. When you go to the test center for the official test, you'll feel more at ease because you practiced.

All the information you need to answer the reading questions is given in the passages or in the text of the questions that accompany the passages. You're not expected to recognize the passage and answer questions about what comes before it or what comes after it in context of the entire work. The passages are complete in themselves, so just focus on what you read.

Many people get hung up on the drama passages. Don't stress. Keep in mind that these literary genres are just different ways of telling a story and conveying feelings. If you're not familiar with them, read plays before taking the test. Discuss what you've read with others; you may even want to consider joining (or starting) a book club that discusses novels and plays.

# Chapter 6

# RLA Question Types and Solving Strategies

. . . . . . . . . . . . . . . . . . . . . . . . . . . . . . . . . . . . . . . . . . . . . . . . . . . . . . . . . . . . . .

## In This Chapter

▶ Focusing on key strategies for mastering the RLA writing component

▶ Discovering some test-taking tricks for surviving the RLA reading component

▶ Letting your language skills shine in the Extended Response

. . . . . . . . . . . . . . . . . . . . . . . . . . . . . . . . . . . . . . . . . . . . . . . . . . . . . . . . . . . . . .

The 150-minute Reasoning through Language Arts (RLA) test evaluates your ability to write clear and effective English and to read, analyze, and accurately assess and respond to the content of written passages. We go into detail about the RLA test particulars in Chapter 5. In this chapter, we help you navigate through the different question types on the RLA test and how to answer them.

## Tackling Items in the Writing Component

Because the GED test is now done on computer, the format of the questions varies, but they're essentially some variation of multiple-choice, with the occasional fill-in-the-blank item. (See Chapter 2 for samples of how questions appear on the computerized GED.)

In this section, we give you some sample questions based on the following business letter, along with advice on the best way to approach and answer them.

**BETA Café Equipment, Inc.**
**700 Millway Avenue, Unit 6**
**Concord, MA 12345**

John Charles
Executive Director
American Specialty Coffee Association
425 Pacific Drive, Suite 301
San Diego, CA 56789

Dear Mr. Charles:

(A)

(1) Thank you for you're interest in our new company, which serves the rapidly expanding specialty coffee industry. (2) BETA Café Equipment, Inc., were formed in 2014 to provide an affordable source of reconditioned Italian espresso/cappuccino machines for new businesses entering the industry.

(B)

(3) During our first year of operation BETA plans to repair and recondition 500 machines for use in restaurants and cafés. (4) This will generate revenue of more then $1,000,000. (5) Almost $500,000 will be created for returning 13 jobs to the local economy.

(C)

(6) BETA will have purchase used equipment, which will be shipped to our centralized repair and reconditioning depot. (7) After total rebuilding, equipment will be forwarded to regional sales offices to be sold to local restaurants and cafés at a much lower price than comparable new equipment. (8) Entrepreneurs wishing to start new specialty coffee businesses particularly should be interested in our products.

(D)

(9) To learn more about BETA please consult our website at www.betace.com, or give us a call at our toll-free number, 1-800-TRY-BETA. (10) Any assistance you can provide in sharing this information with your membership will be very much appreciated.

Yours truly,
Edwin Dale, President

# Mastering traditional multiple-choice questions

The multiple-choice questions on the writing component of the RLA test provide four answer choices, one of which is the best answer. If you aren't sure which one is correct, guessing is better than skipping the question and leaving it blank — that is, you don't get any points for not answering a question, and wrong answers don't count against you. Each question takes a sentence from a passage and asks you what changes you could make to improve it. Sometimes, the question is about just one part of the sentence, and sometimes you're asked to select from different options that pertain to the entire sentence, as in the following example.

Sentence 1: **Thank you for you're interest in our new company, which serves the rapidly expanding specialty coffee industry.**

Which correction should be made to Sentence 1?

(A) change *you're* to *your*

(B) place a comma after *serves*

(C) change *interest* to *concern*

(D) insert *but* after *rapidly*

The error in this sentence is that it confuses the homonyms *your* and *you're*. To correct the grammar error, you need to make the change suggested by Choice (A). Choice (B) tests your knowledge of punctuation rules — no comma is necessary in this case (when you read the sentence, notice how no natural pause occurs after the word *serves*). Choice (C) tests your ability to use vocabulary properly — changing *interest* to *concern* changes the meaning of the sentence and is incorrect. Similarly, Choice (D) tests your ability to use words appropriately — inserting the word *but* separates the verb *expanding* from the adverb *rapidly* and incorrectly suggests one has nothing to do with the other.

In the following example question, you're asked to pick the best wording for just one part of the sentence.

Sentence 2: **BETA Café Equipment, Inc., <u>were formed</u> in 2014 to provide an affordable source of reconditioned Italian espresso/cappuccino machines for new businesses entering the industry.**

What is the best way to write the underlined portion of this sentence?

(A) was being formed

(B) had formed

(C) was formed

(D) is formed

Look at the answer choices, one by one. Choice (A), *was being formed,* is the progressive past tense in the passive voice. That means the activity was ongoing, but the company was formed once, and that process is now over. So Choice (A) is wrong. Choice (B) uses the past perfect tense in the active voice. You don't need to worry about the name, but do remember this: In the active voice, the subject is doing the action; in the passive voice, the action is being done to the subject. Because someone was forming the company (the subject of the sentence), the voice must be passive. Therefore, Choice (B) is also wrong. Choice (C) uses the simple past tense. BETA Café Equipment, Inc., was created once in past. Because the sentence doesn't refer to another time or other events in the past, the proper tense here is the simple past. So Choice (C) is correct. Choice (D) is wrong because it's in the present tense. The action happened in the past, so using the present tense doesn't work.

Another way to answer problems like this is to read the sentence and substitute the choices for the underlined portion one at a time; you can often pick out the right answer just because it "sounds" right.

## Deciding on drop-down menu items

Besides the traditional multiple-choice option that asks a question and gives you four choices, the GED test also includes drop-down menus filled with multiple-choice options. On the computerized test, you click on the drop-down arrow and select the best choice for a word, phrase, or sentence from the options provided, and then that choice appears in the sentence. The following question gives you an example of the types of choices you may have to choose from in a drop-down menu. (*Note:* We couldn't simulate the look and feel of the drop-down menu in the print book, so we ask that you use your imagination and check out Chapter 2 for an example of how this question appears on the computerized GED test.)

Sentence (6) **BETA <u>will have purchase used equipment, which</u> will be shipped to our centralized repair and reconditioning depot.**

Select the most effective revision of the underlined portion of Sentence 6.

(A) will have purchased used equipment, which

(B) will purchase used equipment, which

(C) had purchased used equipment, which

(D) will purchase used equipment which

You can often find the correct answer to a question by eliminating the obviously incorrect choices. Looking at the answer choices here, Choice (A) simply makes no sense, because it uses the future perfect tense. That implies actions completed in the future, but this event is yet to happen. So, you can eliminate that choice right away. Choice (D) can be eliminated because you must have a comma in front of *which* because it starts a subordinate clause.

That leaves Choices (B) and (C). Because all the action in the passage is yet to happen, the purchase can't have been completed in the past, so the tense in Choice (C) is wrong. Choice (B) uses the simple future tense, appropriate for an action that will happen. So Choice (B) is the correct answer.

## Dealing with drag-and-drop items

The drag-and-drop item is essentially another multiple-choice question (because you get to select from a list of possible answers and don't have to come up with one all on your own). The difference is that you often have to sort the choices in a particular order, select which words apply and which one(s) doesn't, or even rank choices in some order of priority or importance. Here's an example of a sorting drag-and-drop question.

Look at the following series of events. According to the letter, in which order did they happen? Drag (or write, in this case) the sentences into the boxes in the appropriate order.

(A) BETA sends used equipment to regional sales offices.

(B) BETA reconditions used coffee equipment.

(C) BETA forms a company to sell refurbished coffee machines.

(D) BETA creates 13 new jobs for the economy.

**Order of Events**

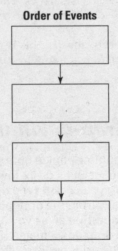

The answer to this question is right in the business letter. You just have to sort the events in the order they happened. The correct order is Choice (C), (B), (A), then (D). First, BETA establishes the company (Choice [C]), and then it reconditions the equipment (Choice [B]). BETA then sends the refurbished equipment to regional offices for resale (Choice [A]), and as a result, it creates 13 new jobs (Choice [D]). This item is quite simple; it just requires careful reading of the source text.

## Filling the blank with the correct answer

One of the question types is a variation of the old standby, the fill-in-the-blank item. This type of question is different from the others only because you have to provide your own answer.

Sentence 9: **To learn more about BETA** ⬚ **please consult our website at** www. betace.com, **or give us a call at our toll-free number, 1-810-TRY-BETA.**

Insert the proper punctuation, if any, required after the word *BETA*.

In an item like this, you simply type the correct answer into the box (or, for the practice questions in this book, *write* the answer in the box). However, you have to know what your options are and select the correct one from your own knowledge. For adding punctuation in the middle of a sentence, you have only three choices: a colon, a semicolon, or a comma. You use colons to introduce a subordinate clause or start a list or quote. You're not doing either here, so that doesn't work. You use a semicolon to join two independent clauses into one sentence or sometimes to separate items in special types of lists. You're not doing that here, either. That leaves the comma or nothing. Read the sentence again. When you read it, notice the slight pause after the word *BETA*, just like after the word *it* in this sentence. Because the beginning phrase *To learn more about BETA* is a prepositional phrase, it needs to be followed by a comma. The correct answer is to write a comma into the blank.

# Choosing Wisely in the Reading Component

The RLA test reading portion consists of excerpts from fiction and nonfiction. You're presented with a reading passage, followed by a series of questions, usually some form of multiple-choice items, based on that reading material.

When working through the reading component of the real GED test, read the questions first so you get an idea of what you need to look for in the passage as you read it. Read the questions carefully — they aren't trick questions, but they do require you to be a good reader. Finally, be sure to read the passage carefully. Look for errors and hard-to-read sentences. If you encounter words that you don't recognize, look at the surrounding text, which can often give you clues about the mystery word's meaning.

In this section, we walk you through a few sample questions based on this short newspaper column.

> Vaccination is important to all of us. It is not only about individual health but also protection for the collective. Many people in the last 15 years have refused measles vaccine for their children. According to a 1998 U.K. study written by a Dr. Wakefield, children given the MMR vaccine had a higher risk of developing autism. Many celebrities got involved, promoting this idea. The resulting publicity caused a significant drop in the rate of immunization.
>
> Since then, that study has been totally discredited. In fact, Dr. Wakefield has had his British medical license revoked. But the malady is still present; the after-effects linger on. Some people are still not convinced of the safety of vaccination. Others object on principle or for reasons of faith.
>
> As the rate of vaccination has dropped, more cases of measles are being reported. Health authorities in the United Kingdom reported some 2,000 cases of the measles in 2012. So far this year, they have recorded more than 1,200 cases. U.K. health authorities have started a massive public health effort to immunize as many children as quickly as possible.
>
> Measles spreads from person to person whenever an infected person sneezes or coughs. While most people will recover completely within ten days, a small percentage of people develop serious complications. Some require hospitalization or end up with permanent disabilities. This is an especially serious risk for small children.
>
> In 2002, the World Health Organization stated that measles was virtually eradicated in North and South America. However, as the rate of immunization dropped, measles made a significant comeback. The United States and Canada have seen a number of recent outbreaks, one in Quebec in 2007 and another in Ontario in 2008 and again in 2012. Many outbreaks are linked to unvaccinated travelers returning from Mexico, India, or Europe, where the risk of exposure is higher. Outbreaks continue wherever vaccination rates are

lower. There are usually about 60 cases a year in the United States, but in 2011 there were over 200. In the first half of 2013, the CDC reported 160 cases, the highest in decades, including more than 60 cases in New York City alone.

One reason outbreaks have been relatively small so far is a sort of "herd immunity." Because measles spreads by proximity, if 95 percent of the population has been vaccinated, the chances of spreading the infection are significantly reduced. If most people are vaccinated, it confers a sort of herd immunity on the entire population. But the rate of immunization has dropped for the last decade. It is now less than 90 percent in many areas, and measles is making a comeback. A few people need to be concerned about vaccines, especially if they have allergies. But for most people, vaccines are safe and effective. Don't put yourself, your children, or the community at risk; make sure your vaccinations are up-to-date. Everyone benefits if you do.

The normal number of measles cases in the United States annually is approximately ⬚ .

This question is a perfect example of when reading the questions first, before you read the passage, can really benefit you. If you know that you're looking for a specific number, you have the answer as soon as you find it in the passage. On the other hand, if you read the passage first and then have to go back and skim the passage and don't read carefully, you may feel rushed and accidentally choose one of the other numbers in the article. The correct answer in this case is *60,* which you can find in the second-to-last sentence of the fifth paragraph.

There are only small outbreaks of measles, despite fewer people being vaccinated in the United States because

(A) measles has been almost eradicated around the world

(B) few people are traveling to Mexico or Europe

(C) enough people are vaccinated to give a herd immunity

(D) none of the above

If you search the article for reasons measles has been relatively controlled, despite reduced vaccination rates, you come across this: "If most people are vaccinated, it confers a sort of herd immunity. . . ." So Choice (C) is the correct answer. Choices (A) and (B) are simply wrong, and Choice (D) doesn't apply.

Measles is making a comeback for a number of reasons. Which of the following is a reason for renewed measles outbreaks?

(A) the gradual reduction of herd immunity

(B) continued fear of the side effects of vaccines

(C) measles has not been eradicated in Europe and Asia

(D) all of the above

The article mentions that measles has been virtually eradicated in North and South America. That implies that it hasn't been eradicated in the rest of the world. So Choice (C) could be a reason for measles outbreaks. Choice (B) is stated at the beginning as a reason some people weren't being vaccinated. This is also a reason measles is returning. That leaves only one reason, Choice (A). As the article states, herd immunity is only present if a significant proportion of the population is immunized. However, more people are refusing vaccinations, so you can deduce that herd immunity is declining. So because Choices (A), (B), and (C) are all correct, the correct answer is Choice (D).

# Writing the RLA Extended Response

The RLA Extended Response item asks you to write an essay in 45 minutes on an assigned topic. This part of the test assesses your literacy and understanding. Even if you can understand the essay topic, you must now demonstrate that you're thoroughly familiar with the process of writing an essay and know correct spelling and the grammar and language usage rules. You're asked to read one or two source texts that present different viewpoints on an issue. You must determine which argument is better supported and write an essay supporting your position.

Keep in mind that writing this essay isn't that different from writing a letter or a blog — except that you must explain and clarify the subject for the reader without rambling on until you run out of space.

The way the RLA test is scored, you most likely won't pass without a passing mark on the Extended Response. That means if you don't do well on the Extended Response, you'll have to take the entire test over again. That fact alone should be all the incentive you need to practice writing.

In the following sections, we walk you through the four steps to writing an effective Extended Response and provide a few pointers for making sure you ace this part of the RLA test.

## Managing your time

You have 45 minutes to finish your essay for the Extended Response on the RLA test, and, in that time, you have four main tasks:

- Plan
- Draft
- Edit and revise
- Rewrite

The following sections take a closer look at these tasks and explain how you can successfully complete each one in the time allotted.

A good plan for action is to spend 10 minutes planning, 20 minutes drafting, 5 minutes editing and revising, and 10 minutes rewriting. Keep in mind that this schedule is a tight one, though, so if your keyboarding is slow, consider allowing more time for rewriting. No one but you will see anything but the final version.

### Planning

Before you begin writing your essay, read the topic carefully several times and ask yourself what the topic means to you. Determine what the two positions presented in the source text(s) are. Then, on the erasable tablet, write down all the points in the source documents that support one argument or the other. Don't worry about the order you write these ideas, but do rate them in terms of their importance to the thesis. Just let everything you think of flow onto the paper. You can sort through all the information in the next phase.

For example, if the essay item presents you with two source texts, one in favor of unions and the other opposed, and then asks you to evaluate the arguments, you need to begin by considering which text is more convincing, which text presents the better and stronger argument. Then you need to look at and evaluate all the supporting evidence presented by the two sides of the argument. The planning stage of your essay writing begins when you jot down every piece of supporting evidence you find about the issue in the source texts. It's important to stick with the points presented in the source texts and not wander off into your own opinions of the topic.

After you write down these points, sit back for a moment to reflect. (Don't reflect too long, though, because you still have an essay to write. Just take a few minutes.) Look over your points and find an introduction, such as, "The argument that the Union Movement has outlived its usefulness makes the stronger case." Write this sentence beneath your brainstorming notes. Then write down the points you came up with earlier that strongly back up your position.

Now, write a concluding sentence, such as, "The anti-union argument is stronger. Although historically significant, unions are no longer necessary to ensure that the working class has a workplace that offers decent working conditions, a fair wage, and a workplace free of discrimination." Glancing at your introduction and the essay topic itself, select points that strengthen your conclusion. Some of these points may be the same ones you used in your introduction.

Next, plan a path from your introduction to your conclusion. The path may be several points long. Here's an example:

- ✓ **Introduction:** "The argument that the Union Movement has outlived its usefulness makes the stronger case."

- ✓ **Body:** Here's the path from your introduction to your conclusion:

  - • List the appropriate supporting evidence in order of importance.

  - • Discuss several of the most important points in detail, in your own words, backed by quotes from the source text.

  - • Discuss false arguments or flawed arguments made by either side of the discussion.

- ✓ **Conclusion:** "Although historically significant, the stronger case argues that unions are no longer necessary to ensure that the working class has a workplace that offers decent working conditions, a fair wage, and a workplace free of discrimination."

Now reflect again. Can you add any more points to improve the essay? Don't just add points to have more points, though. This isn't a contest for who can come up with the most points. You want to have logically written points that support your argument.

Look over your planning path and your points. Can you combine any parts of the path to make it tighter? For example:

- ✓ **Introduction:** "The stronger argument states that the Union Movement has outlived its usefulness."

- ✓ **Body:** Here's the tightened path from your introduction to your conclusion:

  - • List relevant points presented in the source materials.

  - • Expand on each point, based on the source text.

  - • Tie in these points to your thesis. Explain which side makes the better argument, and why that's the case.

  - • Expose any flawed logic.

- ✓ **Conclusion:** "Although historically significant, the stronger argument proves that unions are no longer necessary to ensure that the working class has a workplace that offers decent working conditions, a fair wage, and a workplace free of discrimination."

Now that you have the outline, you're ready to go on to the next step: drafting your essay.

### Drafting

During the drafting stage, you think in more detail about the main points you came up with in the planning stage. As you add new details (called *subpoints*) under each main point, you begin to see your essay take shape.

Each paragraph starts with an *introductory sentence,* which sets up the paragraph content, and ends with a *transition sentence* that leads from the paragraph you're on to the next one. If you put your sentences in a logical order from introduction to transition, you start to see paragraphs — as well as your essay — emerge.

### Editing and revising

Now comes the hard part. You have to be your own editor. Turn off your ego and remember that every word is written on an erasable tablet, not carved in stone. Make your work better by editing and revising it. Make this the best piece of writing you've ever done — in a 45-minute time block, of course.

### Checking your final draft

When you've written your essay, scroll through it again. Only this time, read just the first and last sentences of every paragraph. If you've used proper linkage between paragraphs and put your arguments into a logical order, everything should flow neatly. If it doesn't, you may need to rewrite. Ask yourself whether each paragraph contributes to your argument. If it doesn't, you may need to do more rewriting. It could be something as simple as changing the order of paragraphs, deleting something, or adding transitional phrases. It could be more difficult, requiring a rethink of your argument. Your essay has to be well written, logical, and persuasive but completed. If you don't have time to finish keyboarding your final draft, you don't have an essay for someone to mark.

## Putting together a winning essay

Some of the key points in the essay evaluation include the following list. If you have all these characteristics in your essay, your chances of receiving a high score are pretty good:

- ✔ You've read and understood the (two) source item(s) and selected the position that has the best support.
- ✔ Your essay clearly explains why you made your choice, using proof from the source text.
- ✔ Your essay is clearly written and well organized.
- ✔ The evidence you present is developed logically and clearly.
- ✔ You use transitions throughout the essay for a smooth flow among ideas.
- ✔ You use appropriate vocabulary, varied sentence structure, and good grammar and spelling.

Here are a few other tips and ground rules to keep in mind as you prepare for the Extended Response:

- ✔ **You have only 45 minutes to write an essay based on a single topic and very specific source text.** An essay usually consists of a number of paragraphs, each of which contains a topic sentence stating a main idea or thought. Be sure each paragraph relates to the overall topic of the essay. And, for the most part, make sure to place a topic sentence at the beginning of each paragraph to help readers focus on the main point you want them to understand.

✔ **You can prepare your essay by using the erasable notepad provided.** You're given this pad at the test site. Use it to make notes and write down your rough work so your final essay is well organized and neat. No one will look at the pad, so what you write on it is just for you.

✔ **You must write about the topic and only about the topic.** You're graded for writing an essay on the topic, so make sure you really do write on the topic you're given. One of the easiest ways to fail this test is to write about something that isn't on topic. The source text presents divergent views. Your job is to analyze, reflect, and respond.

✔ **The essay tests your ability to write about an issue that has positive and/or negative implications.** Whether you agree or disagree with the issue presented is immaterial. The essay doesn't test how much you know about a given topic or your personal opinions. Rather, it tests your ability to analyze and express yourself in writing.

✔ **Effective paragraphs use a variety of sentence types: statements, questions, commands, exclamations, and even quotations.** Vary your sentence structure and choice of words to spark the readers' interest. Some sentences may be short, and others may be long to catch the readers' attention.

✔ **Paragraphs create interest in several ways: by developing details, using illustrations and examples, presenting events in a time or space sequence, providing definitions, classifying persons or objects, comparing and contrasting, and demonstrating reasons and proof.** Organize your paragraphs and sentences in a way that both expresses your ideas and creates interest.

✔ **The evaluation requires you to express your ideas clearly and logically.** Make sure you stick to the topic.

# Chapter 7

# Working through Some Practice RLA Questions

● ● ● ● ● ● ● ● ● ● ● ● ● ● ● ● ● ● ● ● ● ● ● ● ● ● ● ● ● ● ● ● ● ● ● ● ● ● ● ● ● ● ● ● ● ● ● ● ● ● ● ●

*T*his chapter provides sample Reasoning through Language Arts (RLA) questions, including a sample Extended Response item, to help you prepare for taking that section of the GED test.

Record your answers directly in this book or on a separate sheet of paper, if you think you'll want to try these practice questions again at a later date. Mark only one answer for each item, unless otherwise indicated. And be sure to have a couple extra sheets of paper handy, or use your computer's word processor, to practice outlining and writing an Extended Response. Remember that most computer word processors have a spell-checker and grammar-checker but the actual test doesn't.

At the end of each section, we provide detailed answer explanations for you. Check your answers. Take your time as you move through the explanations. Read them carefully, because they can help you understand why you missed the answers you did and confirm or clarify what you got right.

Remember, this is just preliminary practice. We want you to get used to answering different types of RLA questions. Use the complete practice tests in Parts VI and VII later in the book to time your work and replicate the real test-taking experience.

## RLA Writing Skills Practice

The questions in the writing component of the RLA test are doubly important because not only do they give you a chance to practice reading a passage and answering questions based on it, but they also teach you a bit about proper grammar. Understanding proper grammar adds to your overall score on the RLA test but also counts toward your mark on the Extended Response item. One of the important things about proper grammar is that it sounds and reads well. These questions give you an opportunity to develop your ear and eye for proper sentences.

For the questions in this section, pay special attention to the mechanics of writing, spelling, and grammar. Work carefully, but don't spend too much time on any one question. Be sure you answer every question. You can find the answers for these items later in this section.

# The questions

*Questions 1–10 refer to the following executive summary.*

**Marketing**

**Dry-Cleaning and Laundering Industry Adjustment Committee Report on the Local Labor Market Partnership Project**

**April 2007–August 2009**

**Executive Summary**

(A)

(1) Over the past two years, the Dry-Cleaning and Laundering Industry Adjustment Committee has worked hard to become a cohesive group focused on assessing and addressing the human resource implications associated with changes in the fabricare industry. (2) As of August 2009, the Committee has an active membership of over 15 individuals involved in all aspects of the project. (3) The Committee, which has great difficulty speaking with one voice, has taken responsibility for undertaking actions that will benefit this large, highly fragmented industry.

(B)

(4) During the initial period that the Committee was in existence, its work focused on out-reaching to and building a relationship with key individuals within the industry. (5) One of its first steps was to undertake a Needs Assessment Survey within the industry.

(C)

(6) During the first year, the Committee explored ways of meeting the needs identified in the Needs Assessment Survey, including raising the profile of the industry and offering on-site training programs, particularly in the areas of spotting and pressing. (7) A great deal of feasibility work was undertaken during this phase yet each possible training solution proved to be extremely difficult and costly to implement.

(D)

(8) As the Committee moved into its second year, it officially established a joint project with the National Fabricare Association to achieve goals in two priority areas: mentorship, training, and profile building.

(E)

(9) During this passed year, much effort and vision has gone into achieving the goals established by the Industry Adjustment Committee and the Association. (10) The new priority areas have provided an opportunity for the industry to do the following

- Introduce technology
- Build capacity and knowledge
- Enhance skills
- Build partnerships and networks

1. Sentence 1: **Over the past two years, the Dry-Cleaning and Laundering Industry Adjustment Committee has worked hard to become a cohesive group focused on assessing and addressing the human resource implications associated with changes in the fabricare industry.**

   Which is the best way to improve Sentence 1?

   (A) remove the comma after *years*

   (B) place a period after *group* and start a new sentence beginning with *It has focused on*

   (C) place a comma after *group*

   (D) change *focused* to *focussed*

2. Sentence 2: **As of August 2009, the Committee has an active membership of over 15 individuals involved in all aspects of the project.**

   Which revision should be made to Sentence 2?

   (A) change *has* to *have*

   (B) change *individuals* to *individual's*

   (C) change *aspects* to *aspect*

   (D) remove *over*

3. Sentence 3: **The Committee, which has great difficulty speaking with one voice, has taken responsibility for undertaking actions that will benefit this large, highly fragmented industry.**

   Which revision is required to improve Sentence 3?

   (A) remove the comma after *large*

   (B) change *Committee* to *committee*

   (C) move *, which has great difficulty speaking with one voice,* to the end of the sentence after *industry*

   (D) no correction required

4. Sentence 4: **During the initial period that the Committee was in existence, its work focused on outreaching to and building a relationship with key individuals within the industry.**

   Which correction should be made to Sentence 4?

   (A) change *its* to *it's*

   (B) change *outreaching to* to *reaching out to*

   (C) place a comma after the period

   (D) change *outreaching* to *out-reaching*

5. Sentence 5: **One of its first steps was to undertake a Needs Assessment Survey within the industry.**

   Which change should be made to Sentence 5?

   (A) change *first* to *1st*

   (B) change *within* to *with*

   (C) change *was* to *were*

   (D) no correction required

6. Sentence 6: **During the first year, the Committee explored ways of meeting the needs identified in the Needs Assessment Survey, including raising the profile of the industry and offering on-site training programs, particularly in the areas of spotting and pressing.**

   Which is the best way to improve Sentence 6?

   (A) insert a comma after *including*

   (B) place a period after *Survey* and start a new sentence with *These included*

   (C) replace the comma after *survey* with a semicolon and add a comma after *including*

   (D) no correction required

7. Sentence 7: **A great deal of feasibility work was undertaken during this phase yet each possible training solution proved to be extremely difficult and costly to implement.**

   Which correction should be made to Sentence 7?

   (A) change *was* to *were*

   (B) change *undertaken* to *undertook*

   (C) insert a comma after *undertaken*

   (D) insert a comma after *phase*

8. Sentence 8: **As the Committee moved into its second year, it officially established a joint project with the National Fabricare Association to achieve goals in three priority areas: mentorship, training, and profile building.**

   What correction should be made to Sentence 8?

   (A) change *its* to *it's*

   (B) change *its* to *their*

   (C) change the comma after *year* to a semicolon

   (D) no correction required

9. Sentence 9: **During this passed year, much effort and vision has gone into achieving the goals established by the Industry Adjustment Committee and the Association.**

   What correction should be made to Sentence 9?

   (A) insert a comma after *Committee*

   (B) change *passed* to *past*

   (C) change *into* to *in*

   (D) change *goals* to *goal*

10. Sentence 10: **The new priority areas have provided an opportunity for the industry to do the following**

    - **Introduce technology**
    - **Build capacity and knowledge**
    - **Enhance skills**
    - **Build partnerships and networks**

    What punctuation should be added to Sentence 10?

    (A) place a semicolon after *technology*

    (B) place a semicolon after *knowledge*

    (C) place a semicolon after *skills*

    (D) place a colon after *following*

*Questions 11–20 refer to the following information piece.*

**Prior Learning Assessment and Recognition**

**Introduction**

(A)

(1) This course is based on a Prior Learning Assessment and Recognition (PLAR) model, as a component of the PLAR, which utilizes preparation for a standardized challenge examination. (2) In addition candidates are guided through the creation of a portfolio, which can be evaluated by a college for admission or advanced standing. (3) This is an opportunity for adults, who have learned in non-formal as well as formal venues to document and assess there prior learning. (4) The course is intents and concentrated and is not meant for every applicant.

(B)

(5) Candidates, who score low in the pre-test, should be directed to remedial programs before beginning such a rigorous course. (6) Those who extremely score well in a pre-test may be advised to arrange immediately to take a challenging test, such as one of the GED tests. (7) This course is meant for candidates who will gain from review and re-mediation but do not require extensive teaching.

**Rationale**

(C)

(8) This course is designed to help adult learners gain acknowledgement and accreditation of their prior learning in preparation for post secondary study. (9) Students will learn methods for documenting prior knowledge and will develop skills while becoming reacquainted with educational environments and developing the skills needed to succeed in such environments. (10) Through the use of assessment tools and counciling, students will gain a realistic understanding of their levels of competence, personal strengths, weaknesses, and learning styles.

11. Sentence 1: **This course is based on a Prior Learning Assessment and Recognition (PLAR) model, as a component of the PLAR, which utilizes preparation for a standardized challenge examination.**

    Which is the best way to improve Sentence 1?

    (A) no improvement required

    (B) delete *as a component of the PLAR,*

    (C) change *is* to *has*

    (D) change *utilizes* to *utilized*

12. Sentence 2: **In addition candidates are guided through the creation of a portfolio, which can be evaluated by a college for admission or advanced standing.**

    Which correction should be made to Sentence 2?

    (A) add a comma after *In addition*

    (B) change *are guided* to *is guided*

    (C) change *by* to *through*

    (D) add a comma after *admission*

13. Sentence 3: **This is an opportunity for adults, who have learned in non-formal as well as formal venues to document and <u>assess there prior learning</u>.**

    Which is the best way to write the underlined portion of Sentence 3?

    (A) assess their prior learning

    (B) assess there prior learning

    (C) assess they're prior learning

    (D) assess people's prior learning

14. Sentence 4: **The course is intents and concentrated and is not meant for every applicant.**

    Which correction should be made to Sentence 4?

    (A) change *is not* to *are not*

    (B) change *not* to *only*

    (C) change *meant* to *mend*

    (D) change *intents* to *intense*

15. Sentence 5: **Candidates, who score low in the pre-test, should be directed to remedial programs before beginning such a rigorous course.**

    Which improvement should be made to Sentence 5?

    (A) remove the comma after *candidates*

    (B) remove the comma after *pre-test*

    (C) remove the comma after *candidates* and the comma after *pre-test*

    (D) change *before* to *after*

16. Sentence 6: **<u>Those who extremely score well</u> in a pre-test may be advised to arrange immediately to take a challenging test, such as one of the GED tests.**

    Which is the best way to write the underlined portion of this sentence?

    (A) Extremely those who score well

    (B) Those who score well extremely

    (C) Those who score extremely well

    (D) Those extremely who score well

17. Sentence 7: **This course is meant for candidates who will gain from review and re-mediation but do not require extensive teaching.**

    Which correction should be made to Sentence 7?

    (A) change *review* to *revue*

    (B) place a comma after *candidates*

    (C) place a comma after *remediation*

    (D) change *re-mediation* to *remediation*

18. Sentence 8: **This course is designed to help adult learners gain acknowledgment and acreditation of their prior learning in preparation for postsecondary study.**

    Which change should be made to Sentence 8?

    (A) change *acreditation* to *accreditation*

    (B) change *acknowledgment* to *acknowledge*

    (C) change *prior learning* to *prior-learning*

    (D) change *their* to *there*

19. Sentence 9: **Students will learn methods for documenting prior knowledge and will develop skills while becoming reacquainted with educational environments and developing the skills needed to succeed in such environments.**

    Which is the best way to improve Sentence 9? Write the unneeded section of the sentence in the box.

    ```
    ┌─────────────────────────────┐
    │                             │
    │                             │
    │                             │
    └─────────────────────────────┘
    ```

20. Sentence 10: **Through the use of assessment tools and counciling, students will gain a realistic understanding of their levels of competence, personal strengths, weaknesses, and learning styles.**

    Which correction should be made to Sentence 10?

    (A) change *realistic* to *real*

    (B) change *levels* to *level*

    (C) change *students* to *students'*

    (D) change *counciling* to *counseling*

    *Questions 21–25 are based on the following business letter.*

    **CanLearn Study Tours, Inc.**
    **2500 Big Beaver Road**
    **Troy, MI 70523**

    Dr. Dale Worth, PhD, Registrar
    BEST Institute of Technology
    75 Ingram Drive
    Concord, MA 51234

    Dear Dr. Worth:

    (A)

    (1) Our rapidly changing economic climate has meant both challenges never before known. (2) It has been said that only those organizations who can maintain loyalty and commitment among their employees, members, and customers will continue to survive and prosper in this age of continuous learning and globalization.

    (B)

    (3) Since 1974, CanLearn Study Tours, Inc., have been working with universities, colleges, school districts, voluntary organizations, and businesses to address the unique learning needs of their staff and clientele. (4) These have included educational travel programs that explore the following, artistic and cultural interests, historic and archeological themes, environmental and wellness experiences, and new service patterns. (5) Professional development strategies have been organized to enhance international understanding and boost creativity. (6) Some organizations' have used study tours to build and maintain their membership or consumer base. (7) Other organizations discover a new soarce of revenue in these difficult economic times.

    (C)

    (8) The formats has varied from a series of local seminars to incentive conferences or sales promotion meetings. (9) Our professional services, including the best possible transportation and accommodation at the most reasonable rates, have insured the success of these programs.

(D)

(10) We would appreciate the opportunity to share our experiences in educational travel and discuss the ways we may be of service to your organization.

Yours sincerely,

Todd Croft, MA, President
CanLearn Study Tours, Inc.

21. Sentence 1: **Our rapidly changing economic climate has meant both challenges never before known.**

    Which improvement should be made to Sentence 1?

    (A) insert *and opportunities* between *challenges* and *never*

    (B) change *has meant* to *have meant*

    (C) change *known* to *none*

    (D) change *challenges* to *challenge*

22. Sentence 2: **It has been said that only those organizations who can maintain loyalty and commitment among their employees, members, and customers will continue to survive and prosper in this age of continuous learning and globalization.**

    Which change should be made to Sentence 2?

    (A) insert a comma after *commitment*

    (B) change *has been* to *had been*

    (C) change *who* to *that*

    (D) change *those* to *these*

23. Sentence 3: **Since 1974, CanLearn Study Tours, Inc., <u>have been working</u> with universities, colleges, school districts, voluntary organizations, and businesses to address the unique learning needs of their staff and clientele.**

    Which is the best way to write the underlined portion of Sentence 3?

    (A) had been working

    (B) has been working

    (C) will be working

    (D) shall be working

24. Sentence 4: **These have included educational travel programs that explore the following, artistic and cultural interests, historic and archeological themes, environmental and wellness experiences, and new service patterns.**

    Which correction should be made to Sentence 4?

    (A) insert a comma after *have included*

    (B) change the comma after *following* to a colon

    (C) change the comma after *interests* to a colon

    (D) change the comma after *themes* to a colon

25. Sentence 5: **Professional development strategies have been organized to enhance international understanding and boost creativity.**

    Which change should be made to Sentence 5?

    (A) change *strategies* to *strategy*

    (B) change *boost* to *boast*

    (C) change *enhance* to *enhancing*

    (D) no correction required

# The answers

1. **B. place a period after *group* and start a new sentence beginning with *It has focused on.*** With this change, you avoid the overly long and complex sentence and create two new sentences: "Over the past two years, the Dry-Cleaning and Laundering Industry Adjustment Committee has worked hard to become a cohesive group. It has focused on assessing and addressing the human resource implications in the fabricare industry."

2. **D. remove *over.*** Removing *over* clarifies the meaning of the sentence. If you know that the group has more than 15 members, say so.

3. **C. move *, which has great difficulty speaking with one voice,* to the end of the sentence after *industry.*** The sentence in question says that the *committee* has great difficulty speaking in one voice, which may be true. However, a more accurate statement is that the *industry* has great difficulty speaking in one voice. You know this statement is true because the sentence describes the industry as *fragmented.* A better organization for the sentence is, "The Committee has taken responsibility for undertaking actions that will benefit this large, highly fragmented industry, which has great difficulty speaking with one voice."

4. **B. change *outreaching to* to *reaching out to.*** *Outreaching* isn't a verb; *reaching out* is.

5. **D. no correction required.** None of the answer choices improves the sentence, so in this case, no correction is required.

Are you thinking that we made a mistake in preceding sentence? Well, we didn't. The noun *none* goes with the verb *improves.* The prepositional phrase *of the other options* doesn't determine how the noun and verb agree. *None* is a singular noun and, therefore, goes with *improves,* not *improve.* If this situation comes up on your test, or you choose to use it in your essay, replace *none* with *not one* (in your head only), ignore everything else between *none* and the verb, and see whether *not one* agrees with the verb given.

6. **B. place a period after *Survey* and start a new sentence with *These included.*** The sentence is simply too long as is. It needs to be broken into two sentences to be understood. So find a logical place to do that. The first part of the sentence discusses the uses of the Needs Assessment Survey; the second part discusses the type of training. You can split the sentence into two smaller, more easily understood sentences, such as, "During the first year, the Committee explored ways of meeting the needs identified in the Needs Assessment Survey. These included raising the profile of the industry and offering on-site training programs, particularly in the areas of spotting and pressing."

    When writing your essay, keep in mind that sentences shouldn't be so long that you have to take multiple breaths just to read them aloud. Short sentences are easier to read and understand.

7. **D. insert a comma after *phase.*** Inserting a comma after *phase* improves the sentence structure because this compound sentence is joined by the conjunction *yet* and needs the comma to ensure that the two thoughts remain separate.

A *compound sentence* contains two independent clauses or thoughts. The clauses have to be separated by a conjunction like *and, but,* or *yet,* and the conjunction needs a comma before it.

8. **D. no correction required.** This sentence is correct as is and requires no change.

9. **B. change *passed* to *past*.** Correct the homonym spelling error from *passed* to *past*. The word *passed* means "to go by," as in "they passed the intersection," or to complete a test successfully, as in "he passed the test." The word *past* means "in times gone by, in a prior time," as in "In the past, there were no computers.'

10. **D. place a colon after *following*.** The introductory clause needs a colon at the end.

If you thought the items in the list needed semicolons, you're not entirely wrong. Whether you use semicolons in a list depends on *house style* (the style used and followed religiously by the company or publishing house writing or editing the text). Formal reference texts, such as *Fowler's Modern English Language Usage,* by R. W. Burchfield (Oxford), recommend semicolons for lists. However, if you use semicolons, you need to use them with every component in the list, and that isn't one of the answer choices. Further, semicolons are generally not necessary in bulleted lists.

11. **B. delete *as a component of the PLAR*.** The phrase *as a component of the PLAR* is unnecessary.

12. **A. add a comma after *In addition*.** The only change required is to add a comma after the introductory phrase *In addition*.

Not sure about commas? Check out *English Grammar For Dummies,* 2nd Edition, by Geraldine Woods (Wiley), for the lowdown on this sometimes tricky form of punctuation.

13. **A. assess their prior learning.** *Their* is possessive (showing belonging) and is the correct choice in this sentence. Correct the spelling error from *there* to *their*.

The homonyms *there, their,* and *they're* probably trip up more high-school and college students than any other homonyms. Before heading into the GED Reasoning through Language Arts test, be sure you know the difference among these three words!

14. **D. change *intents* to *intense*.** *Intense* and *concentrated* are synonyms used in this sentence for emphasis, but *intense* is misspelled as *intents*. *In tents* is where you sleep on a camping trip.

15. **C. remove both the comma after *candidates* and the comma after *pre-test*.** The clause *who score low in the pre-test* is a *restrictive clause,* which means it refers to a specific noun — *candidates,* in this case — and specifies something about the noun that the sentence needs to make sense to readers. Restrictive clauses aren't separated by commas because they're an integral part of the sentence.

Contrast the restrictive clause with the *nonrestrictive clause,* which adds information about the noun that isn't essential to the meaning of the sentence. If you remove a nonrestrictive clause from the sentence, you can still fully understand the meaning of the sentence. Nonrestrictive clauses require commas to separate them from the sentence.

16. **C. Those who score extremely well.** *Those who score extremely well* is the best order of the words. *Extremely,* an adverb, is best placed next to the word it modifies, which is *well*.

17. **D. change *re-mediation* to *remediation*.** This is a spelling error; no hyphen is needed in this case.

Although exceptions exist, when a prefix that ends in a vowel (as *re-* does) precedes a consonant, no hyphen is used. In many (but not all) cases, when a prefix that ends in a vowel precedes another vowel, a hyphen is used.

18. **A. change *acreditation* to *accreditation*.** This is a simple spelling mistake. While *credit* is spelled with one *c*, to give credit, or *accredit*, requires two *c's*.

19. **and developing the skills needed to succeed in such environments.** The sentence is far too complex and repetitive as is. The simplest and correct option is to delete the entire phrase *and developing skills needed to succeed in such environments*.

Unless you're being paid by the word, always try to say what you mean in as few words as possible.

20. **D. change *counciling* to *counseling*.** This sentence contains a spelling error. Correct the spelling error by changing *counciling* to *counseling*.

21. **A. insert *and opportunities* between *challenges* and *never*.** The word *both* refers to two options, but here you're given only one option: *challenges*. If you insert *and opportunities* between *challenges* and *never,* you include a second option and correct the sentence.

22. **C. change *who* to *that*.** An organization is never a *who;* only people can be referred to as *who*. An organization is a collective noun made up of people, but the collective noun itself is an impersonal entity and doesn't qualify as a *who*.

Although this sentence may appear long and, therefore, may benefit from rewriting, the sentence isn't technically incorrect. Although commas do serve to make sentences clearer, you don't want to insert them unless punctuation rules make them correct.

23. **B. has been working.** CanLearn Study Tours is a single entity because it's one company. Therefore, it's a singular noun and needs the singular verb *has* instead of the plural *have*.

People like to refer to companies as *them* when, in fact, a company is always an *it*. Even though a company is made up of a lot of people, it's still a singular entity.

24. **B. change the comma after *following* to a colon.** You need to insert a colon before the list to introduce it.

25. **D. no correction required.** The options presented either make the sentence difficult to understand or introduce errors, so the correct answer is *no correction required.*

# RLA Extended Response Practice

In this section, we provide an example of an Extended Response prompt with two passages that present arguments in favor of and against mandatory vaccination. Your task is to practice writing an essay, analyzing both positions presented in the passages to determine which one is best supported. Be sure to use relevant and specific evidence from each article to support your response.

For this Extended Response practice, read and evaluate the two passages, think about how to respond, plan your essay, and then draft, edit, and write your final response. Then, review your essay with the self-evaluation criteria we provide and check out a sample essay based on this prompt.

## A sample Extended Response prompt

**Passage One**

Vaccines have been proven to be one of the safest forms of medical intervention that exists. They have virtually eradicated diseases such as smallpox and polio and made outbreaks of mumps, measles, and rubella rare occurrences. Thanks to vaccines, these diseases have become rare, and when outbreaks do occur, they spread much more slowly. If someone catches one of these diseases, the consequences are far less serious.

Unfortunately, some individuals have decided, for various reasons, to reject immunization. By doing so, they put everyone at risk. No one should have the right to put the health and safety of others at risk. It is time to make vaccination mandatory for all, unless there are verifiable medical reasons against such a course.

That vaccines work is beyond doubt. It is virtually unheard of today for anyone in a developed nation to contract smallpox or polio. Smallpox spreads easily, kills about 30 percent of those infected, and leaves the rest with severe scarring. We first learned how to vaccinate against smallpox, and, since then, the number of cases each year has dropped. There has not been a single outbreak in America since 1977. Polio epidemics were rampant in the early 1900s, paralyzing tens of thousands of people and killing thousands. One of those left paralyzed by polio was President Franklin D. Roosevelt, who spent the rest of his life in a wheelchair. At the peak of the polio outbreaks in 1952, some 57,000 people were infected with polio. Of those, more than 3,000 died, and about 20,000 suffered some degree of paralysis. Fortunately a vaccine was developed, and since the 1990s, there have been no outbreaks in America, Only in a few countries in the world — Afghanistan, India, and Pakistan among them, where anti-vaccination pressures remain — are there still regular outbreaks of this disease.

Measles can cause hearing loss, severe infections and in a few cases, death. However, according to the American Pediatric Society, when vaccinated children are exposed to diseases such as measles or mumps, they contract a much milder case, with far fewer complications, and recover much faster. More importantly, when a large percentage of the population is vaccinated, it creates a form of herd immunity. The spread of the disease is dramatically slowed down, protecting all people, not just those vaccinated. Sadly, recent outbreaks of measles in America prove that this herd immunity is fading as larger proportions of the population avoid vaccination.

Today, vaccines can prevent Hepatitis B, which can cause liver disease and lead to liver cancer. Vaccines can protect against HPV, a virus that can cause cervical cancer in women. There are 10,000 new cases of cervical cancer in America each year, most of which could be prevented with this simple immunization. The rotavirus vaccine has reduced the annual infant hospitalizations from 50,000 to 70,000 annually to less than 10,000. Vaccines work.

Some people fear that vaccines can harm children and even suggest the risk of disorders such as autism. Famous people get behind such campaigns, and even when they are shown to be wrong, the opposition continues. The study claiming the measles vaccine could cause autism has been proven wrong, and the doctors behind it lost their licenses, yet the campaign continues.

**Passage Two**

The decision to vaccinate must be an individual choice. We live in a free society, which constitutionally protects individual rights. That includes the right to make decisions based on one's conscience or religious beliefs and the right to be free from unreasonable government interference. Reasons to refuse vaccination range from moral, ethical, or religious beliefs, to concerns about the usefulness or even safety of vaccines. According to a recent study, more than 30 percent of individuals believe they should have the right to refuse vaccinations for their children as a precondition of admission to school. In a free society, no one should have the right to force individuals to agree to vaccinations in the face of such beliefs.

Let's start by looking at the refusal of vaccination based on religious, ethical, or moral beliefs. Some religions state that the body is sacred, and any tampering would go against religious injunctions. Disease is just part of God's Great Plan, and human intervention would be sacrilegious. Other faiths state that the power of faith and prayer will give their followers the protection they require, and human medical intervention is anathema. Other religions that might accept vaccination are concerned about the use of human cells in the creation of vaccines. Some of those cells come from aborted fetuses, a use highly offensive to some faiths. Other vaccines are made by using pig cells. Both Judaism and Islam prohibit the ingestion of pork. They cannot permit such vaccines. People with strong religious, moral, or ethical beliefs find such vaccines completely unacceptable.

Others reject vaccinations because of concerns of side effects. They believe that the degree of protection vaccines provide does not outweigh the risk of serious and severe side effects. For example, there's a common belief, backed by some medical studies, that vaccines can, in rare instances, trigger auto-immune disorders, including arthritis, multiple sclerosis, and lupus. Others are concerned about the side effects of commonly used flu vaccines. A few people have had significant reactions, and it's well known that flu vaccines do not protect against all variations of the flu present at any time. They argue that the risk of the vaccination does not outweigh the risks associated with catching the flu.

Many people reject measles, rubella, and mumps vaccinations because of the fear that this may trigger autism in young children. They again believe that the risks associated with these diseases are far less than the risk of triggering autism. Some parents reject HPV (human papilloma virus) vaccinations for similar reasons. The HPV vaccine can prevent an infection that may cause cervical cancer at some time in the future. The vaccine is known to, on rare occasions, cause Guillain-Barré syndrome, spinal cord inflammation, and pancreatitis, sometimes resulting in death. They would argue that the immediate risk of these side effects is far higher than the chance that the infection could lead to cancer. Other concerning side effects of various vaccines include brain inflammation that can lead to permanent brain damage and even death.

There's even a concern that by reducing the overall risk of infection by various child-hood diseases, we reduce the body's own immune system's ability to protect. Vaccines all suppress the natural immune system. This argument suggests that vaccines weaken the body instead of strengthening it or making it more able to resist infection.

## Evaluating your response

After writing your own response to the essay prompt in the previous section (and before you read the sample essay in the next section), review and evaluate your answer with these key points in mind:

- ✔ Do you clearly state which position was stronger and better argued?
- ✔ Are the arguments presented in the two source texts credible?
- ✔ Do you explain which position you selected as the better supported position?
- ✔ Do you explain why you came to that conclusion? (You don't have to agree with the position.)
- ✔ Does your introduction clearly state your position?
- ✔ Do you include multiple pieces of evidence from the passages to support your position?
- ✔ Is your evidence presented in a logical order to build your case?
- ✔ Does your conclusion contain an appropriate summary of the evidence and why you took the stand you did?
- ✔ Is your essay written in a clear, concise manner?
- ✔ Does your essay stay on point?
- ✔ Do you use proper linkages between paragraphs?
- ✔ Do you use varied and clear sentences and sentence structure?
- ✔ Is your use of grammar, spelling, and language correct?

## Checking out a sample response

Here's an example of a solid RLA Extended Response for the given prompt:

> The two passages both make excellent points. Which argument is stronger in this instance depends, at least in part, on your own personal opinion. The first passage makes excellent points about the importance of immunization, both for individuals and the community at large. The second passage also makes a number of excellent points, related to both individual freedoms and the safety of vaccines. However, on the whole, the first passage makes the stronger case.
>
> The first passage points out how effectively vaccination has eliminated diseases that have been a problem for hundreds of years and affected the lives of millions of people. It mentions that both smallpox and polio have been virtually eliminated in North America when as little as 60 years ago some 50,000 people a year suffered from those diseases. It then contrasts how diseases like polio in measles continue to be a major health problem in other countries where efforts to vaccinate the population have been resisted. That contrast alone makes a major point. The first passage also states that when a large proportion of the population is immunized, it creates a "herd immunity" that protects the entire population. As more and more people are refusing vaccinations, this herd immunity has lessened. That reinforces the idea that it is necessary to ensure people are immunized to maintain that herd immunity.
>
> The second passage does have valid points. It outlines the various moral, ethical, and religious grounds that some people have for refusing vaccinations. It makes the point that as citizens, we are guaranteed the right to freedom of religion and belief. Forcing someone to accept vaccination in the face of such beliefs would violate that freedom. The passage also presents arguments based on risk-benefit assessment. Many people seem to be concerned that the benefits of vaccination do not outweigh the risks associated with those vaccines. The author suggests that such risks have been noted in medical research.
>
> To me, the use of mass vaccinations to eliminate diseases such as polio and smallpox is key. That argument shows the ultimate benefit of vaccinations for all. But we cannot achieve those benefits unless all participate. The first passage makes that case very strongly, and nothing in the second passage is as effective. Although I can see the objections based on risk or ethics or religion, none of these arguments is strong enough to outweigh the arguments in the first passage.

# RLA Reading Skills Practice

The reading component of the RLA test consists of excerpts from fiction and nonfiction. Each excerpt is followed by multiple-choice items based on the reading material.

You have two choices of approach when answering the items on this part of the test. You can read each excerpt first, read the question to make sure you understand what's being asked, and then answer the questions (referring back to the reading material as often as necessary). Or you can read each question first, look for the answer in the passage, and answer the questions as you go. If you can keep the question in mind, searching the text for the answer is much easier and faster. You save time because you know what's being asked of you. Try both ways to see which approach is more comfortable for you.

For the questions in this section, choose the one best answer to each question. Work carefully, but don't spend too much time on any one question. Be sure you answer every question. You can find the answers for these items later in this section.

# The questions

*Questions 1–6 refer to the following article from the United States Geological Service Newsroom (www.usgs.gov).*

USGS scientists and Icelandic partners found avian flu viruses from North America and Europe in migratory birds in Iceland, demonstrating that the North Atlantic is as significant as the North Pacific in being a melting pot for birds and avian flu. A great number of wild birds from Europe and North America congregate and mix in Iceland's wetlands during migration, where infected birds could transmit avian flu viruses to healthy birds from either location.

By crossing the Atlantic Ocean this way, avian flu viruses from Europe could eventually be transported to the United States. This commingling could also lead to the evolution of new influenza viruses. These findings are critical for proper surveillance and monitoring of flu viruses, including the H5N1 avian influenza that can infect humans.

"None of the avian flu viruses found in our study are considered harmful to humans," said Robert Dusek, USGS scientist and lead author of the study. "However, the results suggest that Iceland is an important location for the study of avian flu. . . . "

During the spring and autumn of 2010 and autumn of 2011, the USGS researchers and Icelandic partners collected avian influenza viruses from gulls and waterfowl in southwest and west Iceland. . . . By studying the virus' genomes . . . the researchers found that some viruses came from Eurasia and some originated in North America. They also found viruses with mixed American-Eurasian lineages.

"For the first time, avian influenza viruses from both Eurasia and North America were documented at the same location and time," said Jeffrey Hall, USGS co-author and principal investigator on this study. "Viruses are continually evolving, and this mixing of viral strains sets the stage for new types of avian flu to develop."

1. How dangerous is this new potential source of avian flu to humans?

   (A) very dangerous

   (B) not very dangerous, for now

   (C) a concern but not particularly dangerous

   (D) serious enough that it requires monitoring

2. Before this discovery, where did scientists believe most birds carrying the avian flu intermingled with North American birds?

   (A) South Pacific

   (B) Central America

   (C) Eurasia

   (D) North Pacific

3. Why was the finding of Eurasian, North American, and mixed virus genomes in the same locale significant?

   (A) It proved that birds carrying the disease from both Eurasia and North America were present.

   (B) It proved that the avian flu was spreading between continents via Iceland.

   (C) It proved that the avian flu virus had mingled in Iceland.

   (D) All of the above.

4. Why is the mixing of avian flu viruses in Iceland an important concern?

(A) It can lead to a new dangerous strain of avian flu.

(B) Cold viruses are constantly evolving.

(C) It provides lead time to develop new vaccines.

(D) It suggests tourists avoid that area.

5. Which of these terms best describes the tone of this passage?

(A) light-hearted

(B) deeply concerned

(C) factual and straightforward

(D) gloomy

6. Which strain of the avian flu virus can infect humans?

(A) the bird flu

(B) the H5N1 strain

(C) the avian H5 flu

(D) the Eurasian avian flu

*Questions 7–12 refer to the following excerpt from Robert Bloch's short story "This Crowded Earth" (1958).*

The telescreen lit up promptly at eight a.m. Smiling Brad came on with his usual greeting. "Good morning — it's a beautiful day in Chicagee!"

Harry Collins rolled over and twitched off the receiver. "This I doubt," he muttered. He sat up and reached into the closet for his clothing. Visitors — particularly feminine ones — were always exclaiming over the advantages of Harry's apartment. "So convenient," they would say. "Everything handy, right within reach. And think of all the extra steps you save!"

Of course most of them were just being polite and trying to cheer Harry up. They knew damned well that he wasn't living in one room through any choice of his own. The Housing Act was something you just couldn't get around; not in Chicagee these days. A bachelor was entitled to one room — no more and no less. And even though Harry was making a speedy buck at the agency, he couldn't hope to beat the regulations.

There was only one way to beat them and that was to get married. Marriage would automatically entitle him to two rooms — *if* he could find them someplace. More than a few of his feminine visitors had hinted at just that, but Harry didn't respond. Marriage was no solution, the way he figured it. He knew that he couldn't hope to locate a two-room apartment any closer than eighty miles away. It was bad enough driving forty miles to and from work every morning and night without doubling the distance. If he did find a bigger place, that would mean a three-hour trip each way on one of the commutrains, and the commutrains were murder. The Black Hole of Calcutta, on wheels. But then, everything was murder, Harry reflected, as he stepped from the toilet to the sink, from the sink to the stove, from the stove to the table.

Powdered eggs for breakfast. That was murder, too. But it was a fast, cheap meal, easy to prepare, and the ingredients didn't waste a lot of storage space. The only trouble was, he hated the way they tasted. Harry wished he had time to eat his breakfasts in a restaurant. He could afford the price, but he couldn't afford to wait in line more than a half-hour or so.

His office schedule at the agency started promptly at ten-thirty. And he didn't get out until three-thirty; it was a long, hard five-hour day. Sometimes he wished he worked in the New Philly area, where a four-hour day was the rule. But he supposed that wouldn't mean any real saving in time, because he'd have to live further out. What was the population in New Philly now? Something like 63,000,000, wasn't it? Chicagee was much smaller — only 38,000,000, this year.

*This* year. Harry shook his head and took a gulp of the Instantea. Yes, this year the population was 38,000,000, and the boundaries of the community extended north to what used to be the old Milwaukee and south past Gary. What would it be like *next* year, and the year following?

Lately that question had begun to haunt Harry. He couldn't quite figure out why. After all, it was none of his business, really. He had a good job, security, a nice place just two hours from the Loop. He even drove his own car. What more could he ask?

7. This story is set sometime in the future. Which of the following clues confirms that this story is set in the future?

(A) the name Chicagee

(B) the population of Chicagee

(C) the hours worked

(D) all of the above

8. This story was published in 1958. What image did Bloch have of the future?

(A) incredibly crowded

(B) suffering from food shortages

(C) well-organized commutes

(D) long working hours

9. Besides population numbers, how does the author build up the idea of a crowded world?

(A) Harry's claustrophobic living space

(B) images of long commuting times

(C) Harry's moaning about waiting times and lineups in restaurants

(D) all of the above

10. Why does Harry sometimes wish he worked in the New Philly area?

(A) shorter commuting time

(B) shorter working hours

(C) better pay

(D) none of the above

11. Why does Harry live in a one-room apartment when he could afford a two-room apartment?

(A) He likes the convenience.

(B) His lady friends like the convenience.

(C) He would have to get married.

(D) He can't afford a larger apartment.

12. What is the population Harry mentions for Chicagee? ☐

*Questions 13–18 refer to the following excerpt from Jack London's "In a Far Country" (1899).*

When the world rang with the tale of Arctic gold, and the lure of the North gripped the heartstrings of men, Carter Weatherbee threw up his snug clerkship, turned the half of his savings over to his wife, and with the remainder bought an outfit. There was no romance in his nature — the bondage of commerce had crushed all that; he was simply tired of the ceaseless grind, and wished to risk great hazards in view of corresponding returns . . . and there, unluckily for his soul's welfare, he allied himself with a party of men.

There was nothing unusual about this party, except its plans. Even its goal, like that of all the other parties, was the Klondike. But the route it had mapped out to attain that goal took away the breath of the hardiest native, born and bred to the vicissitudes of the Northwest. Even Jacques Baptiste, born of a Chippewa woman and a renegade voyageur (having raised his first whimpers in a deerskin lodge north of the sixty-fifth parallel, and had the same hushed by blissful sucks of raw tallow), was surprised. Though he sold his services to them and agreed to travel even to the never-opening ice, he shook his head ominously whenever his advice was asked.

Percy Cuthfert's evil star must have been in the ascendant, for he, too, joined this company of Argonauts. He was an ordinary man, with a bank account as deep as his culture, which is saying a good deal. He had no reason to embark on such a venture — no reason in the world, save that he suffered from an abnormal development of sentimentality. He mistook this for the true spirit of romance and adventure.

13. Which of the following describes Carter Weatherbee? Write the appropriate item(s) in the box.

    (A) tired

    (B) a romantic

    (C) willing to take a risk for a chance of a good return

    (D) a hardy native

☐

14. What is meant by "bondage of commerce" in the second sentence?

    (A) the corresponding returns

    (B) the romance in his nature

    (C) the drudgery of life as a clerk

    (D) the risk of great hazards

15. What was the goal of the party?

    (A) to find the old trails

    (B) to reach the Klondike

    (C) to map out a route

    (D) to tell the tale of the Arctic

16. How would you best describe the chosen route to the Klondike?

    (A) blissful

    (B) hardy

    (C) hushed

    (D) ominous

17. Why was Jacques Baptiste important to the party?

    (A) He was a native of the Northwest.

    (B) He was born of a Chippewa woman.

    (C) He was a renegade voyageur.

    (D) He was born in a deerskin lodge.

18. Why do you think Percy Cuthfert joined the party?

    (A) to show that he is an ordinary man

    (B) to fill his bank account

    (C) to seek romance and adventure

    (D) because of his abnormal development

*Questions 19–24 refer to the following excerpt from "The Man with Two Left Feet" by P. G. Wodehouse.*

The platform was crowded. Friends of the company had come to see the company off. Henry looked on discreetly from behind a stout porter, whose bulk formed a capital screen. In spite of himself, he was impressed. The stage at close quarters always thrilled him. He recognized celebrities. The fat man in the brown suit was Walter Jelliffe, the comedian and star of the company. He stared keenly at him through the spectacles. Others of the famous were scattered about. He saw Alice. She was talking to a man with a face like a hatchet, and smiling, too, as if she enjoyed it. Behind the matted foliage which he had inflicted on his face, Henry's teeth came together with a snap. In the weeks that followed, as he dogged 'The Girl From Brighton' company from town to town, it would be difficult to say whether Henry was happy or unhappy. On the one hand, to realize that Alice was so near and yet so inaccessible was a constant source of misery; yet, on the other, he could not but admit that he was having the very dickens of a time, loafing round the country like this.

He was made for this sort of life, he considered. Fate had placed him in a London office, but what he really enjoyed was this unfettered travel. Some gipsy strain in him rendered even the obvious discomforts of theatrical touring agreeable. He liked catching trains; he liked invading strange hotels; above all, he revelled in the artistic pleasure of watching unsuspecting fellow-men as if they were so many ants.

That was really the best part of the whole thing. It was all very well for Alice to talk about creeping and spying, but, if you considered it without bias, there was nothing degrading about it at all. It was an art. It took brains and a genius for disguise to make a man a successful creeper and spyer. You couldn't simply say to yourself, 'I will creep.' If you attempted to do it in your own person, you would be detected instantly. You had to be an adept at masking your personality. You had to be one man at Bristol and another quite different man at Hull — especially if, like Henry, you were of a gregarious disposition, and liked the society of actors.

The stage had always fascinated Henry. To meet even minor members of the profession off the boards gave him a thrill. There was a resting juvenile, of fit-up calibre, at his boarding-house who could always get a shilling out of him simply by talking about how he had jumped in and saved the show at the hamlets which he had visited in the course of his wanderings. And on this 'Girl From Brighton' tour he was in constant touch with men who really amounted to something. Walter Jelliffe had been a celebrity when Henry was going to school; and Sidney Crane, the baritone, and others of the lengthy cast, were all players not unknown in London. Henry courted them assiduously.

19. What is Henry's profession?

    (A) baritone

    (B) actor

    (C) detective

    (D) none of the above

20. How do you know that Henry enjoys his work?

    (A) He loves being close to Alice.

    (B) The job does not involve any travel.

    (C) He loves to loaf about.

    (D) He believes he was made for this sort of work.

21. What is Walter Jelliffe's role? ☐

22. Why did Henry believe there was nothing degrading about being a detective?

    (A) It took brains to be good at that job.

    (B) It paid very well.

    (C) It gave him an opportunity to travel.

    (D) He got to be close to actors.

23. Why did Henry enjoy this particular assignment?

    (A) He loved to travel.

    (B) He was fascinated by the stage and actors.

    (C) He got to be close to Alice.

    (D) He enjoyed being a different man in the Hull.

24. What does this phrase "the matted foliage which he had inflicted on his face" tell you about Henry's disguise?

    (A) He was hiding in some shrubbery.

    (B) He blended in well with his surroundings.

    (C) He was wearing a dirty beard.

    (D) All of the above.

*Question 25 refers to the following excerpt from "All You Can Eat," by Murray J. Shukyn.*

I'm glad they didn't send a squad car for me. The school administration was only semi-understanding when the police arrested staff members, although the students enjoyed it more than winning a city championship. There was no greater joy to a student's heart than seeing a teacher led away in handcuffs to a police car. I thought it was very thoughtful of the police to let me come down to the station all by myself, and I didn't want to keep them waiting, even if I had no idea why they wanted me there.

Here I am, sitting in the reception area of a police station waiting for Detective Sulliven of the Vice Squad. I don't remember doing anything illegal. I'm just a quiet mathematics teacher at West Village Secondary School. Some of my students think that I should be in jail for having surprise quizzes, but I can't agree with them. There is no more honest and law abiding teacher than me. I'm so legal, I'm boring; just ask any student in my classes.

Nevertheless, here I am, summoned to the local police station to see someone on the Vice Squad, although I don't have any vices. I quit smoking years ago, and by that, I mean tobacco, not any of that other stuff. Gambling — I stay away from that; drinking — never, even though I am legally allowed to; women — seldom go out, even on dates and wouldn't know a woman of the evening if I stumbled over one. Then why am I sitting here waiting to see a detective? Maybe one of my students made up a story about me, and they took it seriously. I've heard stories of teachers being charged with the most outlandish things on the word of one student. Of course, not enough of my students even know my name or care what I do to pull a prank like that. If I were a drama teacher or a coach, then maybe they would pull pranks on me. Nobody pulls pranks on mathematics teachers. We're regarded as too dull even for pranks. I don't think I'm dull. I have fun with other adults. We go out to dinner and coffee, tell jokes, and discuss politics. Just because I haven't gone on a date for almost a year doesn't make me dull, just very busy. So why am I here? All that I've been able to establish in my mind is that I seem dull and don't go on many dates. That's sad but not very much of a reason to be called to the police station.

25. Why does the math teacher think the vice squad police want to see him?

(A) He might know "a woman of the evening."

(B) He may have gambled in his youth.

(C) A student made up a story about him.

(D) A political discussion went wrong.

## *The answers*

1. **D. serious enough that it requires monitoring.** The text states that the comingling of the virus strains is serious enough to require monitoring. Now that a new area of possible comingling is found, the text implies it, too, should be monitored. Choice (A) isn't supported by the text, and even though Choices (B) and (C) are possible, they're not as clear and important a statement as Choice (D).

2. **D. North Pacific.** The text states that this finding shows the North Atlantic is as significant melting pot for birds and avian flu as the North Pacific. Choice (B) isn't mentioned; and although *Eurasia* is mentioned, it isn't mentioned as a place where birds from Europe and North America mingle.

3. **D. All of the above.** According to the text, all of these statements are true. The finding of the various virus's genomes proves that this is a place where birds from both Eurasia and North America were present, it proves that the flu was spreading between continents via Iceland, and it proves that the avian flu virus had mingled in Iceland.

4. **A. It can lead to a new dangerous strain of avian flu.** The text states that the virus evolves readily, and that the mingling of North American and Eurasian strains can lead to new varieties dangerous to humans. Cold viruses and flu viruses aren't the same, so Choice (B) has nothing to do with the topic of this text. Although Choices (C) and (D) may be partially true, they're not the best options.

5. **C. factual and straightforward.** The tone of the passage is very calm, very factual. It isn't *lighthearted, deeply concerned,* or *gloomy.*

6. **B. the H5N1 strain.** The text refers only to the H5N1 strain as a possible human flu. The term *bird flu* refers to the entire category of disease, not just the version dangerous to human. There's no mention in the text of an *H5 flu,* and *Eurasian avian flu* simply refers to one part of the world were many strains of avian flu originate.

7. **D. all of the above.** Chicagee is a new version of the name Chicago. The urban population listed is well beyond anything existing today. Certainly, the hours Harry works are unusual for today. There are other clues in the text as well, but they're not listed in the answer choices.

8. **A. incredibly crowded.** The overwhelming view that Bloch sees is a future of incredible overcrowding. There doesn't appear to be any food shortages based on the content of the story, so Choice (B) is wrong. Working hours appeared to be shorter, so Choice (D) is also incorrect. And although the commutes may be well organized, nothing in the passage suggests that, so Choice (C) is incorrect.

9. **D. all of the above.** Bloch's descriptions constantly reinforced the overwhelming idea of crowding. The description of Harry's one-room apartment, followed by comments about commuting distances and waiting times, all reinforce this idea of a crowded world.

10. **B. shorter working hours.** Harry states that he sometimes wishes he worked there because of the shorter working hours but doesn't say anything about better pay. The text also states that the commuting times would be longer there.

11. **C. He would have to get married.** The text mentions legal restrictions on accommodations. Harry would have to be married to be entitled to a two-room apartment. Harry states that he makes a good income, so money isn't an issue. His lady friends claim to like the convenience, but Harry knows they're just being polite. He certainly doesn't like the small space.

12. **38,000,000.** The text states that the population is 38,000,000 people.

13. **A & C (tired; willing to take a risk for a chance of a good return).** Carter left his job because he was lured by the promise of Arctic gold. The passage states that he's worn down by the daily grind and willing to take a risk for commensurate return. He isn't a hardy native and certainly not a romantic.

14. **C. the drudgery of life as a clerk.** Carter wanted to escape his everyday drudgery in life as a clerk. "Bondage of commerce" refers to his dislike of his daily routine in the business world. His need for wealth (returns), romance, and risk taking are different factors that don't apply to the question.

15. **B. to reach the Klondike.** The text says that "Even its [the party's] goal . . . was the Klondike."

16. **D. ominous.** The chosen route to Klondike was ominous because there was a foreboding of ill-fortune. Throughout the passage, words such as *unluckily, ominously,* and *evil star . . . in the ascendant* give the passage an ominous feeling. The route certainly wasn't *blissful* or *hushed,* and *hardy* refers to a native of the region.

17. **A. He was a native of the Northwest.** The fact that Jacques was native-born and raised in the Northwest made him important to the party. The fact that he was a renegade voyageur, born of a Chippewa woman in a deerskin lodge, isn't as relevant as his knowledge of the area is to his importance to the party.

18. **B. to fill his bank account.** Percy was seeking some romance and adventure in his otherwise mundane life. The fact that he was an ordinary man with a bank account, who spoke a good deal and was abnormally sentimental, aren't the best answers.

19. **C. detective.** Henry is a detective. Several clues give this answer away. Henry talks about observing people without being observed himself. He talks about disguises remaining undetected and the ability to mask one's personality. The main clue, however, is his reference to Alice talking about "creeping and spying."

20. **D. He believes he was made for this sort of work.** Although the text gives numerous reasons Henry enjoys the work, among the answer choices, only Choice (D) fits the bill. ***Remember:*** You must choose the most correct answer from the options offered.

21. **comedian.** According to the text, Walter Jelliffe's is a comedian and the star of the company.

22. **A. It took brains to be good at that job.** In the third paragraph, Henry comments that being a detective was really an art. He states, "it took brains and a genius for disguise" to be successful. Choice (B) is incorrect because there's no mention of pay in the passage. And although Choices (C) and (D) are correct in their content, they have nothing to do with whether being a detective is degrading.

23. **B. He was fascinated by the stage and actors.** The last paragraph contains the answer. It states that Henry is fascinated by the stage and actors, loves to be near them, and loves to hear all about the stage and the goings-on. Choice (A) may be partially correct, but it isn't the most correct answer. Choice (C) is wrong because Henry mentions it's a misery to be close to Alice without being able to talk to her. Choice (D) is irrelevant to the question.

24. **C. He was wearing a dirty beard.** The passage doesn't support anything about hiding in shrubbery, and although Henry probably blended in with his surroundings, that isn't the best choice.

25. **C. A student made up a story about him.** As the math teacher lists all the reasons he's dull and boring, he can't think of any reason he'd be waiting to see someone from the vice squad other than a student might have made up a story about him that the police took seriously. The other choices are wrong. The math teacher states that he doesn't know "a woman of the evening" or gamble. And there's no suggestion that a political discussion was anything other than a political discussion, so Choice (D) doesn't apply, either.

# Part III

# Finding Your Way: The Social Studies Test

## Five Ways to Get Ready for the Social Studies Test

- ✔ Read news stories and highlight key points; look at graphics and list the information they provide. Information can be anywhere, and you may have to find it to answer questions about it, so being able to locate and identify information is key.

- ✔ Get familiar with how the government works and how civil rights evolved. A large part of the Social Studies test focuses on civics, the Constitution, and similar issues.

- ✔ Review American history for issues that come up again and again, from poverty or unemployment, unions or civil rights movements, to individual liberties versus social rights. Look at what these issues are and why they keep coming up. The Extended Response deals mainly with these types of issues in American history or civics and your analysis of those issues.

- ✔ Watch documentaries about history or social issues. Doing so is a great way to get an overview of topics that may be on the GED test.

- ✔ Check out some high-school geography or economics textbooks (you can often find them at the local library), or even read the economics or business sections of newspapers and magazines. Do what you can to get familiar with the terminology in these subject areas.

Knowing how to do your best on the GED test's Extended Responses (the essays) can make the difference between passing and having to retake the test. Why spend unnecessary time and money on retaking a test when there's more valuable advice at www.dummies.com/extras/gedtest?

## In this part . . .

✔ Find out what skills the Social Studies test expects you to know, what subject areas the test covers, and how the test is laid out.

✔ Take advantage of key test-taking strategies so you're prepared to deal with any question type, evaluate any passage or visual material presented to you, and write up an Extended Response that will get you extra credit.

# Chapter 8

# A Graph, a Map, and You: Getting Ready for the Social Studies Test

......................................................

## In This Chapter

▶ Getting familiar with the Social Studies test's topics and components

▶ Surveying the types of questions and passages on the test

▶ Using strategies to help you achieve the best results

......................................................

**D**o you enjoy knowing about how events in the past may help you foretell the future? Do the lives of people in faraway places interest you? Are politics something you care about? If you answered yes to any of these questions, you're going to like the Social Studies test! After all, social studies helps you discover how humans relate to their environment and to other people.

The GED Social Studies test assesses your skills in understanding and interpreting concepts and principles in civics, history, geography, and economics. Consider this test as a kind of crash course in where you've been, where you are, and how you can continue living there. You can apply the types of skills tested on the Social Studies test to your experience in visual, academic, and workplace situations as a citizen, a consumer, or an employee.

This test includes questions drawn from a variety of written and visual passages taken from academic and workplace materials as well as from primary and secondary sources. The passages in this test are like the ones you read or see in most daily newspapers and news magazines. Reading either or both of these news sources regularly can help you become familiar with the style and vocabulary of the passages you find here.

The Social Studies test consists of two timed sections. The first is a 65-minute question-and-answer segment. The second consists of an Extended Response (an essay), just like in the Reasoning through Language Arts test. On the Social Studies test, however, you have only 25 minutes to produce a somewhat shorter essay. You may not transfer time between the two sections, and there's no break between the two sections. In this chapter, we take a look at the skills required for the Social Studies section of the GED test, the format of the test, and what you can do to prepare.

## Looking at the Skills the Social Studies Test Covers

The question-and-answer items of the Social Studies test evaluate several specific skills, including the ability to read and understand complex text, interpret graphs and relate graphs to text, and relate descriptive text to specific values in graphs. For example, an item could ask about the relationship between a description of unemployment in text and a graph of the unemployment rate over time.

You don't have to study a lot of new content to pass this test. Everything you need to know is presented to you with the questions. In each case, you see some content, either a passage or a visual, a question or direction to tell you what you're expected to do, and a series of answer options.

The questions do require you to draw on your previous knowledge of events, ideas, terms, and situations that may be related to social studies. From a big-picture perspective, you must demonstrate the ability to

- ✔ Identify information, events, problems, and ideas and interpret their significance or impact.

- ✔ Use the information and ideas in different ways to explore their meanings or solve a problem.

- ✔ Use the information or ideas to do the following:

  - • Distinguish between facts and opinions.

  - • Summarize major events, problems, solutions, and conflicts.

  - • Arrive at conclusions using material.

  - • Influence other people's attitudes.

  - • Find other meanings or mistakes in logic.

  - • Identify causes and their effects.

  - • Recognize how writers may have been influenced by the times in which they lived and a writer's historical point of view.

  - • Compare and contrast differing events and people and their views.

  - • Compare places, opinions, and concepts.

  - • Determine what impact views and opinions may have both at this time and in the future.

  - • Organize information to show relationships.

  - • Analyze similarities and differences in issues or problems.

  - • Give examples to illustrate ideas and concepts.

  - • Propose and evaluate solutions.

- ✔ Make judgments about the material's appropriateness, accuracy, and differences of opinion. Some questions will ask you to interpret the role information and ideas play in influencing current and future decision making. These questions ask you to think about issues and events that affect you every day. That fact alone is interesting and has the potential to make you a more informed citizen of the modern world. What a bonus for a test!

About one-third of the questions test your ability to read and write in a social studies context. That means you'll be tested on the following:

- ✔ Identifying and using information from sources

- ✔ Isolating central ideas or specific information

- ✔ Determining the meaning of words or phrases used in social studies

- ✔ Identifying points of view, differentiating between fact and opinion, and identifying properly supported ideas

Another third of the questions ask you to apply mathematical reasoning to social studies. Much of that relates to the ability to

- ✔ Interpret graphs.

- ✔ Use charts and tables as source data and interpret the content.

- ✔ Interpret information presented visually.

- ✔ Differentiate between correlation and cause and effect.

The remaining third deals with applying social studies concepts. That includes the following:

- ✔ Using specific evidence to support conclusions

- ✔ Describing the connections between people, environments, and events

- ✔ Putting historical events into chronological order

- ✔ Analyzing documents to examine how ideas and events develop and interact, especially in a historical context

- ✔ Examining cause-and-effect correlations

- ✔ Identifying bias and evaluating validity of information, in both modern and historical documents

Being aware of what skills the Social Studies test covers can help you get a more accurate picture of the types of questions you'll encounter. The next section focuses more on the specific subject materials you'll face.

# Understanding the Social Studies Test Format

You have a total of 90 minutes to complete the Social Studies test. That time is split between the two components of the test. You have 25 minutes for the Extended Response item, and 65 minutes to answer a variety of question-and-answer items. You can't transfer time from one section to the other. The question-and-answer section consists mostly of multiple-choice questions with a few fill-in-the-blank questions. The multiple-choice questions come in various forms. Most are the standard multiple-choice you know from your school days. Other formats include drop-down menu, drag-and-drop, and hot-spot items. For a general overview of the types of questions on the Social Studies test, check out Chapter 2. For a specific look at the Social Studies types of questions, see Chapter 9.

In the following sections, we explore the subject areas the Social Studies test covers, give you an overview of the types of passages you can expect to see, and take a look at what the Extended Response is all about.

## Checking out the subject areas on the test

The question-and-answer section of the Social Studies test includes about 50 questions. The exact number varies from test to test, as the difficulty level of the questions varies. Most of the information you need will be presented in the text or graphics accompanying the questions, so it's important to read and analyze the materials carefully but quickly. The questions focus on the following subject areas:

- ✔ **Civics and government:** About 50 percent of the Social Studies test includes such topics as rights and responsibilities in democratic governance and the forms of governance.

- ✔ **American history:** About 20 percent of the test covers a broad outline of the history of the United States from pre-colonial days to the present, including such topics as the War of Independence, the Civil War, the Great Depression, and the challenges of the 20th century.

✔ **Economics:** Economics involves about 15 percent of the test and covers two broad areas, economic theory and basic principles. That includes topics such as how various economic systems work and the role of economics in conflicts.

✔ **Geography and the world:** In broad terms, the remaining 15 percent covers the relationships between the environment and societal development; the concept of borders, region, and place and diversity; and, finally, human migration and population issues.

The test materials cover these four subject areas through two broad themes:

✔ **Development of modern liberties and democracy:** How did the modern ideas of democracy and human and civil rights develop? What major events have shaped democratic values, and what writings and philosophies are the underpinning to American views and expressions of democracy?

✔ **Dynamic systems:** How have institutions, people, and systems responded to events, geographic realities, national policies, and economics?

The Extended Response item (that is, the essay you write at the end of the test) is based on enduring issues, which cover issues of personal freedoms in conflict with societal interests and issues of governance — states' rights versus federal powers, checks and balances within government, and the role of government in society. These are all issues that require you to evaluate points of view or arguments, and determine how such issues represent an enduring issue in American history. You need to be able to recognize false arguments, bias, and misleading comparisons.

If you're a little worried about all of these subject areas, relax. You're not expected to have detailed knowledge of all the topics listed. Although it helps if you have a general knowledge of these areas, most of the test is based on your ability to reason, interpret, and work with the information presented in each question. Knowing basic concepts, such as checks and balances or representative democracy, will help, but you don't need to know a detailed history of the United States.

## Identifying the types of passages

The passages in the Social Studies test are taken from two types of sources:

✔ **Academic material:** The type of material you find in a school — textbooks, maps, newspapers, magazines, software, and Internet material. This type of passage also includes extracts from speeches or historical documents.

✔ **Workplace material:** The type of material found on the job — manuals, documents, business plans, advertising and marketing materials, correspondence, and so on.

The material may be from primary sources — that is, the original documents, such as the Declaration of Independence — or secondary sources — material written about an event or person, such as someone's opinions or interpretation of original documents or historic events, sometimes long after the event takes place or the person dies.

## Readying for the Extended Response

The Extended Response on the Social Studies test is similar to the one on the Reasoning through Language Arts (RLA) test (which you can read about in Chapter 5). The major difference between this Extended Response and the one for the RLA test is length. The RLA test gives you 45 minutes to write the Extended Response, and you're expected to write about 600 to 800 words The Social Studies Extended Response allocates only 25 minutes, so the stimulus text is shorter, and you're expected to write only about 250 to 500 words.

For the Social Studies Extend Response item, you're given sample source texts presenting and defending a particular position. You must read and analyze each source text and write an essay based on that text. You're asked to discuss the source texts in terms of presenting an enduring issue in American history and society. You must use quotes from the source documents to support your argument. You may also use your own personal knowledge to support your arguments. Read the instructions carefully. Write the key words down on your tablet to ensure you don't misread. As you prepare your answer, go back to the basic question and make sure you're staying on topic and that all of your answering points relate strictly to that topic.

Because the GED test is now administered on the computer, you'll also use the computer's word processor to write your response. The word processor has all the functions you'd expect — copy, paste, do, and undo — however, it doesn't include either a grammar-checker or a spell-checker. That is part of your job.

The evaluation looks at three specific areas of essay writing:

✔ **Creation of argument and use of evidence:**

- Your argument must show not only that you understand the arguments being presented but also that you understand the relationship between the ideas presented and their historical or social context.

- You must effectively use relevant ideas from the source text to back your arguments.

✔ **Development of ideas and organizational structure:**

- Your arguments develop logically and clearly.

- You connect details and main ideas.

- You explain details as required to further your argument.

✔ **Clarity and command of standard English:**

- You use proper English.

- You demonstrate a command of proper writing conventions.

- You show correct usage of subject-verb agreement, homonyms, capitalization, punctuation, and proper word order.

To prepare for the Extended Response item, we say read, read, and then read some more. Look for magazine and newspaper editorials. Look for documentaries on television, DVD, or even online about such issues in American history. For example, look for a documentary on school bussing in the 1950s. List the issues surrounding the decision to bus pupils in one area to schools in another area. Consider the issues of personal freedom, the rights to choose, and civil liberties in a larger community sense. Look at the changing views on the role of government in our daily lives. What forces drove decision making at that time? How were those decisions a reflection of their times, and to what extent do similar views and decisions still apply today?

# Examining Preparation Strategies That Work

To improve your skills and get better results, we suggest you try the following strategies when preparing for the Social Studies test:

- **Take as many practice tests as you can get your hands on.** The best way to prepare is to answer all the sample Social Studies test questions you can find. Work through practice tests (see Chapters 19 and 27), practice questions (see Chapter 10), and examples, such as those at www.gedtestingservice.com/educators/freepracticetest. (*Note:* This site is intended for educators teaching the GED prep courses. Because you're your own educator while using this book, try it. If you're in a prep class, check with your teacher.)

  Consider taking a preparation class to get your hands on even more sample Social Studies test questions, but remember that your task is to pass the test — not to collect every question ever written.

- **Practice reading a variety of different documents.** The documents you need to focus on include historic passages from original sources (such as the Declaration of Independence and U.S. Constitution) as well as practical information for consumers (such as voters' guides, atlases, budget graphs, political speeches, almanacs, and tax forms). Read about the evolution of democratic forms of government. Read about climate change and migration, about food and population, and about American politics in the post-9/11 world. Read newspapers and news magazines about current issues, especially those related to civics and government, and social and economic issues.

- **Prepare summaries of the passages you read in your own words.** After you read these passages, summarize what you've read. Doing so can help you identify the main points of the passages, which is an important part of succeeding on the Social Studies test. Ask yourself the following two questions when you read a passage or something more visual like a graph:

  - **What's the passage about?** The answer is usually in the first and last paragraphs of the passage. The rest is usually explanation. If you don't see the answer there, you may have to look carefully through the rest of the passage.

  - **What's the visual material about?** Look for the answer in the title, labels, captions, and any other information that's included.

  After you get an initial grasp of the main idea, determine what to do with it. Some questions ask you to apply information you gain from one situation in another similar situation. If you know the main idea of the passage, you'll have an easier time applying it to another situation.

- **Draft a series of your own test questions that draw on the information contained in the passages you read.** Doing so can help you become familiar with social studies–based questions. Look in newspapers and magazines for articles that fit into the general passage types that appear on the Social Studies test. Find a good summary paragraph and develop a question that gets to the point of the summary.

- **Compose answers for each of your test questions.** Write down four answers to each of your test questions, only one of which is correct based on the passage. Creating your own questions and answers helps reduce your stress level by showing you how answers are related to questions. It also encourages you to read and think about material that could be on the test. Finally, it gives you some idea of where to look for answers in a passage.

- **Discuss questions and answers with friends and family to make sure you've achieved an understanding and proper use of the material.** If your friends and family understand the question, you know it's a good one. Discussing your questions and answers with others gives you a chance to explain social studies topics and concepts, which is an important skill to have as you get ready to take this test.

✔ **Don't assume.** Be critical of visual material and read it carefully. You want to be able to read visual material as accurately as you read text material, and doing so takes practice. Don't assume something is true just because it looks that way in a diagram, chart, or map. Visual materials can be precise drawings, with legends and scales, or they can be drawn in such a way that, at first glance, the information appears to be different than it really is. Manipulating the scale for graphs is one way to skew the information and make it appear different from what it actually represents. At first glance, you never know the purpose for which the visual was created. Even visuals can be biased, so "read" them carefully. Verify what you think you see by making sure the information looks correct and realistic. Finally, before coming to any conclusions, check the scale and legend to make sure the graph is really showing what you think it does.

✔ **Be familiar with general graphical conventions.** Maps and graphs have conventions. The top of a map is almost always north. The horizontal axis is always the *x*-axis, and the vertical axis (the *y*-axis) is dependent on the *x*-axis. Looking at the horizontal axis first usually makes the information clearer and easier to understand. Practice reading charts and tables in an atlas or check out government websites where information is displayed in tables, charts, and maps.

See Chapter 3 for general test-taking strategies that apply to all the GED test sections.

# Chapter 9

# Social Studies Question Types and Solving Strategies

The Social Studies test consists of two sections, the question-and-answer items, followed by a separately timed Extended Response (the essay). You have 65 minutes for the first section and then 25 minutes for the essay, and there's no break between the sections. Having a basic understanding of what's in these two sections can help you prepare and avoid any surprises when you sit down to the take the test.

The Social Studies test requires you to read a passage or study a visual, analyze the information, evaluate its accuracy, and draw conclusions according to the printed text or visual materials presented. It doesn't measure your ability to recall information, such as dates, facts, or events. In most cases, you select an answer from four choices. You then choose the one best answer to each item. So although there's not much you can do to study for this test, you can improve your chances of passing by reading and writing summaries of what you've read — and by checking out our test-taking strategies in this chapter.

In this chapter, we explores the types of materials and questions you encounter on the Social Studies test and offer you advice on how to solve them with ease.

## Answering Questions about Text and Visual Materials

There are three broad categories of source materials for the question-and-answer items facing you on the test. The materials require you to extract information and come to conclusions and then determine the correct answer. These source materials consist of textual materials, something with which you're probably already quite familiar; visuals, like maps and diagrams; and statistical tables. Each of these categories requires careful reading, even the visuals, because information can be buried anywhere, and you need to extract it.

## Questions about text passages

About half of the question-answer portion of the Social Studies test includes textual passages with a series of questions following based on that passage. Your job is to read the passage and then answer questions about it.

When you're reading these passages on the test (or in any of the practice questions or tests in this book), read between the lines and look at the implications and assumptions in the passages. An *implication* is something you can understand from what's written, even though it isn't directly stated. An *assumption* is something you can accept as the truth, even though proof isn't directly presented in the text.

Be sure to read each item carefully so you know exactly what it's asking. Read the answer choices and go through the text again, carefully. If the question asks for certain facts, you'll be able to find those right in the passage. If it asks for opinions, you may find those opinions stated directly in the passage or they may simply be implied (and they may not match your own opinions, but you still have to answer with the best choice based on the material presented).

If a question doesn't specifically tell you to use additional information that isn't presented in the passage, use *only* the information given. An answer may be incorrect in your opinion, but according to the passage, it's correct (or vice versa). Go with the information presented unless you're told to do otherwise and select the most correct answer choice.

## Questions about visual materials

To make sure you don't get bored, the other half of the question-answer portion of the Social Studies test is based on maps, graphs, tables, political cartoons, diagrams, photographs, and artistic works. Some items combine visual material and text. You need to be prepared to deal with all of these types of items.

If you're starting to feel overwhelmed about answering questions based on visual materials, consider the following:

- ✔ **Maps aren't there only to show you the location of places.** They also give you information, and knowing how to decode that information is essential. A map may show you where Charleston is located, but it can also show you how the land around Charleston is used, what the climate in the area is, and whether the population there is growing or declining. Start by examining the print information with the map, the legend, title, and key to the colors or symbols on the map. Then look at what the question requires you to find. Now you can find that information quickly by relating the answer choices to what the map shows.

  For example, the map in Figure 9-1 shows you the following information:

  - The population of the United States for 2010

  - The population by state by size range

  Indirectly, the map also shows you much more. It allows you to compare the population of states with a quick glance. For example, you can see that Florida has a larger population than Montana, North Dakota, South Dakota, and Wyoming together. If you were asked what the relationship is between a state's size and population, you could argue, based on this map, that there isn't much relationship. You could also show that the states around Lakes Erie and Ontario have a higher population density than the states in the Midwest. This is part of the skill of analyzing maps.

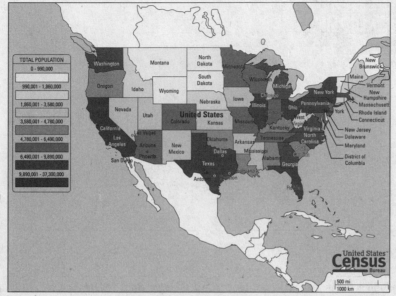

**Figure 9-1:**
Most
Populated
States, 2010
Census Map.

*Illustration courtesy of U.S. Census Bureau*

✔ **Every time you turn around, someone in the media is trying to make a point with a graph.** The types of graphs you see in Figure 9-2 are very typical examples. The real reason people use graphs to explain themselves so often is because a graph can clearly show trends and relationships between different sets of information. The three graphs in Figure 9-2 are best suited for a particular use. For example, the bar graphs are great for comparing items over time, the line graphs show changes over time, and the pie chart shows you proportions. The next time you see a graph, such as the ones in Figure 9-2, study it. Be sure to look carefully at the scale of graphs; even visual information can fool you. A bar graph that shows a rapid rise of something may in fact show no such thing. It only looks that way because the bottom of the chart doesn't start with values of zero. Check carefully to make sure you understand what the information in the graph is telling you. (***Note:*** Graphs are also called *charts.*)

✔ **Tables are everywhere.** If you've ever looked at the nutrition label on a food product, you've read a table. Study any table you can find, whether in a newspaper or on the back of a can of tuna. The population data table in Figure 9-3 is an example of the kinds of data you may see on the test. That table shows you a lot of information, but you can extract quite a bit more information that isn't stated. Just a quick look at the numbers tells you that nearly 1.6 million people are enlisted in the Armed Forces. How do you know that? Subtract the number in the *Civilian Population* column from the *Resident Population Plus Armed Forces Overseas* column. You can also calculate the change in the overall population, the rate of increase of both the population and the Armed Forces personnel, and even the size of the Armed Forces stationed in the United States compared to serving overseas.

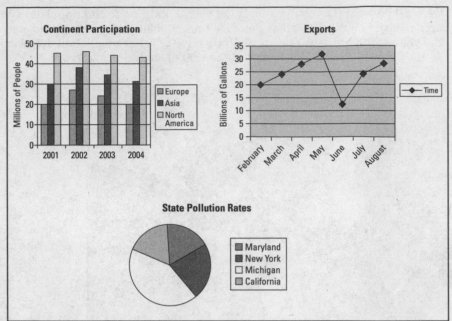

**Figure 9-2:**
Examples
of different
graphs.

© John Wiley & Sons, Inc.

| Monthly Population Estimates for the United States: April 1 to December 1, 2010 | | | |
|---|---|---|---|
| **Year and Month** | **Resident Population** | **Resident Population Plus Armed Forces Overseas** | **Civilian Population** |
| **2010** | | | |
| April 1 | 308,747,508 | 309,180,459 | 307,517,564 |
| May 1 | 308,937,636 | 309,361,879 | 307,702,883 |
| June 1 | 309,122,451 | 309,544,899 | 307,889,928 |
| July 1 | 309,326,225 | 309,745,660 | 308,091,141 |
| August 1 | 309,540,608 | 309,956,285 | 308,313,027 |
| September 1 | 309,768,270 | 310,173,518 | 308,531,330 |
| October 1 | 309,994,453 | 310,395,556 | 308,761,399 |
| November 1 | 310,179,397 | 310,589,914 | 308,957,140 |
| December 1 | 310,353,742 | 310,774,403 | 309,141,425 |

**Figure 9-3:**
Population
data table.

*Illustration courtesy of U.S. Census Bureau*

Tables are also sometimes called charts, which can be a little confusing, because graphs can also be called charts. Regardless of what they're called, you need to be prepared to extract information, even if it isn't stated directly. That's what makes maps and tables and charts such fun. The thing to remember is that it doesn't matter whether a visual passage is a table, a cartoon, a drawing, or a graph — as long as you know how to read it.

✔ **Political cartoons appear in the newspapers every day.** If you don't read political cartoons in the daily newspaper (usually located in the "Editorial" or "Op-Ed" pages), give them a try. Some days, they're the best entertainment in the paper. Political cartoons in the newspaper are usually based on an event in the last day or week. They can be nasty or funny and are always biased. If you want to get the most out of political cartoons, look for small details, facial expressions, and background clues. The cartoons on the test are obviously older than the ones in daily newspapers, so you may not get the context unless you've been reading the newspapers or watching the news for the past several weeks or months.

✔ **You've no doubt seen countless photographs in your day.** Photos are all around you. All you need to do to prepare for the photograph-based questions on the test is to begin getting information from the photographs you see. Start with the newspapers or magazines, where photos are chosen to provide information that connects directly to a story. See whether you can determine what message the photograph carries with it and how it relates to the story it supports.

✔ **You probably like to look at works of art.** On the Social Studies test, you have a chance to "read" works of art. You look at a work of art and gather information you can use to answer the item. To get yourself ready to gather information from works of art on the test, take a look at art galleries, the Internet, and library books. Lucky for you, some books even give some background or other explanation for these works.

If you're unsure of how to read a map, go to any search engine and search for "map reading help" to find sites that explain how to read a map. If any of the other types of visual materials cause you concern, do the same thing — with the exception of political cartoons. If you try to follow the same procedure for political cartoons, you'll get a lot of actual cartoons but not a lot of explanations about them. Instead, look at some examples of political cartoons (either in the newspaper or online) to try to understand what the cartoonist is saying to you. Then look up the topic of the cartoon and the date to read some of the news stories it refers to. Talk about the cartoon with your friends. If you can explain a cartoon or carry on a logical discussion about the topic, you probably understand its contents.

All the visual items you have to review on this test are familiar. Now all you have to do is practice until your skills in reading and understanding them increase. Then you, too, can discuss the latest political cartoon or pontificate about a work of art.

# Acing the Question-Answer Portion of the Social Studies Test

The types of questions you encounter on the Social Studies test include multiple-choice, fill-in-the-blank, and drag-and-drop. In the following sections, we provide strategies for examining information, whether a passage or visual, and for answering sample questions in each of these formats.

## Choosing an answer from multiple choices

Multiple-choice questions basically ask you to choose a correct answer from four choices. You can handle these questions in several ways. Read the question and answer choices, and then go through the text carefully to find which answer choice is correct. If you can't decide based on that reading, review the answer choices. You can probably eliminate one or two of them because they're obviously wrong. Then skim the text again, looking for information based on the choices left. If that doesn't provide you with an answer, then you may have to guess. If you've eliminated the improbable choices, you may have to choose from only two or three options, which gives you reasonable odds of picking the correct answer. The answer choices must reflect something in the text. Or, if none of the answer choices fulfill the question, you may have to choose *none of the above* if that option is provided. Remember, you need to work quickly because you have only about 90 seconds per question.

In the rest of this section, we walk you through answering some multiple-choice questions based on the following passage.

> Bridging both temperate and tropical regions, Mexico's terrain includes mountains, plains, valleys, and plateaus. Snow-capped volcanoes slope down to pine forests, deserts, and balmy tropical beaches. This diverse topography supports a variety of industries, including manufacturing, mining, petroleum, and agricultural production. As a member of the North American Free Trade Agreement (NAFTA), Mexico has the United States and Canada as main trading partners. In economic terms, Mexico boasts a GDP (gross domestic product) of $370 billion ($8,100 per person), which ranks it 13th in the world. Mexico currently enjoys an annual growth rate of more than 6 percent. Beginning in 1985, Mexico began a process of trade liberalization and privatization. From 1982 to 1992, government-controlled enterprises were reduced from 1,155 to 217.

Which of the following is not part of Mexico's terrain?

(A) plateaus

(B) polar ice caps

(C) mountains

(D) valleys

The key to this question is realizing that it's asking for something that *isn't* included in the passage. Be sure you watch for words such as *not* and *except* and *double negatives,* such as *not impossible* or *not unlikely,* especially in multiple-choice questions. In this case, the correct answer is Choice (B) because Mexico doesn't lie either at the North or South Pole, where polar ice caps are found. The passage mentions the other answer choices — *plateaus, mountains,* and *valleys* — but this question asks for what isn't mentioned.

Which adjectives demonstrate that the Mexican climate represents extremes in temperature?

(A) sunny and rainy

(B) dark and misty

(C) plains and valleys

(D) snow-capped and balmy

Here's an example of a question and answer choices whose wording can be misleading if you don't read carefully. The question asks for the answer choice that represents extremes in *temperature.* So the only choice that works here is Choice (D) because it's the only one that deals with temperatures. *Snow-capped* volcanoes represent an extremely low temperature, while *balmy* beaches refer to the higher temperatures found in a tropical climate. Other adjectives — such as *sunny* and *rainy* or *dark* and *misty* — don't refer to changes in temperature but rather weather. *Plains* and *valleys* are nouns that refer to terrain, not temperature.

In this example, "diverse topography" refers to

(A) differences in terrain

(B) uniqueness in manufacturing

(C) differences in agriculture

(D) diversity of tropical beaches

This question shows why understanding subject-appropriate vocabulary is importatnt. *Topography* is another word for terrain. *Diverse* means different, so Choice (A) is the correct answer. *Manufacturing* and *agriculture* are types of industries, and *tropical beaches* are just one type of terrain.

Which countries are Mexico's trading partners in NAFTA?

(A) the United States and the United Kingdom

(B) France and Germany

(C) the United States and Canada

(D) Canada and the United Kingdom

The correct answer is Choice (C). The text states that the United States and Canada joined with Mexico to form the North American Free Trade Agreement. The United Kingdom, France, and Germany aren't partners in NAFTA.

What happened in Mexico between 1982 and 1992?

(A) Government control of enterprises increased.

(B) The government controlled fewer enterprises.

(C) Mexico achieved the highest GDP in the world.

(D) Mexico's growth rate was less than 6 percent.

The correct answer is Choice (B). According to the passage, during the decade from 1982 to 1992, Mexico's government reduced its control of enterprises from 1,155 to 217. It didn't increase enterprise control, nor did Mexico achieve the highest GDP in the world — 12 countries were higher. The country's growth rate was more than 6 percent.

## Coming up with an answer for fill-in-the-blank questions

Fill-in-the-blank questions require you to insert the correct answer, usually one or two words or numbers, into a blank. No answer choices are provided, so you have to extract the information from the passage or visual carefully.

For practice, find the info you need to answer fill-in-the-blank questions based on the following graph.

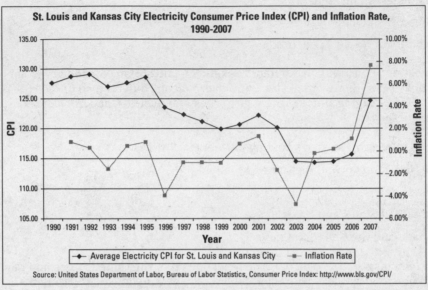

**St. Louis and Kansas City Electricity Consumer Price Index (CPI) and Inflation Rate, 1990-2007**

Source: United States Department of Labor, Bureau of Labor Statistics, Consumer Price Index: http://www.bls.gov/CPI/

*Illustration courtesy of United States Department of Labor, Bureau of Labor Statistics*

In what year was the inflation rate the lowest? ☐

The graph shows two sets of data, the Electricity CPI for Kansas City and the inflation rate. You need to identify that the lighter line represents the inflation rate. The legend on the bottom of the graph will help you. Since the graph shows two sets of data, there are two scales. You need to identify that the vertical scale on the right refers to the inflation data. Every year is listed on the horizontal axis, but the data is marked on the chart in the middle of the space above the year. The tick marks represent the end or beginning of years. You need to estimate where the actual year data would be on the graph. The dots on the graph lines help you locate those individual years. The lowest point on the graph for the inflation rate line (the one with the square dots) occurs in the year 2003. You have to take that information from the data given. The lowest point on that graph is at the 13th point on the lower line. That is your answer.

The longest period that the inflation rate stayed below zero was from ☐ to ☐.

This graph shows two sets of data for comparison. Remember to use the correct line (the one with the square dots). Note also the horizontal lines across the graph. They help you read the values for the data. However, to make your work more difficult, the horizontal lines refer only to the CPI, the left scale, not the inflation rate. Those values are marked only by tick marks, which means you have to figure out where a horizontal line would be on the chart area for those values. You need to draw an imaginary line using the tick marks on the right scale.

The first time the inflation line on this graph passes through the imaginary horizontal line labeled *0* on the inflation scale is sometime in 1992. However, it stays there for only about 18 months (another estimate). The second, and longer, period is between 1995 to almost the end of 1999. The correct answer is *1995* to *1999*.

The CPI rate in 1992 was ⬚.

This question is more difficult because it asks for information that isn't shown directly. The graph doesn't have labels for every unit of CPI increase. You need to work out that value from the scale by estimating. If you look at the labels on the CPI scale (left vertical axis), it's marked at intervals of five points, with corresponding lines across the chart area. You need to fill in your own lines for the in-between CPI values on the graph. The CPI for 1992 is marked by the third dot on the darker line (with the round dots). It's close to the 130 CPI line but below. Estimating the distance between this line and the lower one (CPI of 125) suggests your answer should be *129*.

# *Dragging and dropping answers where they belong*

Dragging and dropping items require more understanding than basic multiple-choice items because, in most instances, you need to prioritize or sort items, not just pick a correct answer.

Here's an example of a drag-and-drop item based on the following excerpt from *U.S. History For Dummies,* by Steve Wiegand (Wiley).

> As time passed, however, the country began to side more often with Britain, France, and other countries that were fighting Germany. The sinking of the British passenger ship, *Lusitania,* by a German submarine in 1915, which resulted in the deaths of 128 Americans, inflames U.S. passions against "the Huns." Propagandistic portrayals of German atrocities in the relatively new medium of motion pictures added to the heat. And finally, when it was revealed that German diplomats had approached Mexico about an alliance against the United States, Wilson felt compelled to ask Congress for a resolution of war against Germany. He got it on April 6, 1917.

Drag (or write, in this case) the list of events into the boxes in chronological order.

(A) sinking of the *Lusitania*

(B) declaration of war against Germany

(C) anti-German propaganda in the movies

(D) Germany negotiates with Mexico to attack the United States

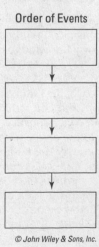

The correct sequence of events is Choice (A), (C), (D), and then (B) (*the sinking of the* Lusitania, *anti-German propaganda in the movies, Germany negotiates with Mexico to attack the United States,* and then *declaration of war against Germany*). The only somewhat tricky part of these choices is the timing for the anti-German propaganda, but the key phrase is in the sentence, "Propagandistic portrayals . . . added to the heat." The word *added* implies it happened after the sinking of the *Lusitania,* which already generated anti-German "heat."

# Writing the Social Studies Extended Response

The Social Studies Extended Response requires you to relate materials to key issues in American economic, political, and social history. Although you don't need a detailed knowledge of American history, you must have a broad sense of key issues because your answer needs to go beyond just the facts and attitudes presented in the text.

Here's a sample Extended Response prompt, like you may see on the Social Studies test.

**Stimulus:** The following statements were made about slavery sometime before the Civil War. The Jay letter, written almost a hundred years before the Civil War reflects the views of abolitionists, common right up to the Civil War. Hammond's speech reflects the continuing justification of, and for, slavery. In what way is this an enduring issue to this day?

*It is much to be wished that slavery may be abolished. The honour of the States, as well as justice and humanity, in my opinion, loudly call upon them to emancipate these unhappy people. To contend for our own liberty, and to deny that blessing to others, involves an inconsistency not to be excused. (John Jay, letter to R. Lushington, March 15, 1786.)*

*In all social systems there must be a class to do the menial duties, to perform the drudgery of life. That is, a class requiring but a low order of intellect and but little skill. Its requisites are vigor, docility, fidelity. Such a class you must have, or you would not have that other class which leads progress, civilization, and refinement. It constitutes the very mud-sill of society and of political government; and you might as well attempt to build a house in the air, as to build either the one or the other, except on this mud-sill. Fortunately for the South, she found a race adapted to that purpose to her hand. A race inferior to her own, but eminently qualified in temper, in vigor, in docility, in capacity to stand the climate, to answer all her purposes. We use them for our purpose, and call them slaves. We found them slaves by the common "consent of mankind," which, according to Cicero, "lex naturae est." The highest proof of what is Nature's law. (The "Mudsill Theory," James Henry Hammond, speech to the U.S. Senate, March 4, 1858.)*

**Prompt:** Isolate the main issue presented in these two quotes, identify the points of view of the authors, consider how these positions reflect an enduring issue in American history, and use your own knowledge of the issue to show how this continues to be one of the enduring issues.

To start drafting your response, first make a list of key points each author uses to support his position. List them as pro and con, and relate them to the enduring issue you've identified. Now think back to your own general knowledge of the issue, and consider what other information you can bring to the essay to explain how and why this is an enduring issue. For example, you could consider why the Founding Fathers argued non-whites should count as only three-fifths of a person. You could consider that there will always be people at the bottom of the food chain, regardless of race, and there will always have to be people who do the drudge work. Go beyond the idea of racial discrimination and consider the idea of equality of opportunity. Whatever points you choose to use, you need to go beyond the text and build on your own knowledge of American history and issues.

When composing your response, you should select a few key statements. In the Jay letter, the most significant statement is "To contend for our own liberty, and to deny that blessing to others, involves an inconsistency not to be excused." How can society argue that it is acceptable to have some deprived of freedom when regarding freedom essential for itself? The Hammond speech is more practical. In essence, he states that in order for some to be wealthy, others must be poor. Now, you have the enduring issue. You can discuss it in several ways: the dissonance between slavery and freedom, or the necessity of poverty to have wealth. In modern terms, you could argue about "the 99 percent and the 1 percent." That then allows you to develop an argument about the enduring issue. You need to use quotes from these two source documents to show that this is indeed an enduring issue, and add your own information to that to back the argument.

# Managing Your Time for the Social Studies Test

You have a total of 65 minutes to answer about 50 question-and-answer items and then an additional 25 minutes to write an essay on the Social Studies test. The exact number of questions varies from test to test, but the time remains the same. So that means you have less than 90 seconds for each item. Answering those items first that you find easy should allow you to progress faster, leaving you a little more time per item at the end so you can come back to work on the harder ones.

The questions on the Social Studies test are based on both regular textual passages and visual materials, so, when you plan your time for answering the questions, you have to consider the amount of time it takes to read both types of materials. (See the "Questions about visual materials" section for advice on how you can get more comfortable with questions based on graphs, charts, and the like.)

When you come to a prose passage, read the questions first and then skim the passage to find the answers. If this method doesn't work, read the passage carefully, looking for the answers. This way, you take more time only when needed.

Because you have such little time to gather all the information you can from a visual material and answer questions about it, you can't study the map, chart, or cartoon for long. You have to skim it the way you skim a paragraph. Reading the questions that relate to a particular visual first helps you figure out what you need to look for as you skim the material. The practice tests in Chapters 19 and 27 contain examples of questions based on visual materials and so do the sample problems in Chapter 10.

 If you're unsure of how quickly you can answer questions based on visual materials, time yourself on a few and see. If your time comes out to be more than 1.5 minutes, you need more practice.

Realistically, you have about 20 seconds to read the question and the possible answers, 50 seconds to look for the answer, and 10 seconds to select the correct answer. Dividing your time in this way leaves you less than 20 seconds for review or for time at the end of the test to spend on difficult items. To finish the Social Studies test completely, you really have to be organized and watch the clock. Check out Chapter 4 for more general time-management tips.

For time-management tips for the Extended Response, refer to the strategies for the Reasoning through Language Arts Extended Response in Chapter 7.

# Chapter 10

# Getting Some Practice on Social Studies Questions

•••••••••••••••••••••••••••••••••••••••••••••••••••••••

This chapter provides sample Social Studies test questions, including a sample Extended Response item, to help you prepare for taking that section of the GED test.

Record your answers directly in this book or on a separate sheet of paper, if you think you'll want to revisit these practice questions at a later date. Mark only one answer for each item, unless otherwise indicated. And be sure to have a couple extra sheets of paper handy, or use your computer's word processor, to practice preparing and writing an Extended Response.

At the end of this chapter, we provide detailed answer explanations for you to check your answers. Take your time as you move through the explanations. They can help you understand why you missed the answers you did and confirm or clarify the thought process for the answers you got right.

Remember, this is just preliminary practice. We want you to get used to answering different types of Social Studies test questions. Use the complete practice tests in Parts VI and VII to time your work and replicate the real test-taking experience.

## Social Studies Practice Questions

The official Social Studies test consists mainly of multiple-choice items but also has some technologically enhanced items of the type we outline in Chapter 3. They measure general social studies concepts. The items are based on short readings that often include a map, graph, chart, cartoon, or figure. Study the information given and then answer the item(s) following it. Refer to the information as often as necessary in answering. Work carefully, but don't spend too much time on any one question. Be sure you answer every question.

*Questions 1–2 refer to the following excerpt from the U.S. Embassy's IIP Digital website (iipdigital.usembassy.gov).*

Democracies fall into two basic categories, direct and representative. In a direct democracy, citizens, without the intermediary of elected or appointed officials, can participate in making public decisions. Such a system is clearly most practical with relatively small numbers of people — in a community organization, tribal council, or the local unit of a labor union, for example — where members can meet in a single room to discuss issues and arrive at decisions by consensus or majority vote.

Some U.S. states, in addition, place "propositions" and "referenda" — mandated changes of law — or possible recall of elected officials on ballots during state elections. These practices are forms of direct democracy, expressing the will of a large population. Many practices may have elements of direct democracy. In Switzerland, many important political decisions on issues, including public health, energy, and employment, are subject to a vote by the country's citizens. And some might argue that the Internet is creating new forms of direct democracy, as it empowers political groups to raise money for their causes by appealing directly to like-minded citizens.

However, today, as in the past, the most common form of democracy, whether for a town of 50,000 or a nation of 50 million, is representative democracy, in which citizens elect officials to make political decisions, formulate laws, and administer programs for the public good.

1. The federal government of the United States is an example of [              ] democracy (direct democracy or representative democracy).

2. One example of allowing the population as a whole to vote on an issue in America would be

   (A) a recall election

   (B) election of a local mayor

   (C) the election of the president

   (D) a school board election

*Questions 3–4 refer to the following excerpt from the U.S. Embassy's IIP Digital website* (`iipdigital.usembassy.gov`).

In a democracy, government is only one thread in the social fabric of many and varied public and private institutions, legal forums, political parties, organizations, and associations. This diversity is called pluralism, and it assumes that the many organized groups and institutions in a democratic society do not depend upon government for their existence, legitimacy, or authority. Most democratic societies have thousands of private organizations, some local, some national. Many of them serve a mediating role between individuals and society's complex social and governmental institutions, filling roles not given to the government and offering individuals opportunities to become part of their society without being in government.

In an authoritarian society, virtually all such organizations would be controlled, licensed, watched, or otherwise accountable to the government. In a democracy, the powers of the government are, by law, clearly defined and sharply limited. As a result, private organizations are largely free of government control. In this busy private realm of democratic society, citizens can explore the possibilities of peaceful self-fulfillment and the responsibilities of belonging to a community — free of the potentially heavy hand of the state or the demand that they adhere to views held by those with influence or power, or by the majority.

3. One example of an authoritarian society would be

   (A) Canada

   (B) Kingdom of Sweden

   (C) the former Union of Soviet Socialist Republics

   (D) the Republic of Korea (South Korea)

4. America is a democratic country. All citizens have the right to do all of the following except

   (A) elect their senator

   (B) elect local magistrates and sheriffs

   (C) elect their state governors

   (D) elect the president

*Questions 5–9 refer to the following excerpt from* U.S. History For Dummies, *by Steve Wiegand (Wiley).*

Partly because of error and partly because of wishful thinking, Columbus estimated the distance to the Indies at approximately 2,500 miles, which was about 7,500 miles short. But after a voyage of about five weeks, he and his crew, totaling 90 men, did find land at around 2:00 a.m. on October 12, 1492. It was an island in the Bahamas, which he called San Salvador. The timing of the discovery was good; it came even as the crews of the *Nina, Pinta,* and *Santa Maria* were muttering about a mutiny.

Columbus next sailed to Cuba, where he found a few spices and little gold. Sailing on to an island he called Hispaniola (today's Dominican Republic and Haiti), the *Santa Maria* hit a reef on Christmas Eve, 1492. Columbus abandoned the ship, set up a trading outpost he called Navidad, left some men to operate it, and sailed back to Spain in his other two ships.

So enthusiastically did people greet the news of his return that on his second voyage to Hispaniola, Columbus had 17 ships and more than 1,200 men. But this time he ran into more than a little disappointment. Natives had wiped out his trading post after his men became too grabby with the local gold and the local women. Worse, most of the men he brought with him had come only for gold and other riches, and they didn't care about setting up a permanent colony. Because of the lack of treasures, they soon wanted to go home. And the natives lost interest in the newcomers after the novelty of the Spanish trinkets wore off.

5. By how much was Columbus in error in guessing the distance to the Indies? Write the answer in the box.

   (A) 7,500 miles

   (B) 5,000 miles

   (C) 2,500 miles

   (D) 0 miles

6. On what date did Columbus arrive in the Bahamas?

   (A) Christmas Eve, 1492

   (B) October 2, 1492

   (C) October 12, 1492

   (D) December 12, 1493

7. Why did so many people want to sail with Columbus on his second trip?

   (A) They were eager to settle new lands.

   (B) They wanted adventure.

   (C) They had heard stories of beautiful native women.

   (D) They had heard stories of the gold Columbus had found.

8. Why did Columbus cut his first voyage short?

   (A) The *Santa Maria* had hit a reef and sank.

   (B) His men were ready to mutiny.

   (C) He had completed his task by setting up a small colony.

   (D) He had not found the riches he had hoped for.

9. Why might the people on the second voyage have disappointed Columbus?

   (A) They were interested only in finding gold.

   (B) They did not want to create a colony.

   (C) Choices (A) and (B).

   (D) None of the above.

*Questions 10–11 refer to the following excerpt from* U.S. History For Dummies, *by Steve Wiegand (Wiley).*

On his second trip to the Americas in 1493, Columbus stopped by the Canary Islands and picked up some sugar cane cuttings. He planted them on Hispaniola, and they thrived. In 1516, the first sugar grown in the New World was presented to King Carlos I of Spain. By 1531, it was as commercially important to the Spanish colonial economy as gold.

Planters soon discovered a by-product as well. The juice left over after the sugar was pressed out of the cane and crystallized was called *melasas* by the Spanish (and *molasses* by the English). Mixing this juice with water and leaving it out in the sun created a potent and tasty fermented drink. They called it *rum* — perhaps after the word for sugar cane, *saccharum officinarum*. The stuff was great for long sea voyages because it didn't go bad.

Sugar and rum became so popular that sugar plantations mushroomed all over the Caribbean.

10. What is molasses?

   (A) juice pressed out of sugar cane

   (B) leftover juice after sugar was pressed out of the cane

   (C) sugar cane mixed with water

   (D) *saccharum officinarum*

11. How many years did it take before the first sugar cane grown in the New World was presented to King Carlos of Spain?

   (A) 33 years

   (B) 23 years

   (C) 13 years

   (D) 1 year

*Questions 12–13 refer to the following chart.*

### Educational Attainment by Sex for the Population of Tennessee 25 Years and Over

| | Total:* | One Race | | | | | |
| --- | --- | --- | --- | --- | --- | --- | --- |
| | | White | Black or African American | American Indian and Alaska Native | Asian | Native Hawaiian and Other Pacific Islander | Some Other Race |
| **Total:** | 4,250,890 | 3,457,513 | 631,508 | 10,736 | 61,011 | 1,397 | 45,004 |
| Male: | 2,027,848 | 1,661,912 | 284,869 | 5,599 | 27,597 | 646 | 25,953 |
| Less than high school diploma | 347,716 | 267,868 | 57,602 | 1,356 | 3,458 | 83 | 12,982 |
| High school graduate, GED, or alternative | 678,789 | 551,185 | 106,812 | 1,820 | 4,709 | 225 | 7,848 |
| Some college or associate's degree | 520,050 | 424,918 | 79,805 | 1,471 | 4,192 | 234 | 3,188 |
| Bachelor's degree or higher | 481,293 | 417,941 | 40,650 | 952 | 15,238 | 104 | 1,935 |
| Female: | 2,223,042 | 1,795,601 | 346,639 | 5,137 | 33,414 | 751 | 19,051 |
| Less than high school diploma | 337,674 | 258,351 | 60,623 | 1,099 | 5,469 | 29 | 8,349 |
| High school graduate, GED, or alternative | 722,442 | 597,860 | 105,275 | 1,163 | 6,482 | 224 | 5,439 |
| Some college or associate's degree | 645,545 | 510,006 | 115,366 | 2,056 | 6,353 | 381 | 3,230 |
| Bachelor's degree or higher | 517,381 | 429,384 | 65,375 | 819 | 15,110 | 117 | 2,033 |

*Illustration courtesy of U.S. Census Bureau*

12. What percentage of black or African American females were high-school graduates, GED, or alternative? [          ] %

13. Comparing white and Asian males and females, which group had attained the higher percentage of bachelor's degrees or higher? Write the appropriate answer in the box.

    (A) white males

    (B) Asian males

    (C) white females

    (D) Asian females

*Question 14 refers to the following chart.*

**Births Steady Despite Falling Fertility**

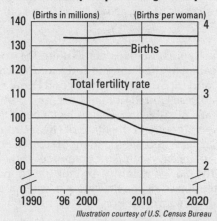

Illustration courtesy of U.S. Census Bureau

14. The chart shows the total number of births over the entire world in one year as compared to the total fertility rate (TFR). The graph shows a steady decline in the TFR — that is, the number of children born to the average woman — yet the total number of births in the world remain the same. Why is that?

    (A) There is an error in the data collection.

    (B) The TFR counts only live births.

    (C) The growing world population means that each woman having fewer children is offset by the fact that there are more women to have children.

    (D) None of the above.

*Questions 15–20 refer to the following excerpt from The Declaration of Independence, 1776.*

*After a long list of grievances, the Declaration of Independence concludes with these words.*

In every stage of these Oppressions We have Petitioned for Redress in the most humble terms: Our repeated Petitions have been answered only by repeated injury. A Prince whose character is thus marked by every act which may define a Tyrant, is unfit to be the ruler of a free people.

Nor have We been wanting in attentions to our Brittish brethren. We have warned them from time to time of attempts by their legislature to extend an unwarrantable jurisdiction over us. We have reminded them of the circumstances of our emigration and settlement here. We have appealed to their native justice and magnanimity, and we have conjured them by the ties of our common kindred to disavow these usurpations, which, would inevitably interrupt our connections and correspondence. They too have been deaf to the voice of justice and of consanguinity. We must, therefore, acquiesce in the necessity, which denounces our Separation, and hold them, as we hold the rest of mankind, Enemies in War, in Peace Friends.

We, therefore, the Representatives of the united States of America, in General Congress, Assembled, appealing to the Supreme Judge of the world for the rectitude of our intentions, do, in the Name, and by Authority of the good People of these Colonies, solemnly publish and declare, That these United Colonies are, and of Right ought to be Free and Independent States; that they are Absolved from all Allegiance to the British Crown, and that all political connection between them and the State of Great Britain, is and ought to be totally dissolved; and that as Free and Independent States, they have full Power to levy War, conclude Peace, contract Alliances, establish Commerce, and to do all other Acts and Things which Independent States may of right do. And for the support of this Declaration, with a firm reliance on the protection of divine Providence, we mutually pledge to each other our Lives, our Fortunes and our sacred Honor.

15. Why did the authors of the Declaration of Independence believe the king was a tyrant?

    (A) The king's only answer was repeated injury.

    (B) Appeals to British parliament failed.

    (C) They had declared that in general Congress.

    (D) None of the above.

16. How did the authors feel about British parliament making laws for the Colonies?

    (A) They were usurpations.

    (B) They were magnanimous.

    (C) They are examples of justice and consanguinity.

    (D) None of the above.

17. Why is the word *united* in "united States of America" not also capitalized?

    (A) The word *united* is used as an adjective, not part of a title.

    (B) The representatives did not see themselves as one country yet.

    (C) This Congress was a meeting of independent states united for action.

    (D) All of the above.

*Questions 18–19 refer to the following passage from* U.S. History For Dummies, *by Steve Wiegand (Wiley).*

By 1787, it was apparent to many leaders that the Articles of Confederation needed an overhaul, or the union of states would eventually fall apart. So Congress agreed to call a convention of delegates from each state to try to fix things. The first of the delegates' (selected by state legislatures) to arrive in Philadelphia in May 1787 was James Madison, a 36-year-old scholar and politician from Virginia who was so frail he couldn't serve in the army during the Revolution. Madison had so many ideas on how to fix things he couldn't wait to get started.

Not everyone else was in such a hurry. Although the convention was supposed to begin May 15, it wasn't until May 25 that enough of the delegates chosen by the state legislatures showed up to have a quorum. Rhode Island never did send anyone.

Eventually, 55 delegates took part. Notable by their absence were some of the leading figures of the recent rebellion against England: Thomas Jefferson was in France, Thomas Paine was in England, Sam Adams and John Hancock weren't selected to go, and Patrick Henry refused.

18. What was the name of the original constitution of the United States?

    (A) Articles of Confederation

    (B) the Constitution of the Confederation

    (C) the Declaration of Independence

    (D) None of the above.

19. Why was James Madison especially important to this convention?

    (A) He was eager to get started.

    (B) He represented one of the southern states, which made him very important.

    (C) He had never served in the military.

    (D) He had many ideas on how to fix things.

*Questions 20–22 are based on this excerpt from a speech by James Madison on the ratification of the new Constitution of the United States.*

What has brought on other nations those immense debts, under the pressure of which many of them labor? Not the expenses of their governments, but war. . . . How is it possible a war could be supported without money or credit? And would it be possible for government to have credit, without having the power of raising money? No, it would be impossible for any government, in such a case, to defend itself. Then, I say, sir, that it is necessary to establish funds for extraordinary exigencies, and give this power to the general government; for the utter inutility of previous requisitions on the States is too well known. Would it be possible for those countries, whose finances and revenues are carried to the highest perfection, to carry on the operations of government on great emergencies, such as the maintenance of a war, without an uncontrolled power of raising money? Has it not been necessary for Great Britain, notwithstanding the facility of the collection of her taxes, to have recourse very often to this and other extraordinary methods of procuring money? Would not her public credit have been ruined, if it was known that her power to raise money was limited? . . . [N]o government can exist unless its powers extend to make provisions for every contingency.

If we were actually attacked by a powerful nation, and our general government had not the power of raising money, but depended solely on requisitions, our condition would be truly deplorable: if the revenues of this commonwealth were to depend on twenty distinct authorities, it would be impossible for it to carry on its operations.

20. According to Madison, what was the major reason for uniting the states under a new constitution?

    (A) to provide a single economic market

    (B) to have the ability to raise money to fund extraordinary exigencies

    (C) to create a stronger state military

    (D) all of the above

21. What was Madison referring to by "the uttered inutility of previous requisitions on the States this too well known"?

    (A) It was difficult to convince all the States to contribute money in emergencies.

    (B) The Federal government had only very limited powers to tax.

    (C) The States control over the Federal government's ability to raise money.

    (D) All of the above.

22. How many states were part of the original Confederation?

    (A) 13

    (B) 17

    (C) 20

    (D) 23

*Questions 23–25 refer to the following passage, excerpted from "A Look Back . . . The Black Dispatches: Intelligence During the Civil War," a CIA Feature Story (www.cia.gov).*

### William A. Jackson

Africans-Americans who could serve as agents-in-place were a great asset to the Union. They could provide information about the enemy's plans instead of reporting how the plans were carried out. William A. Jackson was one such agent-in-place who provided valuable intelligence straight from Confederate President Jefferson Davis.

Jackson served as a coachman to Davis. As a servant in Davis' home, Jackson overheard discussions the president had with his military leadership. His first report of Confederate plans and intentions was in May 1862 when he crossed into Union lines. While there are no records of the specific intelligence Jackson reported, it is known that it was important enough to be sent straight to the War Department in Washington.

### Harriet Tubman

When it comes to the Civil War and the fight to end slavery, Harriet Tubman is an icon. She was not only a conductor of the Underground Railroad, but also a spy for the Union.

In 1860, she took her last trip on the Underground Railroad, bringing friends and family to freedom safely. After the trip, Tubman decided to contribute to the war effort by caring for and feeding the many slaves who had fled the Union-controlled areas.

A year later, the Union Army asked Tubman to gather a network of spies among the black men in the area. Tubman also was tasked with leading expeditions to gather intelligence. She reported her information to a Union officer commanding the Second South Carolina Volunteers, a black unit involved in guerrilla warfare activities.

After learning of Tubman's capability as a spy, Gen. David Hunter, commander of all Union forces in the area, requested that Tubman personally guide a raiding party up the Combahee River in South Carolina. Tubman was well prepared for the raid because she had key information about Confederate positions along the shore and had discovered where they placed torpedoes (barrels filled with gunpowder) in the water. On the morning of June 1, 1863, Tubman led Col. James Montgomery and his men in the attack. The expedition hit hard. They set fires and destroyed buildings so they couldn't be used by the Confederate forces. The raiders freed 750 slaves.

The raid along the Combahee River, in addition to her activities with the Underground Railroad, made a significant contribution to the Union cause. When Tubman died in 1913, she was honored with a full military funeral in recognition for work during the war.

23. What made William Jackson an excellent intelligence source?

    (A) He was an African American.

    (B) He had military experience.

    (C) He worked in the home of Jefferson Davis.

    (D) He was in direct contact with Washington.

24. What is Harriet Tubman best known for?

    (A) the Underground Railroad

    (B) the drinking gourd song

    (C) being a guerilla leader

    (D) none of the above

25. Tubman led a raid on ⬚ in South Carolina.

    (A) the Combahee River

    (B) Montgomery

    (C) Union-controlled areas

    (D) Atlanta

*Questions 26–27 refer to the following excerpt from* U.S. History For Dummies, *by Steve Wiegand (Wiley).*

Despite conflict in war, civilians and soldiers around the world had at least one thing in common in 1918 — a killer flu. Erroneously dubbed "Spanish Influenza" because it was believed to have started in Spain, it more likely started at U.S. Army camps in Kansas and may not have been a flu virus at all. A 2008 study by the National Institute of Allergy and Infectious Diseases suggested bacteria might have caused the pandemic.

Whatever caused it, it was devastating. Unlike normal influenza outbreaks, whose victims are generally the elderly and the young, the Spanish flu often targeted healthy young adults. By early summer, the disease had spread around the world. In New York City alone, 20,000 people died. Western Samoa lost 20 percent of its population, and entire Inuit villages in Alaska were wiped out. By the time it had run its course in 1921, the flu had killed from 25 million to 50 million people around the world. More than 500,000 Americans died, which was a greater total than all the Americans killed in all the wars of the 20th century.

26. Why were various American government agencies unable to do much about this killer flu?

    (A) There was no known cure.

    (B) The Centre for Disease Control did not yet exist.

    (C) The outbreak spread too rapidly to contain.

    (D) All of the above.

27. Why was this flu called the Spanish flu?

    (A) It started in Spanish Harlem.

    (B) It was first seen in Spain at the end of World War I.

    (C) It was called the Spanish flu in error.

    (D) None of the above.

*Questions 28–30 are based on the following graphs.*

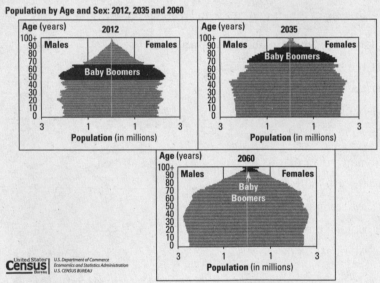

*Illustrations courtesy of U.S. Census Bureau*

28. Look at the population pyramid for the year 2012. Notice that the edges appear ragged. Shorter lines mean fewer people in that age group. There are noticeably fewer people in the 30 to 40 age group. In approximately what time period would these people have been born?

    (A) 1960 to 1970

    (B) 1970 to 1980

    (C) 1980 to 1990

    (D) 1990 to 2000

29. What could have been going on at that time to cause people to have fewer children?

    (A) a major recession and the Vietnam War

    (B) the Korean War

    (C) the first Gulf War

    (D) none of the above

30. Look at the top of the three pyramids. Are there more men or women in the age group of 80+? ☐

*Questions 31–33 refer to the following passage about the 1920s, excerpted from* U.S. History For Dummies, *by Steve Wiegand (Wiley).*

Below the veneer of prosperity, there were indications of trouble. More and more wealth was being concentrated in fewer and fewer hands, and government did far more for the rich than the poor. It was estimated, for example, that federal tax cuts saved the hugely wealthy financier Andrew Mellon (who also happened to be Hoover's treasury secretary) almost as much money as was saved by all the taxpayers in the entire state of Nebraska.

Supreme Court decisions struck down minimum wage laws for women and children and made it easier for big business to swallow up smaller ones and become de facto monopolies. And union membership declined as organized labor was unable to compete with the aura of good times.

Probably worst off were American farmers. They had expanded production during World War 1 to feed the troops, and when demand and prices faded after the war, they were hit hard. Farm income dropped by 50 percent during the 1920s, and more than 3 million farmers left their farms for towns and cities.

31. What events described here for the 1920s are similar to current events?

    (A) tax cuts benefiting the wealthy more than the poor

    (B) declining union memberships

    (C) increasing concentration of wealth in fewer hands

    (D) all of the above

32. Why did union membership decline in the 1920s?

    (A) Unions were illegal.

    (B) Times seemed good so there was no need for union organization.

    (C) Growing corporations made union organization difficult.

    (D) All of the above.

*Questions 33–34 are based on the following excerpt from* The Wealth of Nations, *by Adam Smith (Thrifty Books).*

The increase of revenue and stock is the increase of national wealth. . . . Is this improvement in the circumstances of the lower ranks of the people to be regarded as an advantage or as an inconvenience to the society? The answer seems at first sight abundantly plain. Servants, laborers, and workmen of different kinds, make up the far greater part of every great political society. But what improves the circumstances of the greater part can never be regarded as an inconvenience to the whole. No society can surely be flourishing and happy, of which the far greater part of the members are poor and miserable. It is but equity, besides, that they who feed, clothe, and lodge the whole body of the people, should have such a share of the produce of their own labor as to be themselves tolerably well fed, clothed, and lodged. The liberal reward of labor, as it encourages the propagation, so it increases the industry of the common people. The wages of labor are the encouragement of industry, which, like every other human quality, improves in proportion to the encouragement it receives. A plentiful subsistence increases the bodily strength of the laborer, and the comfortable hope of bettering his condition, and of ending his days perhaps in ease and plenty, animates him to exert that strength to the utmost. Where wages are high, accordingly, we shall always find the workmen more active, diligent, and expeditious than where they are low.

33. What does Smith mean by "what improves the circumstances of the greater part can never be regarded as an inconvenience to the whole"?

    (A) Paying the working class more is an inconvenience to everyone.

    (B) Whatever improves conditions for most people cannot be regarded as bad for society as a whole.

    (C) Only circumstance that helps some improves life for all.

    (D) None of the above.

34. According to Adam Smith, how should employers treat the financial well-being of their employees?

    (A) Keep wages as low as possible.

    (B) Reward a laborer liberally.

    (C) Under no circumstances consider changes.

    (D) Avoid the issue.

35. When Henry Ford's Model T car proved to be a success, he doubled his workers' wages, even when all other car manufacturers at the time would not raise wages. Would he and Adam Smith have agreed on this issue?

    (A) Yes. Well-paid workers are more active and diligent.

    (B) No. Paying workers more only encourages sloth.

    (C) Yes. It is only fair.

    (D) No. A business must remain competitive.

*Questions 35–36 refer to the following passage about the Cuban Missile Crisis, excerpted from* U.S. History For Dummies, *by Steve Wiegand (Wiley).*

During the summer of 1962, the Soviets began developing nuclear missile sites in Cuba. That meant they could easily strike targets over much of North and South America. When air reconnaissance photos confirmed the sites' presence on October 14, JFK had to make a tough choice: Destroy the sites and quite possibly trigger World War III, or do nothing, and not only expose the country to nuclear destruction but, in effect, concede first place in the world domination race to the USSR.

Kennedy decided to get tough. On October 22, 1963, he went on national television and announced the U.S. Navy would throw a blockade around Cuba and turn away any ships carrying materials that could be used at the missile sites. He also demanded the sites be dismantled. Then the world waited for the Russian reaction.

On October 26, Soviet leader Nikita Khrushchev send a message suggesting the missiles would be removed if the United States promised not to invade Cuba and eventually removed some U.S. missiles from Turkey. The crisis — perhaps the closest the world came to nuclear conflict during the Cold War — was over, and the payoffs were ample.

36. Why was the placement of Soviet missiles in Cuba so important to both the Soviet Union and the United States?

    (A) This was the only way missiles of that time could reach into North and South America.

    (B) The Soviets wanted to show their support for Fidel Castro.

    (C) It provided an important trade opportunity.

    (D) None of the above.

37. What triggered the Soviet move to put missiles capable of attacking the United States into bases in Cuba?

    (A) The Soviet Union was preparing to attack the United States.

    (B) Fidel Castro demanded them as protection against an American invasion of Cuba.

    (C) The United States had placed its own missiles in Turkey on the border of the Soviet Union.

    (D) The Soviets wanted to divert attention from the Vietnam War.

*Questions 38–39 are based on the following chart.*

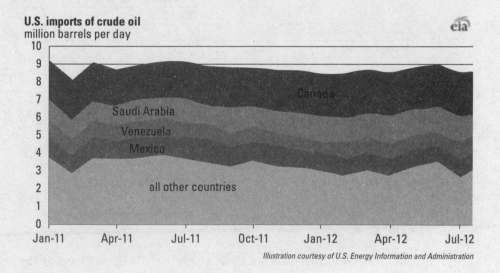

Illustration courtesy of U.S. Energy Information and Administration

38. Which country is the largest single provider of crude oil to the United States? [          ]

39. Why does this graph explain the importance of the oil pipelines between Canada and the southern United States?

    (A) The United States needs to be able to ship oil north.

    (B) The United States cannot ship enough oil using tankers, trucks, or rail.

    (C) Canada is a safe source of crude oil for the United States.

    (D) All of the above.

*Questions 40–41 are based on the following chart.*

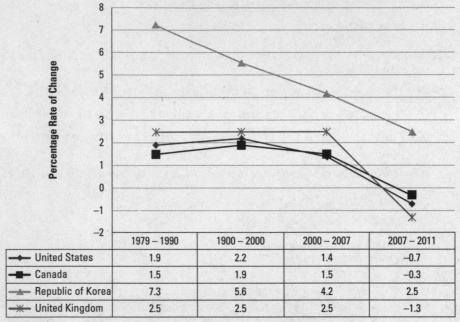

### Rate of Change GDP
### Selected Countries 1979 – 2011

| | 1979 – 1990 | 1900 – 2000 | 2000 – 2007 | 2007 – 2011 |
|---|---|---|---|---|
| United States | 1.9 | 2.2 | 1.4 | −0.7 |
| Canada | 1.5 | 1.9 | 1.5 | −0.3 |
| Republic of Korea | 7.3 | 5.6 | 4.2 | 2.5 |
| United Kingdom | 2.5 | 2.5 | 2.5 | −1.3 |

*Illustration courtesy of U.S. Bureau of Labor Statistics*

40. Which country shows the greatest decline in the rate of GDP growth?

   (A) the United States

   (B) Canada

   (C) Republic of Korea

   (D) United Kingdom

41. Which of these countries does not show a negative GDP growth during the charted period?

   (A) United States

   (B) Canada

   (C) Republic of Korea

   (D) United Kingdom

*Questions 42–45 are based on the following tables.*

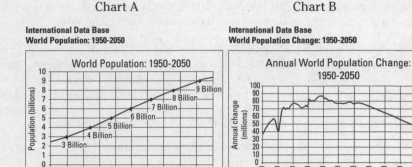

Chart A            Chart B

*Illustrations courtesy of U.S. Census Bureau*

42. The total population of the world continues to [＿＿＿＿].

43. The number of children born each year has [＿＿＿＿] since 1990.

44. What does the graph entitled "Annual World Population Change" actually show?

    (A) the change in the world total population over time

    (B) the actual net change in world population by year

    (C) the actual number of children born each year

    (D) the rate of change in births each year

45. Considering the chart shows that the annual world population change is declining, why is the world population continuing to climb?

    (A) Chart B ignores children who die in the first year of life.

    (B) More people means more children, even if individual women have fewer children. That still adds up to an increasing population.

    (C) The rate of growth is still climbing.

    (D) None of the above.

*Questions 46–48 are based on the following excerpt from* U.S. History For Dummies, *by Steve Wiegand (Wiley).*

While the war on terrorism dominated Bush's presidency, he did attempt to make changes on domestic issues as well. Within a few days of taking office, Bush proposed an ambitious education reform program, called the No Child Left Behind Act. Approved by Congress, the plan posted federal education funding; increased standards expected of schools, including annual reading and math skills testing; and gave parents more flexibility in choosing schools. The program was variously praised for making schools more accountable and criticized for forcing educators to take cookie-cutter approaches to teaching.

In late 2003, Bush pushed a plan through Congress to reform Medicare, the federal health insurance program for the elderly. The plan gave senior citizens more choice when picking a private insurance plan through which they received medical services, as well as in obtaining prescription drugs.

Bush had far less success in trying to reform Social Security and the U.S. immigration policies. Bush proposed to replace the government-run pension program with a system of private savings accounts. But the plan died in the face of criticism that it would put too much of a burden on individuals and be too expensive in the transition.

Bush also supported a bipartisan plan that would allow an estimated 12 million illegal immigrants to remain in the country on a temporary basis and to apply for citizenship after returning to their own countries and paying a fine. The plan was crushed by the weight of opposition from those who thought it was too draconian and those who thought it was too soft.

46. Why were some people opposed to the No Child Left Behind Act?

(A) Some objected to standardized reading and math tests.

(B) Some felt it would reduce education choices.

(C) It was considered too expensive by some in Congress.

(D) Congress would not approve the plan.

*Question 47–48 refer to the following excerpt, taken from the CIA World Factbook (`www.cia.gov`).*

As a high-tech industrial society in the trillion-dollar class, Canada resembles the U.S. in its market-oriented economic system, pattern of production, and high living standards. Since World War II, the impressive growth of the manufacturing, mining, and service sectors has transformed the nation from a largely rural economy into one primarily industrial and urban. The 1989 U.S.-Canada Free Trade Agreement (FTA) and the 1994 North American Free Trade Agreement (NAFTA) (which includes Mexico) touched off a dramatic increase in trade and economic integration with the U.S., its principal trading partner. Canada enjoys a substantial trade surplus with the U.S., which absorbs about three-fourths of Canadian merchandise exports each year. Canada is the U.S.'s largest foreign supplier of energy, including oil, gas, uranium, and electric power. Given its abundant natural resources, highly skilled labor force, and modern capital plant, Canada enjoyed solid economic growth from 1993 through 2007. Buffeted by the global economic crisis, the economy dropped into a sharp recession in the final months of 2008, and Ottawa posted its first fiscal deficit in 2009 after 12 years of surplus. Canada's major banks, however, emerged from the financial crisis of 2008–09 among the strongest in the world, owing to the financial sector's tradition of conservative lending practices and strong capitalization. Canada achieved marginal growth in 2010–13 and plans to balance the budget by 2015. In addition, the country's petroleum sector is rapidly expanding, because Alberta's oil sands significantly boosted Canada's proven oil reserves. Canada now ranks third in the world in proved oil reserves behind Saudi Arabia and Venezuela.

47. How does the CIA World Factbook describe Canada's economy before World War II?

(A) primarily industrial and urban

(B) a modern capitalist society

(C) largely rural

(D) a major petroleum power

48. How is Canada's economy linked with that of America?

(A) Both are members of the North American Free Trade Agreement (NAFTA).

(B) Canada is the largest supplier of oil and uranium to America.

(C) Three-quarters of Canada's exports go to the United States.

(D) All of the above.

*Questions 49–50 refer to the following excerpt from the Australian War Memorial website on the topic of the Australian contribution to the Vietnam War, 1962–1975 (www.awm.gov.au).*

[A]lmost 60,000 Australians, including ground troops and air force and navy personnel, served in Vietnam; 521 died as a result of the war and over 3,000 were wounded. . . .

Australian support for South Vietnam in the early 1960s was in keeping with the policies of other nations, particularly the United States, to stem the spread of communism in Europe and Asia. . . .

By early 1965, . . . the U.S. commenced a major escalation of the war. By the end of the year, it had committed 200,000 troops to the conflict. As part of the build-up, the U.S. government requested further support from friendly countries in the region, including Australia. The Australian government dispatched the 1st Battalion, Royal Australian Regiment (1RAR), in June 1965 to serve alongside the U.S. 173d Airborne Brigade in Bien Hoa province. . . .

By 1969, anti-war protests were gathering momentum in Australia. Opposition to conscription mounted, as more people came to believe the war could not be won. . . . The U.S. government began to implement a policy of "Vietnamisation," the term coined for a gradual withdrawal of U.S. forces that would leave the war in the hands of the South Vietnamese. With the start of the phased withdrawals, the emphasis of the activities of the Australians in Phuoc Tuy province shifted to the provision of training to the South Vietnamese Regional and Popular Forces.

In early 1975, the communists launched a major offensive in the north of South Vietnam, resulting in the fall of Saigon on 30 April. During April a RAAF detachment of 7–8 Hercules transports flew humanitarian missions to aid civilian refugees displaced by the fighting and carried out the evacuation of Vietnamese orphans (Operation Babylift), before finally taking out embassy staff on 25 April.

49. In what way was Australian experience in their participation in the Vietnam War similar to that of America?

(A) They were reluctant to become involved.

(B) They contributed only humanitarian aid.

(C) There was strong popular opposition on the home front to participation in this war.

(D) All of the above.

50. How did the Australian military react to the American policy of "Vietnamization"?

(A) They slowly withdrew their forces.

(B) They stopped active combat.

(C) They concentrated on training South Vietnamese forces.

(D) All of the above.

### Social Studies Extended Response practice

The Extended Response requires you to write an essay examining an issue raised in the stimulus text. Your job is to explain how that issue is an enduring issue in American history. You may recognize the issue from the headlines of newspapers, the in-depth analysis stories in television news, from your history books, or something that continues to arise in history, that never seems to be solved completely, that reappears in a somewhat different form generation after generation, reflecting how attitudes change over time. The stimulus text presents the issue and perhaps an opposing view(s) on the issue. As you write your response, use the content of the stimulus text and your own knowledge to show how and why this issue is and continues to be an enduring issue.

**Stimulus**

**Amendment XIV.** *Passed by Congress June 13, 1866. Ratified July 9, 1868.*

*Note:* Article I, section 2, of the Constitution was modified by section 2 of the 14th amendment.

**Section 2.**

Representatives shall be apportioned among the several States according to their respective numbers, counting the whole number of persons in each State, excluding Indians not taxed. But when the right to vote at any election for the choice of electors for President and Vice-President of the United States, Representatives in Congress, the Executive and Judicial officers of a State, or the members of the Legislature thereof, is denied to any of the male inhabitants of such State, being twenty-one years of age, and citizens of the United States, or in any way abridged, except for participation in rebellion, or other crime, the basis of representation therein shall be reduced in the proportion which the number of such male citizens shall bear to the whole number of male citizens twenty-one years of age in such State.

**Amendment XV.** *Passed by Congress February 26, 1869. Ratified February 3, 1870.*

**Section 1.**

The right of citizens of the United States to vote shall not be denied or abridged by the United States or by any State on account of race, color, or previous condition of servitude.

**Section 2.**

The Congress shall have the power to enforce this article by appropriate legislation.

**ACLU Statement on Voter Suppression Campaigns.** *(Excerpted from the American Civil Liberties Union website:* www.aclu.org*)*

Voting rights are under attack in this country as state legislatures nationwide pass voter suppression laws under the pretext of preventing voter fraud and safeguarding election integrity. These voter suppression laws take many forms, and collectively lead to significant burdens for eligible voters trying to exercise their most fundamental constitutional right.

During the 2011 legislative sessions, states across the country passed measures to make it harder for Americans — particularly African-Americans, the elderly, students and people with disabilities — to exercise their fundamental right to cast a ballot. Over thirty states considered laws that would require voters to present government-issued photo ID in order to vote. Studies suggest that up to 11 percent of American citizens lack such ID, and would be required to navigate the administrative burdens to obtain it or forego the right to vote entirely.

Three additional states passed laws to require documentary proof of citizenship in order to register to vote, though as many as 7 percent of American citizens do not have such proof. Seven states shortened early voting time frames, even though over 30 percent of all votes cast in the 2008 general election were cast before Election Day. Two state legislatures voted to repeal Election Day registration laws, though Election Day registration increases voter turnout by 10–12 percent. Finally, two states passed legislation making it much more difficult for third-party organizations to register voters — so difficult, in fact, that some voter registration organizations are leaving the states altogether.

Despite this frenzy of state legislation . . . proponents of such voter suppression legislation have failed to show that voter fraud is a problem anywhere in the country. Aside from the occasional unproven anecdote or baseless allegation, supporters of these laws simply cannot show that there is any need for them.

**Prompt:** Using the quotations from the Bill of Rights and the statement from the ACLU, explain how campaigns of voter suppression represent an enduring issue in American politics. Incorporate specific evidence from the excerpts, the ACLU statement, and your own knowledge of the enduring issue and circumstances surrounding voting rights to support your analysis.

# Answers and Explanations

1. **representative democracy.** In America, citizens elect officials, from state representative to federal senators, who represent the interests of individual citizens in the administration of the country.

2. **A. a recall election.** Choices (B), (C), and (D) are all examples of indirect or representative democracy, where someone is elected to *represent* the voter. For example, mayors, who citizens elect directly, are in office to represent them. The voters don't make political decisions; the mayor in council does. Only in recall elections is the voters' voice directly applied to a decision.

3. **C. former Union of Soviet Socialist Republics.** The former USSR, also known as the Soviet Union, was a government that allowed elections but allowed only one political party. The party, not the people, decided who would run for office. Although the form resembled democracy, it didn't allow for pluralism or political choice. The other countries are all pluralist. Canada is a parliamentary democracy that has four major federal political parties and numerous minor ones based on popular will. Sweden is also a parliamentary democracy, and like Canada, has a Monarch as head of state. It, too, has several political parties contending for office in free elections. South Korea is a republic, run by a legislative assembly and a president elected by popular vote.

4. **D. elect the president.** The first three choices are all true, but the last choice isn't. American voters don't elect the president, at least not directly. They vote for a group of people who form an electoral college. The members of that electoral college actually elect the president. For a detailed explanation, look up the history of the electoral college.

5. **A. 7,500 miles.** Columbus miscalculated by 7,500 miles. He thought the world was considerably smaller than it actually is.

6. **C. October 12, 1492.** The Christmas Eve date refers to his subsequent arrival at the island he called Hispaniola. The other two dates are simply wrong.

7. **D. They had heard stories of the gold Columbus had found.** According to the text, they were all focused on gold. Choice (B) may be partially correct, that they were looking for adventure, but Choices (A) and (C) are simply wrong.

8. **A. The *Santa Maria* had hit a reef and sank.** Choice (B) is incorrect at this stage of his trip, and although Choices (C) and (D) may be partially correct, they're not the best answers.

9. **C. Choices (A) and (B) (They were interested only in finding gold; they did not want to create a colony).** Both of the first two choices are correct.

10. **B. leftover juice after sugar was pressed out of the cane.** The text states that molasses is "the juice left over after the sugar was pressed out of the cane and crystalized." The juice pressed out of the cane still contains sugar to be extracted. The cane isn't mixed with water, but rather the extracted juices are. And the name *saccharum officinarum* is simply the Latin name for the sugar cane plant.

11. **B. 23 years.** This problem requires some simple arithmetic. The first crop, assuming Columbus' workers planted the cane as soon as they landed, was planted in 1493. The first sugar cane was presented to the King in 1516. Subtract 1493 from 1516, and you get 23. The correct answer is 23 years.

12. **30.4.** To find the percentage, you divide the number of people in question by the total number in the group and multiply the result by 100. In this case, you divide the number of black or African American females who are high-school graduates, GED, or alternative (105,275) by the total number of black or African American females (346,639) and multiply the result by 100 for your answer: (105,275/346,639)100 = 30.37, or 30.4 percent. Rounding the answer to 30 percent would also be acceptable.

13. **B. Asian males.** You use the same method of calculation as in Question 12 to work out a percentage for each of the four options: white males, Asian males, white females, and Asian females. For white males, you divide 417,941 (the number who had a bachelor's degree or higher) by 1,661,912 (the total number of white males in the study) and then multiply by 100, which works out to 25.148, or 25 percent rounded to the nearest whole number. Do the same for the other three categories: Asian males, (15,238/27,597)100 = 55.216, or 55 percent; white females, (429,384/1,795,601)100 = 23.913, or 24 percent; and Asian females, (15,110/33,414)100 = 45.220, or 45 percent. The correct answer is, therefore, *Asian males*.

14. **C. The growing world population means that each woman having fewer children is offset by the fact that there are more women to have children.** Even though the number of children women are having has declined, far more women exist and are available to have children. That balances out the individual birth rate decline and results in a steady number of births.

15. **A. The king's only answer was repeated injury.** The first line of the text states the answer. Choice (B) has nothing to do with the belief that the king was a tyrant. Choice (C) may be correct but also has nothing to do with the reasons the king was considered a tyrant.

16. **A. They were usurpations.** The colonial states felt that the king and British parliament were taking upon themselves powers to which they had no right. They certainly didn't feel that this was *magnanimous* or *examples of justice and consanguinity*.

17. **D. All of the above.** At this time, the various states considered themselves independent countries. That means all the choices are correct. It's interesting to read documents from the time that say "the United States are . . . " as opposed to "the United States is. . . . "

18. **A. Articles of Confederation.** The original constitution of the United States was called the *Articles of Confederation*, not *the Constitution of the Confederation* or *the Declaration of Independence*.

19. **D. He had many ideas on how to fix things.** The text describes Madison as a man of many ideas about how to fix the Articles of Confederation. Choice (A) is a minor consideration, and Choices (B) and (C) are irrelevant.

20. **B. to have the ability to raise money to fund extraordinary exigencies.** Madison had seen that one of the major shortcomings of the Articles of Confederation was that the federal government depended on the states to raise money. It was the need to raise money in the face of extraordinary dangers that was a key element. Although the ability *to fight wars* and *to create a new military* are partially correct, these points aren't major.

21. **D. All of the above.** All these points explain the need for greater union of all the states.

22. **A. 13.** The correct answer is 13. The confederation of 1776 consisted of the original 13 colonies — Connecticut, Delaware, Georgia, Maryland, Massachusetts, New Hampshire, New Jersey, New York, North Carolina, South Carolina, Pennsylvania, Rhode Island, and Virginia. These were the first states in the union. Other states were added at later dates.

23. **C. He worked in the home of Jefferson Davis.** The most important element of the choices offered is the fact that William Jackson worked in the home of Jefferson Davis, where he had direct access to all the discussions that took place. There's no suggestion that Jackson had any military experience, and his direct contact with Washington grew out of his service in the Davis's home. The fact that he was African American is relevant only to the extent that he was a servant in that home.

24. **A. the Underground Railroad.** Harriet Tubman is best known for her key work in the Underground Railroad.

25. **A. the Combahee River.** *Montgomery* was the name of a military officer working with Tubman, and she was attacking confederate controlled areas, not union areas.

26. **D. All of the above.** The Spanish flu was spread very rapidly; there was no known cure at that time, and the Centre for Disease Control (CDC), which works on issues such as this outbreak, didn't yet exist.

27. **C. It was called the Spanish flu in error.** According to the text, the first instance of the Spanish flu was actually seen on an American military camp in Kansas. Spanish Harlem had nothing to do with the origins of this outbreak.

28. **B. 1970 to 1980.** Subtract 30 and 40 from 2012 to get the high and low end of the range, 1970 to 1980.

29. **A. a major recession and the Vietnam War.** The period of 1970 to 1980 was a time of recession and the winding down of the Vietnam War. With many men at war, high unemployment, and worry about finances, people were less likely to have children at that time. The Korean War had ended many years earlier, and the Gulf War was still to come.

30. **women.** If you look at the top of the three pyramids, you can see that the right side is wider than the left. The right side reflects the number of females and the population.

31. **D. all of the above.** All of those events are similar to events in our present time. Union membership among employees in the private sector is at an all-time low. There have been many tax cuts in the last 20 years; however, they have offered more benefits to those at the upper end of the income scale and to corporations than to middle and lower class individuals and families. And, certainly, the concentration of wealth owned by the richest 1 percent of the population is at an all-time high. The top 1 percent of the wealthiest in America control more than 30 percent of all wealth, while the bottom half of the population controls less than 3 percent. Further, the proportion of wealth controlled by the bottom 80 percent of the population continues to decline.

32. **B. times seemed good so there was no need for union organization.** For most people, times appeared to be good, even if they weren't. As long as that was the feeling, there was no real need for labor to organize. Although the growing power of corporations may have made union organization more difficult (as stated in Choice [C]), that isn't stated or even implied in the text. Unions were no longer illegal, so Choice (A) is also incorrect.

33. **B. Whatever improves conditions for most people cannot be regarded as bad for society as a whole.** Adam Smith proposes that anything that helps those less well-off can only improve society as a whole.

34. **B. Reward a laborer liberally.** According to Smith, employers should reward their laborers generously. The other options are contradicted by the text, when Smith states "no society can surely be flourishing and happy, of which the far greater part of the members are poor and miserable."

35. **A. Yes. Well-paid workers are more active and diligent.** Smith and Ford would have been of one mind on this issue. Ford came under attack by other wealthy industrialists for granting his workers this pay increase, but he argued that paying his workers well allowed them to buy his cars, thereby improving his own business while making the workers happy.

36. **A. This was the only way missiles of that time could reach into North and South America.** At that time, missiles couldn't cross intercontinental distances. As a result, locations close to your intended target were important. That's why the United States placed missiles into Turkey that could attack the Soviet Union. The U.S.S.R. was simply responding in kind when it decided to build missile bases in Cuba. There was no trade benefit to the Soviet Union, and although it may have wanted to show support for Fidel Castro, that wasn't the main reason.

37. **C. The United States had placed its own missiles in Turkey on the border of the Soviet Union.** The United States had placed missiles in Turkey that directly threatened the heartland of the Soviet Union. Soviet actions in Cuba were a direct response. The Vietnam War hadn't yet begun, and there's no evidence that the Soviet Union was preparing to attack the United States. Although Castro may have demanded the missiles as protection, that wasn't the key element in the Soviet's decision, nor is that argument supported by the text.

38. **Canada.** You read this chart by examining the thickness of various bands, representing petroleum imports from various sources. The band representing Canada is the widest for a single source. While *all others countries* is thicker, it represent a number of countries, not just one.

39. **C. Canada is a safe source of crude oil for the United States.** From a political point of view, Canada is certainly the safest source of crude oil for the United States. It's considered a politically friendly country for the United States. Choice (A) is incorrect because crude oil is being shipped south. Although limits exist on the amount of crude oil that can be shipped using tankers or rail, that isn't the most important reason. Remember, you must evaluate the importance of the options and choose the most correct answer.

40. **C. Republic of Korea.** South Korea shows the greatest decline. It shows a decline of nearly 5 percent in the improvement to GDP over the designated period. The other three countries showed a much lesser decline in the rate of change. The graph may lead you to think that some of the lower lines suggest the correct answer because they end up at a much lower percentage rate of change, but that isn't what you're being asked. It's that change, not the absolute lowest value, that matters.

41. **C. Republic of Korea.** South Korea is the only country where the rate of change doesn't slip into a negative value. All countries show positive values for all the listed periods, but in 2007 to 2011, that changes. The United States (–0.7 percent), Canada (–0.3 percent), and the United Kingdom (–1.3 percent) all show negative growth, but Korea continues to show growth of 2.5 percent during that same period. All the lines show a decline, and all but one slip below the 0 percent line. The only one that doesn't slip below is the Republic of Korea, and the table confirms that.

42. **increase.** The line for *World Population* continues to climb upward to the right. Using the scale, that shows an increasing population. The number values on the line confirm that.

43. **declined.** The chart shows the change in the net world population. Because all the numbers on the scale are in the positive domain, the world population is growing. However, the growth peaks around 1990, and declines — unevenly — after that. People are living longer in some parts of the world, and life expectancy in most other parts of the world hasn't changed. So the decline in the growth of the world population must mean that there are fewer children being born.

44. **B. the actual net change in the world population by year.** That is, it shows the number of births minus the number of deaths. Choice (A) is partially correct, but Choice (B) is the best option. Choices (C) and (D) are wrong because they don't take into account both birth and death rates.

45. **B. More people means more children, even if individual women have fewer children. That still adds up to an increasing population.** Although the actual number of children by individual women is declining, the population as a whole is growing. That means there are more women available to have children. So even with fewer children for women, the population continues to grow.

46. **A. Some objected to standardized reading and math tests.** The only option mentioned in the text is Choice (A). According to the text, the act increased parental choice, and the plan was passed by Congress. Although some people in Congress may have considered it too expensive, there's nothing in the text to support that point.

47. **C. largely rural.** You have to read carefully to find this answer. The text states that since World War II, Canada became an industrial society. Then it states that this transformed it from a largely rural economy. Choices (A), (B), and (D) are all true but only after World War II.

48. **D. All of the above.** Canada is a major trading partner with America and is part of NFTA, the free trade agreement among Mexico, the United States, and Canada.

49. **C. There was strong popular opposition on the home front to participation in this war.** According to the text, some people in Australia strongly objected to participation in Vietnam, very much like what happened in the United States. The reluctance to become involved isn't the best choice, and there's no evidence that there was a demand to contribute only humanitarian aid.

50. **C. They concentrated on training South Vietnamese forces.** The cessation of active combat by Australian forces and slow withdrawal are implied as part of the training concentration but aren't actually stated, so these are the lesser choices. Remember to pick the most correct answer.

## Sample Extended Response

The following is a sample of an Extended Response based on this prompt. Compare it to your own response and refer to Chapter 7 for the scoring criteria and what the evaluator's look for in a response.

> Even before we had the expression "voter suppression," efforts to take away the vote from individuals existed. That was the key reason for the 15th amendment, which was ratified back in 1870. There are many more current examples, especially in the 2000 Presidential vote in Florida. Thousands of African and Hispanic Americans were removed from voters' lists, often improperly, and few were told they could request reinstatement. Since African Americans in Florida were seen as predominantly democratic voters, this certainly had an impact on the vote outcome.

> A similar situation came up in the 2012 elections. Eventually, the courts ruled illegal the efforts by the Governor of Florida to remove people from the voters list a mere 90 days prior to the election.

> As the ACLU article states, some state governments are putting rules in place which make it harder for average working people to vote. Many working class people do not travel outside the United States and have no need for expensive passports. The requirement to provide photo identification is also a hardship for the many elderly who do not have cars, and hence, no driver's license. As the article states, some 7 percent of voters, mostly the lower classes, have no such ID. Further, efforts to shorten voting times or ban organized voter drives make the situation worse. In the South in the fifties, it was these voter drives that finally managed to get black voters on the voters' list. The efforts to disallow voter registration on election day, combined with these other restrictions, certainly seems aimed at reducing voter turnout among the effected groups.

> While no amendment to the Constitution states flatly that citizens have the right to vote, the amendments do say that voting rights shall not be abridged. Unfortunately, deciding who is on the voters list is in state control, even when it involves federal elections. It seems that some states, especially states controlled by Republicans, are determined to make it more difficult for people who are suspected of favoring Democrats to vote. There is even a petition on the White House website, urging the Supreme Court to intervene. Voter suppression happened in the past and seems destined to continue.

# Part IV

# Peering at Your Specimen: The Science Test

## Five Ways to Build Your Science Knowledge before Test Day

✔ Read as much material on science as you can and make notes on any words you don't understand. Look up definitions for these words and make notes.

✔ Review your list of words regularly and make sure you understand what they mean. Mastering the vocabulary will help you understand the basic concepts.

✔ Make sure you know how to use the calculator available to you on the Science test. Check out the video presentation at www.youtube.com/watch?v=VoLZLsRXuKE.

✔ Spend time reading scientific articles on the Internet. Articles from NASA are always interesting and are aimed at the general public.

✔ If you're having real problems understanding scientific principles or language, consider enrolling in a preparation class or a study group. At least then you'll have someone to help you and other people around you to talk to about science.

Build your science vocabulary with some studying tips at www.dummies.com/extras/gedtest.

# In this part . . .

✔ Discover the secrets to the Science test, including what you need to know for the test, how the test is formatted, and some tips for preparing for the different question types and materials.

✔ Put your science knowledge to the test with some strategies for answering the questions and for writing up a couple of Short Answer responses.

# Chapter 11

# From Aardvarks to Atoms: Confronting the Science Test

● ● ● ● ● ● ● ● ● ● ● ● ● ● ● ● ● ● ● ● ● ● ● ● ● ● ● ● ● ● ● ● ● ● ● ● ● ● ● ● ● ● ●

### In This Chapter

▶ Discovering what skills you need to succeed on the Science test

▶ Checking out the format and content of the Science test

▶ Mastering effective preparation strategies

● ● ● ● ● ● ● ● ● ● ● ● ● ● ● ● ● ● ● ● ● ● ● ● ● ● ● ● ● ● ● ● ● ● ● ● ● ● ● ● ● ● ●

The GED Science test doesn't test you on the depth of your knowledge of science. You're not expected to memorize any scientific information to do well on this test. Instead, this test assesses your ability to ferret out information presented in passages or visual materials. However, you should have at least a passing knowledge of scientific vocabulary.

One of the best ways to improve your scientific vocabulary is to read scientific material, science magazines, websites, and even old textbooks. Look up any words you don't know. Rest easy that you aren't expected to know the scientific difference between terms like *fission* and *fusion* — but just being familiar with them can help you on the test.

The Science test covers material from life science, physical science (chemistry and physics), and earth and space science. Don't panic — you don't need to memorize material from those subjects. You just need to be able to read and understand the material and correctly answer questions. In this chapter, we help you get a feel for the Science test, the skill it requires, and some techniques you can use to prepare.

## Looking at the Skills the Science Test Covers

If you're totally unfamiliar with science and its vocabulary, you'll likely have trouble with the questions on the Science test. You're expected to have some basic knowledge about how the physical world works, how plants and animals live, and how the universe operates. This material tests you on ideas that you observe and develop throughout your life, both in and out of school. You probably know a little about traction, for example, from driving and walking in slippery weather. On the other hand, you may not know a lot about equilibrium aside from what you read in school.

As you prepare to take the Science test, you're expected to understand that science is all about inquiry. In fact, inquiry forms the basis of the *scientific method* — the process every good scientist follows when faced with an unknown. The steps of the scientific method are as follows:

1. **Ask questions.**

2. **Gather information.**

3. **Do experiments.**

4. **Think objectively about what you find.**

5. **Look at other possible explanations.**

6. **Draw one or more possible conclusions.**

7. **Test the conclusion(s).**

8. **Tell others what you found.**

Look at your studying for the Science test as a scientific problem. The question you're trying to answer is, "How can I increase my scientific knowledge?" Follow the scientific method to come up with a procedure to fix the problem. Your solution should include reading, reading, and more reading! In addition to this book, one or more high-school science books is a great tool to use or even a course that teaches the basics of high-school science. (Go to your local library to get your hands on a copy of one of these books, and check with your local school board to find basic science courses in your area.) If there are a group of people that are preparing for the GED tests at the same time as you are, forming a study group may also be helpful.

# Understanding the Test Format and What Topics Are Covered

The Science test contains about 50 questions of different formats, which you have 90 minutes to answer. Within this time limit are two Short Answer items that the GED Testing Service suggests should take you about ten minutes each to complete. This leaves you about 70 minutes for the other 48 items. The Short Answer items aren't timed separately. As with the other test sections, the information and questions on the Science test are straightforward — no one is trying to trick you. To answer the questions, you have to read and interpret the passages or other visual materials provided with the questions (and you need a basic understanding of science and the words scientists use when they communicate).

In terms of organization, some of the items are grouped in sets. Some items are stand-alone questions based on one issue or topic. Some questions follow a given passage, chart, diagram, graph, map, or table. Your job is to read or review the material and decide on the best answer for each question based on the given material.

In terms of subject matter, the questions on the Science test check your knowledge in the following areas:

✔ **Physical science:** About 40 percent of the test is about *physical science,* which is the study of atoms, chemical reactions, forces, and what happens when energy and matter get together. As a basic review, keep the following in mind:

• Everything is composed of atoms. (The paper this book is printed on is composed of atoms, for example.)

• When chemicals get together, they have a reaction — unless they're *inert* (which means they don't react with other chemicals; inert chemicals are sort of like anti-social chemicals).

• You're surrounded by forces and their effects. (If the floor didn't exert a force up on you when you stepped down, you would go through the floor.)

For more information about physical science (which includes basic chemistry and basic physics), read and review a basic science textbook. You can borrow one from your local library (or from your local high school, if you call the office in advance and ask whether the school has any extras). You can also find one on the Internet. When reading this material, you may need definitions for some of the words or terms to make understanding the concepts easier. Use a good dictionary or the Internet to find these definitions. (If you use the Internet, type any of the topics into a search engine and add "definition" after it. Become amazed at the number of hits produced, but don't spend time reading them all.)

✔ **Life science:** Another 40 percent of the test covers *life science* — the study of cells, heredity, evolution, and other processes that occur in living systems. All life is composed of *cells,* which you can see under a microscope. If you don't have access to a microscope and a set of slides with cells on them, most life science–related books and the Internet have photographs of cells that you can study. When someone tells you that you look like your parents or that you remind them of another relative, they're talking about *heredity.* Reading a bit about heredity in biology-related books can help you practice answering some of the questions on the Science test.

Use a biology textbook to help you review for this portion of the test. (Get your hands on a copy of one at your local library or high school.)

✔ **Earth and space science:** The remaining 20 percent of the test covers earth and space science. This area of science looks at the earth and the universe, specifically weather, astronomy, geology, rocks, erosion, and water.

When you look down at the ground as you walk, you're interacting with earth sciences. When you look up at the stars on a clear night and wonder what's really up there, you're thinking about earth sciences. When you complain about the weather, you're complaining about earth sciences. In a nutshell, you're surrounded by earth sciences, so you shouldn't have a problem finding materials to read on this subject.

You don't have to memorize everything you read about science before you take the test. All the answers to the test questions are based on information provided in the passages or on the basic knowledge you've acquired over the years about science. However, any science reading you do prior to the test not only helps you increase your basic knowledge but also improves your vocabulary. An improved science vocabulary increases your chances of being able to read the passages and answer the related questions on the test quickly.

As the basis for its questions, the Science test uses the National Science Education Standards (NSES) content standards, which are based on content developed by science educators from across the country.

# Examining Preparation Strategies That Work

To get better results from the time and effort you put into preparing for the Science test, we suggest you try the following strategies:

✔ **Take practice tests.** Take as many practice tests as you can. You can find two practice tests in this book (in Parts VI and VII). Be cautious about time restrictions, and check the answers and explanations when you're finished. If you still don't understand why some answers are correct, ask a tutor, take a preparation class, or look up the information in a book or on the Internet. Be sure you know why every one of your answers is right or wrong.

✔ **Create your own dictionary.** Get a notebook and keep track of all the new words (and their definitions) that you discover as you prepare for the Science test. Make sure you understand all the science terminology you see or hear. Of course, this chore isn't one you can do in one night. Take some time and make sure this terminology becomes part of your everyday vocabulary.

✔ **Read as many passages as you can.** We may sound like a broken record, but reading is the most important way to prepare for the Science test. After you read a paragraph from any source (textbook, newspaper article, novel, and so on), ask yourself some questions about what you read. You can also ask friends and family to ask you questions about what you read.

Check out Chapter 3 for some general test-taking strategies to help you prepare for all of the sections of the GED test.

# Finding science on the Internet

The Internet can increase your scientific knowledge or simply introduce you to a new area of interest. If you don't have an Internet connection at home, try your local library or community center.

To save yourself time as you begin your online search for additional practice in reading science material, we suggest you check out the following sites:

✔ `www.els.net`: Contains tons of information about life sciences

✔ `www.earth.nasa.gov`: Contains lots of intriguing earth- and space-related info

✔ `www.chemistry.about.com`: Contains interesting info related to chemistry (Note that this is a commercial site, which means you'll see pesky banners and commercial links amidst the interesting and helpful information.)

✔ `www.colorado.edu/physics/2000/index.pl`: Contains some interesting physics lessons that are presented in an entertaining and informative manner

You can also find a great deal of information general and specific regarding the science test on the GED Testing Service's site: `www.gedtestingservice.com`

To explore on your own, go to your favorite search engine and type the science key words you're most interested in (*biology, earth science,* and *chemistry,* just to name a few examples). You can also use the same key words for a YouTube search and find many excellent videos explaining these topics.

# Chapter 12

# Science Question Types and Solving Strategies

• • • • • • • • • • • • • • • • • • • • • • • • • • • • • • • • • • • • • • • • • • • • • • • • •

### In This Chapter

▶ Getting a feel for the test format

▶ Figuring out how to tackle the different question types

▶ Managing your time carefully

• • • • • • • • • • • • • • • • • • • • • • • • • • • • • • • • • • • • • • • • • • • • • • • • •

The Science test is one long 90-minute test. Within the test are two Short Answer items that take about ten minutes each to complete. You're not limited to ten minutes, but any time you use above that takes away from the time you have to answer the rest of the questions. The Short Answer items require you to write short essays, several paragraphs long. These items begin with a passage (stimulus) followed by a *prompt,* a short instruction regarding the topic on which you're to write your short essay.

The Science test shares most of the same features and question formats as the other GED test sections. Although the items are mostly in the traditional multiple-choice format, you'll also find fill-in the-blank, drop-down, drag-and-drop, and hot-spot question formats. The questions are based on scientific text passages or visual images, including diagrams, graphs, maps, and tables. In this chapter, we explore the different question types and strategies for solving them.

## Tackling the Science Test Questions

Like the Social Studies test, the Science test has two main question types — questions about textual passages and questions about visual materials. Having a basic understanding of the item formats can help you avoid any surprises when you sit down to take the test.

You want to make sure you read every word and symbol that appears in the Science test questions, including every chart, diagram, graph, map, table, passage, and question. Information — both relevant and irrelevant — is everywhere, and you never know where you'll find what you need to answer the questions quickly and correctly, especially when dealing with visuals, graphs, tables, and diagrams. Don't skip something because it doesn't immediately look important.

### Questions about text passages

The text passages on this test — and the questions that accompany them — are very similar to a reading-comprehension test: You're given textual material, and you have to answer questions about it. The passages present everything you need to answer the questions, but you usually have to understand all the words used in those passages to figure out what they're telling you (which is why we recommend that you read as much science information as you can prior to the test).

The difference between the text passages on the Science test and other reading-comprehension tests is that the terminology and examples are all about science. Thus, the more you read about science, the more science words you'll know, understand, and be comfortable seeing on the test — which, as you may imagine, can greatly improve your chances of success.

Keep the following tips and tricks in mind when answering questions about text passages:

✔ **Read each passage and question carefully.** Some of the questions on the Science test assume that you know a little bit from past experience. For example, you may be expected to know that a rocket is propelled forward by an engine firing backward. (On the other hand, you won't have to know the definition of *nuclear fission* — thank goodness!)

Regardless of whether an item assumes some basic science knowledge or asks for an answer that appears directly in the passage, you need to read each passage and corresponding question carefully. As you read, do the following:

- Try to understand the passage, and think about what you already know about the subject.

- If a passage has only one question, read that question extra carefully.

- If the passage or question contains words you don't understand, try to figure out what those words mean from the rest of the sentence or the entire passage.

✔ **Read each answer choice carefully.** Doing so helps you get a clearer picture of your options. If you select an answer without reading all the choices, you may end up picking the wrong one because, although that answer choice may seem right at first, another answer choice may be more correct. As you read the answer choices, do the following:

- If one answer is right from your reading and experience, note it.

- If you aren't sure which answer is right, exclude the answers you know are wrong and then exclude answers that may be wrong.

- If you can exclude all but one answer, it's probably correct, so choose it.

Try out these tips on the sample passages and questions in the "Practicing with Sample Items" section, later in this chapter.

## Questions about visual materials

*Visual materials* are pictures that contain information you may need to answer the corresponding questions. They can be in the form of tables, graphs, diagrams, or maps. Understanding information in visual materials takes more practice than textual passages because you likely aren't as familiar with getting information from pictures as you are with getting info from text. This section (and the practice tests) can help you get the practice you need.

Any visual object is like a short paragraph. It has a topic and makes comments or states facts about that topic. When you come across a question based on a visual material, the first thing to do is to figure out the content of the material. Usually, visual objects have titles that help you understand their meanings. After you figure out the main idea behind the visual object, ask yourself what information you're being given; rereading the question can be helpful. After you know these two pieces of information, you're well on your way to answering the question.

The following sections take a more detailed look at the different visual materials that you may find on the Science test. As a bonus, this advice also applies to the Social Studies test. (Check out Part III for more on the Social Studies test.)

### Tables

A *table* is a graphical way of organizing information. This type of visual material allows for easy comparison between two or more sets of data. Some tables use symbols to represent information; others use words.

Most tables have titles that tell you what they're about. Always read the titles first so you know right away what information the tables include. If a table gives you an explanation (or *key*) of the symbols, read the explanation carefully, too; doing so helps you understand how to read the table.

### Graphs

A *graph* is a picture that shows how different sets of numbers are related. On the Science test, you can find the following three main types of graphs:

- **Bar or column graphs:** Bars (horizontal) or columns (vertical) present and often compare information.

- **Line graphs:** On line graphs, one or more lines connect points drawn on a grid to show the relationships between data, including changes in data over time.

- **Pie graphs (also called pie charts or circle graphs):** Arcs of circles (pieces of a pie) show how data relates to a whole.

All three types of graphs usually share the following common characteristics:

- **Title:** The title tells you what the graph is about, so always read the title before reviewing the graph.

- **Horizontal axis and vertical axis:** Bar, column, and line graphs have a horizontal axis and a vertical axis. (Pie graphs don't.) Each axis is a vertical or horizontal reference line that's labeled to give you additional information.

- **Label:** The label on the axis of a graph usually contains units, such as feet or dollars. Read all axis labels carefully; they can either help you with the answer or lead you astray (depending on whether you read them correctly).

- **Legend:** Graphs usually have a *legend,* or printed material that tells you what each section of the graph is about. They may also contain labels on the individual parts of the graph and explanatory notes about the data used to create the graph, so read carefully.

Graphs and tables are both often called *charts,* which can be rather confusing. To help you prepare for problems with graphs, make sure you look at and problem solve plenty of graphs before the test. Remember that many graphs show relationships. If the numbers represented on the horizontal axis are in millions of dollars and you think they're in dollars, your interpretation of the graph will be more than a little incorrect.

### Diagrams

A *diagram* is a drawing that helps you understand how something works.

Diagrams on the Science test often have the following two components:

- **Title:** Tells you what the diagram is trying to show you
- **Labels:** Indicate the names of the parts of the diagram

When you come to a question based on a diagram, read the title of the diagram first to get an idea of what the diagram is about. Then carefully read all the labels to find out the main components of the diagram. These two pieces of information can help you understand the diagram well enough to answer questions about it.

### Maps

A *map* is a drawing of some section — large or small — of the earth or another planet, depending on how much space exploration has been done. Because the entire world is too large to show you on one piece of paper, a section of it is drawn to scale and presented to you on the test.

Most maps give you the following information:

- ✓ **Title:** Tells you what area of the world the map focuses on and what it shows
- ✓ **Legend:** Gives you general information about the colors, symbols, compass directions, or other graphics used on the map
- ✓ **Labels:** Indicate what the various points on the map represent
- ✓ **Scale:** Tells you what the distance on the map represents in real life (For example, a map with a scale of 1 inch = 100 miles shows a distance of 500 miles on the real earth as a distance of 5 inches on the map.)

Although maps are seldom used in science passages, they are used occasionally, so you want to at least be familiar with them. The best way to get familiar with maps is to spend some time looking at road maps and world atlases, which you can find in your local library or bookstore.

The exact meaning of any visual materials may not be obvious or may even be misleading if not examined carefully. You must understand what the legends, scale, labels, and color coding are telling you. Numbers on a table also may be misleading or even meaningless unless you read the legend and labels carefully. Colors on a map aren't just for decoration; each color has a meaning. Each piece of a visual represents meaning from which you can put together the information you need to determine the correct answers.

## Practicing with Sample Items

To help increase your odds of doing well on the Science test, you want to be as familiar as you can be with what you'll encounter on the real GED test. The following questions are some sample problems for the Science test. Read each question carefully, and find the best answer based on the passages.

### Multiple-choice questions

Most of the questions on the Science test are in the traditional multiple-choice format, where you get four answer choices. Your job is to pick the best answer that's supported by the passage or visual material presented to you. If the material is in the form of a text passage, read the passage quickly to answer the question. If the material is in the form of a visual, read the title and the verbal information so you understand what the visual is all about. Be careful of scientific language. You should be familiar with most, if not all, of the words from your reading of science materials.

If one answer must be correct, then three answers must be wrong. If you can exclude the wrong answers, you'll be left with the right one. Read the passage carefully to figure out the right or wrong choices.

The example questions in this section refer to the following passage.

> One of the great discoveries in earth science is rocks. Rocks have many useful purposes in science. They can be used as paperweights to keep academic papers from flying away in the wind. Rocks can be used to prop laboratory doors open when the experiments go wrong and horrible smells are produced. Smooth rocks can be rubbed when pressure builds and you just need a mindless activity to get through the day.

According to the passage, one of the great discoveries in science is

(A) atomic energy

(B) static electricity

(C) rocks

(D) DNA

The correct answer is Choice (C). The important words in the question are *According to the passage.* When you see this phrase, you know to look in the passage for the answer. Because none of the answers except rocks is even remotely mentioned, rocks must be the best answer.

How do rocks help scientists when experiments go horribly wrong and produce terrible odors?

(A) They can be used to smash the windows.

(B) They can prop open the doors.

(C) They can be thrown in anger.

(D) They can be rubbed.

The correct answer is Choice (B). According to the passage, the rocks can be used to hold open the door of the lab. Rocks can also be used to smash windows and can be thrown in anger, but the passage doesn't specifically mention these uses. The passage mentions rubbing rocks as a use of rocks, but it does so in another context.

## Fill-in-the-blank questions

For Science fill-in-the-blank questions, you have to provide your own answer(s) — a specific calculation, word, or words — to show that you understand a concept, to complete a definition, or to describe a trend on a graph. This is another example of why you should read as much scientific material as possible. A misspelled word is scored as incorrect. Keeping that vocabulary list we suggest as a review method before the test will really help.

Here's an example fill-in-the-blank question based on the following excerpt from a job posting on the Federal Government Jobs website (`www.federalgovernmentjobs.us`).

> A career with the Forest Service will challenge you to manage and care for more than 193 million acres of our nation's most magnificent lands, conduct research through a network of forest and range experiment stations and the Forest Products Laboratory, and provide assistance to State and private forestry agencies.
>
> It's an awesome responsibility — but the rewards are as limitless as the views.

Based on the information in the passage, what would the person hired for this job do in conjunction with range experiment stations? ☐

The correct answer is *conduct research.* The successful applicant would conduct research with the range experiment stations as part of their duties. This is stated explicitly in the passage.

Try another fill-in-the-blank question on for size, based on the following excerpt from the USDA Animal and Plant Health Inspection Service website (www.aphis.usda.gov).

> The Lacey Act combats trafficking in "illegal" wildlife, fish, and plants. The 2008 Farm Bill (the Food, Conservation, and Energy Act of 2008), effective May 22, 2008, amended the Lacey Act by expanding its protection to a broader range of plants and plant products. The Lacey Act now, among other things, makes it unlawful to import certain plants and plant products without an import declaration. This page will serve as a clearinghouse for all information related to the implementation of the Lacey Act declaration requirement and will be updated promptly as new information becomes available.

The Lacy Act is an American government piece of legislation to control the transportation and selling of ⬚ plants.

The passage states that this act was passed to combat the trafficking of illegal wildlife, fish and plants. So the correct answer is *illegal.*

## Drag-and-drop questions

For this question format, you have to drag answer choices from a list to a designated position — whether that's placing labels on a graph or diagram or dropping words or images on a specific location on a chart or other type of visual. This question format requires a bit more than just picking the correct answer. In drag-and-drop questions, you may have to sort and prioritize your selections. Although you're given a list of possible answers, more than one may be correct. Read the passage carefully to either eliminate wrong answers or choose correct ones.

Here's an example of a question in the drag-and-drop format.

In Miss Fleming's graduating class, three of her students want to specialize in science:

> Gilda wants to study physics.

> Domenic wants to study biology.

> Freida wants to learn everything she can about NASA's missions

Drag (or write, in this case) the appropriate name into the column labeled with the general area each student wants to study.

(A) Gilda

(B) Domenic

(C) Freida

| Earth and Space Science | Life Science | Physical Science |
|---|---|---|
|  |  |  |

The correct response here is Gilda wants to study physical science, Domenic wants to study life science, and Freida wants to study earth and space science. General knowledge from your experience and reading would enable you to fit the specific interests into the general areas.

## Drop-down menu questions

The drop-down menu is a type of multiple-choice question, in that you're given a number of answer choices to choose from to complete a sentence so it reads correctly and accurately. Usually, drop-down menu questions involve more science vocabulary, so your reading in science will help you choose the correct answer. Like with most multiple-choice items, the drop-down menu includes correct and incorrect answers, but there can be more than one correct answer.

The following drop-down menu question refers to this excerpt from the Missions page on NASA's website (`www.nasa.gov`).

> The Post-landing Orion Recovery Tests (PORT) began in late March at the Naval Surface Warfare Center, Carderock Division in Bethesda, Md. This first round took place in a controlled water environment. Testing near Kennedy Space Center in April will be done in the rougher, uncontrolled waters of the Atlantic Ocean. Crews will head out over several days and at varying distances from land to assess the vehicle's performance in open water landing conditions. Recovery teams will gain experience dealing with Orion in water. The tests will also help NASA understand the motions astronauts will experience within the craft. The same boats that have been used to recover the space shuttle's solid rocket boosters will tow the capsule for these tests.

The Orion will be tested in open waters in Atlantic to

(A) ensure that the astronauts can swim

(B) ensure the safety and security of the astronauts

(C) test the water tightness of the Orion

(D) allow the astronauts to fish to provide them with provisions

The correct answers are Choices (B) and (C), *ensure the safety and security of the astronauts* and *test the water tightness of the Orion*. Dropping a sealed capsule into the ocean wouldn't test swimming ability nor fishing possibilities. The other two are reasonable answers to the question based on the passage.

## Hot-spot questions

The computer screen on the test has several virtual hot spots on it. It's very similar to a piece of graph paper with several intersections marked on the back. When you poke a pin through the paper and strike a marked point, you hit the correct spot. This type of item is very difficult to reproduce on paper because there's no way of making a point on the page "live." To see what the computer screen looks like on the actual test, check out some examples at `www.gedtestingservice.com`. While you're there, look at some of the other variation of these common types of items.

*Note:* In this book, we alter the format of hot-spot questions by asking you to circle the correct spot on the corresponding graph or figure.

# Short Answer item

Although the term *short answer* usually means a few words or phrases in response to a statement or question, on the GED Science test, the Short Answer is closer to a full-blown essay. Introducing the Short Answer item is a stimulus or passage that outlines the material you're supposed to base your response on. This material may be several paragraphs long; be sure to read it carefully. Following the stimulus is the prompt, which tells you what's expected of you in response to the stimulus. At this point, you're in charge of your own destiny. You have to write the equivalent of a short essay (about 200 to 250 words) based on the information in the stimulus and corresponding to what's needed to satisfy the prompt. Remember, you should spend no more than about ten minutes to read the item, think about your answer, make notes, and write your response.

Here's an example:

**Stimulus**

Scientists finally have their hands on a piece of Mars, sort of. Technology seemingly straight out of Star Trek allowed the replication of a rock on Mars, using a 3D printer.

The result is a realistic-looking, true-size facsimile of a Martian meteorite called *Block Island*. NASA's Mars Exploration Rover Opportunity found it in 2009. Block Island is the largest meteorite yet found on Mars. It is an iron-nickel meteorite about the size of a small ice chest. The real Block Island probably weighs a half-ton. You could easily carry its plastic twin under your arm.

Most meteorites break up when hitting the ground because today's Martian atmosphere is not dense enough to slow them down enough. Scientists say this meteorite could have landed on Mars intact only if it had two things: a very specific entry point into the atmosphere and a very shallow flight path. That would slow it down enough to keep it from breaking apart upon landing.

**Prompt**

Earthlings have been curious about Mars for centuries. Explain how these findings are satisfying, in part, our curiosity.

Write your response on a separate sheet of paper. This task may require approximately ten minutes to complete.

Here's a sample response.

The existence of a reproduction of a piece of rock from Mars is a miraculous event. First, the invention of 3D printers has been a recent event and the use of such a printer to reproduce an object found on the surface of Mars is even more exciting. Without such modern advances in technology, we would not be able to look at an object from so far away, even if it is only an accurate reproduction.

In addition, the discovery of such a rock on Mars is even more exciting. Because of the thin atmosphere on Mars, most meteorites hit the surface with such velocity that they are shattered. This one hit just right and was saved. Between the luck of the landing and the wonders of modern technology, we are able to satisfy our curiosity, in part, about Mars. Who knows what will be discovered next?

The Short Answer item is scored on a scale from 0 to 3 points, based on the following criteria.

✔ **A score of 3 points:** You write a clear, well-developed explanation in response to the prompt, using the material in the stimulus. Instead of just copying sections of the stimulus, you paraphrase it to demonstrate understanding. Your writing demonstrates complete support from the stimulus.

✔ **A score of 2 points:** You write a response that demonstrates partial or adequate understanding of the material in the stimulus and follows the guide in the prompt. Your writing shows partial support from the stimulus without just quoting passages.

✔ **A score of 1 point:** You write a response that demonstrates minimal understanding of the stimulus with minimal or implied support from the stimulus.

✔ **A score of 0 points:** You write a response that demonstrates neither explanation nor understanding of the material in the stimulus and a complete disregard for the direction in the prompt. You copy material from the stimulus or prompt with no attempt to explain or understand what was presented in the stimulus and prompt. Your response is incomprehensible or written in a language other than English. Or you didn't even bother to answer the item.

Make sure that your response is clear, concise, readable, and properly written. Although the scoring criteria in the preceding list doesn't mention spelling and grammar, both are important and give a reader an idea of your skill level in written English.

# Managing Your Time for the Science Test

The Science test has about 50 questions (the exact number varies from test to test) that you must answer in 90 minutes, which means you have about 90 seconds to read each textual or visual passage and its corresponding question(s) and determine the correct answer. If a passage has more than one question, you have slightly more time to answer those questions because you should read the passage only once. You'll also have two Short Answer items, each of which should take you about ten minutes or less to complete. The Short Answer items aren't timed separately, so some speed in keyboarding and passage completion will give you more time for the other items.

To help you manage your time, check out Chapters 2 and 3 for some general time-management strategies that you can use on all the test sections. For the Science test, specifically, we suggest you focus on these two time-saving strategies:

✔ **For questions about passages, read the question first and then skim the material for the answer.** The passage always contains the answer, but your background knowledge in science and your familiarity with scientific terms can help you understand the material more easily and quickly. Reading the question first provides you with a guide to what's being asked and what the passage is about so you know what to look for as you read it.

✔ **For questions about a visual material, such as a graph or table, read the question first and then scan the visual material.** Look at the visual material to see the big picture; questions usually don't ask about minute details.

As a general tip, answer the easiest questions first. You can then go back and spend a little more time on the more difficult questions. Remember, though, to plan ahead and leave a few minutes at the end to review your answers.

And don't panic! Your worst enemy on this or any other test is panic. Panicking takes time and energy, and you don't have a surplus of both. On the Science test, you're expected to recognize and understand some scientific vocabulary, but, if you come across a word you don't understand, try to figure out its meaning from the rest of the sentence. If you can't do so quickly, leave it. Return to the problem at the end of the test when you know exactly how much time is left.

# Chapter 13

# Building Your Skills with Some Science Practice Questions

This chapter provides sample Science test questions, including two Short Answer items, to help you prepare for taking that section of the GED test.

Record your answers directly in this book or on a separate sheet of paper, if you think you'll want to revisit these practice questions at a later date. Mark only one answer for each item, unless otherwise indicated. And be sure to have an extra sheet of paper handy, or use your computer's word processor, to practice preparing and writing the Short Answer items. At the end of the chapter, we provide detailed answer explanations for you to check your answers.

Remember, this is just preliminary practice. We want you to get used to answering different types of Science test questions. Use the complete practice tests in Parts VI and VII to time your work and replicate the real test-taking experience.

## Science Practice Questions

The Science test consists of a series of items intended to measure general concepts in science. The items are based on short readings that may include a graph, chart, or figure. Study the information given and then answer the question(s) following it. Refer to the information as often as necessary in answering the questions. Work carefully, but don't spend too much time on any one question. Be sure you answer every question.

*Questions 1–2 refer to the following diagram and excerpt from NASA's Glenn Research Center website for Space Flight Systems (*exploration.grc.nasa.gov*).*

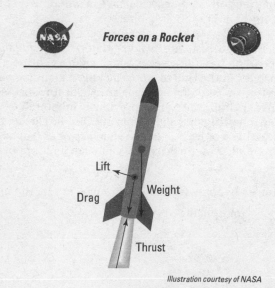

**Forces on a Rocket**

Lift

Weight

Drag

Thrust

*Illustration courtesy of NASA*

Many differences exist between the forces acting on a rocket and those acting on an airplane.

1. On an airplane, the **lift force** (the aerodynamic force perpendicular to the flight direction) is used to overcome the **weight**. On a rocket, **thrust** is used in opposition to weight. On many rockets, lift is used to stabilize and control the direction of flight.

2. On an airplane, most of the aerodynamic forces are generated by the wings and the tail surfaces. For a rocket, the aerodynamic forces are generated by the fins, nose cone, and body tube. For both airplane and rocket, the aerodynamic forces act through the center of pressure (the dot with the black center on the figure) while the weight acts through the center of gravity (the solid dot on the figure).

3. While most airplanes have a high lift to drag ratio, the drag of a rocket is usually much greater than the lift.

4. While the magnitude and direction of the forces remain fairly constant for an airplane, the magnitude and direction of the forces acting on a rocket change dramatically during a typical flight.

1. In the diagram, which force must be the greatest for the rocket to leave the earth?

(A) drag

(B) lift

(C) thrust

(D) weight

2. Short Answer Prompt: Although the purpose of both rockets and airplanes is to lift people and payloads off the earth, because of the differences in distances traveled and the medium through which they travel, explain how the forces acting on each and propelling each are different.

Write your response on a separate sheet of paper. This task may require approximately ten minutes to complete.

*Questions 3–4 refer to the following excerpt from the U.S. Environmental Protection Agency's website on climate change (www.epa.gov/climatechange).*

As temperatures increase, the habitat ranges of many North American species are moving northward in latitude and upward in elevation. While this means a range expansion for some species, for others it means a range reduction or a movement into less hospitable habitat or increased competition. Some species have nowhere to go because they are already at the northern or upper limit of their habitat.

For example, boreal forests are invading tundra, reducing habitat for the many unique species that depend on the tundra ecosystem, such as caribou, arctic fox, and snowy owl. Other observed changes in the United States include expanding oak-hickory forests, contracting maple-beech forests, and disappearing spruce-fir forests. As rivers and streams warm, warmwater fish are expanding into areas previously inhabited by coldwater species. Coldwater fish, including many highly valued trout species, are losing their habitats. As waters warm, the area of feasible, cooler habitats to which species can migrate is reduced. Range shifts disturb the current state of the ecosystem and can limit opportunities for fishing and hunting.

3. As temperatures become warmer and ranges move, the new territory may prove to be less _____ for specific species.

4. When warmwater fish move into territories previously occupied by coldwater species, this creates problems for human beings because

   (A) humans depend on fish as a source of protein

   (B) fishing is a sport that aids local economies

   (C) many coldwater fish are valued as food or prey

   (D) all of the above

*Question 5 refers the following excerpt from* Womenshealth.gov.

"Mirror, Mirror on the wall . . . who's the thinnest one of all?" According to the National Eating Disorders Association, the average American woman is 5 feet 4 inches tall and weighs 140 pounds. The average American model is 5 feet 11 inches tall and weighs 117 pounds. All too often, society associates being "thin" with "hard-working, beautiful, strong and self-disciplined." On the other hand, being "fat" is associated with being "lazy, ugly, weak and lacking will-power." Because of these harsh critiques, rarely are women completely satisfied with their image. As a result, they often feel great anxiety and pressure to achieve and/or maintain an imaginary appearance.

Eating disorders are serious medical problems. Anorexia nervosa, bulimia nervosa, and binge-eating disorder are all types of eating disorders. Eating disorders frequently develop during adolescence or early adulthood, but can occur during childhood or later in adulthood. Females are more likely than males to develop an eating disorder.

5. Why are females more likely to develop an eating disorder than males?

   (A) Males are not concerned about their appearance.

   (B) Females strive for a perfect appearance.

   (C) Males are generally taller and weigh more.

   (D) Not enough information is given.

*Question 6 refers to the following definition from the U.S. Environmental Protection Agency's climate change glossary (*www.epa.gov/climatechange*).*

Adaptive capacity is the ability of a system to adjust to climate change (including climate variability and extremes) to moderate potential damages, to take advantage of opportunities, or to cope with the consequences.

6. How would increasing the insulation in the walls and ceiling of a house be considered part of adaptive capacity?

   (A) It saves money on heating costs.

   (B) It allows the inhabitants to adapt to a colder climate.

   (C) It allows the inhabitants to adapt to changes in energy costs.

   (D) The inhabitants can be more comfortable.

*Question 7 refers to the following definition from the U.S. Environmental Protection Agency's climate change glossary (*www.epa.gov/climatechange*).*

Black carbon (BC) is the most strongly light-absorbing component of particulate matter (PM), and is formed by the incomplete combustion of fossil fuels, biofuels, and biomass. It is emitted directly into the atmosphere in the form of fine particles.

7. Based on this information, how would reducing automobile use result in a cleaner environment?

(A) Traffic would be lighter.

(B) Most automobiles run on fossil fuel.

(C) Subways are a more efficient form of moving people.

(D) Electricity is less expensive than fossil fuels.

*Question 8 refers to the following definition from the U.S. Environmental Protection Agency's climate change glossary (www.epa.gov/climatechange).*

The greenhouse effect is the trapping and build-up of heat in the atmosphere (troposphere) near the Earth's surface. Some of the heat flowing back toward space from the Earth's surface is absorbed by water vapor, carbon dioxide, ozone, and several other gases in the atmosphere and then reradiated back toward the Earth's surface. If the atmospheric concentrations of these greenhouse gases rise, the average temperature of the lower atmosphere will gradually increase.

8. Heat reradiated from the earth's surface is absorbed by several ⬜ in the earth's atmosphere.

*Question 9 refers to the following excerpt from NASA's Science website (science.nasa.gov).*

Examples of the types of forecasts that may be possible are: the outbreak and spread of harmful algal blooms, occurrence and spread of invasive exotic species, and productivity of forest and agricultural systems. This Focus Area also will contribute to the improvement of climate projections for 50–100 years into the future by providing key inputs for climate models. This includes projections of future atmospheric $CO_2$ and $CH_4$ concentrations and understanding of key ecosystem and carbon cycle process controls on the climate system.

9. Long-term forecasts of this type are important to people because

(A) it will help hunters know when their favorite sport will become impossible

(B) it will allow scientists to develop research projects that will address the consequences of dramatic climate change

(C) people will know what type of winter clothing to buy for their children

(D) it will spur research into more efficient subway systems

*Question 10 refers to the following excerpt from NASA's Science website (science.nasa.gov).*

Throughout the next decade, research will be needed to advance our understanding of and ability to model human-ecosystems-climate interactions so that an integrated understanding of Earth System function can be applied to our goals. These research activities will yield knowledge of the Earth's ecosystems and carbon cycle, as well as projections of carbon cycle and ecosystem responses to global environmental change.

10. This type of research should lead to advances in our understanding of how the carbon cycle and our ecosystem respond to ⬜.

*Questions 11–12 refer to the following excerpt from NASA's Jet Propulsion Laboratory website (www.jp.nasa.gov).*

We live on a restless planet. Earth is continually influenced by the sun, gravitational forces, processes emanating from deep within the core, and by complex interactions with oceans and atmospheres. At very short time scales we seem to be standing on terra firma, yet many processes sculpt the surface with changes that can be quite dramatic (earthquakes, volcanic eruptions, landslides), sometime slow (subsidence due to aquifer depletion), seemingly unpredictable, and often leading to loss of life and property damage.

Accurate diagnosis of our restless planet requires an observational capability for precise measurement of surface change, or deformation. Measurement of both the slow and fast deformations of Earth are essential for improving the scientific understanding of the physical processes, and for optimizing responses to natural hazards, and for identifying potential risk areas.

11. Although people often talk about standing on solid ground, the truth is that

(A) the earth is capable of supporting huge buildings anywhere on its surface

(B) the ground is solid and stable

(C) the ground is capable of sudden dramatic movement

(D) people should not live near an active volcano

12. Accurate scientific research into surface change is essential to

(A) discuss the physical processes

(B) warn people about volcanoes

(C) ensure better responses to natural hazards

(D) make more accurate weather forecasts

*Question 13 refers to the following diagram from NASA's Glenn Research Center website (www.grc.nasa.gov).*

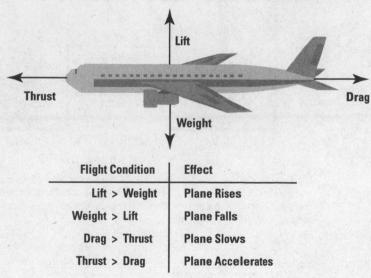

| Flight Condition | Effect |
| --- | --- |
| Lift > Weight | Plane Rises |
| Weight > Lift | Plane Falls |
| Drag > Thrust | Plane Slows |
| Thrust > Drag | Plane Accelerates |

*Illustration courtesy of NASA*

13. For the plane to take off, [_____] and [_____]. Write the appropriate answers in the boxes.

(A) lift > weight

(B) weight > lift

(C) drag > thrust

(D) thrust > drag

*Question 14 refers to the following excerpt from NASA's website (`www.nasa.gov`).*

It would be impractical, in terms of volume and cost, to completely stock the International Space Station (ISS) with oxygen or water for long periods of time. Without a grocery store in space, NASA scientists and engineers have developed innovative solutions to meet astronauts' basic requirements for life. The human body is two-thirds water. It has been estimated that nearly an octillion (1027) water molecules flow through our bodies daily. It is therefore necessary for humans to consume a sufficient amount of water, as well as oxygen and food, on a daily basis in order to sustain life. Without water, the average person lives approximately three days. Without air, permanent brain damage can occur within three minutes. Scientists have determined how much water, air, and food a person needs per day per person for life on Earth. Similarly, space scientists know what is needed to sustain life in space.

14. Why is it necessary to recycle air and water on a space ship?

(A) to keep the interior smelling clean

(B) to keep their plants alive

(C) to keep the astronauts alive

(D) so that they don't get thirsty between meals

*Question 15 refers to the following diagram from NASA's Glenn Research Center website (`www.grc.nasa.gov`).*

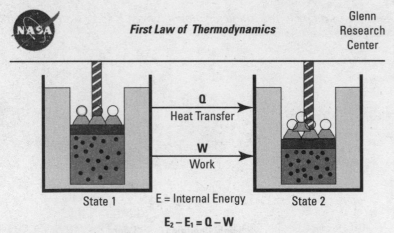

Glenn Research Center

**First Law of Thermodynamics**

Q
Heat Transfer

W
Work

State 1    E = Internal Energy    State 2

$E_2 - E_1 = Q - W$

Any thermodynamic system in an equilibrium state possesses a state variable called the internal energy (E). Between any two equilibrium states, the change in internal energy is equal to the difference of the heat transfer <u>into</u> the system and work done <u>by</u> the system.

*Illustration courtesy of NASA*

15. Circle the vessel on the diagram with the higher temperature.

*Question 16 refers to the following excerpt from NASA's website (`www.nasa.gov`).*

On the space shuttle, fuel cells combine hydrogen and oxygen to produce electricity. A fuel cell uses a chemical reaction to provide an external voltage, as does a battery, but differs from a battery in that the fuel is continually supplied in the form of hydrogen and oxygen gas. A by-product of this reaction ($2H_2 + O_2 \rightarrow 2H_2O$ + electricity) is water, which can be used in a future oxygen generator system to produce oxygen for breathing. Fuel cells can produce electrical energy more safely and efficiently than just burning the hydrogen, to produce heat to drive a generator. The water supply is the limiting factor on the ISS when the space shuttle cannot routinely provide water from its fuel cells. With only two crew members, it is manageable to "truck" water tanks in the Russian Progress resupply ship.

16. How is water supplied to the space shuttle?

    (A) by-product of electricity production

    (B) stored onboard

    (C) delivered by resupply ship

    (D) manufactured from hydrogen and oxygen

*Question 17 refers to the following excerpt from NASA's Science website (science.nasa.gov).*

As basic research leads to prediction of solid earth processes, so is the need to adapt this research to real societal problem solving. Knowledge that improves human abilities to prepare and respond to disasters involving the dynamism of the Earth's interior has an immediate benefit to saving lives and property. Earth Surface and Interior focus area (ESI) seeks to coordinate the efforts of the NASA's Research and Analysis Program in Solid Earth with the Applied Sciences Disaster Management Program to provide a continuum of development from research to applications that will enable first responders, planners, and policy makers to improve decision tools through NASA science and technology.

17. Why is the work of ESI important?

    (A) It coordinates research areas that lead to life-saving developments.

    (B) It provides employment for scientists.

    (C) It produces interesting videos for education.

    (D) It provides real societal problems.

*Question 18 refers to the following definition from the U.S. Environmental Protection Agency's climate change glossary (www.epa.gov/climatechange).*

Weather is atmospheric condition at any given time or place. It is measured in terms of such things as wind, temperature, humidity, atmospheric pressure, cloudiness, and precipitation. In most places, weather can change from hour-to-hour, day-to-day, and season-to-season." On the other hand, "[c]limate . . . is usually defined as the 'average weather,' or more rigorously, as the statistical description in terms of the mean and variability of relevant quantities over a period of time ranging from months to thousands or millions of years. The classical period is 30 years, as defined by the World Meteorological Organization (WMO). These quantities are most often surface variables such as temperature, precipitation, and wind. Climate in a wider sense is the state, including a statistical description, of the climate system. A simple way of remembering the difference is that climate is what you expect (e.g. cold winters) and 'weather' is what you get (e.g. a blizzard).

18. If you were sitting around with a group of friends complaining about how the rain forecast for tomorrow was going to ruin your baseball game, you would be complaining about the ☐☐☐☐☐.

*Question 19 refers to the following definition from the U.S. Environmental Protection Agency's climate change glossary (www.epa.gov/climatechange).*

Atmospheric lifetime is the average time that a molecule resides in the atmosphere before it is removed by chemical reaction or deposition. This can also be thought of as the time that it takes after the human-caused emission of a gas for the concentrations of that gas in the atmosphere to return to natural levels. Greenhouse gas lifetimes can range from a few years to a few thousand years.

19. Why is it important for humans to become more aware of the pollution they are causing by overuse of fossil fuels?

(A) Gasoline is becoming expensive.

(B) The greenhouse gases can remain in the atmosphere for many years.

(C) Traffic congestion is causing health problems.

(D) Humans are turning the blue sky gray.

*Question 20 refers to the following excerpt from the U.S. Department of Energy's website (`www.energy.gov`).*

In 2009, President Barack Obama signed an Executive Order creating the White House Council on Women and Girls. In his remarks at the signing, the President underscored that the purpose of the Council is "to ensure that each of the agencies in which they're charged takes into account the needs of women and girls in the policies they draft." The Energy Department's chapter of the Council continues to pull program offices and National Laboratories together to work on confronting the challenges faced by women and girls.

At the Clean Energy Ministerial held in London in April 2012, the Department launched the U.S. Clean Energy, Education, and Empowerment (C3E) program to advance the careers and leadership of women in clean energy fields. The program, led by the Department in partnership with the MIT Energy Initiative, includes an ambassador network, annual symposium and the C3E Awards program.

A year later, inspired by the success of C3E, Energy Secretary Ernest Moniz launched the Minorities in Energy (MIE) Initiative. The initiative includes a network of more than 30 senior-level Ambassadors across the public and private sector working alongside the Department to increase the participation of minorities in energy careers as well as support their advancement to leadership positions.

20. The effect of President Obama's initiative was to ⬚ the participation of women and minorities in careers in energy-related fields.

(A) increase

(B) leave the same

(C) decrease

*Question 21 refers to the following excerpt from NASA's Earth Observatory website (`www.earthobservatory.nasa.gov`).*

If Kepler's laws define the motion of the planets, Newton's laws define motion. Thinking on Kepler's laws, Newton realized that all motion, whether it was the orbit of the Moon around the Earth or an apple falling from a tree, followed the same basic principles. "To the same natural effects," he wrote, "we must, as far as possible, assign the same causes." Previous Aristotelian thinking, physicist Stephen Hawking has written, assigned different causes to different types of motion. By unifying all motion, Newton shifted the scientific perspective to a search for large, unifying patterns in nature. Newton outlined his laws in *Philosophiae Naturalis Principia Mathematica* ("Mathematical Principles of Natural Philosophy"), published in 1687.

21. Newton was inspired by

    (A) Hawkings

    (B) Aristotle

    (C) Kepler

    (D) Einstein

*Question 22 refers to the following information, taken from the U.S. Department of Labor's Occupational Safety & Health Administration website (`www.osha.gov`).*

Unexpected releases of toxic, reactive, or flammable liquids and gases in processes involving highly hazardous chemicals have been reported for many years. Incidents continue to occur in various industries that use highly hazardous chemicals which may be toxic, reactive, flammable, or explosive, or may exhibit a combination of these properties. Regardless of the industry that uses these highly hazardous chemicals, there is a potential for an accidental release any time they are not properly controlled. This, in turn, creates the possibility of disaster.

Recent major disasters include the 1984 Bhopal, India, incident resulting in more than 2,000 deaths; the October 1989 Phillips Petroleum Company, Pasadena, TX, incident resulting in 23 deaths and 132 injuries; the July 1990 BASF, Cincinnati, OH, incident resulting in 2 deaths, and the May 1991 IMC, Sterlington, LA, incident resulting in 8 deaths and 128 injuries.

Although these major disasters involving highly hazardous chemicals drew national attention to the potential for major catastrophes, the public record is replete with information concerning many other less notable releases of highly hazardous chemicals. Hazardous chemical releases continue to pose a significant threat to employees and provide impetus, internationally and nationally, for authorities to develop or consider developing legislation and regulations to eliminate or minimize the potential for such events.

On July 17, 1990, OSHA published in the *Federal Register* (55 FR 29150) a proposed standard, — "Process Safety Management of Highly Hazardous Chemicals" — containing requirements for the management of hazards associated with processes using highly hazardous chemicals to help assure safe and healthful workplaces.

22. Short Answer Prompt: Often, highly dangerous materials are necessary for use in the manufacture of products people need or want. It is the government's responsibility to ensure that the use of such materials does not pose a massive danger to the population. Explain why the government must step in to safeguard the population from the devastating effects of an incident involving hazardous materials.

Write your response on a separate sheet of paper. This task may require approximately ten minutes to complete.

*Question 23 is based on the following excerpt from the National Oceanic and Atmospheric Administration's Office of Response and Restoration website (`response.restoration.noaa.gov`).*

Reactivity is the tendency of substances to undergo chemical change, which can result in hazards — such as heat generation or toxic gas by-products. The CRW (Chemical Reactivity Worksheet) predicts possible hazards from mixing chemicals and is designed to be used by emergency responders and planners, as well as the chemical industry, to help prevent dangerous chemical incidents.

The chemical datasheets in the CRW database contain information about the intrinsic hazards of each chemical and about whether a chemical reacts with air, water, or other materials. It also includes case histories on specific chemical incidents, with references.

23. What is the most important contribution of the CRW to the prevention of hazardous accidents?

    (A) provides information

    (B) enforces the regulations

    (C) creates laws

    (D) closes companies for infractions

*Question 24 refers to the following excerpt from the U.S. Environmental Protection Agency's website on climate change (`www.epa.gov/climatechange`).*

Climate change, along with habitat destruction and pollution, is one of the important stressors that can contribute to species extinction. The IPCC estimates that 20–30% of the plant and animal species evaluated so far in climate change studies are at risk of extinction if temperatures reach levels projected to occur by the end of this century. Projected rates of species extinctions are 10 times greater than recently observed global average rates and 10,000 times greater than rates observed in the distant past (as recorded in fossils).

24. One of the great dangers to the earth as a result of climate change is the [          ] of species.

*Question 25 refers to the following excerpt from the U.S. Environmental Protection Agency's website on climate change (`www.epa.gov/climatechange`).*

[W]hen coral reefs become stressed, they expel microorganisms that live within their tissues and are essential to their health. This is known as coral bleaching. As ocean temperatures warm and the acidity of the ocean increases, bleaching and coral die-offs are likely to become more frequent. Chronically stressed coral reefs are less likely to recover.

25. Coral bleaching refers to

    (A) chemical reaction between the ocean waters and microorganisms in the coral

    (B) expulsion of microorganisms from within coral reefs

    (C) the effect of extremely strong sunlight on coral reefs

    (D) not enough information

*Question 26 refers to the following excerpt from the U.S. Environmental Protection Agency's website on climate change (`www.epa.gov/climatechange`).*

For many species, the climate where they live or spend part of the year influences key stages of their annual life cycle, such as migration, blooming, and mating. As the climate has warmed in recent decades, the timing of these events has changed in some parts of the country. Some examples are:

- Warmer springs have led to earlier nesting for 28 migratory bird species on the East Coast of the United States.

- Northeastern birds that winter in the southern United States are returning north in the spring 13 days earlier than they did in the early 20th century.

- In a California study, 16 out of 23 butterfly species shifted their migration timing and arrived earlier.

Changes like these can lead to mismatches in the timing of migration, breeding, and food availability. Growth and survival are reduced when migrants arrive at a location before or after food sources are present.

26. Severe climate changes can lead to extinction of a species though [_____] in aspects of their lives upon which their survival depends.

*Question 27 refers to the following excerpt from NASA's Science website (`science.nasa.gov`).*

New remote sensing technologies are empowering scientists to measure and understand subtle changes in the Earth's surface and interior that reflect the response of the Earth to both the internal forces that lead to volcanic eruptions, earthquakes, landslides and sea-level change and the climatic forces that sculpt the Earth's surface. For instance, InSAR [interferometric synthetic aperture radar] and LiDAR [light detection and ranging] measurements from satellite and airborne sensors are used to provide images of millimeter scale surface changes that indicate an awakening of volcanic activity long before seismic tremors are felt. Ground based geodetic GPS instruments provide time continuous measurements of this activity though they are often lost during intense volcanic activity. Thermal infrared remote sensing data from NASA satellites signal impending activity by measuring ground temperatures and variations in the composition of lava flows as well as the sulfur dioxide in volcanic plumes. The combination of instruments provide accurate information that can be used for both long term and short hazard assessment. These same LiDAR, InSAR and thermal instruments also provide accurate information on the velocity of ice steams, sub glacial lake activity, glacial rebound of the Earth's crust, and the retreat and advance of mountain glaciers that are related to climatic changes.

27. New remote sensing technologies provide [_____] that may lead to long- and short-term hazard assessment.

*Question 28 refers to the following excerpt from the National Science Foundation website (`www.nsf.gov`).*

By observing galaxies formed billions of years ago, astronomers have been able to paint an increasingly detailed picture of how the universe evolved. According to the widely accepted Big Bang theory, our universe was born in an explosive moment approximately fifteen billion years ago. All of the universe's matter and energy — even the fabric of space itself — was compressed into an infinitesimally small volume and then began expanding at an incredible rate. Within minutes, the universe had grown to the size of the solar system and cooled enough so that equal numbers of protons, neutrons, and the simplest atomic nuclei had formed.

28. Astronomers believe that the universe evolved about [_____] billion years ago.

*Question 29 refers to the following excerpt from NASA's Earth Observatory website (`www.earthobservatory.nasa.gov`).*

Within a single frame of reference, the laws of classical physics, including Newton's laws, hold true. But Newton's laws can't explain the differences in motion, mass, distance, and time that result when objects are observed from two very different frames of reference. To describe motion in these situations, scientists must rely on Einstein's theory of relativity.

At slow speeds and at large scales, however, the differences in time, length, and mass predicted by relativity are small enough that they appear to be constant, and Newton's laws still work. In general, few things are moving at speeds fast enough for us to notice relativity. For large, slow-moving satellites, Newton's laws still define orbits. We can still use them to launch Earth-observing satellites and predict their motion. We can use them to reach the Moon, Mars, and other places beyond Earth. For this reason, many scientists see Einstein's laws of general and special relativity not as a replacement of Newton's laws of motion and universal gravitation, but as the full culmination of his idea.

29. Einstein's theory provides a frame of reference for explanation of differences in time, length, and mass from

    (A) two very different speeds

    (B) two very different scales

    (C) observations from two very different frames of reference

    (D) two very different perspectives

*Question 30 refers to the following excerpt from NASA's Science website (`science.nasa.gov`).*

As basic research leads to prediction of solid earth processes, so is the need to adapt this research to real societal problem solving. Knowledge that improves human abilities to prepare and respond to disasters involving the dynamism of the Earth's interior has an immediate benefit to saving lives and property. Earth Surface and Interior focus area (ESI) seeks to coordinate the efforts of the NASA's Research and Analysis Program in Solid Earth with the Applied Sciences Disaster Management Program to provide a continuum of development from research to applications that will enable first responders, planners, and policy makers to improve decision tools through NASA science and technology.

30. ESI provides first responders with ☐ to improve their decision making in the event of a disaster.

*Question 31 refers to the following excerpt from the U.S. Environmental Protection Agency's website on climate change (`www.epa.gov/climatechange`).*

The impact of climate change on a particular species can ripple through a food web and affect a wide range of other organisms. . . . Declines in the duration and extent of sea ice in the Arctic leads to declines in the abundance of ice algae, which thrive in nutrient-rich pockets in the ice. These algae are eaten by zooplankton, which are in turn eaten by Arctic cod, an important food source for many marine mammals, including seals. Seals are eaten by polar bears.

31. The declines in the number of ☐ can contribute to declines in polar bear populations.

*Question 32 refers to the following excerpt from the U.S. Environmental Protection Agency's stratospheric ozone glossary (`www.epa.gov/ozone`).*

Consumer aerosol products in the US have not used ozone-depleting substances (ODS) since the late 1970s because of voluntary switching followed by federal regulation. The Clean Air Act and EPA regulations further restricted the use of ODS for non-consumer products. All consumer products, and most other aerosol products, now use propellants that do not deplete the ozone layer, such as hydrocarbons and compressed gases.

32. The propellants that are currently used in aerosol products are ☐ and ☐.

*Question 33 refers to the following definition from the U.S. Environmental Protection Agency's climate change glossary (`www.epa.gov/climatechange`).*

Biofuels are gas or liquid fuels made from plant material (biomass). They include wood, wood waste, wood liquors, peat, railroad ties, wood sludge, spent sulfite liquors, agricultural waste, straw, tires, fish oils, tall oil, sludge waste, waste alcohol, municipal solid waste, landfill gases, other waste, and ethanol blended into motor gasoline.

33. Biofuels are ecologically sound because

    (A) they are inexpensive

    (B) they do not pollute the earth

    (C) they are made from recyclable materials

    (D) they can be used as fuels

_Question 34 refers to the following definition from the U.S. Environmental Protection Agency's climate change glossary (www.epa.gov/climatechange)._

Carbon cycle is all parts (reservoirs) and fluxes of carbon. The cycle is usually thought of as four main reservoirs of carbon interconnected by pathways of exchange. The reservoirs are the atmosphere, terrestrial biosphere (usually includes freshwater systems), oceans, and sediments (includes fossil fuels). The annual movements of carbon, the carbon exchanges between reservoirs, occur because of various chemical, physical, geological, and biological processes. The ocean contains the largest pool of carbon near the surface of the Earth, but most of that pool is not involved with rapid exchange with the atmosphere.

34. The largest pool of carbon on earth is the ⬚ .

_Questions 35–36 refer to the following definition from the U.S. Environmental Protection Agency's climate change glossary (www.epa.gov/climatechange)._

Carbon footprint is the total amount of greenhouse gases that are emitted into the atmosphere each year by a person, family, building, organization, or company. A person's carbon footprint includes greenhouse gas emissions from fuel that an individual burns directly, such as by heating a home or riding in a car. It also includes greenhouse gases that come from producing the goods or services that the individual uses, including emissions from power plants that make electricity, factories that make products, and landfills where trash gets sent.

35. People could reduce their individual carbon footprint by

    (A) driving their cars less

    (B) lowering their thermostats during the cold weather

    (C) not barbequing meat

    (D) all of the above

36. People's personal carbon footprint is also affected by processes out of their control, such as

    (A) grocery shopping

    (B) recycling depots

    (C) power plants

    (D) all of the above

*Question 37 refers to the following definition from the U.S. Environmental Protection Agency's climate change glossary (`www.epa.gov/climatechange`).*

The most abundant greenhouse gas, water vapor is the water present in the atmosphere in gaseous form. Water vapor is an important part of the natural greenhouse effect. While humans are not significantly increasing its concentration through direct emissions, it contributes to the enhanced greenhouse effect because the warming influence of greenhouse gases leads to a positive water vapor feedback. In addition to its role as a natural greenhouse gas, water vapor also affects the temperature of the planet because clouds form when excess water vapor in the atmosphere condenses to form ice and water droplets and precipitation.

37. Water vapor is a positive influence on the earth because

(A) it moisturizes your skin

(B) it counteracts carbon emissions

(C) it has a positive effect on the temperature of earth

(D) it cools the mountains

*Question 38 refers to the following excerpt from NASA's website (`www.nasa.gov`).*

Saving lives does not have to be as complex as robotic surgery, but can be as simple as providing the life-giving source of clean water. This specifically is of utmost importance to a community in rural Mexico, showing the far-reaching benefits of the water purification component of NASA's Environmental and Life Control Support System (ECLSS). ECLSS provides clean water for drinking, cooking and hygiene aboard the space station. This technology has been adapted on Earth to aid remote locations or places devastated by natural disaster that do not have access to clean drinking water.

In Chiapas, Mexico, many people are at risk of illness from drinking contaminated water from wells, rivers or springs not treated by municipal water systems. Children in Chiapas, previously sickened by parasites and stomach bugs, now have access during school to clean, safe drinking water. This is due to the installation of the ECLSS-derived water purification plant. Renewable solar energy powers the water treatment technology for the community in Chiapas. Results include improved overall health and cost-savings from not having to buy purified water or medication to treat water-borne illnesses.

38. How do innovations by NASA help a little town in Mexico?

(A) by setting up space industries

(B) by providing for clean water

(C) by supplying food

(D) by ridding the area of parasites

*Question 39 refers to the following excerpt from the U.S. Department of Labor's Occupational Safety & Health Administration website (`www.osha.gov`).*

Chemicals have the ability to react when exposed to other chemicals or certain physical conditions. The reactive properties of chemicals vary widely and they play a vital role in the production of many chemical, material, pharmaceutical, and food products we use daily. When chemical reactions are not properly managed, they can have harmful, or even catastrophic consequences, such as toxic fumes, fires, and explosions. These reactions may result in death and injury to people, damage to physical property, and severe effects on the environment.

39. Chemical reactions have proven to be a great asset to humanity, but there is a darker side to chemical reactions. What is it?

    (A) They can poison food supply.

    (B) They can have dire consequences if not handled properly.

    (C) They can explode spontaneously.

    (D) All of the above.

*Question 40 refers to the following chart.*

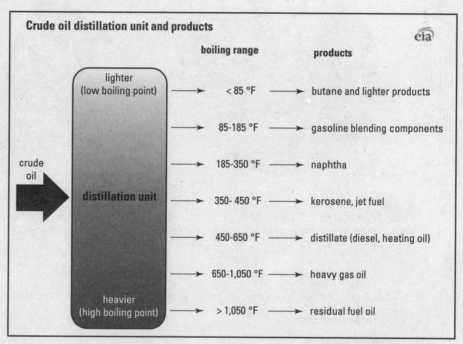

**Crude oil distillation unit and products**

| boiling range | products |
| --- | --- |
| < 85 °F | butane and lighter products |
| 85-185 °F | gasoline blending components |
| 185-350 °F | naphtha |
| 350- 450 °F | kerosene, jet fuel |
| 450-650 °F | distillate (diesel, heating oil) |
| 650-1,050 °F | heavy gas oil |
| > 1,050 °F | residual fuel oil |

lighter (low boiling point)

crude oil

distillation unit

heavier (high boiling point)

*Illustration courtesy of U.S. Energy Information Administration*

40. Why is it easier to obtain naphtha from crude oil in a distillation unit than diesel oil?

    (A) It naturally floats to the surface where it can be skimmed off.

    (B) It has a lower boiling point, so it evaporates sooner than diesel oil.

    (C) It has a higher boiling point, so it remains behind as diesel is evaporated.

    (D) Naphtha can be filtered out.

*Questions 41–42 refer to the following chart.*

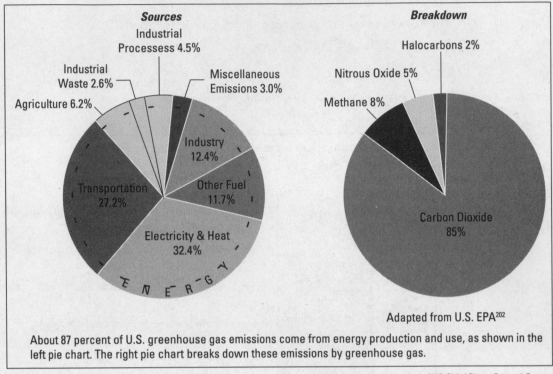

**Sources**

Industrial Processess 4.5%

Industrial Waste 2.6%

Agriculture 6.2%

Miscellaneous Emissions 3.0%

Transportation 27.2%

Industry 12.4%

Other Fuel 11.7%

Electricity & Heat 32.4%

ENERGY

**Breakdown**

Halocarbons 2%

Nitrous Oxide 5%

Methane 8%

Carbon Dioxide 85%

Adapted from U.S. EPA[202]

About 87 percent of U.S. greenhouse gas emissions come from energy production and use, as shown in the left pie chart. The right pie chart breaks down these emissions by greenhouse gas.

*Illustration courtesy of U.S. Global Change Research Program*

41. What is the largest single source of greenhouse gas emissions in the United States?

(A) electricity and heat

(B) transportation

(C) industry

(D) agriculture

42. According to the Intergovernmental Panel of Climate Change, methane gas has 34 times the effect of carbon dioxide, pound for pound, over a 100-year period. Based on the chart, how does methane compare to carbon dioxide as an issue in climate change?

(A) It is a bigger problem than carbon dioxide.

(B) It is approximately equal to carbon dioxide as a problem.

(C) It is less of a problem than carbon dioxide.

(D) Cannot be determined from the table.

*Questions 43–45 refer to the following diagram.*

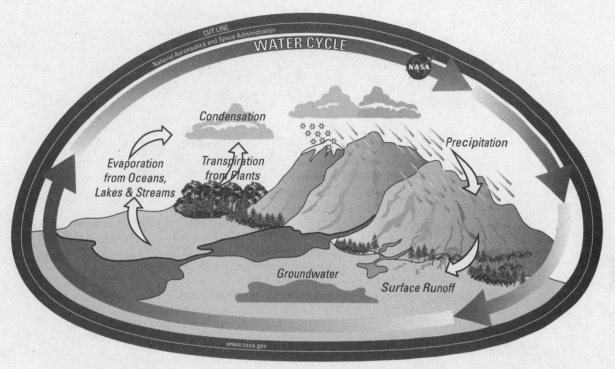

Illustration courtesy of NASA

43. What is the energy source that powers the water cycle?

   (A) wind

   (B) solar energy

   (C) geothermal energy, heating the earth

   (D) none of the above

44. How does surface runoff of water eventually end up as precipitation?

   (A) It collects in lakes and streams and evaporates.

   (B) It eventually runs into the oceans from which it evaporates.

   (C) It is absorbed by plants and reaches the atmosphere by a transpiration.

   (D) All of the above.

45. Large areas of the arctic and Antarctic are covered by ice. How does that ice cover affect climate change?

   (A) The white surface reflects incoming solar energy, reducing the amount of heat absorbed by the earth.

   (B) The ice creates an insulating surface that retains heat in the earth, preventing it from heating the air above.

   (C) The ice itself keeps the air cold.

   (D) The white surface absorbs more solar energy, releasing more heat into the air above.

*Question 46 refers to the following diagram.*

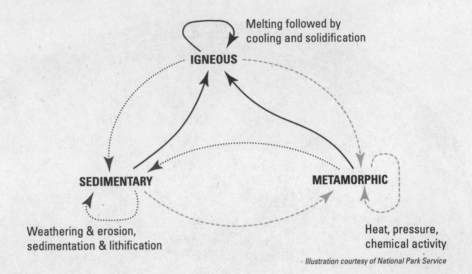

*Illustration courtesy of National Park Service*

46. According to the diagram, how is igneous rock created?

　(A) weathering and erosion

　(B) chemical activity

　(C) chemical activity

　(D) melting, cooling, and solidification

*Question 47 refers to the following diagram.*

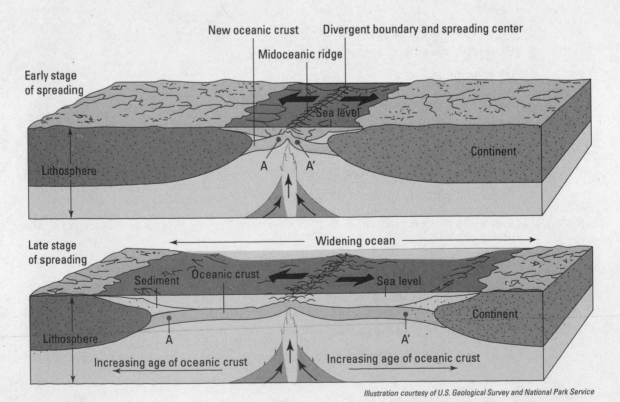

*Illustration courtesy of U.S. Geological Survey and National Park Service*

47. The diagram shows an area where a "hot spot" in the lithosphere allows magma to work its way through the earth's crust to the surface. Because this is taking place under the ocean, it has resulted in a ridge that runs most of the way from Antarctica to the arctic down the middle of the North and South Atlantic. How does that explain the continent's moving farther apart as the arrows in the diagram indicate?

   (A) The magma creates gaps in the sea floor, which are filled by fresh magma.

   (B) The magma cools, forming ridges, which break open as new magma pushes its way up.

   (C) Repeated intrusions of magma widen the gaps, fill them in, and then create new gaps.

   (D) All of the processes above occur, causing the continents to move.

48. How have scientists been able to confirm that this spreading of the sea floor is actually happening and has gone on for millions of years?

   (A) Core sample of the ocean sediments show evidence of increasing age the farther away the samples were taken from the mid ocean ridge.

   (B) Scientists have been able to use lasers to measure the distance between continental coasts.

   (C) Satellite observation has shown continuing movement of the earth's crust.

   (D) All of the above.

*Questions 49–50 refer to the following diagram and excerpt from the U.S. Environmental Protection Agency website (www.epa.gov).*

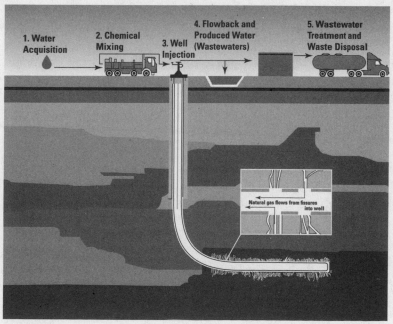

Illustration courtesy of U.S. Environmental Protection Agency

This diagram shows a process for obtaining a natural gas by a method called "fracking" or hydraulic fracturing. In the process, water mixed with chemicals is injected into a well under high pressure. The pressure fractures the earth around the well and allows natural gas to seep into the well. The natural gas, along with waste water comes to the surface where it is separated, treated, and processed.

49. Based on the diagram, what are some concerns people in the area where fracking is taking place may have?

    (A) The process uses a large quantity of both surface and groundwater.

    (B) The natural gas released in the process can contaminate groundwater.

    (C) Not all the chemicals in the fracking water are recovered; some may contaminate groundwater.

    (D) All of the above.

50. What effect has the hydraulic fracturing process had on the availability of crude oil and natural gas in the United States?

    (A) It has resulted in a large increase in crude oil and natural gas production.

    (B) It has had very little effect to date.

    (C) It has had no effect to date.

    (D) Cannot be determined from the information given.

# Answers and Explanations

1. **C. thrust.** The thrust of the rocket engines must provide more energy than the weight of the rocket for it to leave the earth. The other forces have an effect, but the thrust lifts it off the ground.

2. The following is a sample of a Short Answer response. Compare it to your own response and refer to Chapter 12 for the scoring criteria and what the evaluators look for in a response.

   You wouldn't use a rocket to fly to Las Angeles from Washington, and you couldn't use an airplane to fly to the moon. Although each is a method of lifting people and payload off the surface of the earth, each is a specialized form of transportation designed for a specific purpose.

   An airplane is designed to carry people and payloads through the atmosphere in close proximity to the earth in relative comfort. Since the amount of lift needs to be greater than the weight of the aircraft, passengers and payload, modern jet engines can provide the necessary propulsion to move the aircraft forward while the wings provide the lift to enable the airplane to move above the surface of the earth. Airplanes move through the air, albeit thinner air than is found near the ground, it is still able to provide the lift needed. With the advance in current technology of engines, there is enough power to provide a high degree of creature comforts for a large group of passengers.

   Rockets are designed to travel through space across great distances and carry few passengers. Without the lift provided by the wings moving through the air, rockets look different. They have tiny wings relative to their size. Since so much thrust is necessary to escape the pull of the earth's gravity, a rocket engine is huge in comparison to the ones on an airplane. Huge rocket engines require massive amounts of fuel, and since there are no refueling stations in space, all the fuel for the return trip has to be carried upon launch. Not being commercial modes of transportation, yet, rockets do not have to be designed to carry many passengers in relative comfort. The rocket engines provide the thrust required to lift the weight of the rocket and contents through space and back transporting fuel and what else is needed to carry out the purpose of the voyage.

3. **hospitable.** As the passage states, the new territory may be less *hospitable* because of the natural conditions of the territory.

4. **D. all of the above.** All of the choices are possible answers to the question according to the material presented in the passage.

5. **D. Not enough information is given.** Although the choices may seem correct based on generally accepted opinions, they're not supported by the passage. Choice (B) may be close, but the passage states that females may want an imaginary appearance, but the choice indicates a perfect appearance.

6. **B. It allows the inhabitants to adapt to a colder climate.** The passage is about the ability to adjust to climate change, and colder weather is part of climate change over a long period of time. The insulation would allow the inhabitants of the house to adapt to this colder climate. The other choices are concerned with economics and comfort.

7. **B. Most automobiles run on fossil fuel.** Most automobiles run on gasoline, which is a fossil fuel, the incomplete combustion of which forms Black Carbon. The other choices may be important from a traffic congestion or economic point of view but aren't mentioned in the passage.

8. **gases.** The passage states that water vapor, carbon dioxide, ozone, and several other gases are responsible for the reradiation of heat from the earth's surface.

9. **B. it will allow scientists to develop research projects that will address the consequences of dramatic climate change.** More accurate forecasts will allow scientists to work on experiments to address the changes that may be coming. Choices (A) and (C) may be possibilities but aren't mentioned in the passage. Choice (D) is probably a good general idea but has nothing to do with the passage.

10. **global environmental change.** The passage states this as one of the results of this research.

11. **C. the ground is capable of sudden dramatic movement.** Some of the examples given to support this choice are volcanic eruptions, earthquakes, and landslides. The other choices aren't supported by any content in the passage, although Choice (D) is probably a good idea

12. **C. ensure better responses to natural hazards.** The other choices aren't mentioned in the passage.

13. **A, D. lift > weight; thrust > drag.** For a plane to take off, it must accelerate and rise. In order to do that, lift must be greater than weight and thrust must be greater than drag.

14. **C. to keep the astronauts alive.** Without a constant supply of air and water, the astronauts couldn't survive in space, and because carrying a sufficient supply of air and water would be impossible given weight restrictions, they must be recycled.

15. **State 1.** State 1 should be circled because it has the higher temperature. According to the diagram, the heat transfer, Q, would be from State 1 to State 2, indicated by the arrow labeled *Q*.

16. **C. delivered by resupply ship.** The passage states that water is delivered by the Russian resupply ship. This is used for shuttles with two crew members. The by-products of the production of electricity don't supply enough water, nor can it be stored onboard or manufactured onboard.

17. **A. It coordinates research areas that lead to life-saving developments.** ESI coordinates research done by other agencies and research programs that can lead to life-saving developments. Choices (B) and (C) are incorrect and not mentioned in the passage. Choice (D) is the opposite of what's stated in the passage and as such is definitely incorrect.

18. **weather.** *Weather* is current and is a short-term condition. *Climate* is the average weather over a period of time. So *weather* refers to the condition on any given day.

19. **B. The greenhouse gases can remain in the atmosphere for many years.** The passage states that the lifetime of greenhouse gases range from a few years to a few thousand years, and these gases are a danger to people's health. Choice (A) is a *truism* (a commonly heard true statement) and Choice (C) may be true but not in the context of the passage. Choice (D) may be a symptom of the increase in pollution but isn't the best choice.

20. **A. increase.** President Obama's initiative was aimed at increasing the participation of the two groups in science-related careers.

21. **C. Kepler.** The passage is very clear about Kepler's influence on Newton. Hawkings and Einstein both lived after Newton's publication, and Aristotle differed from Newton's conclusion.

22. The following is a sample of a Short Answer response. Compare it to your own response and refer to Chapter 12 for the scoring criteria and what the evaluators look for in a response.

Government and industry often work at cross purposes in the manufacture of needed or wanted goods. The goal and purpose of an industrial endeavour is to show a profit and distribute that profit to its employees and shareholders. Government's purpose is to ensure the safety of the citizens in and around the plant. Sometimes these two purposes are at odds.

Many manufacturing processes use chemicals that in themselves are dangerous but combined can cause catastrophic results. We only have to think about the incident at Bhopal in India that caused in excess of 2,000 fatalities. Numbers such as these are a nightmare to industry and government. There is no doubt that the factory where the disaster occurred was manufacturing a product that required dangerous chemicals. There is no doubt that the government of India would have much preferred never to have had to deal with so many fatalities. But the factory provided jobs for the people in the area, a profit to its owners and shareholders and income to other businesses in the town. Would it have been better if the factory never existed? In light of the resulting carnage, the answer is "yes," but during the time the plant was operating without incident the people and the local economy gained from it.

Should the government have shut the plant down before the accident? That is a question that requires politicians who can foretell the future. They may have been aware that dangerous chemicals were being used in the manufacturing process and might cause a disastrous accident but with what degree of certainty? If someone points a gun at another person at close range and pulls the trigger, there is a high degree of certainty that someone will be injured or killed. But manufacturing plants are not like guns. There may be a chance that a fatality may occur in an industrial accident but not a certainty. With enough proper rigorous inspections, the chances of an accident are reduced. It is the responsibility of the government to ensure that such inspections are carried out and remediation taken if needed.

23. **A. provides information.** The CRW provides information about hazardous materials so companies can use them safely. The other choices are incorrect according to the passage.

24. **extinction.** The passage states that climate change will cause species to become extinct at an accelerated rate.

25. **B. expulsion of microorganisms from within coral reefs.** Stressed coral reefs expel microorganisms essential to their health. Choice (A) sounds correct if you skim the passage, but it's incorrect. Choice (C) is also wrong because there's no mention of the effect of sunlight on the reefs, and Choice (D) is wrong because you have enough information to answer the question.

26. **mismatches.** These mismatches can lead to dramatic changes in the lives of a species, which could lead to eventual extinction.

27. **information.** According to the passage, all of the technologies mentioned provide information that may help scientists in assessing the potential for impending hazards.

28. **15.** The Big Bang theory says that this series of occurrences took place about 15 billion years ago.

29. **C. observations from two very different frames of reference.** As the passage states, Einstein's theory is relevant under these circumstances. The other choices are either incomplete or incorrect.

30. **information.** ESI provides information to the people and departments in charge of making decisions in the case of a disaster.

31. **sea algae.** The passage traces the food chain from sea algae to polar bears; therefore, the decline in numbers of the former would affect the latter.

32. **hydrocarbons; compressed gases.** These two propellants are used because they don't deplete the ozone.

33. **B. they do not pollute the earth.** Materials made from biomass tend to be made from recycled materials, making them less polluting.

34. **ocean.** Although you may not usually think of water as containing carbon, the ocean is the largest pool of carbon on earth because the ocean isn't pure water.

35. **D. all of the above.** Driving your car less, lowering your thermostat during the cold weather, and not barbequing meat all would reduce your carbon footprint.

36. **C. power plants.** Power plants may increase or decrease pollution depending on the process used, which tends to affect your carbon footprint positively or negatively.

37. **C. it has a positive effect on the temperature of earth.** The passage states that water vapor affects the temperature of the earth.

38. **B. by providing for clean water.** NASA used a form of its water purification process to provide the village with clean water.

39. **D. All of the above.** All of the choices are possible negative effects of chemical reactions.

40. **B. It has a lower boiling point, so it evaporates sooner than diesel oil.** Naphtha is a component of crude oil. It has a lower boiling point than diesel fuel and thus evaporates at a lower temperature than diesel fuel. This allows it to be separated from the crude oil before diesel fuel.

41. **A. electricity and heat.** The production of energy and heating in the United States produces more greenhouse gases than any other single activity.

42. **D. Cannot be determined from the table.** The key term here is *by weight*. The pie chart doesn't indicate whether the emissions are by weight or by volume. Therefore, it's impossible to calculate a comparative value.

43. **B. solar energy.** The basic source that drives the water cycle on earth is solar energy. Heat from the sun causes water to evaporate. Heat from the sun causes movement of air mass on earth, thus creating winds and evaporation. Winds carry the evaporated moisture from place to place on earth. Eventually, the evaporated moisture condenses, forming rain or other forms of precipitation.

44. **A. It collects in lakes and streams and evaporates.** Any white surface will reflect solar energy. The polar ice caps reflect solar energy so it can't be reradiated as heat. As the polar ice caps decrease, the effect of incoming solar radiation increases, which contributes to climate change and global warming.

45. **D. The white surface absorbs more solar energy, releasing more heat into the air above.** The appropriate processes are, in order, melting, cooling, and solidification.

46. **D. melting, cooling, and solidification.** The diagram states right beside the word *igneous* that the process consists of melting, cooling, and solidification. The other choices refer to processes involved in creating or changing sedimentary or metamorphic rocks.

47. **D. All of the processes above occur, causing the continents to move.** Sea floor spreading is caused when magma forces its way into faults or thinner or softer area of the earth's crust. The thinnest areas are typically located under an ocean. As the magma forces its way to ocean of level filling cracks in the crust, it forces the crust apart slightly and creates ridges. It cools, solidifies, and then is subjected to pressure from underneath yet again. More cracks are filled with magma, and in the process, ridges are created and the sea floor is forced further and further apart, and the gap is filled with magna.

48. **A. Core sample of the ocean sediments show evidence of increasing age the farther away the samples were taken from the mid ocean range.** The question asks for evidence that this process has been going on for millions of years. The only choice that has any evidence over such a time period is Choice (A). Choices (B) and (C) offer evidence that the continents are continuing to move in the present time, and you can extrapolate from that that this process has been going on for a long time. However, there's no proof, because you can't measure historical data in the present. Therefore, core samples of sediments on the ocean floor are the only useful evidence among the choices presented.

49. **D. All of the above.** According to the EPA, Choices (A), (B), and (C) are all concerns. There has been evidence of all three of these issues in the areas where fracking has taken place.

50. **D. Cannot be determined from the information given.** The diagram shows how the process works but makes no comments on the volume of natural gas or oil products produced by this process.

# Part V

# Counting All the Possible Solutions: The Mathematical Reasoning Test

## Five Ways to Prepare for the Mathematical Reasoning Test

- ✔ **Time yourself as you work through practice math problems.** The Mathematical Reasoning section on the GED test is timed. To get ready for the test, use a timer as you work through practice problems to help you get a feel for the time constraints and to practice working quickly.

- ✔ **Read each item carefully.** A Mathematical Reasoning item is like a story, and you should try to visualize the content. A room with a 30-foot high ceiling isn't normal. Make sure that the question you think about is possible. Here's where your practice tests come in. The more practice you do, the more comfortable you'll become mentally painting mathematical pictures.

- ✔ **Practice conversions.** For example, some questions may require you to convert feet to inches and square yards to square feet. You must answer in the units the item asks for; otherwise, your answer is wrong. Don't risk getting wrong answers because you're rusty on converting.

- ✔ **Tackle the easy questions first.** In some cases, you know exactly what to do just by reading the question. Do those questions first and then go back to the others that require some thinking later. (The only exceptions are the first five questions, which must be done without a calculator on the actual test before you can go on.) Just be sure you go back over the test to catch any questions you may have missed.

- ✔ **Practice using the specified calculator before the test.** Not all calculators are created equal, and you don't want to be figuring out how to use the calculator during a timed test. Getting some practice beforehand will ensure that you're comfortable with it on the actual test. Remember, the calculator is only an aid to calculation and will neither solve problems nor give advice.

Getting familiar with the on-screen calculator before test day is so important. Check out some tips at www.dummies.com/extras/gedtest.

## In this part . . .

✔ Dive into the nuances of the Mathematical Reasoning test, how it's formatted, and what types of skills you need before you show up on test day.

✔ Build your confidence with some key strategies and practice questions, and get familiar with the formula sheet and the calculator specific to the GED Mathematical Reasoning test.

# Chapter 14

# Safety in Numbers: Facing the Mathematical Reasoning Test

**In This Chapter**

▶ Identifying the skills you need for the Math test

▶ Getting a handle on the test format

▶ Preparing for the test using a few tried-and-true strategies

**W**elcome to the dreaded Mathematical Reasoning test (or Math test for short). Although you may have done everything to avoid math in high school, you can't escape this test if you want to pass the GED. To tell you the truth, test-takers really do have nightmares about this test, but don't worry! This chapter helps you prepare, not for having nightmares, but for taking the test successfully.

Most of the questions on the other GED test sections are about reading comprehension: You're given a passage and are expected to understand it well enough to correctly answer the questions that follow. Although you can prepare for the other tests by doing a lot of reading and taking sample tests, you don't have to come in with a lot of knowledge or great skills in the test areas themselves.

The Mathematical Reasoning test is different. It tests your understanding of mathematical concepts and your ability to apply them to situations you may find in the real world. That means you have to spend time solving as many problems as you can and improving your math skills as much as possible before you take this test. This chapter gets you started by introducing the test format and the skills it covers and then providing some tips and tricks for tackling the test.

## Looking at the Skills the Math Test Covers

To do well on the Math test, you need to have a general understanding of numbers, their relationships to one another, measurements, geometry, data analysis and statistics, probability, patterns, functions, and algebra. (If you don't know what we mean by these terms, check out the next section "Understanding the Test Format.") In essence, to be successful on this test, you need to have the mathematical knowledge base that most high-school graduates have, and you need to know how to apply it to solve real-life problems.

The GED Math test provides a formula sheet for you to use during the test. Keep in mind that you may not need all the formulas provided, and you may not need a formula for every question. Part of the fun of math is knowing which formula to use for which problems and figuring out when you don't need one at all.

The Math test assesses the following four areas.

- **Number operations and number sense:** Surprise, surprise — these problems deal with numbers. Here's a breakdown of the two topics in this category:

  - *Number operations* are the familiar actions you take in math problems and equations, such as addition, subtraction, multiplication, and division. You probably mastered these operations in grade school; now all you have to do is practice them.

  - *Number sense* is the ability to understand numbers. You're expected to be able to recognize numbers (not a difficult task), know their relative values (that 5 is larger than 3, for example), and know how to use them (which takes us back to number operations). In addition, number sense includes the ability to *estimate* (or approximate) the result of number operations — which is always a handy skill on a timed test.

- **Measurement and geometry:** Here, you get a chance to play with mathematical shapes and manipulate them in your head. You get to use the Pythagorean relationship (or theorem) to do all sorts of interesting calculations, and you get to use measurements to do things like find the volume of ice cream in a cone or the amount of paint you need to cover a wall. If you relax, you can have fun with these questions and then maybe even use a lot of the knowledge in real life. This category breaks down into two topics:

  - *Measurement* involves area, volume, time, and the distance from here to there. Measurement of time is a good thing to know when taking any test because you want to make sure you run out of questions before you run out of time!

  - *Geometry* is the part of mathematics that deals with measurement. It also deals with relationships and properties of points, lines, angles, and planes. This branch of math requires you to draw, use, and understand diagrams.

- **Data analysis, statistics, and probability:** If you pay attention and practice the concepts in this category, you'll be able to think more clearly about the next political poll that shows that every representative of the party sponsoring the poll is good and all others are evil. This category breaks down into the following types:

  - *Data analysis* allows you to analyze data. You probably already practice this skill without realizing it. When you read about stock performance or lack of performance, calculate or read about baseball statistics, or figure out how many miles per gallon your car gets, you're doing data analysis.

  - Statistics and probability are part of data analysis. *Statistics* is the interpretation of collections of random numbers and can be used to prove one thing or another; *probability* tells you how often an event is likely to happen.

- **Algebra, functions, and patterns:** You most likely use these concepts in everyday life, although you may not know that you do. Here's a breakdown of the three types in this category:

  - *Algebra* is a form of mathematics used to solve problems by using letters to represent unknown numbers, creating equations from the information given, and solving for the unknown numbers — thus, turning them into known numbers. If you ever said something like, "How much more does the $10 scarf cost than the $7.50 one?" you were really solving this equation: $\$7.50 + x = \$10.00$.

  - *Functions* are part of mathematics. They involve the concept that one number can be determined by its relationship with another. A dozen always consists of 12 units, for example. If you were buying two dozen eggs, you'd be buying $12 \times 2 = 24$ eggs.

  - *Patterns* are the predictable repeat of a situation. For example, if someone told you the first four numbers in a pattern were 1, 2, 3, 4 and asked you what the next number was, you'd say "5" pretty fast. This simple pattern involves adding 1 to each number to get the next one. Most patterns get more complicated than this one, but, if you keep your wits about you, you can figure out how to solve them.

Make sure you understand how to solve problems involving these four math concepts. (Check out Chapter 15 for practice problems, where we walk you through strategies on solving each type of math question you'll see on the GED test.) If you already have a firm grasp on these topics, go ahead and take the practice tests in Chapters 23 and 31. However, if you need to review most of this material, read the following section and Chapter 15 for more info, and then take the mini–practice test in Chapter 16. You can check your answers and read the explanations when you're done. If you need to review certain concepts even more, be sure to do so. Then you can take the full practice tests.

# Understanding the Test Format

Math isn't scary, and it has yet to appear as the villain in any major Hollywood horror films (at least that we know about). In fact, math can even be fun when you put your mind to it. In any case, the Mathematical Reasoning test assesses your abilities in math, so you have to be ready for it. This is the one GED test subject that requires a special way of thinking and understanding — improving your ability to think mathematically will make passing this test easier.

The Mathematical Reasoning test is 115 minutes long and consists of multiple-choice, drop-down, fill-in-the-blank, and hot-spot items, but it doesn't have any type of essay question. You really have to be thankful for small mercies.

To get ready for the Math test, you first have to relax and realize that math is your friend — perhaps not a lifetime friend but a friend at least until you finish the test. You also need to consider that you've been using math all your life (and probably didn't even know it). When you tell a friend that you'll be over in 20 minutes, for example, you use math. When you see a sale sign in the store and mentally figure out whether you can afford the sale-priced item, you use math. When you complain about the poor mileage your car gets (and can prove it), you use math. You already know more math than you thought, and we show you the rest in this chapter.

# Revealing Some Helpful Prep Pointers

As you prepare for the Mathematical Reasoning test, do the following:

- **Master arithmetic fundamentals.** About half of the Math test depends on basic arithmetic (addition, subtraction, multiplication, division, decimals, and fractions). The better you know the fundamentals, the better you can do on the test.

- **Understand how to solve problems.** To get a handle on how to solve basic mathematical problems, do a lot of practice problems before the test. The more problems you solve, the more natural solving problems will become. Borrow or buy as many math books as you can, and use the sample questions in them to develop your problem-solving skills. (Be sure to get one that also provides the answers so you can check your work.) Check every answer immediately after you work the question. If you answered it incorrectly, figure out why. If you still have trouble with that problem, ask someone to explain the solution to you. You can also check online for free math quiz websites that provide worksheets with answers. YouTube is also a good place to look for lessons on how to handle a particular math problem.

- **Understand the rules of math.** Textbooks are full of rules, theorems, hypotheses, and so on. Read over as many of these rules as you can, and try to explain the main ones to a friend. If you can explain a particular rule (the Pythagorean theorem, for example) to a friend and he or she understands it, you've mastered the rule. If you can't explain it, ask someone to help you better understand the rule. If you're not sure where to start, begin by looking at the formula sheet provided on the GED test (check out an example in Chapter 23 or 31). Try to explain what each formula does and how it works.

✓ **Sign up for a math prep class or a math study group.** The loneliest time is sitting in a room staring at a wrong answer without anyone to ask why it's wrong. If you're having trouble with math, swallow your pride and enroll for a math class or study group where you can get some help and have access to someone who can answer your questions.

✓ **Take practice tests and check your answers.** See Parts VI and VII in this book for two full-length practice tests. As you take the practice tests, answer every question and adhere to the time limits. Then, be sure to check your answers. Going through the answer explanations can help you figure out which areas you need more work on. Even if you get an answer correct, reading the explanation can be helpful.

The only part of the test you can't duplicate is the feeling of sitting in the examination room just before you start the test. But the more practice tests you take, the more comfortable you'll be when test day finally arrives.

✓ **Get familiar with the calculator ahead of time.** You're probably familiar with calculators that add, subtract, multiply, and divide. The calculator included on-screen in the GED Math test is a scientific calculator, which means it does all those operations and a whole lot more, such as calculating fractions, percentages, exponents, and problems involving parentheses. Note that you won't be able to use the calculator on the first five questions of the test, and you won't necessarily use all the keys on the calculator to take the test. Many test centers require you to preview a short film on how to use the calculator before taking the Math test. Call your local administrator to find out whether the film is available at your site. If not, you can always watch it on the Internet. Check out www.youtube.com/watch?v=VoLZLsRXuKE. It's worth the time to watch it.

✓ **Read and make sure you understand what you read.** What all the GED test sections have in common is that they all assess, in one way or another, reading comprehension; if you can't read and understand the items, you can't answer them. As we mention time and time again in this book, just reading isn't always enough — you have to stop and ask yourself questions about what you read. A good way to practice this skill is to find an old math textbook. Don't worry about the grade level or even the content. If it's full of problems to solve, it'll work. Read through each problem and ask yourself these questions: What does this problem want me to find? How can I calculate it? What is the answer in general terms?

If you need more practice reading and understanding math problems, check out one of the following books (all published by Wiley):

- *Basic Math and Pre-Algebra For Dummies* by Mark Zegarelli

- *Basic Math and Pre-Algebra Workbook For Dummies* by Mark Zegarelli

- *Math Word Problems For Dummies* by Mary Jane Sterling

# Chapter 15

# Mathematical Reasoning Question Types and Solving Strategies

• • • • • • • • • • • • • • • • • • • • • • • • • • • • • • • • • • • • • • • • • • • • • • • • • • •

### In This Chapter

▶ Checking out the different Math test question types and strategies

▶ Getting familiar with the calculator and formula sheet

▶ Doing a little math to help manage your time on the test

• • • • • • • • • • • • • • • • • • • • • • • • • • • • • • • • • • • • • • • • • • • • • • • • • • •

The Mathematical Reasoning (Math) test is 115 minutes long. The first five questions are to be done without a calculator and must be attempted before you can continue, and the rest of the items may or may not need a calculator to complete. If you see the calculator icon on the screen, you can use the calculator to solve the problem. Getting a basic understanding of these question formats helps you avoid any surprises when you sit down to the take the test. The Math test presents you with questions from every area of Math. It includes arithmetic calculations, which you have to do without a calculator, to basic algebra, and more. In this chapter, we explain the four formats of questions you encounter on this test and offer advice on how to solve them with ease.

## Perfecting Your Approach with Sample Problems

New tests usually require new ways of approaching the questions in them. Although the Mathematical Reasoning test has a new format and is given on a computer, it's still about math — the same old math that has been around for several thousand years. Be careful of the format and pay particular attention to the math. The basic operations are still addition, subtraction, multiplication, and division, but you have to know how to use them to solve problems. Practice doesn't make perfect but will increase your chances of getting the correct answer to the question.

Because you're not penalized for guessing, if you don't know the answer to a question, go ahead and guess. Although you can't get a point for a blank answer, you can get a point for eliminating all but the most possible answer and marking it (if you get it right, of course).

### Making the most of multiple-choice questions

Most of the questions on the Math test are a form of multiple-choice. You're given four possible answers, and all you have to do is choose the one best answer.

### Answering basic multiple-choice questions

The multiple-choice questions on the Math test are pretty straightforward. You're given some information or a figure and asked to solve the problem based on that info. Here are a couple examples.

Milton wanted to be taller than his father, who was 2 yards tall. Milton was 5 feet 10 inches tall even when he stretched. How much taller would Milton have to grow to be taller than his father by at least an inch?

(A) 1 inch

(B) 2 inches

(C) 3 inches

(D) 4 inches

The first thing you have to do with questions like this one is make sure all measurements are in the same format. Two yards equals 6 feet (1 yard = 3 feet). So Milton is 2 inches shorter than his father. The question asks how much he would have to grow to be at least 1 inch taller than his father. If he were to grow 3 inches, he would have reached that goal. Choice (C) is correct.

Samantha was a super salesperson and by far the best salesperson at Industrial Chemical and Explosives Ltd. She was so good that she knew that she had to work for only three months not only to beat the sales records of her fellow salespeople but also to boost the total sales for the company substantially. The following chart appeared in the company's annual report. In which quarter do you think Samantha made all her sales?

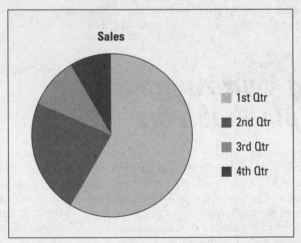

© John Wiley & Sons, Inc.

(A) 1st

(B) 2nd

(C) 3rd

(D) 4th

The graph shows that the majority of sales were made in the first quarter, and if Samantha's boasts were correct, the majority of those sales would have been made by her. In the other nine months of the year, without her sales, the sales slipped considerably. In a graph such as this one, the area of the segment of the circle represents the data.

### Extracting the info you need

Some of the questions on the Math test may have extra information that you don't need; in those cases, just ignore it. Of course, you have to make sure that the information you think is extra really is. For example, if the last question in the previous section said that Irving was the poorest salesperson the company had ever employed, that information really is extra and makes no difference to the rest of the question.

The people who write the test questions include extra information for a reason — extra information can make guessing more difficult and separate the test-takers who are paying attention from those who aren't. Sometimes, extra information is put in to make the question a bit more realistic. You don't want to disregard anything essential to solving the problem.

While reading the following question, try to visualize the situation and consider where the plot takes an extreme turn. This is usually the place where the information turns from important to irrelevant or vice versa.

Kenny, Dharma, and Sophie went out for a snack after school. The wall of their favorite burger place has the following menu:

| Item | Calories (kcal) | Fat (g) | Cost ($) |
| --- | --- | --- | --- |
| Hamburger | 780 | 44 | 4.09 |
| Bacon Cheeseburger | 340 | 15 | 4.09 |
| Chicken Wrap | 450 | 25 | 1.69 |
| French Fries | 360 | 17 | 1.59 |
| Chocolate Muffin | 450 | 15 | 2.10 |
| Chocolate Chip Cookies | 160 | 7 | 1.00 |
| Soda | 220 | 0 | 1.49 |

Their total bill came to $24.31, and after a long discussion, they decided to tip the server 15%. What was the server's tip?

(A) $2.92

(B) $3.00

(C) $3.65

(D) $4.86

The first part of this item may be interesting, but it's irrelevant. The relevant information is the part that asks about the server's tip. The only important information becomes the amount of the bill and the percentage of the tip. So you multiply the total bill by 15% to get a tip of $24.31 × 0.15 = $3.65, rounded to the nearest penny.

### Deciding what to do when you don't have enough info

Some questions may not give you enough information to solve the problem. For example, a question may ask for a conclusion that you can't make from the information given. Even if you know some information that would help you solve the problem, don't use it.

You bring with you to the test the knowledge of what the basic operations are and how to use them. You aren't expected to know the dimensions of some fictional character's room or how well a character does on her reading scores. You're expected to know how to solve problems and to leave the specifics of the problems to the GED test-makers.

Not every question on the GED Math test is solvable. If you come across a question that doesn't include enough information to solve the problem or it can't be answered with the information given, don't panic! Reread the question to make sure it can't be answered and then choose the appropriate answer choice, which is usually "not enough information given" or some variation.

Don't assume that when a question includes the answer choice "not enough information given," it's a clue to mean that you don't have enough information, because some questions that can be solved include this answer choice to make you think. Use this clue only when you've already determined that the question can't be solved.

Carmen bought a new Thunderbolt 8 as a gift to himself. He was impressed with its shiny aluminum wheels, its all-electronic dashboard, and its ventilated leather seats. The acceleration made him feel like a race car driver. He opted for rustproofing and a deluxe GPS and sound system. He negotiated with the salesperson for several hours to get a monthly payment he could barely afford. What were his annual insurance premiums if he was under 25?

(A) $4,159

(B) $4,638

(C) $5,200

(D) not enough information given

This question includes a lot of information; unfortunately, none of it pertains to the question, and Choice (D) is the only answer possible.

## Providing the answer in fill-in-the-blank items

Fill-in-the-blank items require that you fill in the answer without the benefit of four answer choices to choose from. Often, they involve some calculation, using the information provided in the item. We walk you through answering two fill-in-the-blank questions in this section.

Demitri wanted to buy a new television set. His old one had a diagonal measurement of 32 inches, but he wanted to buy a 50-inch diagonal set. The new television set would be ⬜ inches wider, measured diagonally

To answer this question, you have to find the difference between the two TV sets. The new set would be 50 – 32 = 18 inches wider, measured diagonally.

Carol found a part-time job to augment her scholarship. She was paid $13.45 an hour and was promised a 15% raise after three months. Business had been very poor during that period, and the owner of the business called Carol in to explain that he could afford only an 11% raise but would reassess the raise in the next quarter depending on how business was. With this raise, Carol's new hourly rate would be ⬜.

Carol's new salary would be calculated at the rate of $13.45 times 11%, or $13.45 × 1.11 = $14.93 (to the nearest penny). If you want to calculate the amount of an 11% raise, you can multiply by 111% (100% + 11% = 111%, or 1.11 expressed as a decimal).

# Using the Mathematical Reasoning Test's Special Features

During the Mathematical Reasoning test, you can use the built-in calculator for all but the first five questions. Before you start celebrating, remember that the calculator is an instrument that makes calculations easier. It doesn't solve problems or perform other miracles. You still have to solve the problems, using the computer between your ears.

The test also has a formula sheet. This feature also isn't a miracle to work out problems for you. It's just a memory aid if you don't remember the formulas. And as a special treat, the Math test also provides symbols for you to use in the fill-in-the blank items as needed. We explore all these features in the following sections.

## Solving questions with and without a calculator

For all but the first five items in the Math test, you can use a calculator. You have to finish the first five items before you go on to questions that use the calculator. To pull up the calculator on the computerized GED Math test, click on the calculator icon. A calculator — a Texas Instruments TI-30XS calculator to be exact — appears on-screen.

It's a good idea to get familiar with the calculator before taking the GED test. You can either use the one on the GED Testing Service website for practice or find an identical hand-held one. The computer version of the calculator operates just like the hand-held device. Then make sure you know how to solve the various types of mathematical problems and depend on the calculator only to do mechanical operations quicker and easier.

Often, solving a problem without a calculator is easier, especially with multiple-choice questions where you have four answer choices to choose from. And the more questions you practice in your head, the easier it will be. Here are some ways to practice solving problems in your head (without a calculator):

- When you go shopping, add up the items as you put them in the cart.
- Calculate discounts off items you see or buy when you shop.
- Be the first at your table in a restaurant to figure out the tip. And for bonus practice, figure out different tip percentages on your bill, such as 10, 15, 18, and 20 percent tips.

For multiple-choice questions, sometimes estimating the answer to a question is easier and faster. For example, $4.2 \times 8.9$ is almost $4 \times 9$, which equals 36. If you see only one answer choice that's close to 36, that answer is probably correct. If you see that all the answer choices are close to 36, however, you need to spend time calculating the exact answer. Although you may be able to solve problems in your head, always work them out to verify you have the correct answer.

## Refreshing your memory with the formula sheet

The GED Math test includes a formula sheet with a list of formulas you may need for the test. You simply click on the formula icon to make the page of formulas appear. Unfortunately, no genie will appear to tell you which formula to use. Figuring out which formula you need is your job.

To get familiar with the formulas you may need on the GED test, study the formulas in this book (you can find a list of formulas in the practice tests in Chapters 23 and 31), and make sure you know their purpose. Then make sure you understand what kind of problem you can use each formula for. For example, if you have a formula for the volume of a rectangular cube and the question asks you how many cubic feet of water a swimming pool contains, you know this formula will let you work out the answer. If the question asks you how many tiles it'd take to go around the rim of the pool, you need another formula.

## Inserting special symbols

When answering fill-in-the-blank items, you sometimes need special symbols. Fortunately, the Math test provides such symbols on the screen behind the special icon. These formulas are mainly math operators, such as add or subtract, greater than or less than, and so on. You have to know what they mean and how to use them. To make a symbol appear in the fill-in-the-blank box on the test, click on the symbols icon, and then click on the symbol you want to include in the box.

# Managing Your Time for the Math Test

Try not to be intimidated by the word *math* or the subject as a whole. A math teacher once said that mathematicians are lazy people — they always use the easiest way to find the right answer. We don't want to insult or irritate any mathematicians by calling them lazy, but finding the easiest way to solve a problem is usually the right way. If your way is too long and complicated, it's probably not right.

The Mathematical Reasoning test allows you 115 minutes to complete 50 questions. You must answer the first five items without using the calculator, and then the rest follow after you have answered these five questions. The rest of your time is yours to divide any way you see fit. Just remember that you have to answer a question to get a mark.

On the computerized GED test, each question is given a specific number of points depending on how difficult it is. That means that each version of the test may have a different number of questions, but each test has the same number of points. Don't worry if you find out after you leave that you had fewer or more items than a friend. It will all work out.

To help you manage your time for the Math test, check out the following suggestions (refer to Chapters 3 for some general time-management tips):

✔ **Stay on schedule.** Being able to manage your time is the most important indicator of success on the Math test. If you can keep to your schedule of less than 1½ minutes per question, you'll have enough time to go over your answers and make any changes necessary after you finish solving all the questions.

With such a tight schedule for taking the Math test, you have no time to panic. Aside from the fact that panicking distracts you from your overall goal, it also takes time — and you have very little time to spare. So relax and just do your best — save the panicking for another day.

✔ **Know when to move ahead.** If you don't see what's being asked by a question within a few seconds, reread the question and try again. If it still isn't clear, go on to the next question. Spending all your time trying to solve one problem at the expense of the others isn't a good idea. If you have time left at the end, you can always go back.

✔ **Keep an eye on the time.** The timer on the computer screen is your only time-management tool. You're not allowed to bring any electronics into the testing area.

# Chapter 16

# Practicing Sample Mathematical Reasoning Problems

● ● ● ● ● ● ● ● ● ● ● ● ● ● ● ● ● ● ● ● ● ● ● ● ● ● ● ● ● ● ● ● ● ● ● ● ● ● ● ● ● ● ●

*T*he best way to get ready for the Mathematical Reasoning test is to practice. The problems on this test evaluate your skills in a wide variety of areas, so check out the sample problems in this chapter to help you prepare for all of them. At the end of this chapter, you find detailed answer explanations for you to check your answers.

Record your answers either directly in this book or on a separate sheet of paper, if you think you might want to try these practice questions again at a later date. The Mathematical Reasoning test doesn't include an Extended Response or Short Answer item, like the other test sections do, so there's no need for extra sheets of lined paper. (Writing an essay about quadratic equations or the beauty of exponents — now *that* would be painful.)

Remember, this is just preliminary practice. We want you to get used to answering different types of Mathematical Reasoning questions. Use the complete practice tests in Parts VI and VII to time your work and replicate the real test-taking experience.

## *Mathematical Reasoning Practice Questions*

The following Math practice questions test your knowledge of Mathematical operations and reading skills in Math. Read the items carefully, making sure you understand what's being asked. You may have to convert some units of measurement to another, but in all cases, they'll make sense. For example, if you see the measurement for a wall is 120-something high, read the problem carefully because the wall was probably measured in inches and not feet.

1. Vlad is shopping for a new shirt because all the stores are having end-of-season sales. Sam's Special Shirts offers Vlad 20% off all his purchases while Hardworking Harry's Haberdashery has a special sale offering five shirts for the price of four. Which is the better deal?

   (A) neither

   (B) Sam's Special Shirts

   (C) both are the same

   (D) Hardworking Harry's Haberdashery

2. Olga designed a logo consisting of an equilateral triangle in a circle for a new company. She designed it with one vertex of the triangle pointing northeast. The client said she liked the design but preferred that the vertex of the triangle point due south. What rotation would Olga have to perform to satisfy her client?

   (A) 90 degrees to the right

   (B) 110 degrees to the right

   (C) 135 degrees to the left

   (D) 135 degrees to the right

3. Solve the following equation for $x$:

   $x = 2y + 6z - y^2$, if $y = 6$ and $z = 2$

   (A) 12

   (B) 11

   (C) –12

   (D) –11

*Question 4 refers to the following table.*

| Make and Model | Price |
|---|---|
| Hopper Model A1 | $249.99 |
| Vacuous Vacuum Company Model ZZ3 | $679.99 |
| Clean-R-Up Special Series | $179.00 |
| Electrified Home Upright | $749.99 |
| Super Suction 101 | $568.99 |

4. Pierre is looking for a vacuum cleaner for his apartment. He is on a limited budget and wants to spend the least he can for his purchase. He has been told by his best friend that spending around the mean amount for a vacuum cleaner will get him an average unit. His father claims that spending about the median amount is the smartest way to get a good deal. _____ comes the closest to satisfying both criteria.

5. Evaluate the following formula to two decimal places:

   $N = \sqrt{a + c - 2ac}$, if $a = 25$ and $c = 9$

   (A) 34.67

   (B) 20.40

   (C) 22.47

   (D) no answer

6. Solve the following equation for $x$: $3x + 12 = 24$. $x =$

   (A) 12

   (B) 3

   (C) 4

   (D) 5

7. Rachel and Ronda were planning for their first apartment, and they decided to split the required shopping tasks. Rachel was responsible for finding out how much it would cost to carpet their living room, and Ronda was responsible for finding out how much it would cost to paint the walls in the bedroom. What formula would they need to use to get an answer that would let them figure out the price for each job?

   (A) $P = 2(l + w)$

   (B) $A = l \times w$

   (C) $V = l \times w \times d$

   (D) $A = \pi r^2$

8. Lillian is drawing a scale diagram of her apartment to take with her while shopping for rugs. If she has taken all the measurements in the apartment, what mathematical relationship would she use to draw the scale drawing?

    (A) decimals

    (B) exponents

    (C) ratios

    (D) addition

9. Sylvia couldn't fall asleep one night and got to wondering how much water her bedroom would hold if she filled it to the ceiling. She had previously measured all the walls and knew all the measurements, including length, width, and height. She should use [          ] to calculate how many cubic feet of water would be needed to fill the room.

10. Alvin is drawing a diagram of his room. He has drawn the line representing the floor and is ready to draw the line representing the wall. This line would be _____ to the line representing the floor.

    (A) congruent

    (B) parallel

    (C) similar

    (D) perpendicular

11. Aaron wants to paint the floor of his apartment. His living room/dining room is 19 feet by 16 feet, his bedroom is 12 feet by 14 feet, and his hallways are 6 feet by 8 feet. Bowing to pressure from his friends, he has decided not to paint the floor of the kitchen or the bathroom. How many square feet of floor must he paint?

    (A) 304

    (B) 520

    (C) 250

    (D) 216

*Question 12 refers to the following table.*

| Week | Calories Consumed Per Week | Weight (Pounds) | Height (Feet/Inches) |
|------|----------------------------|-----------------|----------------------|
| 1 | 12,250 | 125 | 5 ft. 1.5 in. |
| 2 | 15,375 | 128 | 5 ft. 1.5 in. |
| 3 | 13,485 | 128 | 5 ft. 1.5 in. |
| 4 | 16,580 | 130 | 5 ft. 1.5 in. |
| 5 | 15,285 | 129 | 5 ft. 1.5 in. |

12. Alan kept track of his caloric intake, his weight, and his height for a period of five weeks. What conclusion can you draw from his observations?

    (A) Eating a lot makes you taller.

    (B) Eating more calories will make you gain weight.

    (C) Gaining weight will make you taller.

    (D) There's no correlation between the data presented.

13. On Monday, Mary walked 12 blocks. On Tuesday, she walked 10 blocks, and on Wednesday, she walked 14 blocks. If she wants to beat her average trip for those three days on Thursday, at least how many blocks must she walk?

    (A) 10

    (B) 11

    (C) 9

    (D) 13

14. Hassan has developed a new trick to play on his classmates. He asks them to write down their ages and multiply by 4, divide by 2, then subtract 6, and, finally, add 8. When they tell him the resulting number, Hassan can always tell them their age. If one of his friends tells Hassan the resultant number is 52, how old is he?

    (A) 33

    (B) 25

    (C) 52

    (D) 24

*Question 15 refers to the following table.*

| a | b | F |
|---|---|---|
| 1 | 2 | −16 |
| 2 | 1 | −3 |
| 3 | 2 | −18 |
| 2 | 3 | −35 |
| 3 | 4 | x |

15. Herman developed the following function to amuse himself: $F = 2a + 3b^2 - 2ab$. He kept track of his results in this table.

    Using Herman's function, what is the value of $x$?

    (A) 53

    (B) −82

    (C) 88

    (D) 30

16. Calvin and Kelvin, carpenters extraordinaire, are building a staircase for their clients, the Coalmans. The stairway is to bridge a space 10 feet high, and the distance from the front of the bottom step to the back of the top step is 14 feet. What is the slope of the stairway to 2 decimal places?

    (A) 0.69

    (B) 0.70

    (C) 0.71

    (D) 0.72

*Questions 17–18 refer to the following information.*

April is considering two apartments. They are of equal size except for the bedrooms. Bedroom A is 19 feet by 14 feet, and bedroom B is 17 feet by 16 feet.

17. How many square feet larger is the larger bedroom?

   (A) 8

   (B) 7

   (C) 6

   (D) 5

18. April wants an area rug for the larger bedroom that would cover the floor, leaving a space 1 foot from each wall. If the rug had a 1-inch fringe all the way around it, how many feet long would the fringe be?

   (A) 58

   (B) 29

   (C) 85

   (D) 55

*Questions 19–20 refer to the following table, which shows the results Julio got from measuring and interviewing several of his classmates about their heights and birth months.*

| Month of Birth | Height |
|---|---|
| March | 5 ft. 4 in. |
| June | 5 ft. 6 in. |
| March | 5 ft. 1 in. |
| January | 5 ft. 8 in. |
| August | 5 ft. 5 in. |
| January | 5 ft. 6 in. |

19. What month would produce the shortest people according to these measurements?

   (A) January

   (B) March

   (C) June

   (D) August

20. From the graph of Julio's results, what conclusion, if any, can be reached?

   (A) No conclusions can be reached.

   (B) People born in March are shorter.

   (C) People born in the warm months are similar in height.

   (D) Two of Julio's classmates were born in each of January and March.

21. Susie is shopping for a few groceries. She buys a loaf of bread for $1.29 and a half gallon of milk for $1.47. She sees her favorite cheese on sale for $2.07. If she has $5.00 in her purse, can she buy the cheese if there is no tax on food?

    (A) unsure

    (B) yes

    (C) not enough money

    (D) not enough information

*Question 22 refers to the following table.*

| **Annual Production of the Wonderful World of Widgets** | |
| --- | --- |
| *Year* | *Annual Production (In Million Units)* |
| 2013 | 43 |
| 2012 | 29 |
| 2011 | 72 |
| 2010 | 70 |
| 2009 | 71 |

22. The general manager of the Wonderful World of Widgets wants to present these figures in a visual, easily understood way to the board of directors to help them understand the effect that the downturn in the economy is having on the production of widgets. What would be the best way to present the figures?

    (A) a graph

    (B) a series of tables

    (C) verbal descriptions

    (D) a movie of how widgets are used in America

23. Mark the points (3, 1), (−4, −3), and (−5, 5) on the graph to draw a geometric figure, and identify the figure.

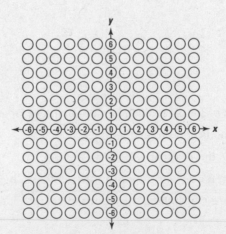

24. Georgio wants to climb a ladder perched beside his house to check the condition of the eaves, which are 22 feet above the ground. For safety, the ladder should be placed 10 feet from the house. The minimum length of ladder he would need to reach the eaves, rounded up to the nearest foot, would be [＿＿＿＿＿] feet.

25. Where are all the points with an *x*-coordinate of –4 located on a graph?

    (A) 4 units above the *x*-axis

    (B) 4 units to the left of the *x*-axis

    (C) 4 units above the *y*-axis

    (D) 4 units to the left of the *y*-axis

*Question 26 refers to the following table.*

### Age at Marriage for Those Who Divorce in America

| Age | Women | Men |
| --- | --- | --- |
| Under 20 years old | 27.6% | 11.7% |
| 20 to 24 years old | 36.6% | 38.8% |
| 25 to 29 years old | 16.4% | 22.3% |
| 30 to 34 years old | 8.5% | 11.6% |
| 35 to 39 years old | 5.1% | 6.5% |

26. Which of the following must be true, based on the information in this table, in order to reduce the chance of divorce?

    (A) Younger women should marry older men.

    (B) Older men should marry younger women.

    (C) Fewer men get divorced than women.

    (D) You can't draw any of these conclusions from this table.

27. The students in a math class are looking at the equation $A = l \times w$. The teacher asks what result doubling the length *(l)* would have on the area *(A)*. What answer is correct?

    (A) makes it two times larger

    (B) makes it four times larger

    (C) makes it three times larger

    (D) can't determine the result without the value of *w*

28. A wall is 20 feet long and 8 feet high. If all of it is to be painted with two coats of blue paint, how many square feet of wall have to be covered?

    (A) 56

    (B) 160

    (C) 230

    (D) 320

29. Where on a graph would the point (–4, –4) be?

    (A) four units to the right and four units below the corresponding axis

    (B) four units to the left and four units below the corresponding axis

    (C) four units to the left and four units above the corresponding axis

    (D) four units to the right and four units above the corresponding axis

30. Roger and Ekua went shopping together. Ekua spent twice as much for clothing as Roger did. If their total expenditure for clothing was $90.00, how much did Roger spend for clothing?
    $ [_____]

    *Question 31 refers to the following table.*

| Subject | Height | Shoe Size |
|---------|--------|-----------|
| 1 | 5 in. 3 ft. | 5 |
| 2 | 5 in. 9 ft. | 8 |
| 3 | 5 in. 6 ft. | 5½ |
| 4 | 6 in. 1 ft. | 10 |
| 5 | 5 in. 7 ft. | 6 |

31. Althea has a theory about the men in her class. She has decided that the taller men have larger shoe sizes than the shorter men. To prove her theory, she asked several of the men to measure themselves and tell her their shoe sizes. From her observations, she created the preceding table.

    Using her observations, Althea decided to see whether there's any credibility to her theory. If she calculated the median height of her subjects, what would be the corresponding shoe size?

    (A) 5

    (B) 6

    (C) 8

    (D) 10

32. Felix and Francis have just bought new cars. Felix, being American, has a car with a speedometer graduated in customary units. Francis, being Canadian, has a speedometer graduated in metric units. When they're driving in Felix's car at a speed of 55 miles per hour and if 1 mile equals approximately 1.6 kilometers, what would Francis's speedometer read in kilometers per hour (rounded to the nearest number)?

    (A) 160

    (B) 88

    (C) 55

    (D) 77

33. The reading on the illustrated meter is [          ].

*Question 34 refers to the following table, which shows Sheila's marks in her final year of high school.*

| Subject | Grade (%) |
|---|---|
| Literature | 94 |
| Mathematics | 88 |
| Physical Education | 86 |
| Science | 92 |
| Spanish | 90 |

34. The result on Sheila's mean grade after a 6-point drop in her Spanish grade would be [          ].

35. Barry earns $1,730 per month after taxes. Each month, he spends $900 for rent and $600 for living expenses like food and utilities. After all his expenses are paid, he has $[          ] left over to buy luxuries and spend on entertainment.

*Questions 36–37 refer to the following table.*

| Car Manufacturer | Sales — July 2013 (In Thousands) | Sales — July 2012 (In Thousands) | % Change |
|---|---|---|---|
| Commonwealth | 90 | 105 | −14 |
| Frisky | 175 | 147 | +19 |
| Goodenough | 236 | 304 | −22 |
| Horsesgalore | 99 | 64 | +55 |
| Silkyride | 24 | 16 | +50 |

36. From the table, which car manufacturer showed the greatest percentage increase in sales?

(A) Commonwealth

(B) Frisky

(C) Goodenough

(D) Horsesgalore

37. From the table, which of the following conclusions could be drawn from the data?

    (A) Car sales are increasing across the board.

    (B) Car sales are decreasing across the board.

    (C) Large manufacturers are selling more cars.

    (D) No generalization is possible from this data.

*Question 38 refers to the following table.*

| Person Interviewed | Flavor Preference | | | |
|---|---|---|---|---|
| | **Chocolate** | **Vanilla** | **Strawberry** | **Peanut** |
| Donalda's mother | No | No | Yes | No |
| Donalda's father | No | No | Yes | No |
| Donalda's brother | No | No | No | Yes |
| Donalda's sister | No | No | Yes | No |

38. Donalda collected the information in the table as part of her research on the most popular flavor of ice cream. After interviewing several subjects and recording her data into the table, she came up with the following conclusions. Which is the most believable?

    (A) Nobody likes chocolate ice cream.

    (B) Nobody likes vanilla ice cream.

    (C) Strawberry ice cream is the most popular flavor in the world.

    (D) No conclusion is possible from this data.

# Answers and Explanations

1. **C. both are the same.** In this case, five shirts for the price of four represents a 20% discount. Consider buying four shirts for $10 each and getting one more free. Your five shirts would cost you $40, or an average price of $8 each, which is 20% off the regular price ($10). Keep in mind that the same prices are often stated in different ways.

2. **C. 135 degrees to the left.** If you visualize the equilateral triangle drawn within the circle with one vertex pointing northeast, you can see that the vertex is 45 degrees above the horizontal, which is due east. Due south would be at the halfway point of the circle or at 180 degrees. Simply subtract 45 degrees (the initial position) from 180 degrees (the final position) to discover that the vertex has traveled 135 degrees to the right. To go from due east to due south requires a rotation of 90 degrees to the right. The entire rotation would consist of 45 degrees + 90 degrees = 135 degrees to the right. If reading about this problem is confusing, draw it. Diagrams often make problems easier to visualize.

3. **C. –12.** You can solve this equation by substituting 6 for $y$ and 2 for $z$, which produces this equation: $2(6) + 6(2) – 6^2 = –12$.

4. **Super Suction 101.** You can calculate the mean price by adding all the prices and dividing the sum by the number of prices: ($249.99 + $679.99 + $179.00 + $749.99 + $568.99)/5 = $485.59. To determine the median price, you put all the prices in order; the middle one is the median. In this case, the median is $568.99 because it's in the middle of the prices: $749.99, $679.99, $568.99, $249.99, and $179.00. The machine that comes closest to satisfying both criteria is the Super Suction 101 because its price is the same as the median. The difference between the price of the Super Suction 101 and the mean price is $568.99 – $485.59 = $83.40. The difference between the price of the Hopper Model A1 and the mean price is $485.59 – $249.99 = $235.60, leaving the Super Suction 101 the clear mathematical winner.

One thing to keep in mind is that the mathematical problems on this test aren't always reflections of reality. The technique used for buying vacuum cleaners in this question isn't a reasonable way of buying anything, but it's a good question because it tests your knowledge of the mean, median, and subtraction.

5. **D. no answer.** You can't find the square root of a negative number, and $2ac$ will always be larger than $a + c$, which makes the difference of the two negative.

6. **C. 4.** If $3x + 12 = 24$, you can subtract 12 from both sides so that $3x = 24 - 12$, or $3x = 12$; then divide both sides by 3 to find $x$, or $x = 4$. Again, remember the cardinal rule of equations: Whatever you do to one side, you must do to the other.

7. **B. $A = l \times w$.** In each case, Rachel and Ronda have to calculate the area of the space they're dealing with to get a price for the carpet and the paint. The formula for area is $A = l \times w$.

8. **C. ratios.** A scale drawing involves representing one dimension with a smaller one while keeping the shape of the room the same. Lillian may have decided to represent 1 foot in real life by 1 inch on her drawing (a ratio of 1 foot to 1 inch), resulting in a 12-foot wall being represented by a 12-inch line. Not all the answers are mathematical relationships and would have to be excluded immediately.

9. **multiplication.** The formula to calculate the volume of a room is to multiply the length by the width by the height. (On the GED test, the formula for calculating volume is listed on the formula sheet.)

10. **D. perpendicular.** The line is perpendicular because walls are perpendicular to floors (if they weren't, the room would probably collapse).

11. **B. 520.** To find the total area, you must multiply the length by the width for each area. The area of the living room/dining room is $19 \times 16 = 304$ square feet, the area of the bedroom is $12 \times 14 = 168$ square feet, and the area of the hallway is $6 \times 8 = 48$ square feet. The total area is the sum of the room areas or $304 + 168 + 48 = 520$ square feet.

12. **B. Eating more calories will make you gain weight.** The more Alan ate, the heavier he became (which represents a possible causal relationship). The table provides no basis for the other answers.

    If two values change in tune with each other, they have a *correlating* relationship. For example, there's a positive correlation between height and age during the teenage years. In other words, you get taller as you get older. If one event leads to another or causes another, the events form a *causal* relationship. For example, eating all the red jellybeans alters the percentage of orange jellybeans in a mixture of equal numbers of each color because eating a red jellybean removes it from the pool of jellybeans, which originally had the same number of each color. As a result, the percentage of orange jellybeans increases.

13. **D. 13.** Mary's average trip for those three days was $(12 + 10 + 14)/3 = 36/3 = 12$ blocks. To beat her average, she has to walk 13 blocks on Thursday. If she walks 12 blocks, she will equal (not beat) her average trip. All the other answers are less than her average.

14. **B. 25.** Hassan knows that multiplication and division are opposite operations, which means that multiplying by 4 and dividing by 2 produces a number twice the original. Addition and subtraction are opposites, too, so subtracting 6 and adding 8 results in a number 2 larger than the original. If the number Hassan's friend tells him is 52, Hassan simply has to subtract 2 from the resultant number (52) and divide by 2, giving him an answer of 25. Or Hassan could start with 52 and then work backward (first subtracting 8 then adding 6 and so on) through the directions to arrive at the correct answer.

15. **D. 30.** Using Herman's function, $x = 2(3) - 3(4)(4) - 2(3)(4) = 6 + 48 - 24 = 30$.

16. **C. 0.71.** To calculate the slope, you have to divide the rise by the run. That is $\frac{10}{14} = 0.7142857$, or 0.71 to 2 decimal places.

The *slope* of a line is rise over run. Thus, the slope of a stairway is equal to the distances above the floor of the last step over the distance from the front of the first step to the back of the top step.

17. **C. 6.** The area of Bedroom A is 19 × 14 = 266 square feet. The area of Bedroom B is 17 × 16 = 272 square feet. Bedroom B is larger by 272 – 266 = 6 square feet.

18. **A. 58.** The measure of the fringe is the perimeter of the rug. Because the rug would cover the floor 1 foot in from each wall, the length of the rug would be 17 – 2 = 15 feet, and the width would be 16 – 2 = 14 feet. The reason you have to subtract 2 from each measurement is that the rug would be 1 foot from each wall, resulting in a rug that was 2 feet shorter than the room in each dimension. Perimeter = 2($l$ + $w$), where $l$ is the length and $w$ is the width, so the perimeter of the rug = 2(15 + 14) = 2(29) = 58 feet.

19. **B. March.** March would produce the shortest person according to the table of observations. With so few subjects, none of them random, this would never be considered a real theory but a bit of mathematical fun.

20. **D. Two of Julio's classmates were born in each of January and March.** The only conclusion that can be reached from such a small sample is about the number of his classmates who were born in each month.

21. **B. yes.** The simplest way to solve this problem is to add the cost of the bread and milk to get $2.76, and then add the price of the cheese ($2.07) to get a total of $4.83, which is less than $5.00. You can also estimate the result by using approximations and adding $1.30 and $1.50 to get $2.80, and then adding $2.10 for the cheese for a total of $4.90, which is less than $5.00. Using approximations can help you answer some questions quickly and give you an idea of whether an answer you achieved using a calculator makes sense.

22. **A. a graph.** A graph is a visual representation of data; it's easily understood and can be used to compare data visually. You could use some of the other choices to represent the data, but they would all be more complex than a graph.

23. Because there are only three points on the graph, the figure is a triangle.

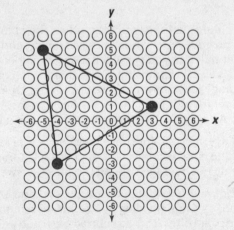

Be prepared to draw graphs from data presented, but always remember that the only way to draw a graph for a question on this test is to use a coordinate-plane grid, which has size limitations. Always be sure that your graph makes sense. If the trend is declining, the graph should be headed downward toward the *x*-axis (horizontal axis). Negative values always appear on the left side of the *y*-axis (vertical axis) or below the *x*-axis.

24. **25.** You can represent a ladder perched against a house by a right-angled triangle with the vertical height of 22 feet and a base of 10 feet. The ladder represents the hypotenuse of the triangle. To calculate the length of the ladder, you have to use the Pythagorean theorem. If you represent the length of the ladder as $x = \sqrt{10^2 + 22^2} = \sqrt{100 + 484} = 24.166091$, because you want the ladder to be long enough to reach the wall, the length has to be rounded up to 25 feet.

Pythagoras, a Greek mathematician, proved that the square of the hypotenuse of a right-angled triangle is equal to the sum of the squares of the other two sides. The *hypotenuse* is the side opposite the right angle. You find the Pythagorean theorem on the formula sheet you get with your test, so don't forget to check it for important information you may need as you work through the questions.

25. **D. 4 units to the left of the *y*-axis.** All points with *x*-coordinates that are negative are located to the left of the *y*-axis (the vertical axis). Therefore, if a point has an *x*-coordinate of –4, it's located on a line 4 units to the left of the *y*-axis.

26. **D. You can't draw conclusions from this table.** This table is a compilation of statistics and reflects the situation as of the date the statistics were gathered. You can't realistically draw conclusions from this type of data, except to state things such as, "5.1 percent of women aged 35 to 39 got divorced." Just because someone presents you with a table of data doesn't mean you can draw general conclusions from it.

27. **A. makes it two times larger.** In this linear equation, any multiple of one term results in the same multiple of the answer. Multiplying *l* by 2 results in multiplying *A* by 2.

As you prepare for the Mathematical Reasoning section of the GED test, you definitely want to remember this rule about equations: Whatever you do to one side, you must do to the other side.

28. **D. 320.** The area of the wall is 20 × 8 = 160 square feet. Each coat requires that you paint 160 square feet, but because you have to paint two coats, the answer is 2 × 160 = 320. If your first choice for the answer was Choice (B), you forgot about the second coat of paint. If you picked Choice (A), you confused perimeter with area. Remember that *perimeter* is the distance all the way around an object — in this case, 2(20 + 8) = 56. Choice (C) is the correct answer with the first two digits reversed (in other words, it's a reminder to check your answers carefully!). Reversing digits under the stress of time limits isn't impossible or unusual.

29. **B. four units to the left and four units below the corresponding axis.** Because both coordinates are negative, the point would have to be the corresponding distance to the left and below the corresponding axis.

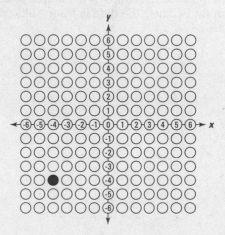

30. **30.00.** If you use $x$ to represent the amount of money Roger spent, the amount of money that Ekua spent is $2x$. You can represent their total spending by the equation $90 = x + 2x$ or $3x = 90$, in which case $x = 30$. So Roger spent $30.00 for clothing.

31. **B. 67.** In order to figure out the corresponding shoe size, you have to calculate the median heights of the subjects. In order to do that, you have to convert all heights into inches.

| Subject | Height (inches) | Shoe Size |
|---------|-----------------|-----------|
| 1 | 63 | 5 |
| 2 | 69 | 8 |
| 3 | 66 | 5½ |
| 4 | 73 | 10 |
| 5 | 67 | 6 |

The median is 67 inches (middle value of values in order).

The shoe size that corresponds to the median height is 6. It is worth noting that Althea doesn't have a statistically significant theory because her sample is too small and not random. Statistics can be useful but not if they are not properly gathered.

32. **B. 88.** Because 1 mile = 1.6 kilometers, 55 miles = 88 kilometers ($55 \times 1.6$). The speeds are both in units per hour, so 55 mph = 88 kph.

33. **1,483.** Read the gauge carefully to find the answer.

34. **88.8.** The mean mark with Sheila's grade in Spanish falling 6 points would be $(94 + 88 + 86 + 92 + 84)/5 = 88.8$.

35. **230.** Barry spends $900 + $600 = $1,500 for rent and living expenses. He has $1,730 − $1,500 = $230 left over.

36. **D. Horsesgalore.** The greatest percentage increase was Horsesgalore with a 55% increase in sales.

37. **D. No generalization is possible from this data.** From the data given, no generalization is possible; some big manufacturers have rising sales, and some have falling sales. This fact eliminates the first three choices.

38. **D. No conclusion is possible from this data.** The sample Donalda used is too small and possibly biased because the subjects are all related. A proper sample in an experiment is selected randomly. Because the data is from a biased sample, no conclusions can be drawn from the results.

# Part VI
# Putting Your Skills to the Test: GED Practice Test 1

## Top Five Ways to Duplicate the GED Test Environment

✔ Find a quiet place to work, where you won't be distracted or interrupted. Put away cell-phones, music players, and all other electronic devices. They won't be permitted on test day.

✔ Use the answer sheet provided and record your answers with a pencil.

✔ Set a timer to count down from the total time allocated for each section of the test.

✔ *Don't* go to the next section of the test until the time allotted for the current section is up. If you finish early, check your work for that section only.

✔ Don't take a break during any test section; however, give yourself exactly one ten-minute break on the Reasoning Through Language Arts test before writing the Extended Response.

# In this part . . .

✔ See how your stamina measures up by taking a full-length GED practice test, including Extended Response prompts for the RLA and Social Studies test sections.

✔ Score your test quickly with the answer key.

✔ Discover how to improve your performance by reading through the answer explanations for all practice test questions and evaluating your Extended Responses.

# Chapter 17

# Practice Test 1: Reasoning through Language Arts

· · · · · · · · · · · · · · · · · · · · · · · · · · · · · · · · · · · · · · · · · · · · · · · · · · · · · · · · · · ·

**Y**ou're ready to take a crack at a full-blown practice GED Reasoning through Language Arts test. You're feeling good and ready to go (well, maybe not, but you're at least smart enough to know that this practice is good for you).

You have 95 minutes to complete the question-and-answer section and then another 45 minutes to write the Extended Response (a separate item). You get a ten-minute break before starting the Extended Response. Remember, you can't save time from one section to use in the other.

The answers and explanations to this test's questions are in Chapter 18. Go through the explanations to all the questions, even for the ones you answered correctly. The explanations are a good review of the techniques we discuss throughout the book.

Unless you require accommodations, you'll be taking the GED test on a computer. Instead of marking your answers on a separate answer sheet, like you do for the practice tests in this book, you'll see clickable ovals and fill-in-the-blank text boxes, and you'll be able to click with your mouse and drag and drop items where indicated. We formatted the questions and answer choices in this book to make them appear as similar as possible to the real GED test, but we had to retain some A, B, C, D choices for marking your answers, and we provide a separate answer sheet for you to do so. Also, to make it simpler for you to time yourself, we present the questions in one unit rather than two units and the Extended Response at the end of the test.

# Answer Sheet for Practice Test 1, Reasoning through Language Arts

| | | | | |
|---|---|---|---|---|
| 1. | A | B | C | D |
| 2. | A | B | C | D |
| 3. | | | | |
| 4. | A | B | C | D |
| 5. | A | B | C | D |
| 6. | A | B | C | D |
| 7. | A | B | C | D |
| 8. | A | B | C | D |
| 9. | A | B | C | D |
| 10. | A | B | C | D |
| 11. | A | B | C | D |
| 12. | A | B | C | D |
| 13. | A | B | C | D |
| 14. | A | B | C | D |
| 15. | A | B | C | D |
| 16. | A | B | C | D |
| 17. | A | B | C | D |
| 18. | A | B | C | D |
| 19. | A | B | C | D |
| 20. | A | B | C | D |
| 21. | A | B | C | D |
| 22. | A | B | C | D |
| 23. | A | B | C | D |
| 24. | | | | |
| 25. | A | B | C | D |
| 26. | | | | |
| 27. | | | | |
| 28. | A | B | C | D |
| 29. | A | B | C | D |
| 30. | A | B | C | D |

| | | | | |
|---|---|---|---|---|
| 31. | A | B | C | D |
| 32. | A | B | C | D |
| 33. | A | B | C | D |
| 34. | A | B | C | D |
| 35. | A | B | C | D |
| 36. | | | | |
| 37. | | | | |
| 38. | A | B | C | D |
| 39. | A | B | C | D |
| 40. | | | | |
| 41. | A | B | C | D |
| 42. | | | | |
| 43. | A | B | C | D |
| 44. | A | B | C | D |
| 45. | | | | |
| 46. | A | B | C | D |
| 47. | A | B | C | D |
| 48. | A | B | C | D |
| 49. | A | B | C | D |
| 50. | | | | |
| 51. | A | B | C | D |
| 52. | A | B | C | D |
| 53. | A | B | C | D |
| 54. | | | | |
| 55. | A | B | C | D |
| 56. | A | B | C | D |
| 57. | A | B | C | D |
| 58. | A | B | C | D |
| 59. | A | B | C | D |
| 60. | A | B | C | D |

# Reasoning through Language Arts Test

**Time:** 95 minutes

**Directions:** You may answer the questions in this section in any order. Mark your answers on the answer sheet provided.

> *Questions 1–5 refer to the following excerpt, written by Dale Shuttleworth (originally printed in the* Toronto Star, *January 2008).*

### What Is the History of the Social Enterprise Movement?

Line    The Center for Social Innovation, a renovated warehouse in the Spadina Ave. area of
Toronto, houses 85 "social enterprises," including organizations concerned with the environment, the arts, social justice, education, health, technology, and design. Tribute has
been paid to the "social enterprise movement" in Quebec and Vancouver for providing the
(05)   impetus for this very successful venture.

Toronto, Ontario, also has provided leadership in the areas of community education and
community economic development — essential components in the creation of social enterprises. In 1974, the Toronto Board of Education assisted in the establishment of the Learnxs
Foundation Inc. as part of its Learning Exchange System.

(10)   The foundation represented an additional source of support for the burgeoning "alternatives in education" movement. In 1973, the Ontario government had imposed ceilings on
educational spending and, together with reduced revenue due to declining enrollment, the
Toronto board had limited means to fund innovative and experimental programs. The
Learnxs Foundation was an independent "arms-length" nonprofit charitable enterprise,
(15)   which could solicit funds from public and private sources and generate revenue through the
sale of goods and services to support innovative programs within the Toronto system.

What followed during the 1970s was a series of Learnxs-sponsored demonstration projects
as a source of research and development in such areas as: school and community programs
to improve inner-city education; a series of small enterprises to employ 14- to 15-year-old
(20)   school leavers; Youth Ventures — a paper recycling enterprise employing at-risk youth;
Artsjunction — discarded material from business and industry were recycled for use as
craft materials for visual arts classes; Toronto Urban Studies Centre — a facility to encourage the use of the city as a learning environment; and Learnxs Press — a publishing house
for the production and sale of innovative learning materials.

(25)   The York Board of Education and its school and community organizations jointly incorporated the Learning Enrichment Foundation (LEF), modeled on Learnxs. Originally devoted to
multicultural arts enrichment, LEF during the 1980s joined with parental groups and the
school board to establish 13 school-based childcare centers for infants, pre-school and
school-age children.

(30)   In 1984, LEF was asked by Employment and Immigrant Canada to convene a local committee
of adjustment in response to York's high rate of unemployment and plant closures.
Outcomes of the work of the Committee included:

York Business Opportunities Centre: In 1985, with support from the Ontario Ministry of
Industry, Trade & Technology, LEF opened the first small business incubator operated by a
(35)   nonprofit charitable organization.

*Go on to next page*

Microtron Centre: This training facility was devoted to micro-computer skills, word and numerical processing, computer-assisted design, graphics and styling, and electronic assembly and repair.

(40) Microtron Bus: This refurbished school bus incorporated eight workstations from the Microtron Centre. It visited small business, industry and service organizations on a sched-uled basis to provide training in word and numerical processing for their employees and clients.

(45) In 1996, the Training Renewal Foundation was incorporated as a nonprofit charity to serve disadvantaged youth and other displaced workers seeking skills, qualifications and employ-ment opportunities. Over the years, TRF has partnered with governments, employers and community organizations to provide a variety of services including job-creation programs for: immigrants and refugees, GED high school equivalency, café equipment technicians, coffee and vending service workers, industrial warehousing and lift truck operators, fully expelled students, youth parenting, construction craft workers and garment manufacturing.

1. The Center for Social Innovation is

   (A) a new restaurant

   (B) a center housing social enterprises

   (C) the head office of a charity

   (D) a small enterprise to employ school leavers

2. The Learnxs Foundation supported

   (A) homeless people

   (B) scholarships for computer studies students

   (C) innovative programs

   (D) art programming

3. Artsjunction specialized in [        ].

4. The Microtron bus helped

   (A) provide transportation for computer science students to their labs

   (B) provide training in word and numerical processing to employees and clients

   (C) train auto mechanics in the digital controls in the new cars

   (D) the center establish social enterprises

5. The Training Renewal Foundation serves

   (A) as a social innovator for youth

   (B) as a patron of the center

   (C) dinner to the homeless

   (D) as a business incubator

---

*Questions 6–10 refer to the following excerpt.*

---

### How Must Employees Behave?

It is expected that employees behave in a respectful, responsible, professional manner. Therefore, each employee must do the following:

- Wear appropriate clothing and use safety equipment where needed.

- Refrain from the use and possession of alcohol and/or illicit drugs and associated para-phernalia throughout the duration of the work day.

- Refrain from associating with those who pass, use, and are under the influence of illicit drugs and/or alcohol.

- Address all other employees and supervisors with courtesy and respect, using non-offensive language.

- Accept the authority of supervisors without argument. If you consider an action unfair, inform the Human Resources department.

*Go on to next page*

- Respect the work environment of this company and conduct oneself in a manner conducive to the growth and the enhancement of our business.

- Refrain from inviting visitors to our place of work to keep the premises secure.

- Promote the dignity of all persons, regardless of gender, creed, or culture and conduct oneself with dignity.

If the employee chooses *not* to comply:

- On the first offense, the employee meets with his or her supervisor. A representative from Human Resources may choose to attend.

- On the second offense, the employee meets with the Vice President of Human Resources before returning to work.

- On the third offense, the employee is dismissed.

6. Which requirement relates to employee appearance?

   (A) The employee must refrain from using alcohol.

   (B) The employee must not use associated paraphernalia.

   (C) The employee must wear appropriate clothing.

   (D) The employee must use courtesy and respect.

7. Which requirement addresses relations with supervisors?

   (A) Accept authority.

   (B) Contribute to business growth and enhancement.

   (C) Use non-offensive language.

   (D) Do not use drugs and alcohol.

8. Which requirement is concerned with the growth and enhancement of the business?

   (A) conducive to growth

   (B) enhancement of self

   (C) dressing unprofessionally

   (D) personal conduct

9. How are safety and security protected?

   (A) by promoting dignity

   (B) by not inviting others in

   (C) by the types of interaction

   (D) through meetings with supervisors

10. What are the penalties for continued noncompliance?

    (A) You meet with the president of the company.

    (B) You must avoid your supervisor.

    (C) You have to take behavior classes.

    (D) You are fired.

*Go on to next page*

Questions 11–20 refer to the following business letter.

**CanLearn Study Tours, Inc.**
**2500 Big Beaver Road**
**Troy, MI 70523**

Dr. Dale Worth, PhD Registrar
BEST Institute of Technology 75 Ingram Drive
Concord, MA 51234

Dear Dr. Worth:

(A)

(1) Our rapidly changing economic climate has meant both challenges never before known. (2) It has been said that only those organizations who can maintain loyalty and commitment among their employees, members, and customers will continue to survive and prosper in this age of continuous learning and globalization.

(B)

(3) Since 1974, CanLearn Study Tours, Inc. have been working with universities, colleges, school districts, voluntary organizations, and businesses to address the unique learning needs of their staff and clientele. (4) These have included educational travel programs that explore the following, artistic and cultural interests, historic and archeological themes, environmental and wellness experiences, and new service patterns. (5) Professional development strategies have been organized to enhance international understanding and boost creativity. (6) Some organizations' have used study tours to build and maintain their membership or consumer base. (7) Other organizations discover a new soarce of revenue in these difficult economic times.

(C)

(8) The formats have varied from a series of local seminars to incentive conferences or sales promotion meetings. (9) Our professional services, including the best possible transportation and accommodation at the most reasonable rates, have insured the success of these programs.

(D)

(10) We would appreciate the opportunity to share our experiences in educational travel and discuss the ways we may be of service to your organization.

Yours sincerely,
Todd Croft, MA, President
CanLearn Study Tours, Inc.

*Go on to next page*

11. Sentence 1: **Our rapidly changing economic climate has meant both challenges never before known.**

    Which improvement should be made to Sentence 1?

    (A) insert *and opportunities* between *challenges* and *never*

    (B) change *has meant* to *have meant*

    (C) change *known* to *none*

    (D) no correction required

12. Sentence 2: **It has been said that only those organizations who can maintain loyalty and commitment among their employees, members, and customers will continue to survive and prosper in this age of continuous learning and globalization.**

    Which change should be made to Sentence 2?

    (A) insert a comma after *commitment*

    (B) change *has been* to *had been*

    (C) change *who* to *that*

    (D) change *those* to *these*

13. Sentence 3: **Since 1974, CanLearn Study Tours, Inc. have been working with universities, colleges, school districts, voluntary organizations, and businesses to address the unique learning needs of their staff and clientele.**

    Which is the best way to write the underlined portion of Sentence 3?

    (A) had been working

    (B) has been working

    (C) will be working

    (D) shall be working

14. Sentence 4: **These have included educational travel programs that explore the following, artistic and cultural interests, historic and archeological themes, environmental and wellness experiences, and new service patterns.**

    Which correction should be made to Sentence 4?

    (A) insert a comma after *have included*

    (B) change the comma after *following* to a colon

    (C) change the comma after *interests* to a colon

    (D) change the comma after *themes* to a colon

15. Sentence 5: **Professional development strategies have been organized to enhance international understanding and boost creativity.**

    Which change should be made to Sentence 5?

    (A) change *strategies* to *strategy*

    (B) change *boost* to *boast*

    (C) change *have been organized* to *has been organized*

    (D) no correction required

16. Sentence 6: **Some organizations' have used study tours to build and maintain their membership and consumer base.**

    Which correction should be made to Sentence 6?

    (A) change *organizations'* to *organizations*

    (B) change *Some* to *All*

    (C) change *their* to *there*

    (D) change *have used* to *has used*

17. Sentence 7: **Other organizations <u>discover a new soarce of revenue in these</u> difficult economic times.**

    Which change should be made to the underlined portion in Sentence 7?

    (A) discovering a new soarce of revenue in these

    (B) discover a new source of revenue in these

    (C) discover a new soarce, of revenue, in these

    (D) recover a new soarce of revenue in these

18. Sentence 8: **The formats has varied from a series of local seminars to incentive conferences or sales promotion meetings.**

    Which revision should be made to Sentence 8?

    (A) add a comma after *seminars*

    (B) add an apostrophe after *sales*

    (C) change *formats* to *format*

    (D) add a period after *seminars*

*Go on to next page*

19. Sentence 9: **Our professional services, including the best possible transportation and accommodation at the most reasonable rates, have insured the success of these programs.**

Which correction should be made to Sentence 9?

(A) change *services* to *service*

(B) replace *insured* with *ensured*

(C) remove the comma after *services*

(D) remove the comma after *rates*

20. Sentence 10: **We would appreciate the opportunity to share our experiences in educational travel and discuss the ways we may be of service to your organization.**

Which revision should be made to Sentence 10?

(A) change *would appreciate* to *appreciate*

(B) insert a comma after *ways*

(C) change *may* to *will*

(D) no correction required

---

*Questions 21–26 refer to the following excerpt from Washington Irving's "Rip Van Winkle" (1819).*

---

Line    Whoever has made a voyage up the Hudson must remember the Kaatskill Mountains. They are a dismembered branch of the great Appalachian family, and are seen away to the west of the river, swelling up to a noble height, and lording it over the surrounding country. Every change of season, every change of weather, indeed, every hour of the
(05)    day, produces some change in the magical hues and shapes of these mountains, and they are regarded by all the good wives, far and near, as perfect barometers. When the weather is fair and settled, they are clothed in blue and purple, and print their bold outlines on the clear evening sky; but, sometimes, when the rest of the landscape is cloudless, they will gather a hood of gray vapors about their summits, which, in the
(10)    last rays of the setting sun, will glow and light up like a crown of glory.

At the foot of these fairy mountains, the voyager may have descried the light smoke curling up from a village, whose shingle-roofs gleam among the trees, just where the blue tints of the upland melt away into the fresh green of the nearer landscape. It is a little village of great antiquity, having been founded by some of the Dutch colonists, in
(15)    the early times of the province, just about the beginning of the government of the good Peter Stuyvesant, (may he rest in peace!) and there were some of the houses of the original settlers standing within a few years, built of small yellow bricks brought from Holland, having latticed windows and gablefronts, surmounted with weather-cocks.

21. How would you set out to find the Kaatskill Mountains?

(A) Ask directions.

(B) Journey up the Hudson.

(C) Look for a dismembered branch.

(D) Notice fresh green.

22. According to Lines 5 and 6, wives tell the weather

(A) with perfect barometers

(B) by the clear evening sky

(C) through gray vapors

(D) with magical hues and shapes

23. What clues might you look for as a sign that you are close to the village?

(A) fairy mountains

(B) shingle-roofs

(C) light smoke curling

(D) blue tints

24. Who originally founded the village?

[          ]

*Go on to next page*

25. Why is the phrase "may he rest in peace!" (Line 16) used after Peter Stuyvesant?

(A) He has since died.

(B) He was an original settler.

(C) He was a soldier.

(D) He was the governor.

26. What materials came from Holland?

[        ]

*Questions 27–32 refer to the following excerpt from Richard Wright's "The Man Who Was Almost a Man," from Eight Men (1961).*

Line Dave struck out across the fields, looking homeward through paling light . . . One of these days he was going to get a gun and practice shooting, then they couldn't talk to him as though he were a little boy. He slowed, looking at the ground. Shucks, Ah ain scareda them . . . even ef they are biggern me! Aw, Ah know whut Ahma do. Ahm going by ol Joe's sto n git that Sears-
(05) Roebuck catlog n look at them guns. Mebbe Ma will lemme buy one when she gits mah pay from ol man Hawkins. Ahma beg her t gimme some money. Ahm ol ernough to hava gun. Ahm seventeen. Almost a man. He strode, feeling his long loose-jointed limbs. Shucks, a man oughta hava little gun aftah he done worked hard all day.

He came in sight of Joe's store. A yellow lantern glowed on the front porch. He mounted
(10) steps and went through the screen door, hearing it bang behind him. There was a strong smell of coal oil and mackerel fish. He felt very confident until he saw fat Joe walk in through the rear door, then his courage began to ooze.

"Howdy, Dave! Whutcha want?"

"How yuh, Mistah Joe? Aw, Ah don wanna buy nothing. Ah jus wanted t see ef yuhd lemme
(15) look at tha catlog erwhile."

"Sure! You wanna see it here?"

"Nawsuh. Ah wants t take it home wid me. Ah'll bring it back termorrow when Ah come in from the fiels."

"You plannin on buying something?"

(20) "Yessuh."

"Your ma lettin you have your own money now?"

"Shucks. Mistah Joe, Ahm gittin t be a man like anybody else!"

27. According to the story, Dave's place of employment was [        ].

28. Dave wanted "to get a gun" (Line 2) to

(A) show he wasn't "scareda" the others

(B) prove he wasn't unemployed

(C) make his Ma proud

(D) impress Joe

*Go on to next page*

29. From where did Dave hope to get a gun?

    (A) from "Joe's sto"

    (B) from "ol man Hawkins"

    (C) from Ma

    (D) from the Sears-Roebuck "catlog"

30. How would you find Joe's store at night?

    (A) by the smell of mackeral

    (B) by a yellow lantern glow

    (C) by the banging screen door

    (D) by the smell of coal oil

31. Why do you think Dave asked to take the catalog home?

    (A) He lost his nerve.

    (B) It was too dark to read.

    (C) He had to be home for supper.

    (D) He makes his own money.

32. What must Dave do to get the gun?

    (A) Find it in the catalog.

    (B) Convince Ma to give him the money.

    (C) Persuade Joe to place the order.

    (D) Get ol man Hawkins's permission.

---

*Questions 33–42 refer to the following excerpt, which is adapted from* Customer Service For Dummies, *by Karen Leland and Keith Bailey (Wiley).*

---

(1) This step requires you to listen to each customers assessment of the problem. (2) Your job when she explains the situation from her perspective is to fully absorb what she is saying about her unique set of circumstances. (3) After you identify the customer's problem, the next step, obviously, is to fix it. (4) Sometimes, you can easily remedy the situation by changing an invoice, redoing an order, waving or refunding charges, or replacing a defective product. (5) At other times fixing the problem is more complex because the damage or mistake cannot be repaired simply. (6) In these instances, mutually exceptable compromises need to be reached.

(7) Whatever the problem, this step begins to remedy the situation and gives the customer what she needs to resolve the source of the conflict. (8) Don't waste time and effort by putting the horse before the cart and trying to fix the wrong problem. (9) Its easy to jump the gun and think that you know what the customer is about to say because you've heard it all a hundred times before. (10) Doing so loses you ground on the recovery front and farther annoys the customer. (11) More often than not, what you think the problem is at first glance, is different from what it becomes upon closer examination.

33. Sentence 1: **This step requires <u>you to listen to each customers assessment</u> of the problem.**

    Which correction should be made to the underlined portion in Sentence 1?

    (A) you to listen each customers assessment

    (B) you to listen to each customers' assessment

    (C) you to listen to each customers asessment

    (D) you to listen to each customer's assessment

34. Sentence 2: **Your job when she explains the situation from her perspective is to fully absorb what she is saying about her unique set of circumstances.**

    To make Sentence 2 more effective, you may consider moving a section of the sentence, beginning with which group of words?

    (A) when she explains the situation from her perspective

    (B) Your job when she explains

    (C) what she is saying about

    (D) no correction required

*Go on to next page*

35. Sentence 4: **Sometimes, you can easily remedy the situation by changing an invoice, redoing an order, waving or refunding charges, or replacing a defective product.**

    Which correction should be made to Sentence 4?

    (A) change *redoing* to *re-doing*

    (B) change *invoice* to *invoise*

    (C) change *waving* to *waiving*

    (D) change *defective* to *defected*

36. Sentence 5: **At other times fixing the problem is more complex because the damage or mistake cannot be repaired simply.**

    After which word would it be most appropriate to place a comma? [        ]

37. Sentence 6: **In these instances, mutually exceptable compromises need to be reached.**

    Enter the one misspelled word from Sentence 6 into the blank. [        ]

38. Sentence 7: **Whatever the problem, this step begins to remedy the situation and gives the customer what she needs to resolve the source of the conflict.**

    Which is the best way to begin Sentence 7? If the original is the best way, choose Choice (A).

    (A) Whatever the problem,

    (B) This step begins to remedy,

    (C) What she needs to resolve,

    (D) To remedy the situation,

39. Sentence 8: **Don't waste time and effort by putting the horse before the cart and trying to fix the wrong problem.**

    Which change should be made to Sentence 8?

    (A) change *waste* to *waist*

    (B) revise to read *the cart before the horse*

    (C) change *trying* to *try*

    (D) change *Don't* to *Doesn't*

40. Sentence 9: **Its easy to jump the gun and think that you know what the customer is about to say because you've heard it all a hundred times before.**

    What word(s) is used incorrectly in Sentence 9? [        ]

41. Sentence 10: **Doing so loses you ground <u>on the recovery front and farther</u> annoys the customer.**

    Which change should be made to the underlined portion in Sentence 10?

    (A) with the recovery front and farther

    (B) on the recover front and farther

    (C) on the recovery front and further

    (D) on the recovery, and farther

42. Sentence 11: **More often than not, what you think the problem is, at first glance, is different from what it becomes, upon closer examination.**

    The comma after which word is used correctly in Sentence 11? [        ]

---

*Questions 43–49 refer to the following business letter.*

---

GED Enterprises LLC
1655 Elizabeth Drive
Ajax, England 51221

To Whom It May Concern:

(1) We are delighted to provide a refference for Michael Jaxon. (2) He was employed by the training division of our company for six years, he provided excellent services, both recruiting and training clients to participate in our coffee vending machine repair division for the period of June 2010 to October 2014.

*Go on to next page*

(3) As part of that programme, he

- prepared PowerPoint presentations for new recruits
- reviewed, revised, and upgraded training procedures
- prepared a repair manual for the graduating technicians
- organizes communications with other companies in the industry

(4) Mr. Jaxon has always been an excellent representative for our company, which has trained some 45 new repair personnel in the past year. (5) Mr. Jaxon's concerted efforts to network with others in the coffee industry contributed greatly to his success. (6) He has showed a high level of commitment to his job; and he will pursue his work with both competence and efficiency.

(7) I have developed a great respect for Mr. Jaxons' personal communications skills, and dedication to his work and our program. I wish him all the best for the future.

Jules Klaus, PhD
President

43. Sentence 1: **We are delighted to provide a refference for Michael Jaxon.**

What revision should be made to Sentence 1?

(A) change *provide* to *provided*

(B) change *refference* to *reference*

(C) change *are delighted* to *would be delighted*

(D) none of the above

44. Sentence 2: **He was employed by the training division of our company for six years, he provided excellent services, both recruiting and training clients to participate in our coffee vending machine repair division for the period of June 2010 to October 2014.**

What revisions should be made to Sentence 2?

(A) break this into two sentences after the word *services* by replacing the comma with a period and capitalizing *both*

(B) replace *was employed* with *had been employed*

(C) break the sentence into two after the word *years,* replacing the comma with a period and capitalizing the word *he*

(D) capitalize *Coffee Vending Machine Repair Division*

45. Sentence 3: **As part of that programme, he**

- **prepared PowerPoint presentations for new recruits**
- **reviewed, revised, and upgraded training procedures**
- **prepared a repair manual for the graduating technicians**
- **organizes communications with other companies in the industry**

What change should be made to Sentence 3?

(A) change *programme* to *program*

(B) change *organizes* to *organized*

(C) remove the comma after *revised*

(D) change *procedures* to *proceedures*

46. **Mr. Jaxon has always been an excellent representative for our company, which has trained some 45 new repair personnel in the past year.**

What is the best rewording for the underlined portion of this sentence?

(A) had always been

(B) always had been

(C) always was

(D) no change required

*Go on to next page* →

47. **He has showed a high level of commit-ment to his job; and he will pursue his work with both competence and efficiency.**

What change should be made to the under-lined portion of this sentence?

(A) change *showed* to *shown*

(B) change *commitment* to *comitment*

(C) change *has* to *had*

(D) no change required

48. **He has showed a high level of commit-ment to his job; and he will pursue his work with both competence and efficiency.**

What change should be made to the under-lined portion of the sentence?

(A) change *will pursue* to *pursues*

(B) replace the semicolon with a comma

(C) change *will pursue* to *will have pursued*

(D) no change required

49. **I have developed a great respect for Mr. Jaxons' personal communications skills, and dedication to his work and our program.**

What correction does this sentence require?

(A) move the apostrophe from *Jaxons'* to *Jaxon's*

(B) change *program* to *programme*

(C) change *personal* to *personnel*

(D) no change required

---

*Questions 50–55 refer to the following excerpt from Saul Bellow's "Something to Remember Me By" (1990).*

---

Line   It began like any other winter school day in Chicago — grimly ordinary. The temperature a few degrees above zero, botanical frost shapes on the windowpane, the snow swept up in heaps, the ice gritty and the streets, block after block, bound together by the iron of the sky. A breakfast of porridge, toast, and tea. Late as usual, I stopped for a moment to look into my

(05)   mother's sickroom. I bent near and said, "It's Louie, going to school." She seemed to nod. Her eyelids were brown, her face was much lighter. I hurried off with my books on a strap over my shoulder.

When I came to the boulevard on the edge of the park, two small men rushed out of a door-way with rifles, wheeled around aiming upward, and fired at pigeons near the rooftop.

(10)   Several birds fell straight down, and the men scooped up the soft bodies and ran indoors, dark little guys in fluttering white shirts. Depression hunters and their city game. Moments before, the police car had loafed by at ten miles an hour. The men had waited it out.

This had nothing to do with me. I mention it merely because it happened. I stepped around the blood spots and crossed into the park.

*Go on to next page*

50. What words from this passage best describe the appearance of a winter school day in Chicago? [          ]

51. What do you find out about the state of Louie's home life in Lines 5 and 6?

   (A) He ate porridge, toast, and tea.

   (B) He carried books on a strap.

   (C) His face was much lighter.

   (D) His mother was sick.

52. What were the men doing in the doorway?

   (A) hunting for game

   (B) having target practice

   (C) staying out of the weather

   (D) hiding from police

53. What is the importance of the term *depression hunters* in this passage?

   (A) It tells you the state of mind of the men.

   (B) A lot of people hunted in the Depression.

   (C) They were reacting to the grim weather.

   (D) It reinforces the image of great hardship, that people had to hunt pigeons for food in the city.

54. What word from the passage identifies the time in which this story is set? [          ]

55. Why didn't Louie tell the police about what he saw?

   (A) He was in a hurry to get to school.

   (B) His mother was sick.

   (C) It had nothing to do with him.

   (D) The guys were his friends.

---

*Questions 56–60 refer to the following excerpt from Russell Hart's* Photography For Dummies, *2nd Edition (Wiley).*

---

Line   If you've ever had to figure out where to stick batteries in your child's latest electronic acquisition, then loading batteries in your point-and-shoot shouldn't be a challenge. Turn off your camera when you install them; the camera may go crazy opening and closing its lens. (Some cameras turn themselves off after you install new batteries, so you have to turn
(05)   them back on to shoot.)

With big point-and-shoot models, you typically open a latched cover on the bottom to install batteries. More compact models have a battery compartment under a door or flap that is incorporated into the side or grip of the camera. You may have to pry open such doors with a coin.

(10)   More annoying are covers on the bottom that you open by loosening a screw. (You need a coin for this type, too.) And most annoying are battery covers that aren't hinged and come off completely when you unscrew them. If you have one of these, don't change batteries while standing over a sewer grate, in a field of tall grass, or on a pier.

Whether loading four AAs or a single lithium, make sure that the batteries are correctly ori-
(15)   ented as you insert them. You'll find a diagram and/or plus and minus markings, usually within the compartment or on the inside of the door.

If your camera doesn't turn on and the batteries are correctly installed, the batteries may have lost their punch from sitting on a shelf too long. Which is where the battery icon comes in.

(20)   If your camera has an LCD panel, an icon tells you when battery power is low.

*Go on to next page*

56. Where will you be installing the batteries?

    (A) an electronic acquisition

    (B) a children's toy

    (C) a big point-and-shoot

    (D) a camera

57. What is the easiest model in which to replace the batteries?

    (A) compact models

    (B) big point-and-shoots

    (C) screw bottoms

    (D) covers not hinged

58. Why should locations such as sewer grates and tall grass be avoided when changing batteries?

    (A) Water can get in the camera.

    (B) Your lens may get dirty.

    (C) Your card might be ruined.

    (D) The battery cover may be lost.

59. How do you ensure that the batteries are correctly oriented?

    (A) Check the LCD panel.

    (B) Use a single lithium.

    (C) Empty the compartment.

    (D) Find a diagram.

60. What tells you whether the batteries are low?

    (A) the LCD panel

    (B) the battery icon

    (C) the battery compartment

    (D) a single lithium battery

**STOP** DO NOT TURN THE PAGE UNTIL TOLD TO DO SO.
DO NOT RETURN TO A PREVIOUS TEST.

# The Extended Response

**Time:** 45 minutes

**Your assignment:** The following articles present arguments both for and against making cyber-bullying a criminal offence. In your response, analyze the positions presented in each article and explain which you think is best supported. You must use specific and appropriate evidence to support your arguments. Use the following sheets of lined paper for your response. You should expect to spend up to 45 minutes in planning, drafting, and editing your response.

### Pro

Some youth deliberately set out to harm others; this act is called bullying. However, when it happens by using social media, texting, and other technologies, it is called cyberbullying. That, too, should be a crime, especially because the intent to hurt and harm is there. Worse, considering how pervasive media technology is today, the bullying never stops; it follows the victims wherever and whenever they try to escape. The resulting evidence of the harm is also clear. The number of young people who have in desperation committed suicide after months and years of horrific abuse shows that.

Cyberbullying is a form of abuse, just like cyberstalking. It relentlessly hounds a designated target, even following the victim when he or she moves or changes schools. In a recent case, a teen was raped, and photographs of the rape were distributed to classmates in her school. Comments that followed taunted her as a slut — it was her fault; she was asking for it — to the point that she transferred schools. The teen reported the rape to the police who took little action, and the perpetrators remained free. She received an endless stream of abusive e-mails and texts. Meetings with the principal of both high schools and parents of the bullies solved nothing. Even after transferring, the bullies found her again and the harassment started again. Only after being faced with community outrage did the police take action, and then only after the teen had committed suicide.

This was not an isolated case. Nearly half of all teens report they have been victims of cyberbullying. There have been multiple suicides in many countries. The police are often unwilling or unable to take action, claiming that cyberbullying itself does not constitute a crime.

Education programs don't work, either. Virtually all schools these days have anti-bullying programs. Even grade-school children are taught about bullying and to show respect for others. They are also educated on how to be safe online. Yet cyberbullying continues.

The threat of a criminal record is a deterrent and, at the very least, will give the police a tool with which to fight cyberbullying. Arresting bullies will certainly stop them in their tracks. It might also give the victims a tool for seeking redress. All the other initiatives have failed, so what choice is left?

### Against

There are several considerations in the debate on criminalizing cyberbullying. There are already laws against cyberbullying if it crosses the line into criminal harassment. That is a chargeable offence. Second, how can one keep a clear line between cyberbullying and an abrogation of the freedom of speech guaranteed by the Constitution? Further, does the threat of a criminal record really deter people from such activities?

The whole issue is unclear: How do you define cyberbullying? Mostly, it consists of wild accusations and name-calling. It may be crude and rude, but it is not a crime unless it crosses the line and becomes slanderous or libelous. If there is no physical harm done and no intent to drive someone to self-harm, why treat verbal abuse as a crime? If it continues and crosses into destruction of reputation, then it does become criminal harassment. Existing laws can deal with this issue. Although this may be interpreted differently in different jurisdictions, it is a criminal offence under existing laws.

There are other tools. A young teen texted nude photos of her boyfriend's ex-girlfriend to friends. She also posted a copy on the former girlfriend's Facebook page. All were minors at the time. She was

*Go on to next page*

recently convicted of distributing child pornography, even though she, too, was a minor at the time. Existing laws punished the crime.

The other issue often raised is that cyberbullying has driven victims to suicide or attempts at self-harm. This is certainly true, but what is not proven is that the cyberbullying was the sole cause. Were the victims already suffering from depression? Were there other issues in their lives that made them unstable and prone to self-harm?

Proponents also argue that the fear of a criminal charge will be a deterrent. But if that is the case, why do so many people still drive drunk or continue to indulge in recreational drugs? There are clear consequences if caught, but they certainly do not stop these incidents. Teens are not the most rational beings, and the idea that their actions might result in criminal charges is not really foremost in their minds.

We must also remember that the Constitution guarantees the right to free speech. When the law tries to tell people they cannot say something, at what point does that infringe on that right? Some social media have taken a solid first step. They no longer permit people to have accounts in false names. Just a limitation of anonymity will reduce cyberbullying and do so without limiting free speech.

Education is a better approach. Let's get the schools and parents, community groups, and churches all involved in teaching our teens to have respect for others. Teach teens that words can hurt, and that hurting others is never an appropriate thing to do.

*Go on to next page*

Go on to next page

# Chapter 18

# Answers for Practice Test 1, Reasoning through Language Arts

••••••••••••••••••••••••••••••••••••••••••••••••••••••••••••

*I*n this chapter, we provide the answers and explanations to every question in the Reasoning through Language Arts practice test in Chapter 17. If you just want a quick look at the answers, check out the abbreviated answer key at the end of this chapter. However, if you have the time, be sure to read the answer explanations. Doing so will help you understand why some answers were correct and others not, especially when the choices were really close. You can discover just as much from your errors as from the correct answers.

## *Answers and Explanations*

1. **B. a center housing social enterprises.** The column specifically states that the center houses 85 social enterprises. Choice (A) is totally wrong and can be instantly eliminated on first reading. The other answers have a ring of correctness because the column is about social enterprises, charities, and school leavers, but they have nothing to do with the center and, thus, are wrong.

2. **C. innovative programs.** The column states that the Learnxs Foundation supports innovative programs. All the other answers except for Choice (A) are mentioned or implied in the column; however, they aren't correct answers to the question. You have to read carefully and double-check the facts. Just because something is mentioned or is familiar doesn't mean it's the right answer to the question.

3. **distributing discarded materials to visual arts classes.** The passage clearly spells out that Artsjunction's function is to distribute discarded materials to visual arts classes.

4. **B. provide training in word and numerical processing to employees and clients.** The column is very specific about the purpose of the Microtron bus. It provided services to employees and clients of small businesses in word and numerical processing. The other answers sound like they could be right, but, after rereading the column, you can see that they aren't.

   When you're trying to answer these questions under time constraints, try to remember exactly what the passage said. If you only think you remember, go back as quickly as you can and skim the piece for key words. In this case, the key word is *Microtron*. It sometimes helps to read the question first before reading the passage.

5. **D. as a business incubator.** The passage very precisely spells out the mandate of the Training Renewal Foundation: to serve disadvantaged youth and displaced workers. Choices (A) and (B) may be worthy activities for any charity, but they aren't stated as part of the mandate and, thus, are wrong as answers. Choice (C) is just wrong and is a play on another meaning of *serves*. You can immediately exclude this answer and have only three others to consider.

6. **C. The employee must wear appropriate clothing.** Employees must wear appropriate clothing to project a professional appearance and maintain safety standards. The other requirements — such as refraining from alcohol use, not associating with paraphernalia, being respectful, and using non-offensive language — don't relate to appearance.

7. **A. Accept authority.** Employees must accept the authority of supervisors, as is stated clearly in the passage. The other choices may be partially correct, but they are not the best answer.

8. **D. personal conduct.** Employees must conduct themselves professionally so that the business grows and improves.

9. **B. by not inviting others in.** To ensure safety and security, employees shouldn't invite other people in. The promotion of dignity, interaction, and supervisors' meetings don't directly relate to ensuring safety and security.

10. **D. You are fired.** Repeated instances of noncompliance lead to dismissal. The other options aren't backed up by the passage.

11. **A. insert *and opportunities* between *challenges* and *never*.** Although the word *both* refers to two options, here, you're given only one option — *challenges*. If you insert *and opportunities* between *challenges* and *never,* you include a second option and correct the sentence.

12. **C. change *who* to *that*.** An organization is never a *who;* only people can be referred to as *who.* An organization is a collective noun made up of people, but the collective noun itself is an impersonal entity and doesn't qualify as a *who.* Although the sentence may appear long and, therefore, may benefit from rewriting, the sentence isn't technically incorrect. Although commas do serve to make sentences clearer, you don't want to insert them unless punctuation rules make them correct.

13. **B. has been working.** CanLearn Study Tours is a single entity because it's one company. Therefore, it's a singular noun and needs the singular verb *has* rather than the plural *have.* A company is always an *it.* Even though a company is made up of a lot of people, it's still a singular entity.

14. **B. change the comma after *following* to a colon.** You need to insert a colon before the list to introduce it.

15. **D. no correction required.** The options presented either make the sentence difficult to understand or introduce errors, so the correct answer is *no correction required.*

16. **A. change *organizations'* to *organizations*.** A stray apostrophe has landed on this sentence. The one after *organizations'* is unnecessary because you're not trying to show possession here. Choice (B) is incorrect, because the passage doesn't refer to *all* organizations. Choice (C) would introduce a homonym error, and Choice (D) inserts the wrong tense. Get comfortable with the uses of apostrophes — especially those used for possession — before taking the GED Reasoning through Language Arts test.

17. **B. discover a new source of revenue in these.** You need to correct the spelling error by changing *soarce* to *source.*

18. **C. change *formats* to *format*.** Formats is plural, but *has* is a singular verb. Verbs and their subjects must agree. There is no need for a comma after seminar or an apostrophe after sales. The apostrophe would indicate ownership, which isn't the case here. A period after *seminars* would create two sentence fragments, also an error. Study both subject-verb agreement and pronoun-antecedent agreement before taking the Reasoning through Language Arts test.

19. **B. replace *insured* with *ensured*.** Choice (B) corrects the spelling error by changing *insured* to *ensured.* Using *insure* is a common error. Use *insure* only when you mean the service you buy to protect your car, house, health, life, and so on. This example has nothing to do with insurance, so use *ensure* instead.

20. **D. no correction required.** The other choices don't improve or correct the sentence.

21. **B. Journey up the Hudson.** To get to the Kaatskill Mountains, you need to journey up the Hudson. A dismembered branch and fresh green aren't locations that can better help you locate the mountains. Although asking directions may work, this approach isn't mentioned in the passage.

22. **D. with magical hues and shapes.** The wives use the magical hues and shapes of the mountains to forecast the weather. Other factors, such as the evening sky or gray vapors, aren't good indicators. A barometer is an instrument to measure air pressure.

23. **C. light smoke curling.** To help you locate the village, you first need to look for light smoke curling from chimneys. You can't see the other sign, shingle-roofs, until after you can see the smoke. Blue tints aren't signs for locating villages.

24. **Dutch colonists.** The Dutch colonists were the newcomers who founded the village. Although there are others named, they're the incorrect answer. Peter Stuyvesant established the government. The great Appalachian family refers to the mountains.

25. **A. He has since died.** Peter Stuyvesant, who had headed the government, had since died. The other answer choices describe Stuyvesant as an original settler, a soldier, and a governor, but they don't refer to his death.

26. **yellow bricks.** Settlers brought yellow bricks from Holland to build the houses. Other materials, such as weather-cocks, windows, and shingle-roofs, were acquired locally.

27. **Hawkins's fields.** Dave worked as a field hand on Hawkins's farm. He hopes his mother will let him buy a gun with his wages from Hawkins.

28. **A. show he wasn't "scareda" the others.** He wants to show the other field hands that he isn't scared of them. Dave mentions that he isn't afraid of them just before he first discusses buying the gun. He might want to impress Joe, but that isn't supported by the text.

29. **D. from the Sears-Roebuck "catlog."** Dave had to purchase the gun through the Sears-Roebuck catalog. Joe didn't keep guns in his store. Neither Mr. Hawkins nor Ma are sources of guns.

30. **B. by a yellow lantern glow.** Joe kept a yellow lantern glowing on the porch. Other answer choices, such as *the smell of mackerel, the banging screen door,* or *the coal oil smell* may also help you find the store, but they aren't the best indicators.

31. **A. He lost his nerve.** Dave lost his nerve and was afraid to ask Joe to see guns in the catalog. The other possibilities — it was too dark, he needed to get home for supper, or he made his own money — aren't the best answers.

32. **B. Convince Ma to give him the money.** Dave would have to convince Ma to give him the money to buy the gun. The other reasons, including finding it in the catalog, persuading Joe, or getting ol' man Hawkins's permission, either aren't relevant or aren't as important as convincing Ma to give him the money.

33. **D. you to listen to each customer's assessment.** The *assessment* belongs to each customer and requires a possessive form of customer: *customer's*. The other answers are neither correct nor do they improve the sentence. Because customer is singular, you must insert the apostrophe before the *s* in *customer*.

34. **A. when she explains the situation from her perspective.** The meaning of this sentence is that the clerk should listen to the customer, so put the most important information first. The best way to start this sentence is with the *when she explains the situation from her perspective* phrase.

35. **C. change *waving* to *waiving*.** Waving means to motion with the hand, while *waive* means to dismiss. It may be interesting to wave at a charge, but the proper meaning of the sentence is to dismiss (or not collect) the charge. These two words are *homonyms* (words that sound the same but have different spellings and meanings). You are expected to understand most homonyms for this test.

36. **times.** The only place you can use a comma in this sentence is after the introductory phrase *At other times.*

37. **exceptable.** *Exceptable* may sound like a word, but it's not. The correct word to use is *acceptable.* The more reading you do as you prepare for the test, the better your chances are for recognizing misspellings.

38. **A. Whatever the problem,.** A gift for you: No correction is required. If you chose Choice (D), keep in mind that this sentence has one subject and two verbs. These types of sentences don't require a comma between the two verbs. Not sure about subjects and verbs? Here, the subject is *step,* and the two verbs are *begins* and *gives.* If the sentence had a second subject before the second verb, it would need a comma.

39. **B. revise to read *the cart before the horse.*** If you live anywhere near Amish country, you know that the horse comes before the cart. Or you may have heard the idiomatic expression, "Don't put the cart before the horse." In either case, the proper correction is to reverse the order of *horse* and *cart.*

40. **Its.** *Its* is possessive (meaning that it shows that something belongs to *it*), whereas *it's* stands for "it is." Here, the sentence clearly means "it is." Confusing these two words is a common error that's usually tested in some way. Master the difference between *its* and *it's*. *It's* means "it is" and is often confused with the possessive form of other words that use the apostrophe.

41. **C. on the recovery front and further.** *Farther* always refers to distance. *Further* is a matter of degree. Here, you want degree, not distance. If you didn't know the answer, this question is a good example of one that you could answer by intelligent guessing. Choice (A) isn't correct because *with* isn't the proper word in this case. Choice (B) doesn't make sense in the context of the sentence. So now you just need to guess between Choices (C) and (D).

42. **not.** Commas used in moderation help sentences. Extra commas hurt sentences. In this sentence, the only comma used properly separates the introductory phrase *More often than not* from the rest of the sentence.

43. **B. change *refference* to *reference*.** The correct spelling is *reference*. Choice (A) introduces a new error, the wrong tense. Choice (C) is a possibility. You could use the subjunctive in this sentence, but the sentence is correct as written. Because a different error occurs in the sentence, Choice (C) isn't the best choice.

44. **C. break the sentence into two after the word *years*, replacing the comma with a period, and capitalizing *he*.** This is an example of a run-on sentence, where two sentences are joined by a comma. The sentences must be separated by either a conjunction or the appropriate punctuation. Choice (A) has the right idea but the wrong location; it would create a sentence fragment after the word *both*. Choice (B) introduces a new error, using the wrong tense under these circumstances. The past perfect is only required when comparing in the past to something in the more distant past. The capitals suggested in Choice (D) aren't required.

45. **B. change *organizes* to *organized*.** This is a case of faulty parallelism. Every bullet is in the past tense except the last one. It should be in the same tense as the rest. The word *programme* is correctly spelled. This is a red herring, taking advantage of the differences between British and American English. In British English, *programme* is the preferred spelling, and the letter return address indicates that the author is from England. Despite that, both spellings are still considered acceptable in American English. The comma in Choice (C) is required, and the suggested change to *proceedure* in Choice (D) introduces a new error, so it's wrong.

46. **D. no change required.** The original wording splits the verb by inserting *always* between the auxiliary verb and the participle. This isn't always an error and, in this case, is fine. Choices (A) and (B) introduce the wrong tense into the sentence, and Choice (C) is no improvement.

47. **A. change *showed* to *shown*.** The sentence uses the wrong form of the participle. Choice (B) introduces a new spelling error, Choice (C) introduces a new tense error, and Choice (D) is wrong because there's an error in the sentence.

48. **B. replace the semicolon with a comma.** The semicolon creates a division between the two independent clauses that isn't required. Choice (A) is an option, but the sentence isn't wrong as is, while the semicolon is an error. You can't use this choice because Choice (B) is the greater error. Choice (C) introduces a tense error, while Choice (D) is simply wrong. Remember to deal only with the underlined portion of the sentence.

49. **A. move the apostrophe from *Jaxons'* to *Jaxon's*.** The sentence refers to the skills Mr. Jaxon possesses. Because his name doesn't end in *s,* the apostrophe needs to come before the *s*. The change in Choice (B) isn't required. Choice (C) introduces a new error, the misuse of the words *personal* and *personnel*. Because the letter is discussing Mr. Jaxon's skills, they are *personal* skills. *Personnel* refers to staff. If the sentence were dealing only with his abilities with staff, such a use may be correct. Choice (D) is wrong because changes are required.

50. **grimly ordinary.** The description states that it was like any other winter school day in Chicago — grimly ordinary.

51. **D. His mother was sick.** Louie was living with his mother, who was very ill and confined to bed. Other answers describing Louie's breakfast, his books, and his complexion aren't good descriptions of the focus of his home life.

52. **A. hunting for game.** The men were hunting pigeons (game) for food. You can see that having target practice, staying out of the weather, and hiding from the police are inappropriate answers. They aren't the key points, if you've read the passage thoroughly.

53. **D. It reinforces the image of great hardship, that people had to hunt pigeons for food in the cities.** The whole scene is grim, but only in that term do you realize the time setting is the Great Depression. That then reinforced the grimness of the scene. Although the men may be depressed and the weather bad, those things have nothing to do with the question. And although Choice (B) may be true, it doesn't answer the question, either.

54. **Depression.** The second to last paragraph, referring to the Depression hunters and their city game, sets the times for the passage.

55. **C. It had nothing to do with him.** What Louie saw had nothing to do with him, and he didn't want to get involved. Other possible answers — that he was hurrying to school, his mother was sick, or he was friends with the guys — don't relate to why Louie wouldn't tell the police.

56. **D. a camera.** The batteries are installed in a camera. Other answer choices, such as electronics or a children's toy, have no meaning in this excerpt. Point-and-shoot, while another term for a camera, isn't the best answer, because not all cameras are point-and-shoot.

57. **B. big point-and-shoots.** The easiest model in which to replace batteries is the point-and-shoot camera. The other answer choices — compact models, screw bottoms, and different types of covers — don't relate directly to the question.

58. **D. The battery cover may be lost.** Avoid all the locations mentioned so you don't lose your battery cover if you drop it. Sewer grates and tall grass are places where the cover could easily be lost. The rest of the answer choices refer to issues other than losing battery covers.

59. **D. Find a diagram.** To ensure that the batteries are correctly oriented, you must find the diagram and use it. The other choices don't answer the question.

60. **B. the battery icon.** You must check the battery icon to see whether the batteries are low. LCD panels show a variety of information, so that option is not the best choice. According to the passage, battery compartment and lithium battery aren't correct answers.

### Sample Extended Response

The following sample essay would receive solid marks. It isn't perfect, but as the GED Testing Service tells you, you're not expected to write the perfect essay. You're expected to write a good, first-draft-quality response. When you prepare your essay, consider using a schedule similar to this: 10 minutes to read and analyze the source passages; 10 minutes to put together the quotes you intend to use to back your argument, 10 minutes to prepare your rough draft, and the remaining 15 minutes to write your actual essay, proofread it, and make any final adjustments.

Compare the following sample to the response you wrote, and check out Chapter 7 for the scoring criteria and what evaluators look for in a response.

By its very nature, this issue is extremely emotional. And that makes it very difficult to prepare a rational argument. The first article describes the harm caused by cyberbullying and describe some unsuccessful efforts to intervene and later punish. The second article explains why criminalizing cyberbullying is unnecessary. Despite the harm cyberbullying causes, the second article is the better argued. It presents a rational case, backed by facts, without resorting to emotional prodding of one's conscience.

The first article very clearly makes the case that cyberbullying should be a crime. There's very little argument about the nature of the horrible crime the first article describes it, nor are the events in dispute. Nor would anyone argue that cyberbullying does no harm. The article further states that often intervention at the parent or school level has little effect. Again, this is not in dispute. However, the passage does use emotionally loaded terms, such as "hounding" and "community outrage." Further, while it presents one case in detail, it does not present little further evidence, neither examples nor statistics to back the case.

In contrast, the second article goes through the arguments against criminalizing cyberbullying in a logical manner. The first argument is the problem of defining what exactly cyberbullying is. It points out that mere name-calling is not a crime. It goes on to state that if and when such actions go too far, there's always recourse to existing laws. Harassments, libel, and slander are all covered under existing laws. Luring someone into self-harm is a criminal offense. Passing on nude or seminude photographs of someone can lead to child pornography charges. In most cases, existing laws will cover cyberbullying when it crosses a line.

The second article also examines the issue of self-harm as it arises from cyberbullying. Just because someone — sadly — commits suicide when bullied, either using electronic media or the old-fashioned bully in the school hallway, that does not automatically mean that the bullying was the cause. Most of us have endured bullying of some form in our lives and have dealt with it without suicide.

The final point that the second article raises, which the first passage ignores, is the right to free speech. While there are obviously reasonable limitations on free speech, we have to be very careful before considering restrictions of such a basic right.

While cyberbullying is an unfortunate reality of the life of today's teens, it is not necessary to expand criminal laws to cover such events. Existing laws will deal with extreme cases, an education, with parental and school involvement, will help limit such events. Finally, the removal of anonymity from social media should have an effect, again without limiting free speech or criminalizing such activities.

# Answer Key

| | | |
|---|---|---|
| 1. B | 2. C | 3. **distributing discarded materials to visual arts classes** |
| 4. B | 5. D | 6. C |
| 7. A | 8. D | 9. B |
| 10. D | 11. A | 12. C |
| 13. B | 14. B | 15. D |
| 16. A | 17. B | 18. C |
| 19. B | 20. D | 21. B |
| 22. D | 23. C | 24. **Dutch colonists** |
| 25. A | 26. **yellow bricks** | 27. **Hawkins's fields** |
| 28. A | 29. D | 30. B |
| 31. A | 32. B | 33. D |
| 34. A | 35. C | 36. **times** |
| 37. **exceptable** | 38. A | 39. B |
| 40. **Its** | 41. C | 42. **not** |
| 43. B | 44. C | 45. B |
| 46. D | 47. A | 48. B |
| 49. A | 50. **grimly ordinary** | 51. D |
| 52. A | 53. D | 54. **hungry** |
| 55. C | 56. D | 57. B |
| 58. D | 59. D | 60. B |

# Chapter 19

# Practice Test 1: Social Studies

· · · · · · · · · · · · · · · · · · · · · · · · · · · · · · · · · · · · · · · · · · · · · · · · · · · · ·

*T*he Social Studies test consists of questions that measure general social studies concepts. The questions are based on short readings that often include a map, graph, chart, cartoon, or figure. Study the information given and then answer the question(s) following it. Refer to the information as often as necessary in answering the questions.

The Social Studies section of the GED test consists of two parts: You have 65 minutes to complete the question-answer portion of the Social Studies component and another 25 minutes to complete the Extended Response (the essay). You may not transfer leftover time between sections.

The answers and explanations to this test's questions are in Chapter 20. Go through the explanations to all the questions, even for the ones you answered correctly. The explanations are a good review of the techniques we discuss throughout the book.

Unless you require accommodations, you'll be taking the GED test on a computer. Instead of marking your answers on a separate answer sheet, like you do for the practice tests in this book, you'll see clickable ovals and fill-in-the-blank text boxes, and you'll be able to click with your mouse and drag and drop items where indicated. We formatted the questions and answer choices in this book to make them appear as similar as possible to the real GED test, but we had to retain some A, B, C, D choices for marking your answers, and we provide an answer sheet for you to do so.

# Answer Sheet for Practice Test 1, Social Studies

| | | | | | | | | | | |
|---|---|---|---|---|---|---|---|---|---|---|
| 1. | Ⓐ | Ⓑ | Ⓒ | Ⓓ | | 24. | Ⓐ | Ⓑ | Ⓒ | Ⓓ |
| 2. | Ⓐ | Ⓑ | Ⓒ | Ⓓ | | 25. | Ⓐ | Ⓑ | Ⓒ | Ⓓ |
| 3. | Ⓐ | Ⓑ | Ⓒ | Ⓓ | | 26. | Ⓐ | Ⓑ | Ⓒ | Ⓓ |
| 4. | Ⓐ | Ⓑ | Ⓒ | Ⓓ | | 27. | Ⓐ | Ⓑ | Ⓒ | Ⓓ |
| 5. | Ⓐ | Ⓑ | Ⓒ | Ⓓ | | 28. | ☐ | ☐ | ☐ | ☐ |
| 6. | Ⓐ | Ⓑ | Ⓒ | Ⓓ | | 29. | Ⓐ | Ⓑ | Ⓒ | Ⓓ |
| 7. | Ⓐ | Ⓑ | Ⓒ | Ⓓ | | 30. | Ⓐ | Ⓑ | Ⓒ | Ⓓ |
| 8. | Ⓐ | Ⓑ | Ⓒ | Ⓓ | | 31. | Ⓐ | Ⓑ | Ⓒ | Ⓓ |
| 9. | Ⓐ | Ⓑ | Ⓒ | Ⓓ | | 32. | Ⓐ | Ⓑ | Ⓒ | Ⓓ |
| 10. | Ⓐ | Ⓑ | Ⓒ | Ⓓ | | 33. | | | | |
| 11. | | | | | | 34. | Ⓐ | Ⓑ | Ⓒ | Ⓓ |
| 12. | Ⓐ | Ⓑ | Ⓒ | Ⓓ | | 35. | Ⓐ | Ⓑ | Ⓒ | Ⓓ |
| 13. | Ⓐ | Ⓑ | Ⓒ | Ⓓ | | 36. | | | | |
| 14. | | | | | | 37. | Ⓐ | Ⓑ | Ⓒ | Ⓓ |
| 15. | Ⓐ | Ⓑ | Ⓒ | Ⓓ | | 38. | Ⓐ | Ⓑ | Ⓒ | Ⓓ |
| 16. | Ⓐ | Ⓑ | Ⓒ | Ⓓ | | 39. | Ⓐ | Ⓑ | Ⓒ | Ⓓ |
| 17. | Ⓐ | Ⓑ | Ⓒ | Ⓓ | | 40. | | | | |
| 18. | Ⓐ | Ⓑ | Ⓒ | Ⓓ | | 41. | Ⓐ | Ⓑ | Ⓒ | Ⓓ |
| 19. | Ⓐ | Ⓑ | Ⓒ | Ⓓ | | 42. | Ⓐ | Ⓑ | Ⓒ | Ⓓ |
| 20. | | | | | | 43. | Ⓐ | Ⓑ | Ⓒ | Ⓓ |
| 21. | Ⓐ | Ⓑ | Ⓒ | Ⓓ | | 44. | Ⓐ | Ⓑ | Ⓒ | Ⓓ |
| 22. | Ⓐ | Ⓑ | Ⓒ | Ⓓ | | 45. | Ⓐ | Ⓑ | Ⓒ | Ⓓ |
| 23. | | | | | | | | | | |

# Social Studies Test

**Time:** 65 minutes

**Directions:** Mark your answers on the answer sheet provided.

---

*Questions 1–5 refer to the following passage, which is excerpted from* CliffsQuickReview U.S. History I, *by P. Soifer and A. Hoffman (Wiley).*

---

### Industry and Trade in the Thirteen Colonies

The colonies were part of an Atlantic trading network that linked them with England, Africa, and the West Indies. The pattern of commerce, not too accurately called the Triangular Trade, involved the exchange of products from colonial farms, plantations, fisheries, and forests with England for manufactured goods and the West Indies for slaves, molasses, and sugar. In New England, molasses and sugar were distilled into rum, which was used to buy African slaves. Southern Europe was also a valuable market for colonial foodstuffs.

Colonial industry was closely associated with trade. A significant percentage of Atlantic shipping was on vessels built in the colonies, and shipbuilding stimulated other crafts, such as the sewing of sails, milling of lumber, and manufacturing of naval stores. Mercantile theory encouraged the colonies to provide raw materials for England's industrializing economy; pig iron and coal became important exports. Concurrently, restrictions were placed on finished goods. For example, Parliament, concerned about possible competition from colonial hatters, prohibited the export of hats from one colony to another and limited the number of apprentices in each hat maker's shop.

1. What did England, Africa, and the West Indies have in common?

   (A) They all had fisheries.

   (B) They all bought slaves.

   (C) They all distilled rum.

   (D) They all exchanged products.

2. What was rum used for?

   (A) colonial farms

   (B) milling of lumber

   (C) purchase of slaves

   (D) molasses and sugar

3. Why were the colonies important to Atlantic trade?

   (A) They built the ships.

   (B) They sewed sails.

   (C) They had naval stores.

   (D) They milled lumber.

4. How did the colonies support British industry?

   (A) They took part in sewing.

   (B) They produced finished goods.

   (C) They developed mercantile theory.

   (D) They provided raw materials.

5. What product was threatened by colonial competition?

   (A) coal

   (B) pig iron

   (C) hats

   (D) lumber

*Go on to next page* ⟶

Questions 6–11 refer to the following passage, which is excerpted from *The Declaration of Independence*, 1776.

### Charges against the King

He has forbidden his governors to pass laws of immediate and pressing importance, unless suspended in their operation till his assent should be obtained; and when so suspended, he has utterly neglected to attend to them.

He has refused to pass other laws for the accommodation of large districts of people, unless those people would relinquish the right of representation in the legislature — a right inestimable to them, and formidable to tyrants only.

He has called together legislative bodies at places unusual, uncomfortable, and distant from the depository of their public records, for the sole purpose of fatiguing them into compliance with his measures.

He has dissolved representative houses repeatedly, for opposing, with manly firmness, his invasions on the rights of the people.

He has refused, for a long time after such dissolutions, to cause others to be elected; whereby the legislative powers, incapable of annihilation, have returned to the people at large, for their exercise, the state remaining in the meantime exposed to all the dangers of invasion from without, and convulsions within.

He has endeavored to prevent the population of these states; for that purpose obstructing the laws for naturalization of foreigners; refusing to pass others to encourage their migration hither, and raising the conditions of new appropriations of lands.

He has obstructed the administration of justice, by refusing his assent to laws for establishing judiciary powers.

He has made judges dependent on his will alone, for the tenure of their offices, and the amount and payment of their salaries.

He has erected a multitude of new offices, and sent hither swarms of officers, to harass our people, and eat out their substance.

He has kept among us, in times of peace, standing armies, without the consent of our legislature.

He has affected to render the military independent of, and superior to, the civil power.

6.  The king neglected the colonies in many ways, especially by

    (A) failing to provide money

    (B) failing to pass laws

    (C) removing their right of condemnation

    (D) giving power to his governors

7.  Which of the listed methods did the king use in an attempt to enforce compliance by legislative bodies to his wishes?

    (A) He never called them together.

    (B) He made them comfortable.

    (C) He made sure they were well rested.

    (D) He made them comply with his wishes.

*Go on to next page*

8. The main measure used by the king that was seen as a threat to the colonists' rights was

   (A) He dissolved representative houses.

   (B) He abdicated the throne.

   (C) He annihilated them.

   (D) He returned them to the people.

9. The king was very concerned about the growth of the colonies, so much so that he

   (A) gave away free land to people willing to settle

   (B) encouraged people to settle

   (C) settled there himself

   (D) discouraged people from settling

10. Were judges able to address the concerns of the people?

    (A) Yes. They had complete freedom to interpret the law.

    (B) No. British law curtailed their freedom of action.

    (C) No. Judges depended on the king's "pleasure" to retain their jobs.

    (D) Yes. The king guaranteed their freedom of action.

11. What was one way the freedom of the people was threatened? [          ]

---

*Questions 12–13 refer to this map.*

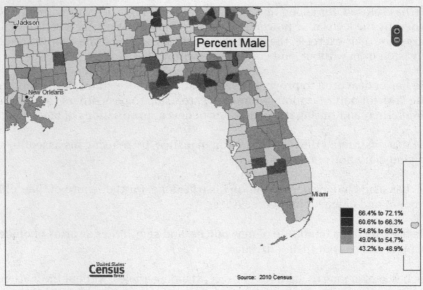

*Illustration courtesy of the U.S. Census Bureau*

---

12. People tend to live in areas with employment opportunities. Look at the areas with the lowest male population density. In these areas, the tourist industry is very important. Based on that information, what factors might explain lower male population density?

    (A) Tourist areas have more service-industry jobs, which are mostly female.

    (B) Because women have a greater life expectancy, there would be more elderly female tourists.

    (C) Men dislike working in the tourist industry.

    (D) Insufficient information is provided.

13. If the area shaded lightly around Miami has a population of 5.6 million people, approximately how many more females are there in the population than males?

    (A) 2.7 million

    (B) 2.9 million

    (C) 400,000

    (D) 1.2 million

*Go on to next page*

Questions 14–16 are based on this chart.

**Median Earnings in the Past 12 Months**
(In 2012 inflation-adjusted dollars)
by Sex by Work Experience in the Past 12 Months for the Population 16 Years And Over With Earnings in the Past 12 Months

San Francisco County, California
Powered by The American Community Survey

| | One Race | | | | | | Two or more races | |
| --- | --- | --- | --- | --- | --- | --- | --- | --- |
| | White | Black or African American | American Indian and Alaska Native | Asian | Native Hawaiian and Other Pacific Islander | Some Other Race | | Hispanic or Latino (any race) |
| Total: | $53,498 | $31,149 | $25,812 | $36,052 | $39,788 | $23,678 | $35,833 | $27,016 |
| Male | $60,910 | $33,915 | $27,766 | $39,346 | $48,347 | $26,758 | $37,400 | $28,456 |
| Worked full-time, year-round in the past 12 months | $79,234 | $50,612 | $48,393 | $53,662 | $62,896 | $40,498 | $62,516 | $39,364 |
| Other | $21,078 | $15,787 | $10,475 | $14,320 | $21,836 | $13,581 | $11,758 | $13,423 |
| Female | $47,729 | $26,962 | $17,365 | $32,893 | $31,386 | $18,692 | $33,719 | $25,012 |
| Worked full-time, year-round in the past 12 months | $65,675 | $43,345 | $34,205 | $49,539 | $43,185 | $35,451 | $56,736 | $40,099 |
| Other | $18,681 | $10,280 | $8,243 | $13,428 | $13,108 | $10,831 | $12,244 | $11,741 |

*Illustration courtesy of the U.S. Census Bureau*

14. Of the various racial groups shown, the group with the highest earning if employed full-time over the past 12 months was

    ☐ .

15. Which group, working full time, had the lowest annual income?

    (A) Female, Black or African American

    (B) Female, American Indian and Alaskan Native

    (C) Female, Asian

    (D) Male, Hispanic or Latino (any race)

16. Where in this chart would a 15-year-old male of Chinese background find statistical information about his income group?

    (A) under Male, Asian

    (B) under Some Other Race

    (C) under Male, Native Hawaiian and Other Pacific Islander

    (D) He could not.

Questions 17–22 refer to the following passage, which is excerpted from Lincoln's Gettysburg Address, November 19, 1863.

**Gettysburg Address**

Four score and seven years ago, our fathers brought forth upon this continent a new nation, conceived in liberty and dedicated to the proposition that all men are created equal. Now we are engaged in a great civil war, testing whether that nation or any nation so conceived and so dedicated can long endure. We are met on a great battlefield of that war. We have come to dedicate a portion of that field as a final resting place for those who here gave their lives that that nation might live. It is altogether fitting and proper that we should do this. But, in a larger sense, we cannot dedicate, we cannot consecrate, we cannot hallow this ground. The brave men, living and dead, who struggled here have consecrated it far above our poor power to add or detract. The world will little note nor long remember what we say here, but it can never forget what they did here. . . .

*Go on to next page*

17. The issue of primary importance in this great civil war is

    (A) happiness and friendship

    (B) safety and security

    (C) liberty and equality

    (D) peace and prosperity

18. Where was President Lincoln's speech delivered?

    (A) on a train

    (B) at the White House

    (C) on a battlefield

    (D) on the radio

19. What does "little note nor long remember" mean?

    (A) The audience is not taking notes.

    (B) Lincoln has a bad memory.

    (C) The soldiers are not there to hear the speech.

    (D) People around the world will not remember the speech.

20. According to the address, a portion of the battlefield is used for [      ].

21. Who has "hallow[ed] this ground"?

    (A) President Lincoln

    (B) those who fought there

    (C) the Confederate government

    (D) the Union government

22. What does "four score and seven" refer to?

    (A) soldiers

    (B) consecration

    (C) time

    (D) the war

---

*Questions 23–28 refer to the following passage, which is excerpted from* CliffsQuickReview U.S. History II, *by P. Soifer and A. Hoffman (Wiley).*

---

### Causes of World War I

On June 28, 1914, a Serbian nationalist assassinated the Archduke Franz Ferdinand, the heir to the throne of Austria-Hungary. Austria demanded indemnities from Serbia for the assassination. The Serbian government denied any involvement with the murder and, when Austria issued an ultimatum, turned to its ally, Russia, for help. When Russia began to mobilize its army, Europe's alliance system, ironically intended to maintain the balance of power on the continent, drew one country after another into war. Austria's ally, Germany, declared war on Russia on August 1 and on France (which was allied with Russia) two days later. Great Britain entered the war on August 4, following Germany's invasion of neutral Belgium. By the end of August 1914, most of Europe had chosen sides: the Central Powers — Germany, Austria-Hungary, Bulgaria, and the Ottoman Empire (Turkey) — were up against the Allied Powers — principally Great Britain, France, Russia, and Serbia. Japan joined the Allied cause in August 1914, in hopes of seizing German possessions in the Pacific and expanding Japanese influence in China. This action threatened the Open Door Policy and led to increased tensions with the United States. Originally an ally of Germany and Austria-Hungary, Italy entered the war in 1915 on the side of Britain and France because they had agreed to Italian territorial demands in a secret treaty (the Treaty of London).

*Go on to next page*

23. The assassin of Archduke Ferdinand came from the country of [          ].

24. Austria initially reacted to the assassination by

    (A) denying any involvement

    (B) demanding indemnities

    (C) asking for Russian help

    (D) declaring war

25. Which countries were not allies?

    (A) Serbia and Russia

    (B) Austria and Hungary

    (C) Germany and France

    (D) France and Great Britain

26. What caused Great Britain to enter the war?

    (A) Germany invaded Belgium.

    (B) Russia attacked Serbia.

    (C) Germany declared war on France.

    (D) Austria invaded Hungary.

27. Which country was not an Allied Power?

    (A) Great Britain

    (B) France

    (C) Germany

    (D) Serbia

28. Place the events in the proper sequence.

    (A) Italy enters on the Allied side.

    (B) Germany declares war on Russia.

    (C) Great Britain declares war on Germany.

    (D) Germany invades Belgium.

---

*Questions 29–32 refer to the following political cartoon.*

*Illustration by Ricardo Checa*

*Go on to next page*

29. How is President Barack Obama portrayed in the cartoon?

    (A) stand-up comedian

    (B) inspiring teacher

    (C) stern disciplinarian

    (D) fashion model

30. What do the smiling faces of the students symbolize?

    (A) happy voters

    (B) a receptive public

    (C) the bright future the President is hoping for

    (D) issues that can be solved

31. Why are two issues written in much smaller print on the spines of two textbooks?

    (A) These issues are very important but often overlooked.

    (B) The president will concentrate more on international rather than domestic issues.

    (C) They are just decoration.

    (D) Not enough room to draw more students.

32. What problems are the students facing in the future?

    (A) unemployment

    (B) shortage of energy

    (C) escalating debt

    (D) all of the above

---

*Questions 33–36 refer to this table.*

**Table 852. Selected Farm Products—U.S. and World Production and Exports: 2000 to 2010**

[In metric tons, except as indicated (60.6 represents 60,600,000). Metric ton = 1.102 short tons or .984 long tons]

| Commodity | Unit | Amount United States | | | Amount World | | | United States as percent of world | | |
|---|---|---|---|---|---|---|---|---|---|---|
| | | 2000 | 2005 | 2010 | 2000 | 2005 | 2010 | 2000 | 2005 | 2010 |
| PRODUCTION [1] | | | | | | | | | | |
| Wheat | Million | 60.6 | 57.2 | 60.1 | 583.1 | 619.1 | 648.1 | 10.4 | 9.2 | 9.3 |
| Corn for grain | Million | 251.9 | 282.3 | 316.2 | 591.4 | 699.7 | 815.3 | 42.6 | 40.3 | 38.8 |
| Soybeans | Million | 75.1 | 83.5 | 90.6 | 175.8 | 220.7 | 262.0 | 42.7 | 37.8 | 34.6 |
| Rice, milled | Million | 5.9 | 7.1 | 7.6 | 399.4 | 418.2 | 451.6 | 1.5 | 1.7 | 1.7 |
| Cotton [2] | Million bales [3] | 17.2 | 23.9 | 18.1 | 89.1 | 116.4 | 114.6 | 19.3 | 20.5 | 15.8 |
| EXPORTS [4] | | | | | | | | | | |
| Wheat [5] | Million | 28.9 | 27.3 | 34.7 | 101.5 | 117.0 | 124.7 | 28.5 | 23.3 | 27.8 |
| Corn | Million | 49.3 | 54.2 | 48.3 | 76.9 | 81.1 | 90.6 | 64.2 | 66.9 | 53.2 |
| Soybeans | Million | 27.1 | 25.6 | 42.2 | 53.7 | 63.4 | 95.6 | 50.5 | 40.3 | 44.1 |
| Rice, milled basis | Million | 2.6 | 3.7 | 3.6 | 24.1 | 29.7 | 31.4 | 10.7 | 12.3 | 11.3 |
| Cotton [2] | Million bales [3] | 6.7 | 17.7 | 15.5 | 26.2 | 44.9 | 37.0 | 25.7 | 39.4 | 41.9 |

[1] Production years vary by commodity. In most cases, includes harvests from July 1 of the year shown through June 30 of the following year. [2] For production and trade years ending in year shown. [3] Bales of 480 lb. net weight. [4] Trade years may vary by commodity. Wheat, corn, and soybean data are for trade year beginning in year shown. Rice data are for calendar year. [5] Includes wheat flour on a grain equivalent.

*Illustration courtesy of the U.S. Department of Agriculture*

33. What percentage of the world's soybean production came from the United States in 2010? [_____]

34. In 2010, approximately how much of the U.S. production of cotton was exported?

    (A) all of it

    (B) most of it

    (C) just under half

    (D) almost none

35. Between 2000 and 2010, world exports of corn

    (A) increased

    (B) decreased

    (C) decreased a lot

    (D) stayed about the same

36. What is the weight of a bale of cotton, according to the table? [_____]

*Go on to next page*

Questions 37–41 refer to the following timeline.

**Timeline of Major Events in U.S. History**

**1900:** Gold standard for currency adopted by United States.
**1914:** World War I begins.
**1918:** World War I ends.
**1929:** Stock market crashes; Great Depression begins.
**1933:** Gold exports banned; daily price established; U.S. citizens ordered to turn in all gold.
**1934:** Price of gold fixed at $35 per troy ounce.
**1939:** World War II begins.
**1945:** World War II ends.
**1950:** Korean Conflict begins.
**1953:** Korean Conflict ends.
**1965:** Vietnam War begins.
**1973:** Vietnam War ends; gold prices allowed to float; U.S. currency removed from gold standard.
**1974:** U.S. citizens allowed to own gold again.
**1979:** Soviet Union invades Afghanistan; U.S. hostages seized in Iran.
**1980:** Historic high prices for gold.
**1987:** Stock market crashes.
**1989:** Berlin Wall falls.
**1990:** Gulf War begins.
**1991:** Gulf War ends.
**2001:** Terrorist attacks on the United States.
**2002:** Invasion of Afghanistan and Iraq.
**2008:** United States elects first black president.
**2009:** United States slips into a recession.

37. In 1900, the value of the United States' dollar was based on

    (A) stock market

    (B) value of gold

    (C) value of silver

    (D) trade surplus

38. What, if anything, is the connection between the stock market crash and the Great Depression in 1929?

    (A) It was the trigger.

    (B) Very little; economic problems had been building for some time before the crash.

    (C) Pure coincidence.

    (D) The stock market crash actually delayed the Great Depression.

39. What does "U.S. citizens ordered to turn in all gold" mean?

    (A) Citizens got to keep their gold.

    (B) Citizens had to tell the government about their gold.

    (C) Citizens could buy gold from each other, for profit.

    (D) Citizens had to take all their gold to government offices.

40. When was U.S. currency removed from the gold standard? ☐

41. Based on what you see in the timeline, what likely caused the price of gold to reach an historic high?

    (A) Citizens were allowed to hold bullion.

    (B) Gold stocks were sold.

    (C) The Soviet Union invaded Afghanistan.

    (D) The Gulf War began.

*Go on to next page*

*Questions 42–44 refer to the following newscast.*

### World Environmental News

Good evening and welcome to World Environmental News.

Our stories this evening: cyclones in Korea, hurricane near Mexico, flooding in Europe and India, volcanic eruptions in New Guinea, drought in Australia, tornadoes in the United States, hailstorms in Italy, earthquakes in Iran, and locusts in Denmark.

Now, let's look at our top stories.

**Drought in Australia:** The wheat fields west of Canberra, New South Wales, are in great danger today because of the ongoing drought. If the drought continues, farmers may have to write off this year's entire crop, and this will likely lead to financial ruin for many of them. To add to the misery, hundreds of thousands of sheep had to be sold because there was not enough water for them to drink.

**Locusts in Denmark:** The unseasonably warm weather in Denmark is proving to be inviting to the lowly locust, a major crop-eating pest. Normally found along the Mediterranean coast, the locust recently has been found far from its normal habitat. These discoveries in southwest Denmark are causing concern because locusts have not been seen in Denmark for more than 50 years.

**Hurricane near Mexico:** Hurricane Herman is losing force off the Pacific coast of Mexico. The country is giving a collective sigh of relief as the hurricane winds down.

**For wine drinkers:** And a last note for you wine drinkers. The recent violent hailstorms in Italy have devastated vineyards, and wine producers are warning of a poor grape harvest. This means lower wine production and, consequently, higher prices.

There's more as nature lashes out. Tune in again for more World Environmental News.

42. The newscast says "cyclones in Korea, hurricane near Mexico"; what is the difference between cyclones and hurricanes?

(A) Location. Meteorologists call these storms *hurricanes* in the Atlantic and northeast Pacific and *cyclones* in the eastern Pacific and Indian Ocean.

(B) Cyclones are a form of tornado.

(C) Cyclones are much more severe.

(D) Unlike hurricanes, cyclones are always associated with flooding.

43. How does extreme drought cause financial problems for farmers?

(A) Farmers lose their entire year's crop and income.

(B) Selling off large herds of sheep at once leads to much lower prices and fewer sheep for future breeding stock.

(C) It doesn't because crop insurance covers any losses.

(D) Choices (A) and (B).

44. Is the finding of locusts in Denmark significant?

(A) Yes, because it reinforces the idea of climate change and global warming.

(B) Yes, because it indicates that prevailing winds have shifted.

(C) Yes, because more stringent inspections of ships are required if ships carried insects.

(D) No, because it is an isolated incident and has no real significance.

*Go on to next page*

---

*Question 45 refers to the following passage, which is excerpted from the Central Intelligence Agency website (www.cia.gov).*

By the time World War I started in 1914, the United States' ability to collect foreign intelligence had shrunk drastically because of budget cuts and bureaucratic reorganizations in the government. The State Department began small-scale collections against the Central Powers in 1916, but it wasn't until the United States declared war on Germany in 1917 that Army and Navy intelligence finally received more money and personnel. By that time, it was too late to increase their intelligence output to aid the cause very much.

The most significant advance for US intelligence during the war was the establishment of a permanent communications intelligence agency in the Army, what would become the forerunner of the National Security Agency. Meanwhile, the Secret Service, the New York Police Department, and military counterintelligence aggressively thwarted numerous German covert actions inside the United States, including psychological warfare, political and economic operations, and dozens of sabotage attempts against British-owned firms and factories supplying munitions to Britain and Russia.

45. How effective was U.S. foreign intelligence gathering during World War I?

(A) Very effective; it stopped much domestic sabotage.

(B) Not very effective; it depended on the New York Police Department.

(C) It was limited because of pre-war budget cuts.

(D) It was excellent at psychological warfare.

*Go on to next page*

# The Extended Response

**Time:** 25 minutes

**Your assignment:** Develop an argument on how the following passage reflects an enduring issue in American history. (*Note:* An enduring issue is one that "reflects the founding principles of the United States and is an important idea that people often grapple with as new situations arise" [GED. com].) Incorporate material from the passage, the 14th Amendment, the Defense of Marriage Act, and your own knowledge of the enduring issues and the controversy surrounding this specific issue to support your argument. You have 25 minutes to plan, draft, and write your response in the space provided.

### 14th Amendment of the Constitution of the United States

**Section 1.** *All persons born or naturalized in the United States, and subject to the jurisdiction thereof, are citizens of the United States and of the State wherein they reside. No State shall make or enforce any law which shall abridge the privileges or immunities of citizens of the United States; nor shall any State deprive any person of life, liberty, or property, without due process of law; nor deny to any person within its jurisdiction the equal protection of the laws.*

**The Defense of Marriage Act** *(excerpted from U.S. Government Printing Office (*`www.gpo.gov`*))*

**Section 2. Powers Reserved to the States.** *No State, territory, or possession of the United States, or Indian tribe, shall be required to give effect to any public act, record, or judicial proceeding of any other State, territory, possession, or tribe respecting a relationship between persons of the same sex that is treated as a marriage under the laws of such other State, territory, possession, or tribe, or a right or claim arising from such relationship.*

**Section 3. Definition of Marriage.** *In determining the meaning of any Act of Congress, or of any ruling, regulation, or interpretation of the various administrative bureaus and agencies of the United States, the word 'marriage' means only a legal union between one man and one woman as husband and wife, and the word 'spouse' refers only to a person of the opposite sex who is a husband or a wife.*

The Defense of Marriage Act (DOMA), passed in 1996, made it possible for state governments to refuse to recognize same-sex marriage granted in other jurisdictions. Section 3 of the Act made it impossible for same-sex couples to receive spousal benefits and any other federal benefits, from health insurance to social security benefits. That section was ruled unconstitutional in 2013. The second section of DOMA continues to exist. It exempts states, tribes, and possessions of the United States from the Constitutional requirements to recognize marriages formalized in another state. Any state can refuse to recognize same-sex marriages formalized elsewhere. The Constitution guarantees that marriages performed in any state are recognized in every other state, but the remnants of DOMA grant states an exemption on same-sex marriage.

For the lesbian, gay, bisexual, and transgender (LGBT) community, this means that discrimination remains in effect in numerous states that have not made same-sex marriage legal. Discrimination of any kind is in theory inappropriate, and yet the continuation of the second section of the Defense of Marriage Act allows it. This, too, is in direct violation of Section 1 of the 14th Amendment. Further, there are no federal laws that prohibit discrimination based on sexual orientation, and in any case, they generally would not apply to the private sector or religious organizations. More than half of the states have no prohibitions against discrimination based on sexual orientation or identity.

There has been obvious progress. The military has ended the policy of "Don't ask, don't tell" and ended discrimination based on sexual orientation. Some states now allow same-sex marriages and more have some degree of legal protections against discrimination based on sexual orientation. Discrimination based on sexual orientation is not permitted in federal health care programs, and there is some limited protection under federal hate crime laws. The Equal Employment Opportunity Commission ruled in 2011 and again in 2012 that job discrimination based on sexual orientation also is a form of discrimination covered by the Civil Rights Act of 1964. Despite all these changes, there is much left to do.

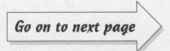
*Go on to next page*

To be a nation truly committed to equal rights for all, there must be federal legislation that applies across the country, public, and private sector alike. The hodgepodge of state legislation is not adequate, and the statement by President Obama that the federal government would no longer enforce Section 2 of the 14th Amendment is not enough. There must be clear direction and leadership. Without such, there is no equality of rights.

*Go on to next page*

*Go on to next page*

# Chapter 20

# Answers for Practice Test 1, Social Studies

*I*n this chapter, we provide the answers and explanations to every question in the Social Studies practice test in Chapter 19. If you just want a quick look at the answers, check out the abbreviated answer key at the end of this chapter. However, if you have the time, it's more useful for study purposes to read all the answer explanations carefully. Doing so will help you understand why some answers were correct and others not, especially when the choices were really close. It will also point you at areas where you may need to do more review. Remember, you learn as much from your errors as from the correct answers.

## Answers and Explanations

1. **D. They all exchanged products.** England, Africa, and the West Indies all traded products: The West Indies traded molasses, sugar, and slaves with England for food and wood; England (via the New England colonies) then made the molasses and sugar into rum and traded it with Africa for more slaves. But these areas did not all have the same commodities to trade; each had its own strengths.

2. **C. purchase of slaves.** Rum was used to purchase slaves for the colonies. The other answer choices — colonial farms, milling of lumber, and molasses and sugar — were all patterns of commerce but weren't uses of rum.

3. **A. They built the ships.** Ships were built in the colonies to increase Atlantic trade. Sewing sails, naval stores, milled lumber, and other crafts were colonial products that shipbuilding stimulated. However, ship building itself was the primary reason the colonies were important to the Atlantic trade — the other choices were secondary.

4. **D. They provided raw materials.** The colonies provided raw materials for British manufacturing industries. According to the passage, "Mercantile theory encouraged the colonies to provide raw materials for England's industrializing economy. . . ." The British government blocked exports of finished goods from the colonies.

5. **C. hats.** The export of hats — a finished good — from the colonies was prohibited because it threatened British manufacturing. Coal and lumber were raw materials, which didn't threaten English manufacturing. Even pig iron needed further manufacturing to sell, so it was allowed.

6. **B. failing to pass laws.** According to the first paragraph of the passage, the king neglected the colonies in a number of ways. Of the ways listed here, only failing to pass laws (ones that would alleviate grievances) is correct. Although the other choices are grievances, they can't be alleviated until the appropriate laws are passed.

7. **D. He made them comply with his wishes.** According to the third paragraph of the passage, the legislative bodies were forced to comply with the king's rule (". . . for the sole purpose of fatiguing them into compliance with his measures . . .").

8. **A. He dissolved representative houses.** According to the fourth paragraph of the passage, when the king dissolved the representative houses, he threatened the rights of the people.

9. **D. discouraged people from settling.** The sixth paragraph of the passage says, "He has endeavored to prevent the population of these states." In other words, he has discouraged newcomers from settling.

10. **C. No. Judges depended on the king's "pleasure" to retain their jobs.** The eighth paragraph of the passage states that judges were completely dependent on the king for their position, tenure and salaries. They could be removed at the king's "pleasure". While they may have had the appearance of freedom of action, the threat of losing their jobs kept judges' decisions in line with the king's wishes.

11. **an independent military.** The king made sure the military was independent from the colonists (last paragraph). This independence meant the colonists didn't have any authority over when to hire or fire soldiers, how large the military was, or who the officers were. Only the king made those kinds of decisions.

12. **D. Insufficient information is provided.** Although both Choices (A) and (B) are potentially correct, nothing in the map supports those statements. Choice (C) is simply speculation and, therefore, doesn't apply. The only option left is Choice (D).

13. **C. 400,000.** You're asked for an approximate answer. First, find that the range of the male population is between 43.2 and 48.9 percent. So using an average of 47 percent, there are about 2.6 million males. That means that there are some 3 million females, for a surplus of about 400,000 females. Because all the numbers are approximate, you can round off your answer. Regardless, the only choice that comes close is Choice (C).

14. **White Male.** Based on the table, the group with the highest income for full-time employment for the year is White Male.

15. **B. Female, American Indian and Alaskan Native.** Based on the chart, the lowest full-time earners are American Indians and Alaskan native females.

16. **D. He could not.** The table doesn't list information for people under the age of 16. That is shown in the subheading of the chart title.

17. **C. liberty and equality.** As stated in the first two sentences of the passage, the issues of prime importance in the Civil War were liberty and equality. Happiness and friendship, safety and security, and peace and prosperity aren't the best answers.

18. **C. on a battlefield.** You know from the passage that President Lincoln was delivering his speech on a battlefield at Gettysburg. This fact rules out every answer choice except on a battlefield and on the radio (he could've recorded his speech, and it could've been broadcasted by radio at the battlefield). However, Lincoln gave this speech in 1863, and radios (or audio recorders for that matter) hadn't yet been invented.

19. **D. People around the world will not remember the speech.** Lincoln was saying that the world would remember the soldiers who died but wouldn't remember his speech. (He was wrong, given that the Gettysburg Address is one of the most famous speeches in American history.)

20. **burial ground.** Some of the battlefield was to become a burial ground for the fallen.

21. **B. those who fought there.** The ground was hallowed by those who fought there. Lincoln doesn't believe the people involved in the dedication of the battlefield can make the place holy or important; only the people who fought on the battlefield can do so.

22. **C. time.** The word *years* follows *four score and seven,* so you can assume that phrase relates to time. (By the way, a *score* is 20 years, so *four score and seven* is 87 years.)

23. **Serbia.** Archduke Ferdinand was assassinated by a Serbian nationalist, so the correct answer is *Serbia*.

24. **B. demanding indemnities.** Austria demanded indemnities in response to the assassination. This answer comes directly from the passage.

25. **C. Germany and France.** Germany and France weren't allies in the war. Although the list of allies is rather confusing, the passage does sum up who was on which side.

26. **A. Germany invaded Belgium.** You know that Great Britain entered the war when Germany invaded Belgium from the sentence that states, "Great Britain entered the war on August 4, following Germany's invasion of neutral Belgium."

27. **C. Germany.** Germany was not an Allied power. About halfway through the passage is a list of the Central powers (on one side of the war) and the Allied powers (on the other side).

28. **B, D, C, A (Germany declares war on Russia; Germany invades Belgium; Great Britain declares war on Germany; Italy enters on the Allied side).** In this sequence, Germany declared war on Russia and then invaded Belgium. Great Britain declared war on Germany because it invaded Belgium. Italy didn't enter into the war on the Allied side until 1915.

29. **B. inspiring teacher.** In the cartoon, Barack Obama is portrayed in front of a chalkboard in a classroom setting. Most of the students are seen as receptive to his role as an inspiring teacher. The other choices — comedian, disciplinarian, or fashion model — don't go with the cartoon.

30. **D. issues that can be solved.** Most of the young people are portrayed as smiling students. They each represent an issue Obama must face, some more obvious than others. They're not happy voters, nor is there any indication that they represent the public in general. Although they may represent a bright future, there are also problems, so Choice (D) is the most logical answer. The smiling faces reinforce the idea that these issues can be solved.

31. **A. These issues are very important but often overlooked.** Each of the students in the cartoon represents a different problem facing America, but the issue of tensions with Iran and Iraq are always in the background and potentially a much larger problem for the president. The smiling faces suggest that the problems attached to them can be solved. But the issues of Iran and Iraq must also be solved, and the suggestion in the cartoon is that they're just waiting to become major.

32. **D. all of the above.** *All of the above* is the only correct choice because each of the students represents one of the problems facing America.

33. **34.6%.** According to the table, the United States produced 34.6 percent of the soybean output that year. It's the third item down on the last column of the table.

34. **B. most of it.** Production that year was 18.1 million bales. Exports amounted to 15.5 million bales. That is just over 85 percent. The best match among the choices is *most of it.*

35. **A. increased.** According to the table, center section, corn exports increased from 76.9 to 90.6 metric tons.

36. **480 pounds.** The explanatory notes under the table give the answer: 480 pounds. On tables and charts, it's important to read the fine print — the explanatory notes, legends, and keys — to make sure you have a complete understanding of the content.

37. **B. value of gold.** The first item on the list states "gold standard for currency adopted." That means that the value of the American dollar was based on the value of gold.

38. **A. It was the trigger.** The Great Depression was caused by a variety of issues, but the immediate cause, the trigger, was the crash of the stock market. The other answers are wrong. Although Choice (B) says that problems had been building, the crash started the panic that resulted in the Great Depression. It wasn't coincidence nor did the crash delay the Depression.

39. **D. Citizens had to take all their gold to government offices.** U.S. citizens had to take all their gold to U.S. offices and not keep any in their own homes. The timeline and graph don't tell you why they had to do so, just that they did. *Turn in* is the key phrase here.

40. **1973.** The U.S. currency was removed from the gold standard in 1973.

41. **C. The Soviet Union invaded Afghanistan.** The best answer is that gold reached a historic high when the Soviets invaded Afghanistan. You have to read the timeline to answer this question.

42. **A. Location. Meteorologists call these storms *hurricanes* in the Atlantic and northeast Pacific and *cyclones* in the eastern Pacific and Indian Ocean.** There is no difference between these storms other than location. Both hurricanes and cyclones are cyclonic storms, and both may bring flooding and heavy rains. A cyclone is not a tornado.

43. **D. Choices (A) and (B).** The extreme drought conditions in Australia led to both crop failures and the need to sell off far more sheep than usual. Both represent financial losses. Therefore, Choices (A) and (B) are correct. Although Choice (C) may be true, no information offered supports the idea that crop insurance exists for these farmers.

44. **A. Yes, because it reinforces the idea of climate change and global warming.** Because of unseasonably warm weather, locusts were found in Denmark. Locusts are drawn to warm weather. The fact that Denmark, a northern European country, is warm enough to allow locusts to survive means that the local climate must be warming. Although the newscast doesn't say so, in the context of all the other information presented, this fact supports the argument for climate change. You must interpret the information to arrive at the correct conclusion.

45. **C. It was limited because of pre-war budget cuts.** The efforts against sabotage, Choice (A), and psychological warfare, Choice (D), weren't part of foreign intelligence gathering and are thus wrong. Choice (B) is also domestic intelligence. The foreign intelligence work was limited because of budget issues. The text states at the end of the first paragraph that foreign intelligence "did not aid the cause very much."

## Sample Extended Response

The following sample essay would receive good marks. It isn't perfect, but you're not expected to write a perfect essay in 25 minutes. Besides, you have only the source passages and your own knowledge on which to base your argument. Part of your mark is earned for content and argument, and part is earned for proper writing and grammar.

Compare the following sample to the response you wrote, and check out Chapter 7 for the scoring criteria and what evaluators look for in a response.

The issue of LGBT rights is one of equal rights for all, as guaranteed by the American constitution, especially in the 14th Amendment. While today the issue is equality regardless of sexual preference, in the past the issue included gender equality and racial equality. The issue of equality has a long history in America, starting with the debate about whether women should have the right to own and control property. That was followed by long conflicts over equal rights for African Americans. While slavery was ended by the Civil War, discrimination was not. Later, there were fierce arguments about granting women the right to vote. In the 1920s, there were debates about whether Native Americans should become American citizens. As recently as the 1960s, we were still debating — sometimes violently — whether whites and blacks should have integrated facilities, especially schools. In the seventies, the equality debate involved equal pay for women doing the same jobs as men.

Today, that debate centers of LGBT rights. While our constitution grants everyone equal rights, these have not been extended to LGBT individuals. Until recently, gay soldiers were expelled from the military just for being gay. As the text states, same-sex couples have few rights to spousal benefits. And despite constitutional guarantees that marriages performed in any state of the United States must be recognized in all states, some states still refuse to accept same-sex marriage.

The efforts to reinforce discrimination on this issue are blatant. The Defense of Marriage Act (DOMA) made it possible for states to refuse to recognize same-sex marriages performed in other states. This is in direct conflict with other portions of the Bill or Rights and the Constitution. Further, the definition of marriage specifically excluded same-sex couples.

However, there are efforts to protect equality rights for LGBT individuals. As the articles show, DOMA has been partially invalidated. And in other areas, the military has stopped discrimination against openly gay individuals. Court rulings have included gender orientation in forms of discrimination covered by the Civil Rights Act.

Yet the application of these moves to reinforce equal right is uneven. In many states, it is not illegal to discriminate on the basis of sexual orientation. Some states still ban same-sex marriage. The ending of the article states that there is still much to do.

The battle for equality for all continues, whether rights for Native Americans, African Americans, women, or anyone else, the issue continues. The focus of the inequality debate may have changed, but the issue — equality for all — has not. Indeed, this is an enduring issue, one that has created a national debate that still rages on.

# Answer Key

| | | |
|---|---|---|
| 1. D | 2. C | 3. A |
| 4. D | 5. C | 6. B |
| 7. D | 8. A | 9. D |
| 10. C | 11. **an independent military** | 12. D |
| 13. C | 14. **White Male** | 15. B |
| 16. D | 17. C | 18. C |
| 19. D | 20. **burial ground** | 21. B |
| 22. C | 23. **Serbia** | 24. B |
| 25. C | 26. A | 27. C |
| 28. **B, D, C, A** | 29. B | 30. D |
| 31. A | 32. D | 33. **34.6%** |
| 34. B | 35. A | 36. **480 pounds** |
| 37. B | 38. A | 39. D |
| 40. **1973** | 41. C | 42. A |
| 43. D | 44. A | 45. C |

# Chapter 21

# Practice Test 1: Science

• • • • • • • • • • • • • • • • • • • • • • • • • • • • • • • • • • • • • • • • • • • • •

*T*he Science test consists of multiple-choice, fill-in-the-blank, drop-down, drag-and-drop, hot-spot, and Short Answer items intended to measure general concepts in science. The questions are based on short passages that may include a graph, chart, or figure. Study the information given and then answer the question(s) following it. Refer to the passage information as often as necessary in answering the questions, but remember that you have a time limit, and you should try to spend as little time on any item as you can and still get the correct answer.

You have 90 minutes to complete this section of the GED test, including answering two Short Answer items, which should take about 10 minutes each. The answers and explanations to this test's questions are in Chapter 22. Go through the explanations to all the questions, even for the ones you answered correctly. The explanations are a good review of the techniques we discuss throughout the book.

Unless you require accommodations, you'll be taking the GED test on a computer. Instead of marking your answers on a separate answer sheet, like you do for the practice tests in this book, you'll see clickable ovals and fill-in-the-blank text boxes, and you'll be able to click with your mouse and drag and drop items where indicated. We formatted the questions and answer choices in this book to make them appear as similar as possible to what you'll see on the computer-based test, but we had to retain some A, B, C, D choices for marking your answers, and we provide an answer sheet for you to do so.

# Answer Sheet for Practice Test 1, Science

| | | | | | | | | | |
|---|---|---|---|---|---|---|---|---|---|
| 1. | Ⓐ | Ⓑ | Ⓒ | Ⓓ | 26. | Ⓐ | Ⓑ | Ⓒ | Ⓓ |
| 2. | Ⓐ | Ⓑ | Ⓒ | Ⓓ | 27. | Ⓐ | Ⓑ | Ⓒ | Ⓓ |
| 3. | Ⓐ | Ⓑ | Ⓒ | Ⓓ | 28. | Ⓐ | Ⓑ | Ⓒ | Ⓓ |
| 4. | Ⓐ | Ⓑ | Ⓒ | Ⓓ | 29. | Ⓐ | Ⓑ | Ⓒ | Ⓓ |
| 5. | | | | | 30. | Ⓐ | Ⓑ | Ⓒ | Ⓓ |
| 6. | Ⓐ | Ⓑ | Ⓒ | Ⓓ | 31. | Ⓐ | Ⓑ | Ⓒ | Ⓓ |
| 7. | | | | | 32. | Ⓐ | Ⓑ | Ⓒ | Ⓓ |
| 8. | Ⓐ | Ⓑ | Ⓒ | Ⓓ | 33. | Ⓐ | Ⓑ | Ⓒ | Ⓓ |
| 9. | Ⓐ | Ⓑ | Ⓒ | Ⓓ | 34. | | | | |
| 10. | | | | | 35. | | | | |
| 11. | | | | | 36. | Ⓐ | Ⓑ | Ⓒ | |
| 12. | Ⓐ | Ⓑ | Ⓒ | Ⓓ | 37. | Ⓐ | Ⓑ | Ⓒ | Ⓓ |
| 13. | Ⓐ | Ⓑ | Ⓒ | Ⓓ | 38. | Ⓐ | Ⓑ | Ⓒ | Ⓓ |
| 14. | Ⓐ | Ⓑ | Ⓒ | Ⓓ | 39. | Ⓐ | Ⓑ | Ⓒ | Ⓓ |
| 15. | Ⓐ | Ⓑ | Ⓒ | Ⓓ | 40. | Ⓐ | Ⓑ | Ⓒ | Ⓓ |
| 16. | Ⓐ | Ⓑ | Ⓒ | Ⓓ | 41. | Ⓐ | Ⓑ | Ⓒ | Ⓓ |
| 17. | Ⓐ | Ⓑ | Ⓒ | Ⓓ | 42. | | | | |
| 18. | Ⓐ | Ⓑ | Ⓒ | Ⓓ | 43. | | | | |
| 19. | Ⓐ | Ⓑ | Ⓒ | Ⓓ | 44. | Ⓐ | Ⓑ | Ⓒ | Ⓓ |
| 20. | Ⓐ | Ⓑ | Ⓒ | Ⓓ | 45. | Ⓐ | Ⓑ | Ⓒ | Ⓓ |
| 21. | | | | | 46. | | | | |
| 22. | Ⓐ | Ⓑ | Ⓒ | Ⓓ | 47. | Ⓐ | Ⓑ | Ⓒ | |
| 23. | Ⓐ | Ⓑ | Ⓒ | Ⓓ | 48. | Ⓐ | Ⓑ | Ⓒ | Ⓓ |
| 24. | Ⓐ | Ⓑ | Ⓒ | Ⓓ | 49. | Ⓐ | Ⓑ | Ⓒ | Ⓓ |
| 25. | Ⓐ | Ⓑ | Ⓒ | Ⓓ | 50. | Ⓐ | Ⓑ | Ⓒ | Ⓓ |

# Science Test

**Time:** 90 minutes

**Directions:** Read each item carefully and mark your answer on the answer sheet provided by filling in the corresponding oval or writing your answer in the blank box.

---

*Questions 1–2 refer to the following passage.*

---

### Insulation

During the winter, you need something to keep warmth in the house and cold air out. In the summer, you need something to keep heat outside and cooler air inside. What you need is insulation.

Insulation reduces or prevents the transfer of heat (called *thermal transfer*) from the inside out or the outside in. Fiberglass and plastic foam provide such insulation because they contain trapped air. Normally, air is not a good insulator because the currents in air transfer the heat from one place to another. Trapping the air in small places, however, slows or prevents the transfer of heat. Think about these little packets of air the next time you sit in a warm house, safe from the frigid air of winter.

Joe "JJ" Johnson, the world-famous architect and building supervisor, has developed a standard vacation home that he builds for his clients. This house has one floor-to-ceiling glass wall that overlooks the best feature of the client's lot. The other walls are cinder block covered with a cosmetic coat of concrete.

Mr. Johnson has been hired to build one of his famous designs for a client who lives in Juno, Alaska, in a huge home with a spectacular view of the Gastineau Channel. The client has requested a variation on the standard design to reduce his heating costs.

1. What variation would make the most sense to reduce the heating costs?

    (A) Have a floor-to-ceiling window facing away from the channel toward the front of the property.

    (B) Replace the floor-to-ceiling window with a cinder block wall.

    (C) Order curtains to cover the floor-to-ceiling window.

    (D) Order an oversized furnace.

2. What other ways could the homeowner consider to reduce the cost of energy to heat the house?

    (A) Add as much additional insulation as possible.

    (B) Use the house only during the summer months.

    (C) Wear clothing with thermal padding in the house.

    (D) All of the above.

*Go on to next page*

Questions 3–5 refer to the following passage.

### Metabolism

The process of metabolism is an essential process in every living cell. Metabolism allows the cell to obtain and distribute energy, which is necessary for survival. Light from the sun is absorbed and converted into chemical energy by photosynthesis, and it is this chemical energy that is necessary for animals to survive.

One of the primary carbohydrates derived from plants is glucose. Through a process called *glycolysis,* energy is obtained from glucose. This reaction takes place in mitochondria, and the glucose molecule is broken down into pyruvic acids, which are further broken down into molecules, such as ethanol and lactic acid. This process is cyclical as the energy produced keeps the fermentation going.

Pyruvic acids are broken down to carbon dioxide and water by respiration, which releases far more energy. What started out as sunlight has become through photosynthesis the energy that keeps animals alive.

3. How do animals depend on plants to stay alive?

   (A) Animals need the shade provided by plants.

   (B) Cures for some diseases originate in plants.

   (C) Plants provide a comfortable environment for animals.

   (D) Plants provide animals with chemical potential energy.

4. What would happen to a plant if you covered it with a cloth that does not allow light to pass through it?

   (A) The plant would stop growing.

   (B) The leaves would shrivel.

   (C) The flower would fall off.

   (D) The plant would starve to death.

5. The chemical that is key to providing animals with energy is [          ].

Questions 6–7 refer to the following passage.

### Velocity and Speed

There is a difference between speed and velocity, though sometimes you see the words used interchangeably. The *velocity* of a body is its rate of motion in a specific direction, such as a bicycle traveling 34 miles per hour due east. Because velocity has both magnitude (34 miles per hour) and direction (due east), it can be represented by a vector.

Speed has a magnitude only. If a bicycle travels at a speed of 28 miles per hour, you know its magnitude (28 miles per hour) but not its direction. Because speed has a magnitude but not a direction, it can be represented as a scalar.

6. If force is defined as that which is required to change the state or motion of an object in magnitude and direction, how should it be represented?

   (A) wavy lines

   (B) straight line

   (C) scalar

   (D) vector

7. If you were involved in a bicycle race over a predetermined route, what would be of greatest interest to you if you wanted to win: your speed, your distance traveled, your direction, or your route? [          ]

*Go on to next page*

> *Questions 8–9 refer to the following diagram, which is excerpted from* Physical Science: What the Technology Professional Needs to Know, *by C. Lon Enloe, Elizabeth Garnett, Jonathan Miles, and Stephen Swanson (Wiley).*

### Newcomen's Steam Engine

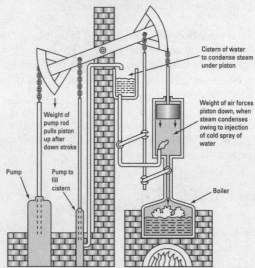

©John Wiley & Sons, Inc.

8. What properties of water and steam allow Newcomen's steam engine to operate?

   (A) Water is heavier than steam.

   (B) Steam condenses when cooled, occupying less space.

   (C) The boiler provides the energy to move the pump.

   (D) The pump rod is heavy enough to pull the arm down.

9. What effect does the condensation of steam in the cylinder with the piston have on the pump that fills the cistern?

   (A) It controls the fire in the boiler.

   (B) It pumps water from the cistern to the boiler.

   (C) It causes the pump to fill the cistern with water.

   (D) It forces the piston down.

*Go on to next page* ⟹

Question 10 refers to the following figure.

**The Food Chain**

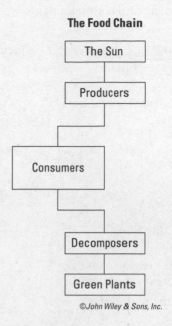

©John Wiley & Sons, Inc.

10. If the number of consumers in an ecosystem began to multiply without control, the result to the balance of the ecosystem would be [          ].

Questions 11–14 refer to the following passage.

**The Big Bang Theory**

It is hard enough to imagine the universe as it is now and even harder to create a theory about how it all began. In the 1940s, George Gamow began to develop such a theory. Georges Lemaitre, another scientist, had also been working on the problem, and Gamow used some of the ideas of Lemaitre to develop his theory.

Gamow proposed the following theory: Somewhere between 10 and 21 billion years ago, there was a giant explosion in space. Before the explosion, the universe was the size of an atomic nucleus, with a temperature of about 10 billion degrees. The explosion started the expansion of the universe. Quarks, or elemental particles, existed in huge numbers.

Within a millisecond, the universe had expanded to the size of a grapefruit. The temperature cooled to 1 billion degrees. The quarks began to clump into protons and neutrons. Minutes later, the universe was still too hot for electrons and protons to form into atoms: a super-hot, fog-like environment.

With passing time and cooling temperatures, nuclear reactions took place, and within 300,000 years, atoms of hydrogen and helium began to emerge. As the atoms formed, light began to shine. The universe was taking shape.

*Go on to next page*

Gravity began to act on the atoms and transform them into galaxies. Within 1 billion years of that first great explosion, galaxies and stars began to form. Within 15 billion years, planets began to emerge from the heavy elements thrown off by the dying of stars. The universe started with a big bang and continues to grow and change according to this theory.

11. The temperature of the first tiny particles was thought to be [_____] billion degrees.

12. For galaxies to have been transformed from atoms, what was necessary?

    (A) heat

    (B) pressure

    (C) centrifugal force

    (D) gravity

13. This theory is called the "Big Bang" because

    (A) An interplanetary war created a void, which the planets were formed to fill.

    (B) An immense explosion created the universe.

    (C) Hydrogen causes immense explosions when ignited.

    (D) The explosion was very loud.

14. How is the formation of hydrogen and helium atoms related to the possible destruction from an atomic bomb?

    (A) Both use hydrogen.

    (B) No relation exists.

    (C) Both result from explosions.

    (D) Both are nuclear reactions.

*Questions 15–17 refer to the following passage.*

**The Jellyfish**

One of the creatures living in all the world's oceans is the jellyfish. Although it lives in the ocean, it is not a fish. The jellyfish is an invertebrate — that is, an animal lacking a backbone. Not only does it lack a backbone, but the jellyfish also has no heart, blood, brain, or gills and is more than 95 percent water.

Around the bell-like structure of the body, the jellyfish has *tentacles* — long tendrils that contain stinging cells — which are used to capture prey. The movement of the prey triggers the sensory hair in the stinging cell, and the prey is then in trouble.

Unfortunately, people are also in trouble if they get too close to the tentacles of a jellyfish. The stings are not fatal to humans but can cause a great deal of discomfort.

*Go on to next page*

15. Why is a jellyfish classified as an invertebrate?

    (A) It has tentacles.

    (B) It has a small brain.

    (C) It has a primitive circulatory system.

    (D) It has no backbone.

16. What are the possible consequences for a swimmer swimming in the vicinity of a school of jellyfish?

    (A) They might scare away the jellyfish.

    (B) Swimmers can get caught in the tentacles.

    (C) Swimmers may accidentally swallow a jellyfish.

    (D) The jellyfish may sting the swimmer, and the stings are painful.

17. Why do most small ocean creatures try to avoid jellyfish?

    (A) Jellyfish get in the way of the fish when they are feeding.

    (B) Jellyfish sting and eat small ocean creatures.

    (C) Fish are afraid of the strange-looking creatures.

    (D) Jellyfish and ocean creatures compete for the same food sources.

---

*Questions 18–25 refer to the following passage.*

---

**Laws of Conservation**

You are faced with laws every day. You cannot speed on the roads, and you cannot park wherever you choose.

Science has its laws as well. One such law states that energy cannot be created or destroyed. This law, called the law of conservation of energy, makes sense because you cannot create something from nothing. If you have an electrical charge, you cannot simply make it disappear.

A further law of conservation is the law of conservation of matter, which says that matter cannot be created or destroyed. This means that when a chemical change occurs, the total mass of an object remains constant. When you melt an ice cube, the water that results is neither heavier nor lighter than the original ice cube.

18. Trees are damaged when struck by lightning, but the lightning is nowhere apparent afterward. Because lightning is a form of energy, what would explain the apparent disappearance of the energy in the lightning?

    (A) The energy in the lightning disappears.

    (B) The energy in the lightning must be conserved and is transformed into another form of energy that affects the tree.

    (C) The tree absorbs the lightning and stores the energy for future use.

    (D) Lightning striking the tree creates new energy, which damages the tree.

19. What is the purpose of laws in science?

    (A) Science is an ordered discipline, and the laws provide the requisite order.

    (B) Laws set parameters within which scientists can proceed with their investigations.

    (C) Laws make it easier to study science because they provide a logical order to the information studied.

    (D) All of the above.

*Go on to next page*

20. When a magician makes a rabbit appear in a hat, it is an example of which law of science?

    (A) conservation of energy

    (B) conservation of matter

    (C) creation of illusion

    (D) conservation of resources

21. When an iceberg melts as a result of temperature changes, the law of science that is being best illustrated is [          ].

22. When you take a dead battery out of your flashlight, what has happened to its original charge?

    (A) It has been converted into light.

    (B) It has disappeared.

    (C) The battery has worn out.

    (D) The energy has been destroyed.

23. How would a scientist categorize the result of adding 3 ounces of water to 1 ounce of salt?

    (A) An example of the law of conservation of energy in that the amount of energy would be the same afterward as before.

    (B) You will end up with 1 ounce of salty water.

    (C) The salt will disappear, and all that will remain is water.

    (D) An example of the law of conservation of mass in that the total mass will remain the same.

24. A ball rolling down a hill cannot stop by itself. What law of science explains this?

    (A) There is a bump on the road.

    (B) The law of gravity.

    (C) The energy from rolling down the hill can't disappear.

    (D) The theory of the laws of conservation keeps the ball from stopping.

25. Why are scientific observations eventually categorized as laws?

    (A) They summarize the results of a group of experimental results in a form that can be understood and remembered.

    (B) They represent the sum of positive reproducible experimental results in a coherent summary statement.

    (C) They represent the mathematical or verbal summary of a series of diverse experimental results that may not otherwise be recognized as related.

    (D) All of the above.

---

*Questions 26–28 refer to the following passage.*

---

### Why Do Birds Fly South for the Winter?

Every fall, the sky is full of birds flying south for the winter. However, you can still see a few birds in the northern part of the country during the winter. Scientists have advanced theories about this phenomenon.

Some birds eat insects for food. In winter, many species of birds fly south, because that's where the food exists. In southern states, insects are available all year long, providing a banquet for the birds, whereas in the northern parts of the country, insects (as well as other food sources, such as seeds and berries) are scarce or even nonexistent during the winter. The birds fly south for winter to follow the food. In the spring, as insects once again become plentiful in the northern states, the birds still follow the food, this time to the north.

*Go on to next page*

26. Why do migratory birds return to the northern states in the spring?

    (A) They miss their summer homes.

    (B) It gets too hot in the southern states.

    (C) They are able to find food again.

    (D) They fly north out of habit.

27. How is the population of insects in a geographical area related to the regular migratory pattern of birds?

    (A) Insects bite the birds.

    (B) The insects lead the birds south.

    (C) Some birds eat insects.

    (D) Birds have a habit of always eating the same insects.

28. Why are scientists interested in the migration of birds?

    (A) It happens regularly and apparently without reason.

    (B) Scientists are investigating a link between prevailing winds and migration routes.

    (C) Scientists regard coincidence as a reason for study.

    (D) Scientists look for connections between caterpillars and travel.

---

*Questions 29–30 refer to the following passage.*

---

### The Law of Unintended Consequences

Lake Victoria is the largest freshwater lake in Africa. It once had abundant fish, which provided protein for the local people who ate the fish. Unfortunately, a new species — the Nile Perch — was introduced into the lake by fishermen looking for a challenging fishing experience to attract their share of tourists interested in exploring the area.

The Nile Perch is an aggressive predator and had no natural enemies in Lake Victoria. It quickly ate up large numbers of the smaller fish, which affected the diets of the local population. These smaller fish ate algae and parasite-bearing snails. Without the smaller fish eating them, the live algae spread over the surface of the lake. Dead algae sank to the bottom of the lake and decayed, a process that consumed oxygen necessary for the fish living deep in the lake.

The snails, without natural predators, and the parasites they carried, multiplied, creating a serious health hazard to the population. The introduction of a fish to encourage tourism had a detrimental effect on the lake and the population that depended on it.

29. What caused the destruction of the ecological balance in Lake Victoria?

    (A) shrinking populations of snails

    (B) freshwater lake

    (C) growing populations of smaller fish

    (D) the Nile Perch

30. Why is it seldom beneficial to introduce a foreign species into a stable environment?

    (A) The foreign species has plenty of predators.

    (B) The other species in the lake would not have to compete for food.

    (C) The foreign species is bad for sport fishermen.

    (D) The foreign species can upset the ecological balance.

*Go on to next page*

*Questions 31–34 refer to the following table, which is adapted from* Hands-On General Science Activities with Real-Life Applications, *by Pam Walker and Elaine Wood (Wiley).*

## Space Travel

| Characteristic | Moon | Mars |
|---|---|---|
| Distance from Earth | 239,000 miles | 48,600,000 miles |
| Gravity | 1/6 Earth's gravity | 1/3 Earth's gravity |
| Atmosphere | None | Thin carbon dioxide, 1% air pressure of Earth |
| Trip time | 3 days | 1.88 Earth years |
| Communication time | 2.6 seconds, round trip | 10 to 41 minutes, round trip |

31. If you were an aeronautical engineer planning a journey to Mars, why would you prefer to go to a space station on the moon and then launch the rocket to Mars instead of going directly from Earth to Mars?

    (A) Lower gravity on the moon means you need less fuel for the launch.

    (B) You have more space to take off and land on the moon.

    (C) No atmosphere means an easier takeoff.

    (D) The moon is closer to Earth than Mars.

32. If you were a communications engineer trying to establish a safety network to warn a rocket ship of dangers, where would you place the transmitter for this rocket ship's journey to Mars?

    (A) on the moon

    (B) on Earth

    (C) on Mars

    (D) not enough information given

33. Why would a trip to the moon be a better first choice than a trip to Mars for space travelers?

    (A) You can see the moon from Earth without a telescope.

    (B) The time of the trip is much shorter.

    (C) The moon has a better atmosphere.

    (D) There are already space vehicles on the moon.

34. If you held a pole-vaulting contest on the moon and Mars, the same contestant would vault higher with the same expenditure of energy on ⬚.

*Go on to next page*

Questions 35–37 refer to the following passage.

### Heredity, Then and Now

How often have you seen a young child and said, "She takes after her parents"? Many traits in a child do come from her parents. Physical and other characteristics, such as hair color and nose shape, are transmitted from one generation to the next. These characteristics, passed from one generation to the next, exist because of genetic code.

The first scientist to experiment with heredity was Gregor Mendel during the 19th century. Mendel experimented with pea plants and noted that characteristics appearing in "child" plants were similar to the "parent" plants. Mendel hypothesized that these characteristics were carried from generation to generation by "factors." It took many years of research to understand why children often look like their parents, but genetic code is now the basis of the study of heredity.

35. According to the passage, ⬚⬚⬚⬚ is a primary determinant for characteristics of the next generation.

36. According to Mendel, what carries traits from one generation to the next?

    (A) RNA

    (B) protons

    (C) genetic code

    (D) mutation

37. If you want to grow monster-sized pumpkins, from what kind of pumpkins do you want to get seeds to increase the probability of growing larger-than-average pumpkins?

    (A) orange pumpkins

    (B) monster-sized pumpkins

    (C) larger-than-average pumpkins

    (D) healthy pumpkins

Questions 38–39 refer to the following passage.

### The Space Shuttle

NASA has designed and built six space shuttles: Atlantis, Challenger, Columbia, Discovery, Endeavor, and Enterprise. The space shuttles are made up of two distinct parts: the orbiter and the booster rocket. The booster rocket provides the additional thrust to get the space shuttle away from the gravitational pull of the earth. The orbiter carries the people and payload as well as the workings of the shuttle. In a space flight, the booster is jettisoned after clearing the earth's gravitational pull, and the orbiter continues on its way.

38. Why would the booster be jettisoned during flight?

    (A) because the shuttle needs to add weight

    (B) to increase the size of the shuttle

    (C) to make the shuttle less maneuverable for landing

    (D) because it is no longer needed

39. Which part of a shuttle carries the payload?

    (A) booster

    (B) cockpit

    (C) orbiter

    (D) rocket

*Go on to next page*

*Questions 40–41 refer to the following figure, which is excerpted from* Physical Science: What the Technology Professional Needs to Know, *by C. Lon Enloe, Elizabeth Garnett, Jonathan Miles, and Stephen Swanson (Wiley).*

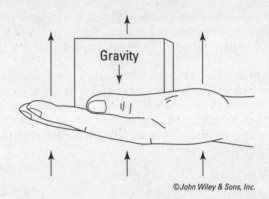

©John Wiley & Sons, Inc.

40. Work is defined as the product of force times displacement. Consider the diagram. If the force of gravity is greater than the forces being exerted by the muscles controlling the hand, what would happen?

(A) Nothing would happen.

(B) The hand would move downward.

(C) The hand would move to the right.

(D) The hand would move upward.

41. If an athlete knows that building muscles requires doing work against a weight, what parameter would the athlete want to change in this diagram?

(A) Move the hand upward faster.

(B) Add weight to the hand.

(C) Close the fist as the arm is raised.

(D) Exhale as the arm is raised.

*Questions 42–43 refer to the following passage, which is adapted from* The Sciences: An Integrated Approach, *3rd Edition, by James Trefil and Robert M. Hazen (Wiley).*

**Copying DNA Sequence**

The polymerase chain reaction (PCR) copies a sequence of DNA. To do this, a strand of DNA is mixed with nucleotides (DNA precursors). Nucleotides target a specific piece of DNA, as well as polymerase, an enzyme that helps to assemble DNA. Heat is applied until the temperature reaches 200°F. The energy from the heating separates the DNA strands. The mixture is then cooled to 140°F. At this temperature, the primers attach themselves to the DNA strands. Raising the temperature to 160°F causes the nucleotides to begin to attach to the DNA strands. After all this, two copies of the DNA are created.

42. To separate the DNA strands during the polymerase chain reaction, the addition of ⬚ is necessary.

43. To clone an organism, you require an identical DNA blueprint. The PCR is something a scientist who is interested in cloning would want to study because ⬚.

*Go on to next page*

Questions 44–45 refer to the following passage.

## Dogs and Wolves — Relatives?

Current scientific theory is that the familiar family pet, the dog, descended from the wolf, but the dog has taken a very different path. The dog was the first animal to be domesticated, right around the end of the Ice Age.

Dogs are part of an extended family called *Canidae,* which contains 38 different species. Jackals, foxes, wolves, and dogs are all part of this family. Although they are related, wolves and dogs are different. Wolves have smaller heads for the same body weight. Dogs have smaller teeth, a more curved lower jaw, and eyes that are more rounded and forward looking. At a distance, however, many of these differences are difficult to spot.

44. What feature makes the wolf better adapted to hunting in the wild?

(A) heavier coat

(B) larger body

(C) larger teeth

(D) larger paws

45. What attribute of dogs makes them a better household pet than other members of the Canidae family?

(A) There are many types of dogs to choose from.

(B) Dogs were domesticated.

(C) Dogs protect people's houses.

(D) Dogs can help the visually impaired.

Questions 46–48 refer to the following passage.

## Isotopes

Isotopes are chemical cousins. They are related to each other, but each isotope has slightly different — but related — atoms. Each of the related atoms has the same number of protons but a different number of neutrons. Because the number of electrons or protons determines the atomic number, isotopes have the same atomic number.

The number of neutrons determines the mass number. Because the number of neutrons in each isotope is different, the mass number is also different. These cousins all have different mass numbers but the same atomic number. Their chemical properties are similar but not the same. Like most cousins, they have family resemblances, but each has a unique personality.

46. Different elements would have different numbers of [          ].

47. Isotopes of a chemical have the same

(A) number of neutrons

(B) mass number

(C) atomic number

(D) chemical properties

48. A scientist has found related atoms in two different substances. If both atoms have the same atomic number but different mass numbers, what preliminary conclusion can be reached about the atoms?

(A) They are the same substance.

(B) They are isotopes.

(C) They are different substances.

(D) One is a compound of the other.

*Go on to next page*

Questions 49–50 refer to the following passage.

### How to Survive the Winter

When the temperature drops and the wind blows cold, you may think of animals that don't have homes to keep out the cold and worry about their ability to survive the winter. Not much food is available, temperatures in northern states go into the sub-zero range, and shelter is limited. How do they survive the winter?

Many animals can find shelter and hibernate for the winter. Hibernation is a sleeplike condition in which the animal's heartbeat, temperature, and metabolism slow down to adapt to the colder temperatures. This dormant condition prevents their starving or freezing during the harsh winters.

49. To survive the winter, bears do what?

(A) Live in warm caves.

(B) Grow heavy winter coat.

(C) Absorb the sun's rays to keep warm.

(D) Find a safe shelter and hibernate.

50. Why should you not disturb a hibernating animal?

(A) It gets grouchy when awakened suddenly.

(B) It could have trouble falling asleep again.

(C) You should never bother a wild animal.

(D) It would not be able to find enough food to survive.

*Go on to next page*

# Short Answer #1

**Time:** 10 minutes

**Your assignment:** Read the excerpt from the USAID website (www.usaid.gov) and write a short response to the following prompt in the space provided.

There has always been a divide between "haves" and "have nots," both within countries and between countries. Recently, there have been efforts made to level the playing field. This may mean a lower standard of living for the "haves" to assist and raise the standard of living of the "have nots." Do you think that this will be an acceptable policy direction even if the extremes are needed, such as increased unemployment here to ship jobs to underdeveloped countries or assisting in the over-throw of corrupt governments? You may include ideas from your personal experience and reading.

### Ending Extreme Poverty

"The United States will join with our allies to eradicate such extreme poverty in the next two decades by connecting more people to the global economy; by empowering women; by giving our young and brightest minds new opportunities to serve, and helping communities to feed, and power, and educate themselves; by saving the world's children from preventable deaths; and by realizing the promise of an AIDS-free generation, which is within our reach." — President Obama, 2013 State of the Union address

### Tackling the Greatest Challenge Known to Man

For the first time in history, we have the tools, technologies, and approaches to end extreme poverty and its most devastating corollaries — including widespread hunger and preventable child death — within two decades. But if we're going to tackle this great challenge, we must take stock of what we know, assess what we don't know, and work together to apply new approaches to help us eradicate extreme poverty. By bolstering inclusive growth and coalescing in partnership around this goal, the end of extreme poverty is within our reach.

- Today, roughly 1.2 billion people live in extreme poverty — nearly 700 million fewer than 1990, when more than 1.9 billion people lived below $1.25/day.

- The world achieved Millennium Development Goal 1 — to halve the poverty rate among developing countries — five years ahead of schedule, in 2010, when the global rate fell to 20.6% (from 43.1% in 1990). Aggregate poverty rates are now falling in every region, including sub-Saharan Africa since around 2000.

- If we accelerate our progress and focus on key turnarounds in some challenging contexts, we believe we can lift one billion more people out of poverty by 2030.

### What Will It Take to End Extreme Poverty in Our Lifetimes?

This will not be an easy task. We can get there, but only if we come together as a global community in support of this effort. We must:

- Leverage existing development capacities and priorities towards this end - such as increasing food security, promoting child survival, combating HIV/AIDS, expanding access to renewable energy, and improving education; AND

- Invite new ideas and fresh perspectives to development efforts, to find innovative solutions to long-standing and seemingly intractable development challenges; TO

- Bolster economic growth and connect people to the global economy, and better engage in fragile contexts, where we project extreme poverty will become increasingly concentrated in the coming decades; AND

*Go on to next page*

**A New Focus**

In the 20 years from 1990 to 2010, poverty reduction has, in most cases, followed economic growth. Connecting more people to the global economy — through, for instance, financial inclusion, greater access to markets, and the institutions that promote decent and sustainable employment — is thus critical to long-term poverty reduction. Yet not every country has seen growth, nor has this rule been without exception. While constraints to poverty reduction are highly context-specific, from a global perspective, two broad trends, in particular, may hamper continued progress:

- Slow or volatile growth

- Vulnerability and non-inclusive growth

Fragility — and weak institutions more broadly — can exacerbate each of these constraints. This can include for example: conflict that halts growth or destroys people's assets; governments that are corrupt or illegitimate and divert public resources from development or exclude certain populations; or recurrent crises that hamper agricultural production or displace populations.

*Go on to next page*

# Short Answer #2

**Time:** 10 minutes

**Your Assignment:** Read the excerpt from the Environmental Protection Agency website (www.epa. gov) and write a short response to the following prompt in the space provided.

From the material provided and your general knowledge, explain why these invasive species are a threat to all of us.

**Invasive Animal Species**

At least 25 non-native species of fish have entered the Great Lakes since the 1800s, including round goby, sea lamprey, Eurasian ruffe, alewife and others. These fish have had significant impacts on the Great Lakes food web by competing with native fish for food and habitat. Invasive animals have also been responsible for increased degradation of coastal wetlands; further degrading conditions are resulting in loss of plant cover and diversity.

Non-native mussels and mollusks have also caused turmoil in the food chain. In 1988, zebra mussels were inadvertently introduced to Lake St. Clair, and quickly spread throughout the Great Lakes and into many inland lakes, rivers, and canals. Since then, they have caused severe problems at power plants and municipal water supplies, clogging intake screens, pipes, and cooling systems. They have also nearly eliminated the native clam population in the ecosystem.

The spiny water flea (*Cercopagis pengoi*) was the most recent species to enter the Great Lakes. This organism, a native of Middle Eastern seas, is a tiny predatory crustacean that can reproduce both sexually and, more commonly, parthenogenically (without fertilization). This allowed them to quickly populate Lake Ontario.

*Go on to next page*

# Chapter 22

# Answers for Practice Test 1, Science

*I*n this chapter, we provide the answers and explanations to every question in the Science practice test in Chapter 21. If you just want a quick look at the answers, check out the abbreviated answer key at the end of this chapter. However, if you have the time, it's more useful for study purposes to read all the answer explanations carefully. Doing so will help you understand why some answers were correct and others not, especially when the choices were really close. It will also point you at areas where you may need to do more review. Remember, you learn as much from your errors as from the correct answers.

Go through the explanations to all the questions, even for the ones you answered correctly. The explanations are a good review of the techniques we discuss throughout the book.

## *Answers and Explanations*

1. **B. Replace the floor-to-ceiling window with a cinder block wall.** A sheet of glass contains no encapsulated air and, thus, provides neither insulation nor greater thermal flow. To answer this question, you need to know that good insulators contain trapped air and that glass doesn't. Thus, replacing the floor-to-ceiling glass walls with a cinder block wall would increase the insulating properties of that wall and reduce the heating costs for the house. The question assumes that this information is general knowledge for someone at this educational level.

2. **C. Wear clothing with thermal padding in the house.** Each of the options would reduce heat loss and reduce energy costs. General knowledge would let you assume that Juno was considerably warmer during the summer, and the word *thermal* indicates a garment that's meant to reduce personal heat loss and, thus, would allow the room temperature to be reduced.

3. **D. Plants provide animals with chemical potential energy.** The last paragraph of the passage implies that animals must eat food with chemical potential energy, which is derived from plants. The other answers are irrelevant to the information in the passage.

4. **D. The plant would starve to death.** Plants produce food using energy from the sun. If you cut off the energy from the sun, you cut off the food supply. The other answers may be symptoms of a plant's starving to death, but Choice (D) sums up the information in one answer.

5. **pyruvic acid.** According to the passage, pyruvic acid is key to energy production. This question is a good example of why a little bit of knowledge and familiarity with the words and names used in science are helpful when taking the GED test.

6. **D. vector.** The passage states that velocity can be represented by a vector because it has both magnitude and direction. Force is defined as changing the state or motion of an object, either in magnitude or direction. Because a force has magnitude and direction, it's represented by a vector. The information needed to answer this question is in the last sentence of the first paragraph. You can ignore the first three answer choices completely because they have very little to do with the question. Choice (D) requires you to know the difference between a vector and a scalar. The last line of each paragraph in the passage contains the definitions you need.

7. **your speed.** As with most bicycle races, the distance traveled is predetermined so that all riders traverse the same distance. The race route, including the direction traveled, is

predetermined by the race organizers. The only variable for the individual rider is his or her speed. If they go fast enough, they'll probably win the race, but if they travel slower than other riders, someone else will win.

8. **B. Steam condenses when cooled, occupying less space.** In the steam engine, water cools the steam, which then condenses, occupying less space. This action starts the entire cycle over again. You can eliminate the other answer choices when guessing is necessary. Choice (A) is incorrect because water and steam are both water, in different states. Their densities may be different, but their weights are the same. Only the volume differs when water turns to steam. Choice (C) is incorrect because the boiler doesn't provide the energy to move the pump, which you can see by looking at the diagram. Choice (D) isn't based on information given in the diagram. Nowhere are you told the weight of the pump rod.

9. **C. It causes the pump to fill the cistern with water.** The pump pushes water into the cistern. The other choices don't answer the question based on the information provided in the diagram. Knowing how to answer questions based on diagrams is a useful skill to have for the GED test.

10. **consumers would starve for lack of food.** The producers provide food for the consumers. If the producers stay the same but the consumers increase, the consumers won't have enough food, so the consumers will starve. Your reading in science topics should have exposed you to this concept. If you read the newspapers regularly, you'll find stories about the lack of food leading to starvation, which is a semi-scientific statement of this principle.

11. **10.** The passage states that the temperature of the first tiny particles was 10 billion degrees.

12. **D. gravity.** The last paragraph states that gravity transformed the atoms into galaxies. This question is an example of when a basic knowledge of science-related words can be helpful.

13. **B. An immense explosion created the universe.** The passage states that immense explosions created the planets when the space debris was attracted to each other by gravity.

14. **D. Both are nuclear reactions.** An atomic bomb uses a nuclear reaction to produce its massive damage. The passage states that hydrogen and helium atoms were formed by nuclear reactions (Choice [D]). The other three choices don't answer the question based on the passage. Choice (A) may be right, but it's irrelevant in this context. Choice (B) is incorrect, and Choice (C) may be interesting in another context, but it's wrong here.

15. **D. It has no backbone.** According to the passage (second sentence in the first paragraph), invertebrates have no backbones. The other choices may be correct, but they don't answer the question. Here, and in all questions on this test, you're looking for the best answer that answers the question posed. Don't get sidetracked by other choices that are correct based on your knowledge or even based on the passage. The answer to the question posed is always the best response on a multiple-choice test.

16. **D. The jellyfish may sting the swimmer, and the stings are painful.** Jellyfish can sting swimmers, and the stings are painful. You find this information in the last sentence of the third paragraph. The other choices don't answer the question based on the passage. For example, Choice (C) may be the stuff nightmares are based on, but the information or misinformation isn't in the passage, so you can't consider it.

17. **B. Jellyfish sting and eat small ocean creatures.** Small ocean creatures are always on the menu for jellyfish. Creatures, in general, avoid predators — a fact that's general science knowledge.

18. **B. The energy in the lightning must be conserved and is transformed into another form of energy that affects the tree.** The passage states that energy can't be created or destroyed, so the energy from the lightning must be transformed into another type of energy. The other answer choices imply that the energy has somehow disappeared, which the passage says can't happen.

19. **D. All of the above.** Science is an ordered discipline and, as such, needs laws to maintain its organization.

20. **C. creation of illusion.** Matter can't be created or destroyed. Thus, a rabbit can't appear except by creation of an illusion, which isn't a true law of science but the best answer of

the choices given. The other answer choices seem scientific but have nothing to do with the question. Always read the question carefully to make sure you're answering it with the best of the answers provided.

21. **conservation of matter.** When ice melts, it turns into water. This is an example of the law of conservation of matter. Although the amount of water in a melting iceberg is tiny compared to the amount of water in the ocean, it does add some water to the ocean, which may be considered another acceptable answer but not the best one.

22. **A. It has been converted into light.** Flashlights provide light by using the energy in the battery. The passage says that energy can't be created or destroyed, so the energy in the battery must have been converted or transformed into something else. In reality, even if you don't use a battery for an extended time, the battery grows weaker because of other reactions inside the cell. But this tidbit isn't mentioned in the passage and is just a reminder not to leave batteries in your flashlight forever.

23. **D. An example of the law of conservation of mass in that the total mass will remain the same.** If you add 3 ounces of water to 1 ounce of salt, you have 4 ounces of combined ingredients. The combined mass is the same as the sum of the individual masses. The volume may be different, but the question doesn't ask you about the volume. If you add 3 ounces of water to a dissolvable substance, you'll get at least 3 ounces of resultant liquid, but that isn't what was asked in the question. Choices (A) and (C) are just incorrect.

24. **C. The energy from rolling down the hill can't disappear.** The law of conservation of energy states that energy can't be created or destroyed. Thus, the energy developed by the ball rolling down the hill can't disappear. Choice (C) is more a statement of the meaning of the law of conservation of energy than naming it, but it is still the best answer. In reality, there's friction between the ball and the ground that slows it down, and the hills don't go on forever — so the ball will eventually come to rest. You may have learned this information elsewhere, but it doesn't answer the question based on the passage.

25. **D. All of the above.** Choices (A), (B), and (C) contribute to a definition of a scientific law, so Choice (D) is the best answer because it indicated that the others are a summary.

26. **C. They are able to find food again.** The passage states that the lack of food in the winter months makes most birds fly south to find sources of food. When the food returns to the northern states, so do the birds. The other choices don't answer the question based on the information in the passage.

27. **C. Some birds eat insects.** Some birds eat insects for their food supply. If an area has no insects, the birds move to find a new source of food. General reading in science tells you that living creatures go where the food is. Even human beings, who can choose where to live, are unlikely to move somewhere that lacks food. Other creatures have a more basic instinct to move to where there's a supply of food. Thus, the insects have a responsibility for the birds' migration — although their main contribution is being eaten. And although some birds always eat the same insects, that's not the best answer.

28. **A. It happens regularly and apparently without reason.** Scientists are curious about anything that happens regularly that can't be easily explained. Migration is one such issue. The key word here is *every* at the beginning of the first sentence.

29. **D. the Nile Perch.** This question may have many answers, from sport fishermen to algae to snails. Of the potential answers given, however, Nile Perch is the best one because the introduction of this species caused all the subsequent problems.

30. **D. The foreign species can upset the ecological balance.** This question asks you to make a general statement about foreign species of fish. Although this question doesn't ask you specifically to consider the Lake Victoria example, you're supposed to think about that example as you answer the question. Using the Lake Victoria example, you can safely say that a foreign species upsets the local ecological balance. You also know from the example that the other three choices are incorrect.

31. **A. Lower gravity on the moon means you need less fuel for the launch.** The less fuel you need to launch, the less you have to carry. The gravity on the moon is less than that on Earth, so you need less force and less fuel to break free of gravity.

32. **D. not enough information given.** The only locations mentioned in the table are Mars and the moon, and you're supposed to answer the question based on the material given. Thus, you don't have enough information to answer the question.

33. **B. The time of the trip is much shorter.** According to the table, it takes just 3 days to get to the moon, which is a much better first choice than the 1.88 years needed to get to Mars. The other choices are irrelevant to the question and the given table.

34. **the moon.** Gravity on the moon is less than that on Mars. Because gravity is the force that attracts you to the moon (or to Earth or to Mars), the less the gravity, the less the attraction between you and the surface on which you stand, and, thus, the higher and farther you can jump — which, as you may know, is the goal of a pole-vaulting contest.

35. **heredity.** The passage states that heredity determines the characteristics of the next generation.

36. **C. genetic code.** The passage states, "These characteristics, passed from one generation to the next, exist because of genetic code." Thus, the best answer is *genetic code.*

37. **B. monster-sized pumpkins.** If children inherit the traits of their parents, you want the desired traits of your child pumpkin to be a part of the traits of the parent pumpkins. Monster-sized pumpkin seeds have a better chance of producing extra-large pumpkins than do the seeds from a regular-sized pumpkin.

38. **D. because it is no longer needed.** All the choices except Choice (D) — that the booster is no longer needed — are incorrect because they're in direct opposition to the passage. If you can quickly eliminate some or most of the answer choices, you can save time answering the question. In this case, you can eliminate three answers, making the final choice easy and quick.

39. **C. orbiter.** Because the booster is jettisoned after takeoff, the orbiter has to carry everything that continues on the trip. Choices (A), (B), and (D) are wrong and can be quickly eliminated.

40. **B. The hand would move downward.** If the force pushing down is greater than the force pushing up, the hand would move down. Although this question is based on the given diagram, which gives a general idea of what happens when a hand holds weight, the answer to the question is in the first part of the question itself. If the force of gravity (the downward force) is greater than the force of the muscles moving upward, the resultant force would be downward.

41. **B. adding weight to the hand.** A larger weight in the hand would produce a greater force downward. Thus, the athlete would have to work harder against this extra weight (and, as a result, would build more muscle). Making the displacement of the hand larger would also increase the work done, but this isn't an answer choice.

42. **heat.** The fourth sentence in the passage tells you that heating is the process that separates DNA strands.

43. **it creates an identical copy of the DNA.** Cloning requires identical DNA. As you can see from the first sentence of the passage, PCR provides identical copies of DNA.

44. **C. larger teeth.** The larger teeth of the wolf are better for hunting. The third sentence of the third paragraph of the passage states that dogs have smaller teeth, which means wolves must have bigger teeth. Although this information isn't stated directly in the passage, it's implied. You're expected to be able to draw conclusions from the information given, so read carefully. The other answer choices are incorrect. True, some dogs have heavier coats, larger bodies, and so on, but this information isn't in the passage. You can answer the question using only information given or implied in the passage — not information from your general knowledge or prior reading.

45. **B. Dogs were domesticated.** The passage states that the dog was domesticated very long ago. A domesticated animal is preferable to a wild one for a household pet. The other answers may be factually correct, but they aren't part of the information included in the passage.

46. **protons.** According to the first sentence of the passage, the atomic number is determined by the number of protons. Skimming the paragraph after reading the question for key words in the question makes choosing the correct answer faster and easier.

47. **C. atomic number.** The last sentence of the first paragraph of the passage states that isotopes have the same atomic number.

48. **B. They are isotopes.** The last sentence of the first paragraph of the passage states that isotopes have the same atomic number. The second sentence of the second paragraph tells you that isotopes have different mass numbers. This question requires using two bits of information from two different locations in the passage to decide on the right answer.

49. **D. Find a safe shelter and hibernate.** According to the first sentence of the second paragraph of the passage, animals, including bears, survive the winter by finding a safe shelter and hibernating.

50. **D. It would not be able to find enough food to survive.** Animals hibernate in the winter when food is scarce (a fact implied from the last sentence in the second paragraph). If you wake up a hibernating animal, that animal awakes to a strange environment without its usual sources of food and probably wouldn't be able to find enough food to survive. The other answer choices may be right in some circumstances, but they don't relate to the passage.

## Sample Short Answer #1

The following is a sample response to the Short Answer #1 in Chapter 21. Your response should be a proper essay — that is, it should include an introduction, appropriate body content, and a conclusion. If you haven't had much practice writing essays, practice writing some before the test. Tests are never a good time to try to learn a new skill.

Compare your response to this sample, and check out Chapter 12 for more information about how these responses are scored.

Everyone I have spoken to has agreed that the eradication of poverty is a worthwhile endeavor but at what cost? If the population of the United States is about 300 million people and there are 1.2 billion people living in poverty in the world, then each and every one of us is responsible for about 400,000 people. That is a staggering responsibility. The president suggests that this can be accomplished in the next two decades. Joining with our friends and enemies would make this easier but still not completely possible.

It is suggested that the impoverished masses be included in the global economy. In simpler terms, that would mean a large majority of them would have to be employed. This is an admirable goal. If we could find employment for some, most or all of these people, a good part of the problem would be solved. But the number of jobs required at any one time is finite and that would mean the loss of one of our jobs to export it to an undeveloped country. That would be unacceptable to the displaced workers and would reimport poverty by exporting employment. I, for one would not be happy donating my job to someone I don't know in some other part of the world.

The article goes on to enumerate areas that could be accelerated, such as increasing food security, promoting child survival, combating HIV/AIDS, expanding access to renewable energy and improving education. These are all admirable goals but each cost money, and internal money is scarce in these countries. Improving education usually means hiring more and better trained teachers, and that costs money. Renewable energy means a massive change in infrastructure. A country requires an acceptable way of recycling and an infrastructure to carry it out and that costs money. Eradicating HIV/AIDS is a massive public health and economic problem requiring untold millions of dollars to just address not to solve. Where will that money come from? An impoverished country cannot afford to build testing facilities and treatment centers or to hire the trained and experienced staffs to implement the program.

The author of the report is clear. We have to work together to achieve this. In this context, "together" means "us."

The route to the solution to extreme poverty is clear, but are we motivated and willing to travel that road? Only time will tell.

### Sample Short Answer #2

The following is a sample response to the Short Answer #2 in Chapter 21. Your response should be a proper essay — that is, it should include an introduction, appropriate body content, and a conclusion.

Compare your response to this sample, and check out Chapter 12 for more information about how these responses are scored.

Fish are a good source of protein for human beings and other aquatic species, but these invasive species are destroying the balance of the lakes. Many of the species that formerly inhabited the lakes provided food and sport for the local residents and food for the other species in the food chain. With the increasing numbers of these invasive species, the food chain is thrown off-balance and the former source of protein is being lost.

Not all of these invasive species provide a good or palliative source of food for humans. In addition, these species are more often the predators and not the source of food for existing species in the lake. This reduces the variety of species in the lake limiting the options for survival for species above them in the food chain.

For example, zebra mussels have caused severe problems at power plants and municipal water supplies, clogging intake screens, pipes, and cooling systems. This alone has increased our costs for hydro-electric power and drinking water because of the increased maintenance costs, especially on the Great Lakes. They have also nearly eliminated the native clam population in the ecosystem. Clams have provided food for other species, but with their disappearance, that food supply is no longer available.

Humans are at the mercy of these invasive species, whether introduced accidentally or deliberately. We have no way of eliminating them without further destruction of the ecosystem. The only solution is to guard against their introduction into our local ecosystems.

# Answer Key

1. B

2. C

3. D

4. D

5. **pyruvic acid**

6. D

7. **your speed**

8. B

9. C

10. **consumer would starve for lack of food**

11. **10**

12. D

13. B

14. D

15. D

16. D

17. B

18. B

19. D

20. C

21. **conservation of matter**

22. A

23. D

24. C

25. D

26. C

27. C

28. A

29. D

30. D

31. A

32. D

33. B

34. **the moon**

35. **heredity**

36. C

37. B

38. D

39. C

40. B

41. B

42. **heat**

43. **it creates an identical copy of the DNA**

44. C

45. B

46. **protons**

47. C

48. B

49. D

50. D

# Chapter 23

# Practice Test 1: Mathematical Reasoning

● ● ● ● ● ● ● ● ● ● ● ● ● ● ● ● ● ● ● ● ● ● ● ● ● ● ● ● ● ● ● ● ● ● ● ● ● ● ● ● ● ● ● ● ● ● ● ● ● ● ● ● ● ● ● ●

**T**he Mathematical Reasoning test consists of a series of questions intended to measure general mathematics skills and problem-solving ability. The questions are based on short readings that may include a graph, chart, or figure.

You have 115 minutes to complete this section. The answers and explanations to this section's questions are in Chapter 23. Go through the explanations to all the questions, even for the ones you answered correctly. The explanations are a good review of the mathematical techniques we discuss throughout the book.

Formulas you may need are given on the page before the first test question. Only some of the questions require you to use a formula, and you may not need all the formulas given. *Note:* If you can memorize the formulas and understand how to use them, you'll save a bit of time on the test; you then can use that time saved for review or for harder items that give you more trouble.

Unless you require accommodations, you'll be taking the GED test on a computer. Instead of marking your answers on a separate answer sheet, like you do for the practice test sections in this book, you'll see clickable ovals and fill-in-the-blank text boxes, and you'll be able to click with your mouse and drag and drop items where indicated. We formatted the question and answer choices in this book to make them appear as similar as possible to what you'll see on the computer-based test, but we had to retain some A, B, C, D choices for marking your answers, and we provide an answer sheet for you to do so.

# Answer Sheet for Practice Test 1, Mathematical Reasoning

1. (A) (B) (C) (D)
2. (A) (B) (C) (D)
3. [          ]
4. (A) (B) (C) (D)
5. [          ]
6. (A) (B) (C) (D)
7. (A) (B) (C) (D)
8. [          ]
9. (A) (B) (C) (D)
10. (A) (B) (C) (D)
11. [          ]
12.
13. (A) (B) (C) (D)
14. (A) (B) (C) (D)
15. (A) (B) (C) (D)
16. [          ]
17.
18. (A) (B) (C) (D)
19. (A) (B) (C) (D)
20. (A) (B) (C) (D)
21. (A) (B) (C) (D)
22. (A) (B) (C) (D)
23. (A) (B) (C) (D)

24. (A) (B) (C) (D)
25. [          ]
26. [          ]
27. (A) (B) (C) (D)
28. [          ]
29. [          ]
30. (A) (B) (C) (D)
31. [          ]
32. [          ]
33. (A) (B) (C) (D)
34. (A) (B) (C) (D)
35. (A) (B) (C) (D)
36. [          ]
37. (A) (B) (C) (D)
38. [          ]
39. (A) (B) (C) (D)
40. (A) (B) (C) (D)
41.
42. (A) (B) (C) (D)
43. (A) (B) (C) (D)
44. (A) (B) (C) (D)
45. [          ]
46. (A) (B) (C) (D)
47. (A) (B) (C) (D)
48. (A) (B) (C) (D)
49. (A) (B) (C) (D)
50. (A) (B) (C) (D)

# Mathematics Formula Sheet

**Area of a:**

parallelogram $A = bh$

trapezoid $A = \frac{1}{2}h(b_1 + b_2)$

**Surface Area and Volume of a:**

rectangular/right prism $SA = ph + 2B$ $V = Bh$

cylinder $SA = 2\pi rh + 2\pi r^2$ $V = \pi r^2 h$

pyramid $SA = \frac{1}{2}ps + B$ $V = \frac{1}{3}Bh$

cone $SA = \pi rs + \pi r^2$ $V = \frac{1}{3}\pi r^2 h$

sphere $SA = 4\pi r^2$ $V = \frac{4}{3}\pi r^3$

($p$ = perimeter of base $B$; $\pi \approx 3.14$)

**Algebra**

slope of a line $m = \frac{y_2 - y_1}{x_2 - x_1}$

slope-intercept form
of the equation of a line $y = mx + b$

point-slope form of the
equation of a line $y - y_1 = m(x - x_1)$

standard form of a
quadratic equation $y = ax^2 + bx + c$

quadratic formula $x = \frac{-b \pm \sqrt{b^2 - 4ac}}{2a}$

Pythagorean theorem $a^2 + b^2 = c^2$

simple interest $I = prt$

($I$ = interest, $p$ = principal, $r$ = rate, $t$ = time)

# Mathematical Reasoning Test

**Time:** 115 minutes

**Directions:** Choose the appropriate answer for each question. Mark your answers on the answer sheet provided by filling in the corresponding oval, writing your answer in the blank box or marking your answer on the graph.

1. Dharma is making sale signs for the Super Summer Sale at the Super Saver Swim Shop. Sales tax in Dharma's state is 5%. She makes a series of signs:

   Sign A: ½ off all merchandise

   Sign B: Buy one item, get the second item of equal value free

   Sign C: 50% off all merchandise

   Sign D: Nine times your sales tax back

   What would a shrewd consumer notice about the signs?

   (A) Sign A offers a better buy.

   (B) Sign C offers the worst deal.

   (C) Sign D offers the worst deal.

   (D) Sign B offers a better deal.

2. Daryl is framing a picture. He draws the following diagram to help him make it:

   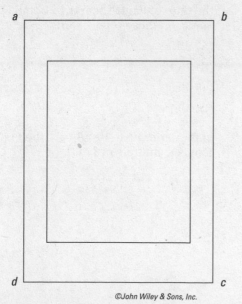

   ©John Wiley & Sons, Inc.

   Which of the following is true about the diagram?

   (A) *ab* must be perpendicular to *ad*.

   (B) *ab* must be parallel to *bc*.

   (C) *ad* must be parallel to *ab*.

   (D) *ab* and *dc* must be perpendicular.

3. The Hammerhill family is building a deck behind their house. The deck is to be 16 feet long and 21 feet wide, and the decking material was priced at $45.00 a square yard. The cost, in dollars, of the decking material would be ⬚.

4. Margaret Millsford, the Chief Financial Officer of Aggravated Manufacturing Corporation, has to report to the Board of Directors. She has been instructed to analyze the sales of each of the company's product lines and recommend dropping the least profitable line. She found that although the per-unit profits of grommets and gadgets were the same, producing widgets off-shore doubled the profit. She prepared the following graph to demonstrate the relative volumes and made an oral presentation to illustrate the differing profitability of off-shore production to back up her recommendation:

   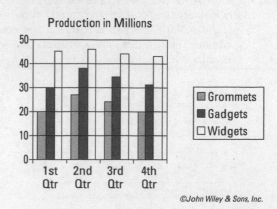

   ©John Wiley & Sons, Inc.

   Based on the graph and Margaret's oral presentation, her recommendation would be to drop

   (A) widgets

   (B) grommets

   (C) gadgets

   (D) grommets and widgets

*Go on to next page* ⟹

5. Quan is obsessive about his marks and how they compare to the rest of his class. On Quan's final report, his results were as follows:

> Computer Studies: 97
>
> English: 98
>
> Mathematics: 99
>
> Physical Education: 87
>
> Science: 97
>
> Social Studies: 94
>
> Spanish: 86

The results for Quan's entire class were

> Average: 93.27
>
> Median: 96
>
> Mode: 97
>
> Range: 14

Calculate Quan's average, median, mode, and range, and then compare them to the results of his class. If Quan is most concerned about being admitted to college, the measure he should be most concerned about is [        ].

6. Alice was trying to explain how the length of time she could run each morning had improved each month since she started, except for the month she twisted her ankle. She drew the following graph to show her friends Mary and Kevin the average length of time (in minutes) she ran each day each month:

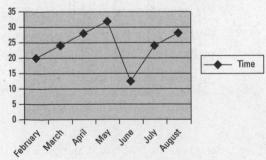

©John Wiley & Sons, Inc.

In which month did Alice likely twist her ankle?

(A) June

(B) February

(C) August

(D) September

7. Dominic and Paula were comparing their report cards, as follows:

**Dominic's Report Card**

| Subject | Grade (%) |
| --- | --- |
| Mathematics | 63 |
| Social Studies | 76 |
| Science | 65 |
| Language Arts | 84 |
| Physical Education | 72 |

**Paula's Report Card**

| Subject | Grade (%) |
| --- | --- |
| Mathematics | 80 |
| Social Studies | 64 |
| Science | 76 |
| Language Arts | 72 |
| Physical Education | 88 |

The teacher told them that the ratio of their total marks was very close. What is the ratio of Paula's marks to Dominic's marks on these report cards?

(A) 9:10

(B) 18:19

(C) 10:9

(D) 19:18

8. In the series, 4, 6, 10, 18, . . . , the first term that is a multiple of 11 is [        ]

*Go on to next page*

9. Simone follows the stock market very carefully. She has been following Cowardly Corporation the last few months, keeping track of her research in the following table:

| Date | Closing Price (In U.S. Dollars) |
|------|----------------------------------|
| August 7 | 15.03 |
| August 17 | 16.12 |
| September 1 | 14.83 |
| September 9 | 15.01 |
| September 16 | 14.94 |
| September 20 | 15.06 |
| September 23 | 15.17 |
| September 24 | 15.19 |

Simone bought shares of the stock on September 24 and wants to make money before selling it. She paid 3% commission to her broker for buying and will pay the same again for selling. What is the lowest price (in U.S. dollars) for which Simone can sell each of her shares to break even?

(A) $16.48

(B) $16.13

(C) $15.66

(D) $20.00

10. If $22.4 = \dfrac{56a}{5a+10}$, what is the value of $a$?

(A) 0

(B) –56

(C) 4

(D) –4

*Questions 11–12 refer to the following graph.*

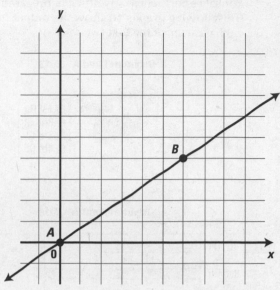

©John Wiley & Sons, Inc.

11. Calculate the slope of the line $AB$. The slope of $AB$ is _____.

12. If the slope of $AB$ remains the same, but it intercepts the $y$-axis at $C$ (0, 4), where does it intersect the $x$-axis? Use the graph on the answer sheet to indicate the point where $AB$ intersects the $x$-axis.

13. If a fire is built in the center of a square barbeque pit, where is the safest place to stand to avoid the intense heat of the fire?

(A) at a corner

(B) along the left side

(C) along the right side

(D) not enough information given

14. Lydia and Wayne are shopping for carpets for their home and are looking for the best carpet at the best price. Carnie's Carpets offers them a wool carpet for $21.50 per square yard. Flora's Flooring says they will match that same carpet for only $2.45 per square foot, while Dora's Deep Discount offers them an 8-x-12-foot rug of the same carpet material for $210.24. What is the lowest price per square foot offered to Lydia and Wayne?

(A) $2.45

(B) $21.90

(C) $2.19

(D) $2.39

*Go on to next page*

**15.** Miscellaneous Appliances Limited is concerned about its output at Plant A. For its annual report, company officials prepared the following graphs to show the output for each quarter of the last two years:

**Output at Plant A – 2013**

- ■ 1st Qtr
- ■ 2nd Qtr
- □ 3rd Qtr
- ▨ 4th Qtr

**Output at Plant A – 2014**

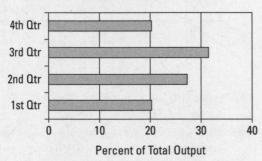

Percent of Total Output

©John Wiley & Sons, Inc.

Which quarter showed a dramatic increase in production in 2014?

(A) 3rd quarter

(B) 1st quarter

(C) 4th quarter

(D) 2nd quarter

**16.** Mr. and Mrs. Ngs are looking to expand their two-story house and have calculated that they need at least another 630 square feet to live comfortably. They want to use the basement level for storage and the rest for living. A contractor quotes them $15.80 per square foot for the renovation without redecoration. A real estate agent tells them that they can increase the value of their home by about $18,000 by building the addition. If they want to add as much additional space as possible for the $18,000 they will recover, they would have to add ⬚ additional square feet.

**17.** An experiment involving throws of a 20-sided die produced the following results:

| Throw | Left-Handed | Right-Handed |
|-------|-------------|--------------|
| 1 | 2 | 4 |
| 2 | 4 | 12 |
| 3 | 5 | 2 |
| 4 | 9 | 6 |
| 5 | 11 | 13 |
| 6 | 10 | 15 |
| 7 | 4 | 17 |
| 8 | 6 | 3 |
| 9 | 7 | 5 |

Use the graph on the answer sheet to indicate the point that represents the combined medians of the throws, using the median of the left-handed results as the $x$-value and the median of the right-handed results as the $y$-value.

**18.** LeeAnne is shopping for a new vehicle. She drives about 18,000 miles per year. She is most concerned about the cost of gasoline. She expects gasoline to average $3.50 a gallon during the five years she will own the car and is basing her decision on that price. As she shops, she creates a chart based on her calculations:

| Type of Vehicle | Miles per Gallon |
|-----------------|------------------|
| SUV | 12.8 |
| Sedan | 19.6 |
| 2-door | 19.5 |
| All-wheel drive | 17.2 |
| Sports car | 18.6 |

Based on her criteria, which car should LeeAnne buy?

(A) SUV

(B) sedan

(C) 2-door

(D) sports car

*Go on to next page* ⟹

19. Tom is worried about getting to the GED testing center on time. He knows that he averages 40 miles per hour on the route to the test. If the test site is 47 miles from Tom's house and he wants to arrive 20 minutes early, how do you figure out how much time he needs to leave for travel and waiting?

    (A) add then divide

    (B) multiply then add

    (C) divide then add

    (D) add then multiply

20. Leonora has just received her mid-term report card. Her grades are as follows:

    ### Leonora's Report Card

    | Subject | Grade (%) |
    | --- | --- |
    | English | 84 |
    | Geography | 78 |
    | Mathematics | 68 |
    | Physical Education | 77 |
    | Physics | 82 |

    Leonora's average grade is 77.8%. To get into the college of her choice, she needs an average of 80%. English is her best subject. By how many percentage points will her English score have to go up, assuming all her other subjects stay the same, to get into college?

    (A) 8

    (B) 9

    (C) 10

    (D) 11

21. Sonia has an amazing recipe for rice. For each 1 cup of rice, she adds 2 cups of vegetable soup and a quarter cup of lentils. This weekend, Sonia is having a large dinner party and figures she needs to cook 3½ cups of rice for her guests. How much of the other two ingredients should she use?

    (A) 7 cups of soup and ⅞ cup of lentils

    (B) 3½ cups of soup and ½ cup of lentils

    (C) 7 cups of soup and 1 cup of lentils

    (D) 1 cup of soup and 7 cups of lentils

22. In drawing cards from a 52-card deck, any single card has an equal chance of being drawn. After six cards have been drawn and removed, what is the probability of drawing an ace of hearts if it has not yet been drawn?

    (A) 1:50

    (B) 1:48

    (C) 1:46

    (D) 1:44

23. The Symons are redecorating a room in their house. They have some interesting ideas. They want to put a rug on the floor surrounded by a border of tiles. They are considering teak paneling halfway up each wall. In addition, they may cut away part of the ceiling to put in a skylight. This is a diagram of their room:

    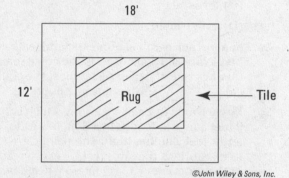

    ©John Wiley & Sons, Inc.

    The rug costs $7.50 a square foot, and tile costs $9.00 a square foot. One rug they like is 16 feet by 10 feet, leaving just a little area around the rug for tiles. At the store, however, they see another rug that is only 12 feet by 8 feet, but it's just the right pattern and colors for their room. Which floor treatment is less expensive?

    (A) both are the same cost

    (B) the larger rug

    (C) the smaller rug without the paneling

    (D) the smaller rug

*Go on to next page*

24. Brad is a secret shopper for the Friendly Furniture store. His job is to go to competitive stores and price a series of items to make sure his employer can advertise that he has the best prices. His boss wants to start a new advertising campaign: "Friendly Furniture — always lower than the average price of our competitors." Brad's job is to shop several stores to make sure the claim is accurate. Brad's results are recorded in the following table:

| Item | Store A | Store B | Store C | Store D | Friendly Furniture |
|------|---------|---------|---------|---------|--------------------|
| Couch | $1,729 | $1,749 | $1,729 | $1,699 | $1,719 |
| Dining room set | $4,999 | $4,899 | $5,019 | $4,829 | $4,899 |
| Loveseat | $1,259 | $1,199 | $1,279 | $1,149 | $1,229 |
| Coffee table | $459 | $449 | $479 | $429 | $449 |
| Reclining chair | $759 | $799 | $739 | $699 | $739 |

Which item cannot be advertised as "lower than the average price"?

(A) couch

(B) dining room set

(C) loveseat

(D) coffee table

25. In a pistachio-eating contest, Sarah eats 48 pistachios in 18 minutes. If she could maintain her rate of eating pistachios, she could eat [          ] pistachios in 2 hours.

26. Kevin wants to paint his room, which is 9 feet 5 inches long, 8 feet 3 inches wide, and 8 feet 2 inches high. The paint can label cautions that air must be exchanged in the room every 12 minutes. When Kevin looks for exhaust fans to keep the air moving, he finds that they are calibrated in cubic feet per minutes. The operation that Kevin has to perform first to figure out which size fan he needs is [          ].

27. Which of these shapes has the same relationship to the horizontal after a 90-degree rotation about a point on the perimeter?

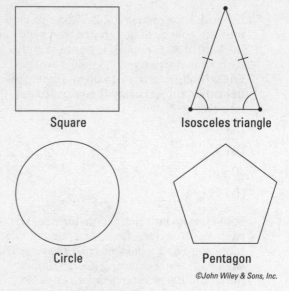

Square     Isosceles triangle

Circle     Pentagon

©John Wiley & Sons, Inc.

(A) isosceles triangle

(B) circle

(C) pentagon

(D) not enough information given

*Go on to next page*

28. In a large company, the top four positions are organized as follows:

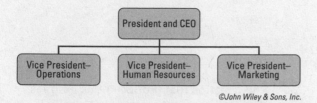

©John Wiley & Sons, Inc.

Each department has the following budget:

| Department | Budget ($ Millions) |
|---|---|
| Operations | 14.7 |
| Human Resources | 2.1 |
| Marketing | 5.6 |

What is the ratio of the largest budget to the smallest budget? [          ]

29. A company has doubled its sales from the first to the third quarters. Graph [          ] indicates this pattern.

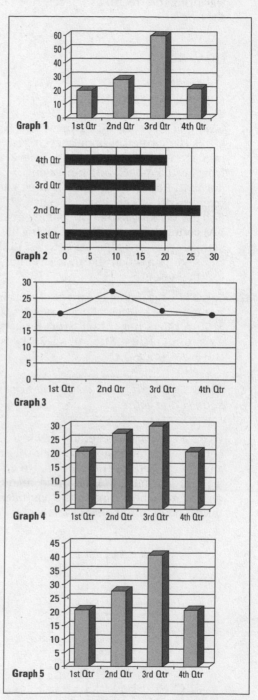

©John Wiley & Sons, Inc.

*Go on to next page*

30. A 6-foot-tall forester standing some 16 feet from a tree uses his digital rangefinder to calculate the distance between his eye and the top of the tree to be 25 feet. How tall is the tree?

    (A) $\sqrt{41}$

    (B) $\sqrt{881}$

    (C) $\sqrt{256}$

    (D) not enough information

31. Lawrie is trying to save money, so she keeps her money in both checking and savings accounts. Each week, she puts $24.00 from her paycheck into her savings account. However, the fourth week, she overdraws her checking account by $7.50, and the bank transfers the money from her savings account. For providing this service, the bank charges Lawrie $10.00. Her savings account balance after the fourth week is $ [           ].

32. Sarah is negotiating the price of a chair for her room. The original price was $96.00. Store A offers her 1/3 off. Store B offers her a discount of 30%. She will save $ by taking the lower price.

---

Questions 33–34 are based on the following information and figure.

---

While a rock band is setting up for a concert, the audio engineer is calibrating the amplifiers used for the concert. He has an instrument that develops and displays a graph for each setting on the amplifier controls. The graph appears like this:

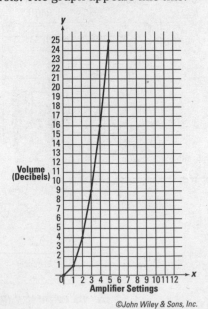

Volume (Decibels)

Amplifier Settings

©John Wiley & Sons, Inc.

33. From the graph, calculate the volume in decibels for a setting of 10 on the amplifier.

    (A) 20

    (B) 30

    (C) 50

    (D) 100

34. The equation that produced this graph is $V = S^2$, where V is the volume in decibels and S is the volume setting. If the volume is 144 decibels, what is the volume setting on the amplifier?

    (A) 9

    (B) 10

    (C) 11

    (D) 12

35. In this particular auditorium, the volume of sound decreases by half for every 10 feet away from the stage a person sits. If the volume at the stage is 144 decibels, the volume in decibels for a person sitting 20 feet from the stage will be

    (A) 36

    (B) 48

    (C) 60

    (D) 72

36. Gary and Georgina George bought a new car and are trying to estimate the gas mileage. The new car travels 240 miles at a cost of $54.00. The price of gasoline is $2.70 per gallon. They estimate that the car will get 18 miles per gallon. The actual mileage would be [           ] miles per gallon.

*Go on to next page*

Question 37 is based on the following figures, which are reprinted from Physical Science: What the Technology Professional Needs to Know, *by C. Lon Enloe, Elizabeth Garnett, Jonathan Miles, and Stephen Swanson (Wiley).*

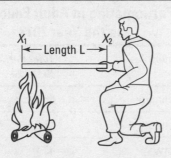

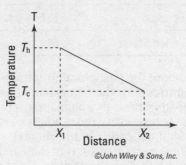

©John Wiley & Sons, Inc.

37. If the person pictured wants to walk but remain at a constant temperature, what geometrical shape should he follow as a path?

(A) ellipse

(B) line

(C) square

(D) circle

38. Igor is in charge of the swimming pool at the local recreation center. The pool is 120 feet long and 24 feet wide and holds 12,902 cubic feet of water. The average depth of the pool in feet is [          ].

Questions 39–42 refer to the following table.

## Average Mileage and Annual Fuel Cost of Selected Vehicles

| Vehicle | Mileage (Miles per Gallon) City | Mileage (Miles per Gallon) Highway | Annual Cost ($)* |
|---------|------------------------------|-----------------------------------|------------------|
| A | 23 | 28 | 840 |
| B | 21 | 29 | 875 |
| C | 19 | 25 | 1,000 |
| D | 18 | 24 | 1,050 |
| E | 17 | 22 | 1,105 |
| F | 16 | 22 | 1,167 |
| G | 15 | 21 | 1,235 |
| H | 14 | 19 | 1,314 |
| I | 13 | 18 | 1,400 |
| J | 12 | 16 | 1,823 |

*Annual cost includes 15,000 miles driven annually; 55% of the miles in the city and 45% on the highway; standard price of fuel*

Go on to next page

39. If you were in the market for a car, how much could you save, in dollars, over a three-year period, by buying the most economical car over the least economical car?

   (A) 983

   (B) 2,520

   (C) 5,469

   (D) 2,949

40. What is the difference in miles per gallon between the mean city mileage and the median of the city mileages for these vehicles?

   (A) 12/3

   (B) 1/3

   (C) 17

   (D) 2½

41. Use the graph on the answer sheet to indicate the results for Vehicle A with the difference between city and highway mileage as the appropriate point on the *y*-axis.

42. To solve a problem in her mathematics class, Jan had to solve the following set of equations:

   $$2x + 3y = 10$$
   $$5x + 6y = 13$$

   What is the correct value of *y?*

   (A) –8

   (B) –6

   (C) +6

   (D) +8

43. An international survey found the following information about participation in adult education:

### Percent of Population over Age 21 Participating in Adult Education in the Year 2013

| Country | Total Participation Rate (%) |
| --- | --- |
| Denmark | 62.3 |
| Hungary | 17.9 |
| Norway | 43.1 |
| Portugal | 15.5 |
| United States | 66.4 |

Compare the participation rates of the countries with the highest and lowest participation rates by calculating approximately how many more adults participate in adult education in the country with the highest participation rate than in the country with the lowest participation rate.

   (A) 2 times as many

   (B) 4 times as many

   (C) 6 times as many

   (D) 8 times as many

*Go on to next page*

44. Gordon has the following six bills to pay this month:

| Bill Payable To | Amount |
|---|---|
| Bedding by Vidalia | $23.00 |
| Chargealot Credit Corp. | $31.00 |
| Dink's Department Store | $48.00 |
| Furniture Fit for a Princess Shoppe | $13.00 |
| Highest Fidelity Sound Shop | $114.00 |
| Overpriced Gas Corporation | $39.00 |

Each month, he allocates $250.00 to pay his bills. This month, his bills are over this budget. How much extra money must he find from other parts of his budget to pay all his bills?

(A) $8.00

(B) $268.00

(C) $28.00

(D) $18.00

45. Georgette needs $185 to buy books for her Geography course, but because her hours at work have been cut back this month, she cannot afford to buy them, even though she needs them. Walking to class, she notices a sign offering to loan her $200 for one month for $20 interest. She calculates that if she can repay the money within the month by working extra hours, she will be able to afford the principal and the interest.

When Georgette applies for the loan, she reads the contract carefully and notices that after the initial one-month period, the interest rate climbs to 15% per month and includes the previous month's principal and interest. If she earns $11.00 per hour, how many extra hours (to the nearest hour) would she have to work to pay the additional second month's interest?

[          ]

46. Andrew just bought a small circular swimming pool for his children. The diameter of the pool is 12 feet, and Andrew can fill it safely to a depth of 9 inches. If a cubic foot of water weighs 62.42 pounds, how many pounds does the water in Andrew's pool weigh?

(A) approximately 27,000

(B) approximately 2,700

(C) approximately 1,300

(D) approximately 5,300

47. If Giorgio borrows $100 for one year and three months and repays $108 including simple interest, what rate of interest was he charged?

(A) 6.4%

(B) 8.0%

(C) 4.0%

(D) 4.6%

*Go on to next page*

48. Chico went shopping for some groceries for his family. His shopping list was as follows:

     2 pounds of apples

     5 bananas

     1 container of milk

     1 loaf of bread

     If apples were $0.79 a pound, bananas $0.23 each, milk $1.27 a carton, and bread $0.98 a loaf, what is the approximate total cost of the groceries?

     (A) $3.90

     (B) $4.10

     (C) $4.90

     (D) $5.50

49. From the numbers listed, what number should go in the box?

     SERIES, 4, 7, 12, 19, [ ], 38, . . . .

     (A) 28

     (B) 26

     (C) 24

     (D) 22

50. A rectangle 5 units long and 4 units high is represented on a graph. If three of the corners are placed at (3, 2), (3, –2), and (–2, 2), where should the fourth corner be placed?

     (A) (–2, 2)

     (B) (2, –2)

     (C) (–2, –2)

     (D) (2, 2)

**STOP** DO NOT TURN THE PAGE UNTIL TOLD TO DO SO.
DO NOT RETURN TO A PREVIOUS TEST.

# Chapter 24

# Answers for Practice Exam 1, Mathematical Reasoning

. . . . . . . . . . . . . . . . . . . . . . . . . . . . . . . . . . . . . . . . . . . . . . . . . . . . . . . . . . . . . . . . .

This chapter provides you with answers and explanations for the Mathematical Reasoning practice test in Chapter 23. The answers tell you whether you answered the questions right or wrong, but the explanations are even more important. They explain why your answers were right or wrong and give you some hints about the areas tested. Reading the explanations and checking the areas where your answers weren't the best will help you identify where you should spend more time preparing for the test.

## Answers and Explanations

1. **C. Sign D offers the worst deal.** This problem tests your understanding of numbers and their equivalents (integers, fractions, decimals, and percents) in a real-world situation. Signs A, B, and C give customers 50% off. Sign D gives them 45% (9 × 5% sales tax). Sign D offers the least discount.

2. **A. *ab* must be perpendicular to *ad*.** This problem involves measurement and geometry and tests your understanding of perpendicular and parallel lines in a geometrical figure. Frames are rectangles. Each pair of opposite sides must be parallel and intersecting sides (*ab* and *ad*) must be perpendicular.

3. **$1,680.** This problem tests your knowledge and mastery of number operations and number sense. Use a calculator, because numerous conversions are involved, including the following:

   Area of the deck is 16 × 21 = 336 square feet

   9 square feet = 1 square yard

   37.33 square yards $\frac{336}{9} = 37\frac{1}{3}$

   Because you have to buy carpet at a full square yard at a time, you'd have to buy 38 square yards.

   One square yard of decking costs $45.00, and $37\frac{1}{3}$ or 38 square yards of decking (rounded to the nearest square yard) costs $1,710.00.

4. **B. grommets.** This problem tests your data-analysis skills. You're asked to interpret and draw inferences from the bar graph and include additional data from the presentation. Because the profit per unit is the same for grommets and gadgets but differs from the profit on widgets, which had twice the profitability, to make a fair comparison, you'd have to double the sales of widgets. In this case, grommets seem to be less profitable than the other two lines but not by much. Because grommets sold the fewest numbers and were the least profitable product, they're recommended as the one to drop.

5. **average.** This problem tests your skills in calculations of statistical measurement. You're asked to use the presented data to calculate the measures of Quan's performance and compare them to those of his classmates. This is a good question on which to use the calculator because it involves a series of calculations.

You find the *average* by adding the marks and dividing by the total number of marks. The *median* is the middle value; in Quan's case, the middle value is the fourth value, which just happens to be equal to the fifth value. Quan's average was 94, his median was 97, and the range of his marks was 13. The *mode* is the most often, or common, value in the list, and the *range* is the difference between the largest and smallest numbers. This question is a good example of why some familiarity with mathematical vocabulary is an asset. The admissions department of a college would put the most weight on Quan's average because it's a reflection of how well he did in all his subjects.

6. **A. June.** Alice has converted her story into a graph, and you're being asked to interpret the line graph in conjunction with her story. Because her average daily time had been increasing until May, dropped in June, and recovered in July and August, you can assume that the twisted ankle slowed her down. It likely happened in June.

7. **D. 19:18.** A number of operations are involved in solving this problem. You're asked to average a set of grades for each person and compare them by using a ratio. You can simplify this question, using a calculator.

    The total of Paula's marks is $80 + 64 + 76 + 72 + 88 = 380$.

    The total of Dominic's marks is $63 + 76 + 65 + 84 + 72 = 360$.

Because you divide each total by 5 to get the average marks for Paula and Dominic, you can simply use the ratio of the totals to get the answer because it will equal the ratio of the averages. (Note that if one of the students had six grades and the other had five, for example, you'd have to use the ratio of the averages, not of the totals.)

The ratio of Paula's marks to Dominic's marks is 380:360, which you can simplify by dividing each number by 20 to get 19:18.

8. **66.** This problem involves algebra, functions, and patterns. The numbers 4, 6, 10, and 18 form a pattern (also called a series). After looking carefully at the series, you see that the second term is formed by subtracting 1 from the first term and multiplying by 2. Try this on the third number: $(6 - 1) \times 2 = 10$. You've found your pattern. Continuing the series: 4, 6, 10, 18, 34, 66, . . . , the first term you come to that is a multiple of 11 is 66.

You could also simply double the difference between the previous two numbers and add it to the second number to create the next one. For example, the difference between 4 and 6 is 2. Double that $(2 + 2 = 4)$ and add it to the 6 $(4 + 6 = 10)$ to get the next number. The difference between 6 and 10 is 4. Double that $(4 + 4 = 8)$ and add it to the 10 $(8 + 10 = 18)$ to get the next number. Continue with this pattern until you find the number you need.

9. **B. $16.13.** This problem involves data analysis and manipulation of numbers and is best done using a calculator. Most of the information given is irrelevant, except to decide that Simone may have bought at a high point. The important price to consider is $15.19. In addition to this price per share, Simone has to pay her broker 3% commission.

Therefore, her final price per share on September 24 is $15.19 + (0.03 \times \$15.19) = \$15.6457$. Because you're dealing with money, you have to round the number to two decimal places, making her final price per share $15.65. This amount of money came out of her bank account for each share she bought.

If Simone decides to sell the shares at this price, $15.65, she has to pay her broker another 3% commission, or $0.03 \times \$15.65 = \$0.4695$. Rounded to two decimals, she has to pay a commission of $0.47 per share. She then receives the value of the shares, $15.65, minus the commission of $0.47, for a total of $15.18 per share — that is, for each share she sells, the broker deposits $15.18 into her account. Notice that this amount is less than the amount she paid for each share.

To break even, Simone has to receive $15.65 per share — after the commission. Set the equation up this way:

$1x - x(0.03) = 15.65$, where $x$ is the selling price

$1x - 0.03x = 15.65$

$0.97x = 15.65$

Now divide both sides by 0.97 to get $x = 16.13$.

10. **D. –4.** This question involves algebra. You have to solve a linear equation, as follows:

$$22.4 = \frac{56a}{5a + 10}$$

Cross-multiply and write this equation as $22.4(5a + 10) = 56a$. Then, getting rid of the parentheses, the equation looks like this: $112a + 224 = 56a$. Next, bring all the $a$'s to the left and the numbers to the right, so you have $112a - 56a = -224$. Then, combine the $a$'s to get $56a = -224$. Finally, divide both sides by 56 to get one $a$ on the left: $a = -4$.

11. **2/3.** This question tests your skills in measurement and geometry. You're asked to find the slope of a line drawn for you.

The $x$-axis runs horizontally across the grid. The $y$-axis runs vertically, up and down the grid. The origin is where the two axes (that's the plural of axis) intersect. Points to the left of the $y$-axis have negative $x$-values. Points below the $x$-axis have negative $y$-values. The $x$-intercept of a line is the point where the line cuts the $x$-axis. The $y$-intercept of a line is the point where the line cuts the $y$-axis. All lines parallel to the $x$-axis have slopes of 0.

The slope of a line is the rise over the run (the difference of the values of $y$ divided by the difference in values of $x$). The rise is 4, and the run is 6. This means that the slope is 4/6 or 2/3 (divide top and bottom by 2 to simplify). Remember, the general formula for a slope is $(y_2 - y_1)/(x_2 - x_1)$.

12. **(–6, 0).** This question tests your skills in measurement and geometry. You're asked to identify the $x$-intercept and the $y$-intercept and to draw a line with a slope of 2/3 on the graph.

If you draw a line through the point on the $y$-axis having the same slope, it crosses the $x$-axis at (–6, 0). Simply count over 3 points to the left (the run), down 2 (the rise), and you're at (–3, 2). But you're asked for the $x$-intercept, so repeat this process. Go over 3 more points to the left and down 2 more, and you're at (–6, 0).

13. **D. not enough information given.** This question doesn't provide enough information for you to give an accurate answer. If the fire were rectangular in shape, the answer would be different from a circular fire or an irregularly shaped fire. The question provides information only about the shape of the barbeque.

14. **C. $2.19.** Consider the price per square foot at each store:

Carnie's Carpets: $21.50 per square yard = $21.50/9 = $2.39 per square foot

Flora's Flooring: $2.45 per square foot

Dora's Deep Discount: The area of an 8-x-12-foot rug is (8)(12) = 96 square feet. The cost for 96 square feet is $210.24 or $210.24/96 = $2.19 per square foot.

15. **A. 3rd quarter.** In this question, you're asked to analyze graphs to identify patterns in a workplace situation.

In the 2013 graph, the third quarter of 2013 produces a little more than 30% of the output. The best answer for this question is the *3rd quarter*.

16. **1,140.** This problem involves measurement, specifically, area and money. Assuming that the estimate for renovation is accurate, the number of square feet of renovation that the Ngs can afford for $18,000 is $18,000/15.80 square feet = 1,139.24 square feet. Round this number to 1,140 because you usually don't add part of a square foot.

17. **(6, 6).** This problem involves data analysis, statistics, and probability. You're being asked to graph a point representing the medians of two sets of data. First, find the median (the middle number, when put in order) of the first set of numbers. The median is 6. Then find the median of the second set of numbers. Again, it's 6.

18. **B. sedan.** This problem is based on measurement, using uniform rates, and it asks you to make a decision based on factual information. The fastest way to answer this question is to realize from the table that the sedan is the most economical option. But if you need to crunch the numbers to figure the cost of gasoline over the five years, set up the problem this way:

$$18,000 \text{ miles} \times \frac{1 \text{ gallon}}{12.8 \text{ miles}} \times \frac{\$3.50}{\text{gallon}} \times 5 \text{ years}$$

To help you decide which car LeeAnne should buy, create a chart like the following:

| Vehicle Type | Miles/Gallon | Total Gas Costs |
|---|---|---|
| SUV | 12.8 | $24,609.38 |
| Sedan | 19.6 | $16,071.43 |
| 2-door | 19.5 | $16,153.83 |
| All-wheel drive | 17.2 | $18,313.94 |
| Sports car | 18.6 | $16,935.47 |

From these figures, you can see that the sedan is the best buy. It gets the most miles per gallon, so LeeAnne wouldn't have to fill the tank as frequently.

19. **C. divide then add.** This problem involves number operations. Instead of asking you for the answer, which is pretty simple, you're asked to provide the operations that are required to solve the problem. First, you divide (miles to site by miles per hour), and then you add (the amount of time Tom wants to arrive early). Remember to keep the units consistent.

20. **D. 11.** This question involves data analysis. You're asked to apply measures of central tendency (the mean) and analyze the effect of changes in data on this measure. If Leonora's present average is 77.8% and she wants to get an average of 80%, she needs enough marks to get an additional 2.2% (80 − 77.8).

Because Leonora is taking five subjects, she requires 5 extra points for each percent increase. Thus, she requires (2.2)(5) = 11 additional points. The problem says that English is her best subject, so she would need the 11 extra points in English.

21. **A. 7 cups of soup and ⅞ cup of lentils.** This question tests your ability to figure out how a change in the amount of rice used results in changes to the amount of soup and lentils needed. Because each cup of rice requires 2 cups of soup, 3½ cups of rice require 2 × 3½ = 7 cups of soup. Because each cup of rice requires ¼ cup of lentils, 3½ cups of rice require 3½ × ¼ = ⁷⁄₂ × ¼ = ⅞ cup of lentils.

22. **C. 1:46.** This question is a test in probability. You're asked to figure out the probability of an event occurring. If you had an entire deck of 52 cards, the probability of drawing an ace of hearts would be 1:52. If you remove 6 cards and none of them is the ace of hearts, you may as well have a 46-card deck (52 − 6). The probability of drawing an ace of hearts from a 46-card deck is 1:46.

23. **B. the larger rug.** This problem tests your measurement skills. You're asked to predict the impact of changes in the linear dimensions of the rug on its area and cost. Choice (C) seems logical, but the question never mentions the cost of the paneling or the skylight, so you can't consider it as an answer.

Draw a sketch of the room with the larger rug. It will have a tiled area around it. You have to figure out how many square feet of tile and carpet you need for this floor treatment, as follows:

The area of the room is (18)(12) = 216 square feet.

The larger rug will cover (16)(10) = 160 square feet of the floor. This leaves 56 square feet (216 − 160) to be covered with tile. The cost of the rug is ($7.50)(160) = $1,200. The cost of the tile is ($9.00)(56) = $504.00. The total cost is $1,200.00 + $504.00 = $1,704.00.

The smaller rug will cover (12)(8) = 96 square feet of the floor. This leaves 216 – 96 = 120 square feet to be covered with tile. The cost of the rug is ($7.50)(96) = $720.00. The cost of the tile is ($9.00)(120) = $1,080.00. The total cost is $720.00 + $1,080.00 = $1,800.00. The smaller rug will cost more for the entire floor treatment.

Tile costs more per square foot than carpeting, so you know without doing any figuring that having more tile will result in higher costs.

24. **C. loveseat.** This question is an exercise in data analysis. You're asked to compare sets of data based on the mean (average) prices of four other stores. You can summarize the average prices on a sketch table like this one:

| Item | Store A | Store B | Store C | Store D | Average Price | Friendly Furniture |
|------|---------|---------|---------|---------|---------------|--------------------|
| Couch | $1,729.00 | $1,749.00 | $1,729.00 | $1,699.00 | $1,726.50 | $1,719.00 |
| Dining room set | $4,999.00 | $4,899.00 | $5,019.00 | $4,829.00 | $4,936.50 | $4,899.00 |
| Loveseat | $1,259.00 | $1,199.00 | $1,279.00 | $1,149.00 | $1,221.50 | $1,229.00 |
| Coffee table | $459.00 | $449.00 | $479.00 | $429.00 | $454.00 | $449.00 |
| Reclining chair | $759.00 | $799.00 | $739.00 | $699.00 | $749.00 | $739.00 |

You can see that the only item Friendly Furniture sells for over the average price is the loveseat, which is the answer to the question.

25. **320.** This question is a unit conversion problem asking you to solve a problem involving calculations. Sarah ate 48/18 pistachios per minute. In 2 hours or 120 minutes, she could eat $120 \times \frac{48}{18} = 320$ pistachios.

26. **multiplication.** This question is about number operations; it asks you to select the appropriate operation to solve a problem. Because the first operation performed is to find the volume of the room, and the formula for volume is *length × width × height*, the first operation you use to solve the problem is multiplication.

27. **D. not enough information given.** This question tests your knowledge of measurement and geometry. You're asked to visualize and describe geometrical figures under a 90-degree rotation. Each of the figures is changed by the rotation. Try drawing each of these shapes, picking a point on the perimeter and rotating it 90 degrees. Because this is a timed test, try drawing one or two, noticing that they change quite a bit. Use your imagination to check the rest. After discovering that none of the four shapes has the same relationship to the horizontal after a 90-degree rotation about a point on its perimeter, you have your answer — not enough information given.

28. **7:1.** This question tests your data-analysis skills by asking you to interpret a chart and answer a question involving calculation.

The largest budget is the Operations budget, while the smallest budget is Human Resources. The ratio between these two budgets is 14.7 to 2.1 or 7:1 (dividing both sides by 2.1).

If you wanted to do this in your head, notice that 14:2 (the approximate ratio between the Operations budget and the Human Resources budget) is double 7:1.

29. **5.** This question tests your knowledge of patterns by asking you to compare information from different types of graphs to extract information. Graph 5 has the first and third quarters in the required ratio and is the correct answer.

30. **D. not enough information.** This problem involves measurement and geometry, and it asks you to use the Pythagorean theorem.

You can't actually solve this problem, however. Because the rangefinder is measuring the distance from the forester's eye and you don't know how high his eye is above the ground, you can't calculate the height of the tree. You can calculate the distance from the forester's eye to the top of the tree by using the Pythagorean theorem, but the question asks for the height of the tree (which is the distance from the ground — not the forester's eye — to the top of the tree). Thus, you don't have enough information.

31. **$78.50.** This question tests your knowledge of number operations by asking you to perform several operations to calculate an answer. After the fourth week, Lawrie would've deposited (4)($24.00) = $96.00. There would've been two withdrawals totaling $7.50 + $10.00 = $17.50. Her balance after the fourth week would be $96.00 – $17.50 = $78.50.

32. **$3.20.** This question tests your skills in using percentages and discounts. Store A offers Sarah 1/3 off or 96/3 = $32.00 off the original price. Store B offers her 30% off; 30% is 0.30, so she'll get (96)(0.30) = $28.80 off the original price. By buying at Store A, she'd get the chair for $32.00 – $28.80 = $3.20 less. Thus, she'd save $3.20.

33. **D. 100.** This question tests your skills by asking you to use information from a graph to solve a problem. From the graph, you can figure out that the volume in decibels is the square of the volume setting. For a volume setting of 4, the volume is 16 decibels. Therefore, for a setting of 10, the volume is 100 decibels ($10^2$).

34. **D. 12.** This question tests your skills in algebra by asking you to solve equations. The equation given is V = $S^2$. If $S^2$ = 144, the square root of 144 is 12. Thus, the answer is 12.

35. **A. 36.** If the volume decreases by half for every 10 feet away from the stage you get and the volume at the stage is 144 decibels, a person sitting 10 feet from the stage would hear at a volume of 72 decibels (144/2), and a person sitting 20 feet from the stage would hear at a volume of 36 decibels (72/2).

36. **12.** This question involves number operations. You're asked to calculate the average miles per gallon for a vehicle. Rather than provide you with the number of gallons used, you're given the cost of gasoline and the cost of the 240-mile trip. To calculate the amount of fuel used, you divide $54.00 by $2.70 to get 20 gallons. You can do this operation mentally to speed things up. Next, you divide the miles, 240, by the fuel used, 20 gallons, to get the mileage, 12 miles per gallon (240/20 = 12).

37. **D. circle.** This question tests your skills in measurement and geometry. To remain at a constant temperature, you have to remain at a constant distance from the fire. The distance $x_1 - x_2$ would be the radius of the circle.

The path of a point that travels a constant distance from a point is a circle.

38. **4.48.** This problem tests your ability to do calculations and use a formula: *Volume = length × width × depth.* Thus, 12,902 cubic feet = 120 feet × 24 feet × average depth. The average depth $= \dfrac{12,902}{(120 \times 24)} = 4.48$ (the answer is rounded).

39. **D. 2,949.** This question tests your ability to make a decision based on data presented in a table and then to use that information to answer a question. The least economical car costs $1,823 to drive for a year, while the most economical car costs $840 for the same time under the same conditions. The difference in cost for one year is $1,823 – $840 = $983. The cost for three years is ($983)(3) = $2,949.

You could also estimate an answer. The difference annually is just under $1,000. For three years, that's just under $3,000. So Choice (D) is the best answer.

40. **B. 1/3.** This question tests your ability to analyze data, using the mean and median to answer a question about the data given. The mean of the city mileages is the sum of the mileages divided by 10 (the number of entries), which equals 16.8. The median of the mileages is the one midway between the two in the middle, or 16.5. The difference between the two numbers (16.8 – 16.5) is 0.3 or 1/3.

41. **(0, 5).** This question tests your ability to analyze data by representing data graphically.

For Vehicle A, the difference between the city and highway mileage is 5 miles per gallon (28 – 23). The point you want on the *y*-axis is (0, 5), which you need to mark on the graph.

42. **D. +8.** This question tests your skill in algebra by asking you to solve a system of linear equations:

$$2x + 3y = 10$$

$$5x + 6y = 13$$

A linear equation is one in which the powers of the variables are all equal to 1. To solve this system, you have to eliminate $x$ by multiplying each equation by a number that allows you to subtract one from the other and end up with just $y$'s. Multiply the first equation by 5 and the second equation by 2:

$$5(2x + 3y = 10) = 10x + 15y = 50$$

$$2(5x + 6y = 13) = 10x + 12y = 26$$

Subtract the second equation from the first, and you get $3y = 24$; $y = 8$. (Note that you can also multiply the first equation by $-2$ and add the two equations together. Either way gets you the same answer.)

43. **B. 4 times as many.** This question asks you to analyze a situation presented in a table. The table tells you that the country with the highest participation rate is the United States, with a participation rate of 66.4. The country with the lowest participation rate is Portugal, with a participation rate of 15.5. Because you're asked for an approximation, you can say that the participation rate in the United States is 60 and in Portugal, it's 15, which means that 4 times as many adults participate in adult education in the United States than in Portugal.

44. **D. $18.00.** This problem involves number operations. The total amount of Gordon's bills is $23.00 + $31.00 + $48.00 + $13.00 + $114.00 + $39.00 = $268.00. If Gordon allocates only $250.00 to pay these bills, he ends up $268.00 − $250.00 = $18.00 short. Be wary of Choice (B), which is a special trap for people who don't read the question carefully.

45. **3 hours.** At the end of the first month, Georgette will owe $185 + $20 = $205. The second month's interest will be ($205)(0.15) = $30.75. At $11 an hour, Georgette would have to work an additional 2.76 hours, or practically 3 hours because no one would hire someone to work 2 hours, 45 minutes, and 36 seconds.

46. **D. approximately 5,300.** This problem tests your knowledge of measurement and geometry by asking you to solve a problem involving volume and weight. You can do this problem in your head, but we take you through the steps using calculations first.

    The formula for volume of a cylinder (the cylinder is the circular inside of the pool to a height of 9 inches) is $\pi r^2 h$, where $\pi$ = approximately 3.14, $r$ = radius, and $h$ = height. If the diameter is 12 feet, the radius is 6 feet. If the height is 9 inches, it's 9/12 feet, which can be simplified to 3/4 feet.

In a formula, don't forget that all units must be the same — that is, feet and feet or inches and inches.

    The volume is (3.14)[(6)(6)](3/4) = 84.78 cubic feet.

    Because 1 cubic foot weighs 62.42 pounds, the weight of 84.78 cubic feet is (84.78)(62.42) = 5,291.96 or 5,300 rounded to the nearest hundred.

To do this problem in your head, multiply 6 by 6 to get 36. Multiply 36 by 3/4 to get 27, and multiply 27 by 3 to get 81. The approximate volume of the pool is 81 cubic feet, which isn't bad for an approximation. For your purposes, say the volume is 80 cubic feet, which is still close. The weight of a cubic foot of water is 62.42 pounds, so round it to 60 pounds. Now, multiply 80 by 60 to get 4,800, which is closest to Choice (D). You can go with that approximation because it's very close to one of the answers.

47. **A. 6.4%.** This question tests your ability to evaluate an answer by using a formula. This formula, $I = prt$, where $I$ is interest, $p$ is principal, $r$ is rate, and $t$ is time. However, this formula needs to be adjusted to provide the information you want, the rate, which means solving for $r$. You can change the equation to $r = \dfrac{I}{p \times t}$, which allows you to calculate the rate from the information given. Substituting into this equation, you get $r = \dfrac{8}{100 \times 1.25}$. (Remember that 1 year and 3 months is 1¼, or 1.25 of a year.) Then $r = \dfrac{8}{125} = 0.064 = 6.4\%$.

48. **C. $4.90.** This question involves number operations. You're asked to calculate — in your head — the answer to a problem.

    To use mental math to solve this problem, round everything. Consider the apples at $0.80 a pound, bananas at $0.20 each, milk at $1.30, and a loaf of bread at $1.00. The total for this approximation is $(2)(\$0.80) + (5)(\$0.20) + \$1.30 + \$1.00 = \$4.90$. Looking at the answer choices, Choice (C) is the only one close to this approximation.

49. **A. 28.** This question tests your knowledge of patterns by asking you to figure out the next number in a series. By looking at the series, it looks like each number is the square of the placement of the number in the list, plus 3. That is, the first number is $1^2$ plus 3, or 4. The second number is $2^2$ plus 3, or 7. The third term is $3^2$ (9) plus 3, or 12. The fifth term would be $5^2$ (25) plus 3, which is 28.

50. **C. (–2, –2).** This question tests your skills in geometry by asking you to visualize a graph of an object. Because the object is a rectangle, the opposite sides are equal in length and are parallel, the fourth corner will be 2 units to the left of the $y$-axis, giving it an $x$-coordinate of –2, and 2 units below the $x$-axis, giving it a $y$-coordinate of –2. Therefore, the point would be (–2, –2).

    The $x$-coordinate is the distance from the $y$-axis, and the $y$-coordinate is the distance from the $x$-axis.

    It may be helpful to draw the diagram, if the answer isn't apparent.

# *Answer Key*

1. **C**

2. **A**

3. **$1,680**

4. **B**

5. **average**

6. **A**

7. **D**

8. **66**

9. **B**

10. **D**

11. **2/3**

12. **(–6, 0)**

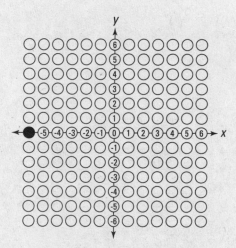

13. **D**

14. **C**

15. **A**

16. **1,140**

17. **(6, 6)**

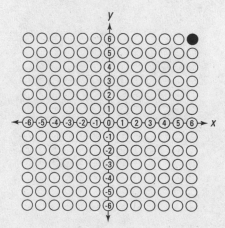

18. B          19. C

20. D          21. A

22. C          23. B

24. C          25. **320**

26. **multiplication**     27. D

28. **7:1**          29. **5**

30. D          31. **$78.50**

32. **$3.20**        33. D

34. D          35. A

36. **12**          37. D

38. **4.48**        39. D

40. B          41. **(0, 5)**

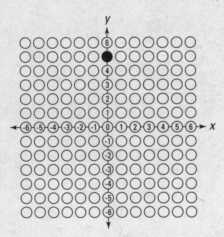

42. D          43. B

44. D          45. **3 hours**

46. D          47. A

48. C          49. A

50. C

# Part VII

# Getting More Test Practice: GED Practice Test 2

## Five Things to Do Before Taking the Next Practice Test

- Review all the items from the previous test on which you didn't do well. Correct any misunderstandings.

- Practice extracting information from various sources, including graphics, maps, diagrams, tables, charts, editorials, old documents, corporate policy statements, and even computer manuals.

- Make sure you know how to use the calculator included on-screen on the real GED test. You may only use that one specific model, so familiarize yourself with the various functions.

- Practice reading on a computer screen. Studies have shown that people read and comprehend on-screen materials very differently compared to paper materials.

- Review the Math formula table. If you understand the formulas and know what they do, you're probably well on your way to a good score on the Math test.

Whether you're in time of war or peace, or simply taking the GED test, you need to be prepared with a strategy to help you succeed. Find some helpful hints on taking the GED test at www.dummies.com/extras/gedtest.

## In this part . . .

✔ Continue building your skills and your confidence with another full-length GED practice test.

✔ Score your answers quickly and compare your results from this practice test with Practice Test 1.

✔ Check out detailed answer explanations for every question and sample scoring criteria for the Extended Response items.

# Chapter 25

# Practice Test 2: Reasoning through Language Arts

· · · · · · · · · · · · · · · · · · · · · · · · · · · · · · · · · · · · · · · · · · · · · · · · · · · · · · · · · · · ·

*R*eady for more practice? You have 95 minutes to complete the question-and-answer section, followed by a ten-minute break, and then another 45 minutes to write the Extended Response (the essay). Remember, on the real GED test, you can't transfer unused time from one section to another.

The answers and explanations to this test's questions are in Chapter 26. Review the explanations to all the questions, not just the ones you didn't get. Going over the answers is a good review technique.

Practice tests work best when you take them under the same conditions as the real test. Unless you require accommodations, you'll be taking the GED test on a computer. You'll see all the questions on a computer screen and use a keyboard or mouse to indicate your answers. We formatted the questions and answers formatted the questions and answer choices in this book to make them visually as similar as possible to the real GED test. We had to retain some A, B, C, D choices for marking your answers, and we provide a separate answer sheet for you to do so. Also, to make it simpler for you to time yourself, we present the question and answer sections as one unit, rather than two, followed by the Extended Response at the end.

# Answer Sheet for Practice Test 2, Reasoning through Language Arts

1. (A) (B) (C) (D)
2. (A) (B) (C) (D)
3. (A) (B) (C) (D)
4. (A) (B) (C) (D)
5. (A) (B) (C) (D)
6. (A) (B) (C) (D)
7. _____
8. 

| Advantages | Disadvantages |
| --- | --- |
|  |  |
|  |  |

9. (A) (B) (C) (D)
10. (A) (B) (C) (D)
11. (A) (B) (C) (D)
12. (A) (B) (C) (D)
13. (A) (B) (C) (D)
14. (A) (B) (C) (D)
15. (A) (B) (C) (D)
16. ☐☐☐☐☐☐
17. (A) (B) (C) (D)
18. (A) (B) (C) (D)
19. (A) (B) (C) (D)
20. (A) (B) (C) (D)
21. (A) (B) (C) (D)
22. (A) (B) (C) (D)
23. (A) (B) (C) (D)
24. (A) (B) (C) (D)
25. (A) (B) (C) (D)

26. (A) (B) (C) (D)
27. (A) (B) (C) (D)
28. _____
29. (A) (B) (C) (D)
30. (A) (B) (C) (D)
31. _____
32. (A) (B) (C) (D)
33. (A) (B) (C) (D)
34. _____
35. (A) (B) (C) (D)
36. (A) (B) (C) (D)
37. (A) (B) (C) (D)
38. (A) (B) (C) (D)
39. (A) (B) (C) (D)
40. (A) (B) (C) (D)
41. (A) (B) (C) (D)
42. _____
43. (A) (B) (C) (D)
44. (A) (B) (C) (D)
45. (A) (B) (C) (D)
46. (A) (B) (C) (D)
47. (A) (B) (C) (D)
48. (A) (B) (C) (D)
49. (A) (B) (C) (D)
50. _____

# *Reasoning through Language Arts Test*

**Time:** 95 minutes

**Directions:** Mark your answers on the answer sheet provided.

---

*Questions 1–10 refer to the following passage.*

---

But not all brands of bottled water are the same. Many bottlers use the same municipal water that comes from your tap. They merely have to completely remove the chlorine and do some additional filtration to enhance the taste. Bottled spring waters are different. The mineral content of waters differs from spring to spring, producing water with a unique taste. Other bottled waters are carbonated, either naturally or artificially in the bottling process, carbonation can add to the clean taste of water.

If you find mineral water whose taste you enjoy and don't mind the cost, enjoy. From our "Green" perspective, the plastic litter is a huge negative. Also, the effect on the environment of moving large quantities of potable water from one area to another make this an undesirable solution.

Many people enjoy there bottle water taste. So how can you get the same clean taste without the waste? The least expensive way is to use a jug with a charcoal filter cartridge. Filling that jug with clean tap water removes the chlorine and unpleasant tastes or odors. It also removes some of the lead found in the water pipes of older buildings. This is an effective and inexpensive choice. Certainly our morning coffee and tea tastes better for this filtration.

A more advanced and expensive counter-top system is a distillation pot. This system boils water, collects the steam, and condenses it into absolutely pure water. But not everyone likes the taste of totally mineral-free water, and the electricity costs add up.

There are also more extensive systems available. If you get tired of changing cartridges or storing the plastic jug in your fridge, you can also have an under-the-counter system installed on your kitchen sink. In townhouses, you can add such a system on the main water pipe and provide the same filtration to the entire house. Some of these systems use carbon blocks and ceramic filters. The blocks are more effective than loose charcoal filters. Also removing traces of pesticides and other chemical contaminants. Ceramic filters remove cloudiness and micro-particles, spores, and other microscopic matter. They deliver excellent drinking water. In either case, there is little waste other than the filters.

*Go on to next page*

1. How would you correct the underlined portion of this sentence?

   <u>But not all brands of bottled water are</u> the same.

   (A) But not all brands of bottled water are

   (B) Not all brands of bottled water are

   (C) But, not all brands of bottled water is

   (D) Not all brands of bottled water is

2. How would you correct the underlined portion of this sentence?

   <u>They merely have to completely remove the chlorine and</u> do some additional filtration to enhance the taste.

   (A) They merely have to completely remove the chlorine and

   (B) They merely have to remove the chlorine completely and

   (C) They merely have completely to remove the chlorine and

   (D) They merely have to remove the chlorine and

3. How would you correct this sentence?

   Bottled spring waters are different.

   (A) Bottled spring waters are different.

   (B) Bottled, spring waters are different.

   (C) Bottled spring waters were different.

   (D) Bottled spring waters is different.

4. How would you correct the underlined portion of this sentence?

   <u>The mineral content of waters differ from spring to spring</u>, producing water with a unique taste.

   (A) The mineral content of waters differ from spring to spring

   (B) The mineral content of water differ from spring to spring

   (C) The mineral content of waters differs from spring to spring

   (D) The mineral content of waters differ; from spring to spring

5. How would you correct the underlined portion of this sentence?

   Other bottled waters <u>are carbonated, either naturally or artificially in the bottling process, carbonation can add</u> to the clean taste of water.

   (A) are carbonated, either naturally or artificially in the bottling process, carbonation can add

   (B) are carbonated naturally or artificially in the bottling process, carbonation can add

   (C) are carbonated. Either naturally or artificially in the bottling process, carbonation can add

   (D) are carbonated, either naturally or artificially in the bottling process. Carbonation can add

6. How would you correct the underlined portion of this sentence?

   Many people enjoy <u>there bottle</u> water taste

   (A) there bottle

   (B) their bottled

   (C) they're bottling

   (D) none of the above

7. Most people object to the taste of chlorine in their drinking water. The easiest way to remove that taste is with a ☐.

8. What are the advantages and disadvantages of using distillation pots? Write the answers in the appropriate column.

   (A) absolutely pure water

   (B) expensive to use

   (C) removes lead

   (D) no mineral taste

9. How would you correct this sentence?

   If you get tired of changing cartridges or storing the plastic jug in your fridge, you can also have an under-the-counter system installed on your kitchen sink.

   (A) change the word *fridge* to *refrigerator*

   (B) change *can also have* to *also can have*

   (C) insert a comma after *jug*

   (D) no change required

*Go on to next page* →

10. How would you correct the underlined portion of these sentences?

    The blocks are more <u>effective than loose charcoal filters. Also removing traces</u> of pesticides and other chemical contaminants.

    (A) effective than loose charcoal filters. Also removing traces

    (B) effective than lose charcoal filters. Also removing traces

    (C) effective than loose charcoal filters; also removing traces

    (D) effective than loose charcoal filters, also removing traces

---

*Questions 11–17 refer to the following business letter.*

---

BEST Institute of Technology
75 Ingram Drive
Concord, MA 51234

To whom it may concern:

(1) I am pleased to comment on the relationship of our organization to Peta Jackson of the York Square Employment resource Center. (2) The BEST Institute of Technology has partnered with the York Square ERC in recruiting candidates for our Café Technician and Operator training programs since April 2010.

(3) In support of the partnership, Peta provided the following services to our programs

- Set up information presentations as part of her job readiness seminars

- Distributed print materials

- Counseled applicants

- Expedited meetings with potential candidates

- Arranged five graduating ceremonies held at York Square ERC

(4) Peta has always been a strong advocate for our program, which has trained more than 50 technicians and operators during the past 18 months. (5) The fact that York Square was our primary source of referrals are a tribute to Peta's efforts. (6) She has, with a high degree of professional competence and efficiency, pursued her responsibilities. (7) On a personal level, it has been a joy to work with Peta, and I wish her the very best in her future endeavors.

Dale Worth, PhD, Registrar

*Go on to next page*

11. Sentence 1: **I am pleased to comment on the relationship of our organization to Peta Jackson of the York Square Employment resource Center.**

Which revision should be made to Sentence 1?

(A) change *to Peta Jackson* to *of Peta Jackson*

(B) change *pleased* to *please*

(C) change *resource* to *Resource*

(D) change *Center* to *Centre*

12. Sentence 2: **The BEST Institute of Technology has partnered with the York Square ERC in recruiting candidates for our Café Technician and Operator training programs since April 2010.**

Which is the best way to improve Sentence 2?

(A) move *since April 2010* to the start of the sentence

(B) change *has partnered* to *have partnered*

(C) change *with* to *between*

(D) change *in recruiting* to *while recruiting*

13. Sentence 3: **In support of the partnership, Peta provided the following services to our programs**

- **Set up information presentations as part of her job readiness seminars**
- **Distributed print materials**
- **Counseled applicants**
- **Expedited meetings with potential candidates**
- **Arranged five graduating ceremonies held at York Square ERC**

Which correction should be made to Sentence 3?

(A) remove the comma after *partnership*

(B) add a semicolon after *seminars*

(C) add a semicolon after *materials*

(D) insert a colon after *programs*

14. Sentence 4: **Peta <u>has always been</u> a strong advocate for our program, which has trained more than 50 technicians and operators during the past 18 months.**

Which is the best way to write the underlined portion of this sentence? If the original is the best way, choose Choice (A).

(A) has always been

(B) always has been

(C) has been always

(D) have always been

15. Sentence 5: **The fact that York Square was our primary source of referrals are a tribute to Peta's efforts.**

Which correction should be made to Sentence 5?

(A) change *Peta's* to *Petas'*

(B) change *are* to *is*

(C) change *was* to *were*

(D) change *our* to *her*

16. Sentence 6:

**(1) She has**

**(2) ,**

**(3) with a high degree of professional competence**

**(4) and efficiency**

**(5) pursued her responsibilities**

**(6) .**

Reorder these sentence fragments into the best possible word order. Insert punctuation only as needed.

17. Sentence 7: **On a personal level, it has been a joy to work with Peta and I wish her the very <u>best in her future endeavors</u>.**

How would you correct the underlined portion of Sentence 7?

(A) best in her future endeavors

(B) best, in her future endeavors

(C) best in her future endeavours

(D) best; in her future endeavors

*Go on to next page*

> *Questions 18–25 refer to the following excerpt from* Customer Service For Dummies, *by Karen Leland and Keith Bailey (Wiley).*

### The Care Token Coupon

(1) A new copy shoppe recently opened near our office. (2) Modern and full of new, streamlined, state-of-the-art copiers. (3) The store was just what I needed. (4) The first time I went over, I waited 45 minutes to get served because of a shortage of trained staff. (5) They bounced back by apologizing, explaining the situation, and gave me a care token coupon that was worth 100 free copies. (6) Okay, I thought, fair enough, they're new and getting their act together, no big deal. (7) A week later, I went back and waited 30 minutes for service. (8) They apologised, explained the situation, and gave me a coupon for 100 free copies. (9) This time I was a little less understanding. (10) Two weeks later, I went back and the same thing happened again. (11) I didn't want another free coupon — they had bounced back just once too often. (12) My opinion of their services were so soured that I began looking for another copy shop.

18. Sentence 1: **A new copy shoppe recently opened near our office.**

    Which correction should be made to Sentence 1?

    (A) change *copy* to *copie*

    (B) change *shoppe* to *shop*

    (C) change *opened* to *is opening*

    (D) change *a* to *an*

19. Sentences 2 and 3: **Modern and full of new, streamlined, state-of-the-art copiers. The store was just what I needed.**

    Which improvement should be made to Sentences 2 and 3?

    (A) combine the two sentences by changing *The* to *the* and replacing the period after *copiers* with a comma

    (B) remove the hyphens from *state-of-the-art*

    (C) change *streamlined* to *streamlining*

    (D) change *store was* to *the copiers were*

20. Sentence 4: **The first time I went over, I waited 45 minutes to get served because of a shortage of trained staff.**

    Which is the best way to begin Sentence 4?

    (A) Because to get served

    (B) I waited 45 minutes

    (C) To get served because

    (D) no correction required

21. Sentence 5: **They bounced back by apologizing, explaining the situation, and gave me a care token coupon that was worth 100 free copies.**

    Which correction should be made to Sentence 5?

    (A) change apologizing to apologized

    (B) replace explaining with explained

    (C) change gave to giving

    (D) no correction required

22. Sentence 6: **Okay, I thought, fair enough, they're new and getting their act together, no big deal.**

    Which revision should be made to Sentence 6?

    (A) change *thought* to *am thinking*

    (B) change the one sentence into three sentences

    (C) change *no* to *know*

    (D) change *getting* to *got*

23. Sentence 7: **A week later I went back and waited 30 minutes for service.**

    Which addition should be made to Sentence 7?

    (A) add a comma after *later*

    (B) add a comma after *back*

    (C) add a colon after *back*

    (D) add *more* after *minutes*

*Go on to next page* ⟹

24. Sentence 8: **They apologised, explained the situation, and gave me a coupon for 100 free copies.**

    Which correction is required for Sentence 8?

    (A) change *apologised* to *apologising*

    (B) change *explained* to *explaining*

    (C) change *apologised* to *apologized*

    (D) no correction required

25. Sentence 9: **This time I was a little less understanding.**

    Which correction should be made to Sentence 9?

    (A) insert a comma after *time*

    (B) change *was* to *am*

    (C) change *less* to *least*

    (D) change *understanding* to *understood*

---

*Questions 26–29 refer to the following excerpt from* The Prince, *by Niccolò Machiavelli (Project Gutenberg;* www.gutenberg.org*).*

---

A prince ought to have no other aim or thought, nor select anything else for his study, than war and its rules and discipline; for this is the sole art that belongs to him who rules, and it is of such force that it not only upholds those who are born princes, but it often enables men to rise from a private station to that rank. And, on the contrary, it is seen that when princes have thought more of ease than of arms they have lost their states. And the first cause of your losing it is to neglect this art; and what enables you to acquire a state is to be master of the art. Francesco Sforza, through being martial, from a private person became Duke of Milan; and the sons, through avoiding the hardships and troubles of arms, from dukes became private persons. For among other evils which being unarmed brings you, it causes you to be despised, and this is one of those ignominies against which a prince ought to guard himself, as is shown later on. Because there is nothing proportionate between the armed and the unarmed; and it is not reasonable that he who is armed should yield obedience willingly to him who is unarmed, or that the unarmed man should be secure among armed servants. Because, there being in the one disdain and in the other suspicion, it is not possible for them to work well together. And therefore a prince who does not understand the art of war, over and above the other misfortunes already mentioned, cannot be respected by his soldiers, nor can he rely on them. He ought never, therefore, to have out of his thoughts this subject of war, and in peace he should addict himself more to its exercise than in war; this he can do in two ways, the one by action, the other by study.

26. Why should a prince concentrate on the study of war?

    (A) It is the knowledge that preserves their position.

    (B) It allows the prince to lead a more comfortable life.

    (C) Not being focused on war makes you more beloved by the people.

    (D) Peaceful men are respected by their soldiers.

27. What is the connection between authority and military power, according to Machiavelli?

    (A) Having a large army grants someone high status.

    (B) People are suspicious of princes without large armies.

    (C) Slaves fear soldiers.

    (D) The armed do not readily yield authority to the unarmed.

28. How does Machiavelli think the population will react to a prince who is unarmed? They will ☐ .

*Go on to next page* ➡

29. Which of these phrases best describes Machiavelli's attitude to the study of the art of war?

    (A) Study hard.

    (B) In times of peace, prepare for war.

    (C) Avoid war to gain the respect of your people.

    (D) Warriors respect only warriors.

    *Questions 30–34 refer to the following passage from* The Adventures of Tom Sawyer, *by Mark Twain (Project Gutenberg; www.gutenberg.org).*

"Hang the boy, can't I never learn anything? Ain't he played me tricks enough like that for me to be looking out for him by this time? But old fools is the biggest fools there is. Can't learn an old dog new tricks, as the saying is. But my goodness, he never plays them alike, two days, and how is a body to know what's coming? He 'pears to know just how long he can torment me before I get my dander up, and he knows if he can make out to put me off for a minute or make me laugh, it's all down again and I can't hit him a lick. I ain't doing my duty by that boy, and that's the Lord's truth, goodness knows. Spare the rod and spile the child, as the Good Book says. I'm a laying up sin and suffering for us both, I know. He's full of the Old Scratch, but laws-a-me! he's my own dead sister's boy, poor thing, and I ain't got the heart to lash him, somehow. Every time I let him off, my conscience does hurt me so, and every time I hit him my old heart most breaks. Well-a-well, man that is born of woman is of few days and full of trouble, as the Scripture says, and I reckon it's so. He'll play hookey this evening, * and [* Southwestern for "afternoon"] I'll just be obleeged to make him work, tomorrow, to punish him. It's mighty hard to make him work Saturdays, when all the boys is having holiday, but he hates work more than he hates anything else, and I've GOT to do some of my duty by him, or I'll be the ruination of the child."

30. Why did Mark Twain write this dialogue in such an ungrammatical manner?

    (A) He did not know any better.

    (B) He was "folksy" at heart.

    (C) He wanted to reflect the character of the speaker.

    (D) Everyone spoke like that back then.

31. Which phrase from the text explains why the speaker, Aunt Polly, thinks she should be stricter with Tom Sawyer? [        ]

32. Why is Tom living with the speaker?

    (A) She likes Tom.

    (B) She needs his help managing her home.

    (C) Tom is her nephew, and his mother is dead.

    (D) She adopted him.

33. What evidence is there in the text to support the idea that the speaker considers herself a good, God-fearing woman?

    (A) She makes numerous references to the Bible.

    (B) She worries about making Tom work on Saturdays.

    (C) She gets mad at Tom for the tricks he pulls.

    (D) All of the above.

34. Who is Old Scratch? [        ]

*Go on to next page*

---

*Questions 35–36 refer to the following excerpt from the Central Intelligence Agency Careers website (www.cia.gov).*

---

### Instilling Inclusive Work Practices

In our organization, we are working to ensure every officer's views are heard and that their ideas and skills are given due consideration. This enables us to fully leverage our talented and dedicated workforce.

The Agency has a variety of employee resource groups comprised of employees who share a common affinity (gender, sexual orientation, disability, ethnic, and racial backgrounds) and their allies. The employee resource groups make the organization stronger by:

- increasing cultural awareness,

- providing insight, practical solutions, and best practices, and

- promoting engagement and collaboration.

In addition, mentoring, coaching, training, and recognition for collaborative and inclusive behaviors foster employee engagement, professional development, and career advancement.

35. What corrections does the following sentence require?

This enables us to fully leverage our talented and dedicated work force.

(A) enables us to fully leverage

(B) enables us to leverage fully

(C) enables you to fully leverage

(D) enables full leverage to

36. Why does the CIA use employee resource groups?

(A) They make the organization stronger.

(B) They promote racial understanding.

(C) They reduce sexual harassment.

(D) They produce diverse employment opportunities.

---

*Questions 37–42 refer to the following passage.*

---

### Facilities for Access to Creative Enterprise (FACE)

Originally founded in 1982 to train unemployed youth in small "hand skill" craft workshops, this project provides occupational and entrepreneurial skills as an alternative to traditional manufacturing jobs. Beginning with glass engraving and sign writing, FACE now offers training in more than 200 hand skill occupations, including antique restoration, clothing manufacturing, graphic design, masonry, sail making, specialist joinery, weaving, and wood turning. Funded through the Youth Training Scheme, FACE provides 800 training places in the west and northeast of England under the premise that even if the young people can't secure employment, they at least will have the skills to create their own businesses.

*Go on to next page* ⟶

Based on its experience, FACE has developed, with the Royal Society of Arts, a Certificate in Small Business and Enterprise Skills. The aim of the certificate is "to develop the basic skills of enterprise across a range of occupational sectors, within small business and in general employment and which are applicable in a wide range of personal and social contexts outside work." Competencies include self-evaluation, decision making, initiative taking, resource and time management, opportunism and self-motivation, problem solving, and learning-to-learn skills, as well as communication and number skills vital to personal effectiveness.

37. What is the overall purpose of the FACE project?

    (A) to provide manufacturing jobs

    (B) to engrave glass

    (C) to train unemployed youth

    (D) to write signs

38. Which of the following is not an example of a hand skill craft occupation?

    (A) weaving

    (B) wood turning

    (C) sail making

    (D) robotic assembly

39. What does the passage suggest is the best advice for youth who want to work?

    (A) engage in traditional manufacturing

    (B) create new enterprises

    (C) join the Royal Society of Arts

    (D) obtain a Certificate in Small Business

40. Who helped FACE develop the Certificate in Small Business and Enterprise Skills?

    (A) Youth Training Scheme

    (B) west and northeast England

    (C) hand skill workshops

    (D) Royal Society of Arts

41. Which competency is not included in training for the Certificate?

    (A) problem solving

    (B) anger management

    (C) decision making

    (D) self-evaluation

42. What in the passage reveals FACE's expectations for its graduates?

    (A) They will succeed if they develop basic skills.

    (B) Finding alternatives to traditional manufacturing jobs are their best bet.

    (C) Training in small "hand skill" craft workshops will guarantee them employment.

    (D) It will not be difficult to obtain general employment.

---

*Questions 43–48 refer to the following letter.*

---

TO: James Tiberius

FROM: Akira Hudson

RE: Consumer Math Book Proposal

We meet mathematical problems everyday in our lives. How we handle them makes the difference between winning and losing. Many of our decisions require knowledge of "survival mathematics," the skills and concepts that help us survive in an increasingly complex world. Many students drop high-school mathematics as soon as they can. Few are willing or able to take in school the life skills courses that would help them later in life. As a result, they never learn some of the important math life skills. This book has a built-in target audience, the people who need "survival mathematics" to get ahead in this world.

*Go on to next page*

The key life skills are the everyday arithmetic that helps one survive in the market place. We propose to help readers learn and practice the following skills:

- Different methods of earning a paycheck: We explain hourly wages and piecework, commission and salary.

- Calculating deductions from pay slips: What comes off and why.

- Budgeting: Making the money last from paycheck to paycheck; creating a household budget.

- The deal: How to read ads. Just how good a deal is "the deal"?

- Credit cards: How you pay, what you pay for, and the real cost of loyalty programs.

- Compound interest: The true cost of money. Comparing interest rates on debt, ranging from bank loans to credit card debt. Working out just how expensive credit card debt is.

- Compound interest: The mortgage. Working out the true costs of "zero down" financing of a home.

- Compound interest: Earning money on money. How can one reinvest to earn more, and the magic of time in accumulating wealth.

- Keeping more of what you earn: Some simple strategies to minimize taxes, from education and retirement savings to mortgage interest deductibility.

- The car: Calculating the pros and cons: We compare used vs. new, purchase vs. lease, and examine the true cost of owning a car. Since the car is probably the second biggest purchase most people will ever make, this is an important part of consumer knowledge. This unit is specially aimed at first-time car purchasers.

The application of basic arithmetic skills will help readers become better consumers and teach them how to deal with mathematical issues in everyday life.

43. Why do the authors suggest "survival mathematics" is a skill many young people need?

(A) Many students cannot or will not take life skills courses.

(B) Many students drop high-school math as soon as possible.

(C) Both Choices (A) and (B) are correct.

(D) Neither Choice (A) nor (B) is correct.

44. What do the authors suggest is the point of budgeting?

(A) to avoid overspending

(B) to make the money last between paychecks

(C) to set aside some savings from each paycheck

(D) all of the above

45. What does *zero down* mean?

(A) a lack of involvement

(B) no interest payments on the first part of a loan

(C) no security deposit

(D) no initial payment on the mortgage before monthly payments start

46. Why are car purchases considered important enough to be given a heading of their own?

(A) Everyone needs a car.

(B) Students in particular want to buy cars.

(C) Car loans are more expensive than credit card debts.

(D) Cars are among the largest purchases most people ever make.

*Go on to next page*

47. If John owns a car, that is _____ car.

   (A) John's

   (B) Johns

   (C) Johns'

   (D) none of the above

48. Which version of the underlined portion of this sentence is correct?

   <u>Their car was they're</u> when we got there.

   (A) Their car was they're

   (B) There car was their

   (C) Their car was there

   (D) They're car was their

---

*Questions 49–50 refer to the following excerpt from the Environmental Protection Agency website (www.epa.gov).*

---

### Weather Versus Climate

- Weather is a specific event or condition that happens over a period of hours or days. For example, a thunderstorm, a snowstorm, and today's temperature all describe the weather.

- Climate refers to the average weather conditions in a place over many years (usually at least 30 years). For example, the climate in Minneapolis is cold and snowy in the winter, while Miami's climate is hot and humid. The average climate around the world is called global climate.

Weather conditions can change from one year to the next. For example, Minneapolis might have a warm winter one year and a much colder winter the next. This kind of change is normal. But when the average pattern over many years changes, it could be a sign of climate change.

49. When scientists consider climate, what length of time is involved?

   (A) 30 years or more

   (B) a decade

   (C) probably a few months

   (D) whatever is going on today

50. What is more likely to be variable from year to year, weather or climate? ⬚

# The Extended Response

**Time:** 45 minutes

**Your assignment:** The following articles present arguments from both supporters and critics of promoting higher education for all. In your response, analyze both positions presented in the two articles to determine which one is best supported. Use relevant and specific evidence from the article to support your response.

Use the following sheets of lined paper for your response. You should expect to spend up to 45 minutes in planning, drafting, and editing your response.

## Higher Education

*(This article was extracted from the White House Support for Higher Ed website:* www.whitehouse.gov.*)*

Earning a post-secondary degree or credential is no longer just a pathway to opportunity for a talented few; rather, it is a prerequisite for the growing jobs of the new economy. Over this decade, employment in jobs requiring education beyond a high school diploma will grow more rapidly than employment in jobs that do not: of the 30 fastest growing occupations, more than half require post-secondary education. With the average earnings of college graduates at a level that is twice as high as that of workers with only a high school diploma, higher education is now the clearest pathway into the middle class.

In higher education, the U.S. has been outpaced internationally. In 1990, the U.S. ranked first in the world in four-year degree attainment among 25-34 year olds; today, the U.S. ranks 12th. We also suffer from a college attainment gap, as high school graduates from the wealthiest families in our nation are almost certain to continue on to higher education, while just over half of our high school graduates in the poorest quarter of families attend college. And while more than half of college students graduate within six years, the completion rate for low-income students is around 25 percent.

Acknowledging these factors early in his Administration, President Obama challenged every American to commit to at least one year of higher education or post-secondary training. The President has also set a new goal for the country: that by 2020, America would once again have the highest proportion of college graduates in the world.

To achieve this bold goal for college completion, ensure that America's students and workers receive the education and training needed for the jobs of today and tomorrow, and provide greater security for the middle class, President Obama and his Administration are working to make college more accessible, affordable, and attainable for all American families.

## Helping Middle Class Families Afford College

America is home to the best colleges and universities in the world — and increasing college attainment has never been more important to our economic competitiveness — yet tuition and fees have skyrocketed over the past decade, making it more difficult for American families to invest in a higher education for their future. Today's college students borrow and rack up more debt than ever before. In 2010, graduates who took out loans left college owing an average of more than $26,000. Student loan debt has now surpassed credit card debt for the first time ever.

Our nation's commitment to placing a good education within reach of all who are willing to work for it helped build a strong American middle class over the past several generations. In keeping this promise alive, President Obama has expanded federal support to help more students afford college, while calling for a shared responsibility in tackling rising college costs. President Obama's efforts of reform in higher education funding have produced the largest investment in student aid since the G.I. Bill, while resulting in a more efficient, reliable, and effective system for students to help them afford college and manage debt.

*Go on to next page* ⟹

### Keeping Costs Down

The President is calling on Congress to advance new reforms to give more hard working students a fair shot at pursuing higher education, because education is not a luxury: it is an economic imperative that every hard working and responsible student should be able to afford. President Obama has emphasized that the federal government, states, colleges, and universities all have a role to play in making higher education more affordable, by reining in college costs, providing value for American families, and preparing students with a solid education to succeed in their careers.

In his State of the Union address, President Obama emphasized this shared responsibility of states and higher education institutions — working with the federal government — to promote access, affordability and attainment in higher education by reining in college costs, providing value for American families, and preparing students with a high quality education to succeed in their careers. It is not enough to increase federal student aid alone — state policymakers and individual colleges and universities bear a shared responsibility to take action against rising college tuition and costs.

Providing greater pathways for students to enter into and succeed in higher education is in the interest of all Americans, and is critical to developing a highly educated, highly skilled economy and workforce that will attract business and lead to lower unemployment. The Administration has taken several steps and advanced several proposals to put higher education greater within reach for more Americans.

### Strengthening Community Colleges

The President has placed a strong emphasis on making America's community colleges stronger, ensuring that they are gateways to economic prosperity and educational opportunities for millions of Americans each year. Each year, over 1,100 community colleges provide students and workers with critical skills to succeed in a 21st century economy. To help reach the President's college attainment goal, the Obama Administration has called for an additional 5 million graduates from community colleges by 2020. Working in partnership with states and communities, community colleges are well suited to promote the dual goal of academic and on-the-job preparedness for the next generation of American workers.

Many community colleges are already working with businesses to develop programs and classes — ranging from degree-granting curricula to certified courses for retraining — that will enhance skills for workers.

### Improving Transparency and Accountability

President Obama has consistently strived to lead the most open, efficient and accountable government in history. Over the last two years, new initiatives have increased public participation in government, opened up new information to Americans on a variety of topics, and improved citizens' everyday lives. In the vein of transparency and accountability, the President tasked his Administration with giving students and families new tools and relevant information that will help them make sound financial decisions in pursuing their higher education goals.

### Higher Education Not For Everyone

*(This opposing article was written by yours truly, Murray Shukyn and Achim Krull.)*

Not everyone needs a postsecondary education. Numerous pathways to successful employment, work well and do not require years of college or university education. Whether it is apprenticeships in trades, training through the military, or entrepreneurial initiative, these approaches work. Moreover, people acquire a position without the huge debts incurred in formal postsecondary education.

It is true that unemployment rates decrease with educational attainment. The rate for people with only a high-school diploma is about 25 percent higher than that of people with a completed university degree. After they start working, that scenario changes. The high-school graduate has been working for at least four years before the college graduate can start looking for work. The median income for a high-school graduate is about $35,000, while the university graduate's is about $54,000. At a median income difference of about $20,000 a year, it will take the college graduate's total earnings at least seven years to catch up to

*Go on to next page*

the high-school graduate, just based on lost income alone. But then you need to consider the cost of going to college. In 2010–2011, private colleges and universities in the United States cost (including residence fees) an average of $36,000 annually, while public institutions cost about $13,000. In the meantime, fees have continued to increase. When you include the cost of education for those four years, it now would take the college graduate from public institutions another two years of employment to catch up to the high-school graduate. If the student went to a private college, it would take an additional seven years.

In effect, just based on median incomes and tuition fees, the college graduate will take between 10 and 15 years to catch up in total earnings. And we have not considered the costs of books and incidentals, which the Department of Education suggests will add approximately another $5,000 annually. That adds at least another year to the time it takes to catch up.

Forbes Magazine, which writes mainly for an audience of wealthy business people, argued in a 2013 article that few jobs require a university education. The article takes the position that most of what you learn at college or university has little relevance to what you end up doing on the job. The main benefit of a degree is that it shows prospective customers that you are smart.

And then there are the people who made it without even finishing high school. That list includes Dave Thomas, founder of Wendy's, John D. Rockefeller, and many others. A whole collection of wealthy entrepreneurs started with just a high-school diploma, like Richard Branson of Virgin Records, Virgin Atlantic airline, and now Virgin Galactic, a private space travel venture. We also know of many successful entrepreneurs who dropped out of university to start businesses, from Steve Jobs to Bill Gates and Marc Zuckerberg.

That does not mean degrees are useless; it does tell us that drive and ideas are more important than formal education.

*Go on to next page*

*Go on to next page*

# Chapter 26

# Answers for Practice Test 2, Reasoning through Language Arts

••••••••••••••••••••••••••••••••••••••••••••••••••••••••••••

**Y**ou've done the test. Now you need to check your answers. If you just want a quick look at what you got right or wrong, check out the abbreviated answer key with just the answers at the end of this chapter. The better approach is to read all the answers and explanations so you find out the reasoning behind the correct answers. You can discover just as much from your errors as from understanding why the right answers are correct.

## Answers and Explanations

1. **B. Not all brands of bottled water are.** Although starting a sentence with *and* or *but* isn't a grammar error, it's generally considered poor style and is a stylistic mistake. It's best simply to leave out such conjunctions when starting sentences or paragraphs.

   Choice (A) gives no change and is therefore wrong. Choice (C) adds a comma after the word *but,* which leaves the same style issue. And Choice (D) doesn't show subject-verb agreement because it uses *is*.

2. **B. They merely have to remove the chlorine completely and.** The mistake here is a split infinitive, which is considered by many to be a grammar mistake. In this case, you shouldn't split *to remove* with the adverb *completely*. Out of the answer choices that don't split the infinitive, Choice (B) is the best one.

3. **A. Bottled spring waters are different.** This is sort of a trick question. The sentence is correct as it stands and requires no change, so Choice (A) is correct. The other options introduce new errors.

4. **C. The mineral content of waters differs from spring to spring.** This is a subject-verb agreement error. The subject of the sentence is *content,* which is singular and requires a singular verb. So the correct form of the verb is *differs*. Changing the word *waters* to *water* has no effect on the sentence and doesn't correct the error. The other choices merely introduce new errors.

5. **D. are carbonated, either naturally or artificially in the bottling process. Carbonation can add.** This is an example of a comma splice or run-on sentence. In fact, there are two sentences here; the second one begins with *Carbonation can add*. The only answer choice that addresses that error is Choice (D), which inserts a period after *bottling process*.

6. **B. their bottled.** In the case of there/their/they're, the correct choice is *their*. The word *there* refers to location, while *their* shows possession, and *they're* is the contraction of *they are*. Because the sentence is talking about someone's water, the possessive form is correct.

In the case of bottle/bottled/bottling, the correct choice is *bottled*. *Bottle* is a noun, *bottled* is an adjective, and *bottling* is a *gerund* — a special form of the verb that can be used as a noun. Here, you want an adjective to describe the water, so *bottled* is the correct form.

7. **charcoal filter.** The third paragraph states that charcoal filters will remove the taste of chlorine.

8. **Advantages: A, C; Disadvantages: B, D.** The only point that may be troublesome here is Choice (C). However, when you think about the answer, the text states that the distillation process removes everything from the water and leaves only pure water behind. So that means it also removes lead.

9. **A. change the word *fridge* to *refrigerator*.** When you're writing an article, you should generally use more formal language. The word *fridge* is vernacular, a shortened version of the word *refrigerator*. The preferred word here is *refrigerator*. Choice (B) is a split verb, and although it's better not to split the verb, this isn't a hard grammar rule, but it's not the best answer. Choices (C) and (D) are incorrect.

10. **D. effective than loose charcoal filters, also removing traces.** The second sentence isn't a complete sentence; therefore, the only way to correct this example without a complete rewrite is to replace the period between *filters* and *also* with a comma. Adding a semicolon after the word *filters* doesn't correct the error, so Choice (D) is the best answer.

11. **C. change *resource* to *Resource*.** In the letter, the York Square Employment Resource Center is a title; therefore, all words except prepositions and articles must be capitalized.

12. **A. move *since April 2010* to the start of the sentence.** Moving *since April 2010* is the only good answer here. The current sentence sounds as though the training programs have been in existence since April 2010 when, in fact, the partnership has been in existence since that time.

13. **D. insert a colon after *programs*.** Most, although not all, lists begin with a colon. You don't need semicolons after *seminars* or *materials*. These are just items in the list; the bullets serve as separators. You do need a comma after the introductory phrase, so Choice (A) is wrong.

14. **A. has always been.** No change is required for this sentence, so Choice (A) is correct.

15. **B. change *are* to *is*.** The subject of the sentence is *fact,* which is singular, but the verb is *are,* which is plural. Verbs must agree with their subjects.

16. **(1) She has (5) pursued her responsibilities (3) with a high degree of professional competence (4) and efficiency (6).** In its current form, this sentence forces the reader to pause too long and remember too much. Rewriting it as "She has pursued her responsibilities with a high degree of professional competence and efficiency" is far more straightforward.

17. **A. best in her future endeavors.** The sentence needs no correction. A comma or semicolon after *best* isn't required. The spelling of *endeavor* with a *u* is the British spelling, not American English.

18. **B. change *shoppe* to *shop*.** The word *shoppe* is quaint, but it isn't common usage. If you were living in Williamsburg 200 years ago, the answer would be different. Today, people use the shorter and more common *shop*.

19. **A. combine the two sentences by changing *The* to *the* and replacing the period after *copiers* with a comma.** The first sentence is missing a verb, making it an incomplete sentence. By joining it to the second sentence, you create one complete sentence. Choice (B) is incorrect because *state-of-the-art* is acting as a single adjective to *copiers,* and multiword adjectives are nearly always hyphenated. Choice (C) is wrong because it introduces a new error, using the wrong form of the word "streamlined". Choice (D) is incorrect because the first sentence is clearly describing the store, not the copiers.

20. **B. no correction required.** No change is required in this sentence. The copy shop may want to consider changing the way it hires and trains its staff, but that's another matter altogether.

21. **C. change *gave* to *giving*.** Lists have to be parallel. In this case, you have *apologizing, explaining,* and *gave,* which aren't parallel. All three are verbs, but the first two are gerunds, while the second is an infinitive. Maintaining parallel structures in sentences is important. Changing *gave* to *giving* makes the list parallel.

22. **B. change the one sentence into three sentences.** This is a classic run-on sentence, so you need to break it apart into separate sentences, in this case, three separate sentences. A good change is as follows: "Okay," I thought, "fair enough. They're new and getting their act together. No big deal." Note that the third sentence doesn't appear to have a verb, but the implied subject and verb are *it is,* as in "It is no big deal."

23. **A. add a comma after *later*.** The correct answer is to add a comma after *later*. Most of the time, you want to set off an introductory clause with a comma; however, be aware that when the introductory clause is very short, the convention isn't always clear: Some people use the comma and others don't. On this test, however, you're always better off putting a comma after any introductory clause.

24. **C. change *apologised* to *apologized*.** Correct the spelling in *apologised*. The other answer choices do nothing to improve the sentence.

25. **A. insert a comma after *time*.** Add a comma after the introductory phrase. Most of the time, you want to set off an introductory clause, even a short one, with a comma.

26. **A. It is the knowledge that preserves their position.** The text clearly states that princes lose their states when they neglect this art. Although Choice (B) may be true, it has nothing to do with the question. Choices (C) and (D) are the opposite to what the text states.

27. **D. The armed do not readily yield authority to the unarmed.** Although Choices (A), (B), and (C) are all possible, they don't answer the question. However, further into the text, Machiavelli states that it's unreasonable for the armed to yield power to the unarmed.

28. **despise him.** The text states that the population will despise him.

29. **B. In times of peace, prepare for war.** The last sentence of the text makes it clear that Choice (B) is the best answer. Although Choices (A) and (D) may be partially correct, they're not the whole answer. Choice (C) is contradicted by the text.

30. **C. He wanted to reflect the character of the speaker.** The speaker in this case is Aunt Polly. She's a simple country woman with little education. This pattern of speech reflects that. Choices (A) and (B) are certainly wrong because Mark Twain was a well-educated writer. Choice (D) is simply wrong.

31. **Spare the rod and spile the child.** The correct section of the text is the speaker's quote from the Good Book.

32. **C. Tom is her nephew, and his mother is dead.** The correct answer refers to the quote "he's my own dead sister's boy" in Lines 18 and 19. The speaker is a good woman who wants to do the right thing for her nephew. Choices (A) and (B) may be true, but are not the best answers. There is nothing in the text to suggest she has adopted Tom, Choice (D).

33. **A. She makes numerous references to the Bible.** The key evidence about the speaker's religiosity consists of her frequent Bible quotes and references. Choices (B) and (C) may be correct but have nothing to do with the fact that she's a God-fearing woman. Choice (D) is simply wrong.

34. **the Devil.** *Old Scratch* was a term used by country people back then when they meant the Devil. There was an old superstition that one didn't use the name of the Devil for fear of conjuring him up. You have to infer that meaning from the context.

35. **B. enables us to leverage fully.** This is a case of a split infinitive. The infinitive is *to leverage*. Placing any words between the *to* and *leverage* is grammatically incorrect. Although splitting infinitives has become quite common practice in spoken English, it's grammatically incorrect.

36. **A. They make the organization stronger.** Although Choices (B), (C), and (D) may be correct, they're not the complete answer. The last part of the second paragraph states the reason: "the employee resource groups make the organizations stronger." Remember, when selecting an answer, select the most correct and complete choice.

37. **C. to train unemployed youth.** The overall purpose of the FACE project is to train unemployed youth. Glass engraving, sign writing, and antique restoring are just some of the skills the youth may develop through FACE. Manufacturing jobs are in short supply, resulting in the need for entrepreneurial skills.

38. **D. robotic assembly.** Robotic assembly is a high-tech computer-assisted approach to manufacturing that seeks to replace workers with robots. The other answers — *weaving, wood turning, sail making,* and *joinery* (carpentry) — are all examples of hand skill craft occupations according to the passage.

39. **B. create new enterprises.** The best way for youth to secure employment is to "create new enterprises," as the passage states. Jobs are being lost in traditional manufacturing. The Royal Society, business certificate, and training places don't refer directly to securing employment.

40. **D. Royal Society of Arts.** The Royal Society of Arts assisted FACE in developing the Certificate in Small Business and Enterprise Skills. Although the Youth Training Scheme provided funding for FACE, it wasn't directly involved with the Certificate. *Hand skill workshops* and occupational sectors have no direct relation to the Certificate. Choice (B), *west and northeast England,* refers only to locations.

41. **B. anger management.** *Anger management* isn't mentioned in the passage as one of the competencies; all the other skills are.

42. **B. Finding alternatives to traditional manufacturing jobs is their best bet.** Choice (B) is the most clear and direct statement in the text that the FACE program doesn't expect graduates to find traditional jobs but instead is preparing them for some alternative form of employment. Choices (A) and (D) could apply to any form of employment, so they're wrong. Choice (C) is somewhat correct, but it still suggests working for an employer, while the text suggests that graduates will need to look at alternatives, such as self-employment.

43. **C. Both Choices (A) and (B) are correct.** According to the introduction to the text, students both drop mathematics courses and are unwilling or unable to take life skills courses.

44. **B. to make the money last between paychecks.** Although a few choices are partially correct, you must select the most correct answer. The item about budgets specifically mentions making the money last between paychecks. So Choice (B) is the most correct answer.

45. **D. no initial payment on the mortgage before monthly payments start.** The term *zero down* means that no down payment is required before you begin making payments on a loan, or in this case, a mortgage. This definition can be inferred from the text.

46. **D. Cars are among the largest purchases most people ever make.** As the proposal states, car loans are the second largest purchase most people will ever make. Although Choices (A) and (B) are partially correct, they don't answer the question. And Choice (C) is wrong.

47. **A. John's.** The correct word is *John's.* The point of the exercise is to use the apostrophe appropriately.

48. **C. Their car was there.** The first their/there/they're choice has to show possession, so the correct choice is *their.* The second their/there/they're choice refers to location, and the correct version for location is *there.*

49. **A. 30 years or more.** The text states that climate refers to the average weather conditions over many years.

50. **weather.** Climate is the average of weather conditions over many years, while weather varies from day to day.

## Sample Extended Response

Here's an example of an essay in response to the articles about higher education. Your essay will look different, but this example can help you compare your response to a well-structured essay. Your essay could raise many of the same points that this essay does, perhaps organized differently, but above all, it should be well organized with a clear introduction, conclusion, and supporting evidence.

Compare the following sample to the response you wrote, and check out Chapter 7 for the scoring criteria and what evaluators look for in a response.

Higher education should be accessible for all, but the reality is that it is not. Both articles point out the problems in attaining that education. The first article discusses plans for promoting higher education and opening doors for people to attain that education. The second article discusses the expense involved in obtaining a postsecondary education. However, neither article offers any real answers to the issue of accessibility to postsecondary education. In terms of argument, the second article certainly provides far greater specific detail on the issues and thus makes a stronger case.

The first article, the White House statement, clearly states that more jobs will require more education, and that at least half of the fastest-growing areas of employment will require postsecondary education. It also points out that the United States is falling behind the rest of the world in terms of the percentage of the population attaining such higher education. It goes on to make a number of statements about how the administration is working toward improving access. Yet these statements are vague and general, offering no concrete answers.

It then goes on to state that the administration wishes to help make college and university affordable, so that everyone has a "fair shot at pursuing higher education." However, that section of the article is also woefully weak in terms of actual specifics on how this is to be done.

The second article, on the other hand, is full of very specific details. It explains the financial challenges facing individuals trying to obtain a postsecondary education. It presents statistics about average income of high-school graduates, comparing it to that of university graduates. It then presents details about the cost of a postsecondary education and the debt loads students acquire. For example, the article states that the average high-school graduate currently earns about $35,000 annually, nearly $20,000 less than a university graduate. It shows that the average college or university student's debt load will take that student anywhere from 10 to 15 years of full employment to catch up with the earnings of the average high-school graduate, providing that both fall into the average income bracket for their education level.

There are problems with both articles. The first article is indeed quite vague. Under the heading of "Improving Transparency and Accountability," it talks about how the president has tasked the administration to give "students and families new tools and relevant information that will help them make sound financial decisions in pursuing their higher education goals." Nowhere does it state any specifics. Earlier, the article talks about the president's emphasis on strengthening the community college system to ensure that the air gateways to economic prosperity. While it states the goal is to provide an additional 5 million graduates, nothing is said about how this will be achieved.

There are similar weaknesses within the second article. After demonstrating how expensive a postsecondary education can be, it goes on to talk about individuals who have obtained amazing careers, all without or with very limited postsecondary education. The weakness of this argument is that the article can only present five or six examples, while we are talking about a potential postsecondary population in the hundreds of thousands. The article says postsecondary education is not for everyone, but most people are not going to have the careers of a Dave Thomas or John D. Rockefeller, not without assistance. Undeniably, for the average person, postsecondary education still opens doors that will remain closed for most without that education.

Both articles have problems. The first article talks about the desirability of a postsecondary education and many possible solutions to the problem of obtaining that education. However, it is woefully weak on specifics. The second article basically says forget about a postsecondary education, by presenting in great detail the financial issues, but also offers no concrete answers on how to get ahead. In the context of supporting their arguments, the second article is the stronger.

# Answer Key

| | | |
|---|---|---|
| 1. B | 2. B | 3. A |
| 4. C | 5. D | 6. B |
| 7. charcoal filter | 8. Advantages: A, C;<br>Disadvantages: B, D | 9. A |
| 10. D | 11. C | 12. A |
| 13. D | 14. A | 15. B |
| 16. (1) She has (5) pursued her responsibilities (3) with a high degree of professional competence (4) and efficiency (6). | 17. A | 18. B |
| 19. A | 20. B | 21. C |
| 22. B | 23. A | 24. C |
| 25. A | 26. A | 27. D |
| 28. despise him | 29. B | 30. C |
| 31. Spare the rod and spile the child | 32. C | 33. A |
| 34. the Devil | 35. B | 36. A |
| 37. C | 38. D | 39. B |
| 40. D | 41. B | 42. B |
| 43. C | 44. B | 45. D |
| 46. D | 47. A | 48. C |
| 49. A | 50. weather | |

# Chapter 27

# Practice Test 2: Social Studies

· · · · · · · · · · · · · · · · · · · · · · · · · · · · · · · · · · · · · · · · · · · · · · · · · · · · · · · ·

*W*e're firm believers that practice makes better, if not perfect. So here's another Social Studies practice test. Give yourself 65 minutes to complete the question-and-answer section and then 25 minutes for the Extended Response to best simulate the real test-taking experience. The answers and explanations to this test's questions are in Chapter 28.

# Answer Sheet for Practice Test 2, Social Studies

1. Ⓐ Ⓑ Ⓒ Ⓓ
2. Ⓐ Ⓑ Ⓒ Ⓓ
3. Ⓐ Ⓑ Ⓒ Ⓓ
4. Ⓐ Ⓑ Ⓒ Ⓓ
5. Ⓐ Ⓑ Ⓒ Ⓓ
6. Ⓐ Ⓑ Ⓒ Ⓓ
7. Ⓐ Ⓑ Ⓒ Ⓓ
8. ◯ ◯ ◯ ◯
9. Ⓐ Ⓑ Ⓒ Ⓓ
10. Ⓐ Ⓑ Ⓒ Ⓓ
11. Ⓐ Ⓑ Ⓒ Ⓓ
12. Ⓐ Ⓑ Ⓒ Ⓓ
13. Ⓐ Ⓑ Ⓒ Ⓓ
14. Ⓐ Ⓑ Ⓒ Ⓓ
15. Ⓐ Ⓑ Ⓒ Ⓓ
16. Ⓐ Ⓑ Ⓒ Ⓓ
17. ◯ ◯ ◯ ◯
18. Ⓐ Ⓑ Ⓒ Ⓓ
19. Ⓐ Ⓑ Ⓒ Ⓓ
20. Ⓐ Ⓑ Ⓒ Ⓓ
21. Ⓐ Ⓑ Ⓒ Ⓓ
22. Ⓐ Ⓑ Ⓒ Ⓓ
23. Ⓐ Ⓑ Ⓒ Ⓓ

24. Ⓐ Ⓑ Ⓒ Ⓓ
25. Ⓐ Ⓑ Ⓒ Ⓓ
26. Ⓐ Ⓑ Ⓒ Ⓓ
27. Ⓐ Ⓑ Ⓒ Ⓓ
28. ◯ ◯ ◯ ◯
29. Ⓐ Ⓑ Ⓒ Ⓓ
30. Ⓐ Ⓑ Ⓒ Ⓓ
31. ☐ ☐ ☐ ☐
32. Ⓐ Ⓑ Ⓒ Ⓓ
33. Ⓐ Ⓑ Ⓒ Ⓓ
34. Ⓐ Ⓑ Ⓒ Ⓓ
35. Ⓐ Ⓑ Ⓒ Ⓓ
36. Ⓐ Ⓑ Ⓒ Ⓓ
37. Ⓐ Ⓑ Ⓒ Ⓓ
38. Ⓐ Ⓑ Ⓒ Ⓓ
39. Ⓐ Ⓑ Ⓒ Ⓓ
40. ▭
41. Ⓐ Ⓑ Ⓒ Ⓓ
42. Ⓐ Ⓑ Ⓒ Ⓓ
43. Ⓐ Ⓑ Ⓒ Ⓓ
44. Ⓐ Ⓑ Ⓒ Ⓓ
45. Ⓐ Ⓑ Ⓒ Ⓓ

# Social Studies Test

> **Time:** 65 minutes
>
> **Directions:** Mark your answers on the answer sheet provided.

> *Questions 1–4 refer to the following passage, which is excerpted from* Cliffs Quick Review U.S. History I, *by P. Soifer and A. Hoffman (Wiley).*

## The First Inhabitants of the Western Hemisphere

In telling the history of the United States and also of the nations of the Western Hemisphere in general, historians have wrestled with the problem of what to call the hemisphere's first inhabitants. Under the mistaken impression he had reached the "Indies," explorer Christopher Columbus called the people he met "Indians." This was an error in identification that has persisted for more than five hundred years, for the inhabitants of North and South America had no collective name by which they called themselves.

Historians, anthropologists, and political activists have offered various names, none fully satisfactory. Anthropologists have used "aborigine," but the term suggests a primitive level of existence inconsistent with the cultural level of many tribes. Another term, "Amerindian," which combines Columbus's error with the name of another Italian explorer, Amerigo Vespucci (whose name was the source of "America"), lacks any historical context. Since the 1960s, "Native American" has come into popular favor, though some activists prefer "American Indian." In the absence of a truly representative term, descriptive references such as "native peoples" or "indigenous peoples," though vague, avoid European influence. In recent years, some argument has developed over whether to refer to tribes in the singular or plural — Apache or Apaches — with supporters on both sides demanding political correctness.

1. What name has been favored since 1960?

   (A) Amerindian

   (B) Native American

   (C) native peoples

   (D) indigenous peoples

2. Why did Columbus call the native inhabitants "Indians"?

   (A) They were in the Western Hemisphere.

   (B) He thought he'd reached the Indies.

   (C) North and South America had not been discovered.

   (D) They were the hemisphere's first inhabitants.

3. Who used the term aborigine?

   (A) historians

   (B) political activists

   (C) Columbus

   (D) anthropologists

4. How was America named?

   (A) after an Italian explorer

   (B) after its first inhabitants

   (C) because of the European influence

   (D) after the native peoples

*Go on to next page*

> *Questions 5–9 refer to the following passage, which is excerpted from* CliffsQuickReview
> *U.S. History I, by P. Soifer and A. Hoffman (Wiley).*

### The Voyages of Christopher Columbus

Christopher Columbus, a Genoese sailor, believed that sailing west across the Atlantic Ocean was the shortest sea route to Asia. Ignorant of the fact that the Western Hemisphere lay between Europe and Asia and assuming the Earth's circumference to be a third less than it actually is, he was convinced that Japan would appear on the horizon just three thousand miles to the west. Like other seafarers of his day, Columbus was untroubled by political allegiances; he was ready to sail for whatever country would pay for his voyage. Either because of his arrogance (he wanted ships and crews to be provided at no expense to himself) or ambition (he insisted on governing the lands he discovered), he found it difficult to find a patron. The Portuguese rejected his plan twice, and the rulers of England and France were not interested. With influential supporters at court, Columbus convinced King Ferdinand and Queen Isabella of Spain to partially underwrite his expedition. In 1492, Granada, the last Muslim stronghold on the Iberian Peninsula, had fallen to the forces of the Spanish monarchs. With the Reconquista complete and Spain a unified country, Ferdinand and Isabella could turn their attention to overseas exploration.

5. Why was Columbus's estimate of the time required to reach Japan wrong?

   (A) He thought Japan was much farther away.

   (B) He thought Japan was much closer.

   (C) He was just taking a blind guess.

   (D) He was using Vespucci's maps.

6. Why did the Spanish Crown sponsor Columbus's exploration?

   (A) The royals were competing with the British for new colonies.

   (B) Queen Isabella admired Columbus.

   (C) The war with the Muslims was over, and they could focus on other things.

   (D) The Crown worried Columbus would be sponsored by a competing nation.

7. Columbus sailed what direction to reach Asia?

   (A) east

   (B) south

   (C) north

   (D) west

8. What about Columbus made finding sponsors for his voyage difficult?

   Write the correct answers in the circles on the answer sheet.

   (A) His demands were out of line.

   (B) He was arrogant.

   (C) He was a shrewd politician.

   (D) He had become fluent in Spanish.

9. How much funding did Columbus finally receive?

   (A) complete funding

   (B) partial funding

   (C) a small percentage

   (D) a commission on whatever he discovered

*Go on to next page*

Questions 10–12 refer to the following graph.

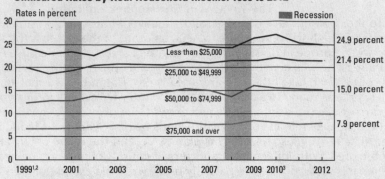

**Uninsured Rates by Real Household Income: 1999 to 2012**

[1] Implementation of Census 2000-based population controls occurred for the 2000 ASEC, which collected data for 1999. These estimates also reflect the results of follow-up verification questions, which were asked of people who responded "no" to all questions about specific types of health insurance coverage in order to verify whether they were actually uninsured. This change increased the number and percentage of people covered by health insurance, bringing the CPS more in line with estimates from other national surveys.

[2] The data for 1999 through 2009 were revised to reflect the results of enhancements to the editing process.

[3] Implementation of 2010 Census population controls.

Notes : Income in 2012 dollars. The data points are placed at the midpoints of the respective years. For information on recessions, see Appendix A. For information on confidentiality protection, sampling error, nonsampling error, and definitions, see <www.census.gov/prod/techdoc/cps/cpsmar13.pdf>.

*Illustration courtesy of U.S. Census Bureau*

10. The highest rate of uninsured by household is among which income group?

(A) $75,000 and over

(B) $50,000 to $74,999

(C) $25,000 to $49,999

(D) less than $25,000

11. Among all households, regardless of income, what has happened to the uninsured rate between 1999 and 2012?

(A) It has decreased.

(B) It has increased.

(C) It has stayed the same.

(D) It shows no pattern.

12. At what point did the uninsured rate change fastest?

(A) around 2001

(B) around 2004 to 2005

(C) around 2008 to 2009

(D) around 2012

*Go on to next page*

Questions 13–14 refer to this graph.

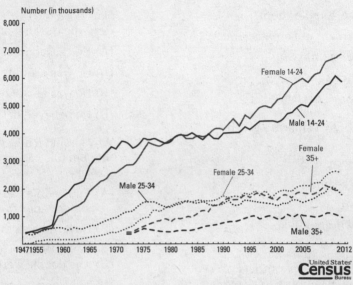

Number of Persons Enrolled in College by Sex and Age, 1947-2012

*Illustration courtesy of U.S. Census Bureau*

**13.** What is the earliest year after which there have been consistently more women enrolled in college than men?

(A) 1975

(B) 1980

(C) 1985

(D) 1990

**14.** Which group has consistently had the lowest college enrollment?

(A) women 25–34

(B) men 25–34

(C) women 35+

(D) men 35+

Questions 15–19 refer to the following passage, which is excerpted from The Declaration of Independence, 1776.

### Declaration of Independence

We hold these truths to be self-evident: that all men are created equal; that they are endowed by their Creator with certain inalienable rights; that among these are life, liberty, and the pursuit of happiness. That to secure these rights, governments are instituted among men, deriving their just powers from the consent of the governed; that whenever any form of government becomes destructive of these ends it is the right of the people to alter or to abolish it, and to institute a new government, laying its foundation on such principles, and organizing its powers in such form, as to them shall seem most likely to effect their safety and happiness. Prudence, indeed, will dictate that governments long established should not be changed for light and transient causes; and accordingly, all experience hath shown, that mankind are more disposed to suffer, while evils are sufferable, than to right themselves by abolishing the forms to which they are accustomed. But when a long train of abuses and usurpations, pursuing invariably the same object, evinces a design to reduce them under absolute despotism, it is their right, it is their duty, to throw off such government, and to provide new guards for their future security. Such has been the patient sufferance of these colonies; and such is now the

*Go on to next page*

necessity which constrains them to alter their former system of government. The history of the present king of Great Britain is a history of repeated injuries and usurpations, all having in direct object the establishment of an absolute tyranny over these states. To prove this, let facts be submitted to a candid world.

15. What truths were self-evident?

    (A) that all men are not created equal

    (B) that men don't have rights

    (C) that men are suffering

    (D) that men have certain rights

16. From where do governments get their power?

    (A) from the people

    (B) from the Creator

    (C) among men

    (D) from a new foundation

17. According to the Declaration of Independence, the people should overthrow their governments when government does what?

    Write the correct answers in the circles on the answer sheet.

    (A) when government prevents abuse

    (B) when government resorts to absolute despotism

    (C) when government abuses and usurps people's rights

    (D) when government taxes without representation

18. How does the Declaration of Independence describe the king of Great Britain?

    (A) He caused injuries.

    (B) He was a kindly ruler.

    (C) He was an absolute tyrant.

    (D) He believed in the equality of all men.

19. Why should a new government be instituted in this case, according to the passage?

    (A) The people were willing to continue to suffer under the king.

    (B) Governments should be changed regularly.

    (C) The people were suffering.

    (D) They needed to abolish the accustomed forms.

---

*Questions 20–22 refer to the following political cartoon.*

Illustration by Ricardo Checa

*Go on to next page*

20. How does the cartoon depict the use of cellphones?

   (A) wonderful invention

   (B) aid to communication

   (C) useful appliance

   (D) injurious to health

21. How would you best describe the cellphone user in the cartoon?

   (A) foolhardy

   (B) talkative

   (C) courageous

   (D) cowardly

22. How do you know that cellphones may represent a risk to health?

   (A) going to the movies

   (B) scientific research

   (C) urban legends

   (D) popular opinion

---

*Questions 23–25 refer to the following passage, which is excerpted from* CliffsQuickReview *U.S. History I, by P. Soifer and A. Hoffman (Wiley).*

---

**Resistance to Slavery**

Resistance to slavery took several forms. Slaves would pretend to be ill, refuse to work, do their jobs poorly, destroy farm equipment, set fire to buildings, and steal food. These were all individual acts rather than part of an organized plan for revolt, but the objective was to upset the routine of the plantation in any way possible. On some plantations, slaves could bring grievances about harsh treatment from an overseer to their master and hope that he would intercede on their behalf. Although many slaves tried to run away, few succeeded for more than a few days, and they often returned on their own. Such escapes were more a protest — a demonstration that it could be done — than a dash for freedom. As advertisements in southern newspapers seeking the return of runaway slaves made clear, the goal of most runaways was to find their wives or children who had been sold to another planter. The fabled underground railroad, a series of safe houses for runaways organized by abolitionists and run by former slaves like Harriet Tubman, actually helped only about a thousand slaves reach the North.

23. Why did the slaves refuse to work?

   (A) They destroyed farm equipment.

   (B) They did their jobs poorly.

   (C) They were ill.

   (D) They longed to be free.

24. According to the text, why is the Underground Railroad still considered "fabled"?

   (A) It offered hope to all slaves of permanent escape.

   (B) It was the most successful option for escaping slaves.

   (C) It supported slave rebellions.

   (D) It is only a story or fable.

25. Who organized the Underground Railroad?

   (A) Harriet Tubman

   (B) former slaves

   (C) abolitionists

   (D) runaways

*Go on to next page*

Questions 26–29 refer to the following report.

### Weather and Traffic Report

Good morning and welcome to America's weather and traffic on WAWT, the voice of the world in the ear of the nation. Today is going to be hot. That's H-O-T, and we all know what that means. The big "P" is coming back for a visit. We are going to have pollution today for sure. With our record heat today on each coast, there is a problem. If you think that it's hot here, it's even hotter up higher. And that means unhealthy air leading to unhealthy people. I can hear the coughs and sneezes coast to coast. I think I hear a whole series of gasps from our nation's capital, good ol' Washington, D.C., and it's not Congress that is producing all that hot air. And out in western California, it's just as bad. Just the other day, I looked up "poor air quality" in the dictionary, and it said "see California." Lots of luck breathing out there.

This morning, once again, there's a layer of hot air just above ground level. That's where we live — ground level. This air acts like a closed gate, and it keeps the surface air from going up and mixing. Of course, we are all going to drive our cars all day in heavy traffic, and some of us will go to work in factories. And, surprise — by afternoon, all those pollutants from the cars mix with the emissions from the factories and get trapped by the layer of hot air, and it's try-to-catch-your-breath time. Unhealthy air is here again. Tomorrow and every day after, we'll probably have more of the same until we learn to take care of our environment.

Well, I'll see you tomorrow, if the air's not too thick to see through.

26. When is the worst time for pollution?

   (A) in the morning

   (B) in the afternoon

   (C) late at night

   (D) before breakfast

27. What are the main sources of pollution?

   (A) record heat

   (B) air rising and mixing

   (C) exhausts and emissions

   (D) warmer air aloft

28. Where will pollution be most serious?

   Write the appropriate factors in the circles on the answer sheet.

   (A) hot air trapping pollution

   (B) cars

   (C) Congress

   (D) California

29. What is the best way to prevent pollution?

   (A) Change the temperature.

   (B) Reduce emissions.

   (C) Get rid of the hot air layer.

   (D) Prevent air from rising.

*Go on to next page*

---

*Questions 30–34 refer to the following passage, excerpted from* CliffsQuickReview U.S. History II, *by P. Soifer and A. Hoffman (Wiley).*

### The End of the Cold War

In July 1989, Gorbachev repudiated the Brezhnev Doctrine, which had justified the intervention of the Soviet Union in the affairs of communist countries. Within a few months of his statement, the Communist regimes in Eastern Europe collapsed — Poland, Hungary, and Czechoslovakia, followed by Bulgaria and Romania. The Berlin Wall came down in November 1989, and East and West Germany were reunited within the year. Czechoslovakia eventually split into the Czech Republic and Slovakia with little trouble, but the end of the Yugoslav Federation in 1991 led to years of violence and ethnic cleansing (the expulsion of an ethnic population from a geographic area), particularly in Bosnia-Herzegovina. The Soviet Union also broke up, not long after an attempted coup against Gorbachev in August 1991, and the Baltic states of Latvia, Estonia, and Lithuania were the first to gain their independence. That December, Gorbachev stepped down, and the old Soviet Union became the Commonwealth of Independent States (CIS). The CIS quickly disappeared, and the republics that had once made up the Soviet Union were recognized as sovereign nations. The end of the Cold War led directly to major nuclear weapons reduction agreements between President Bush and the Russian leaders as well as significant cutbacks in the number of troops the United States committed to the defense of NATO.

**30.** Who or what caused the end of the Cold War?

(A) the Soviet Union

(B) Communist regimes

(C) Gorbachev

(D) Brezhnev

**31.** Indicate the order in which East and West Germany were reunited.

Write the events in the boxes on the answer sheet.

(A) the fall of the Berlin Wall

(B) Brezhnev comes to power

(C) Gorbachev resigns

(D) Communism collapses in Poland

**32.** What is ethnic cleansing?

(A) years of violence

(B) the end of the Yugoslav Federation

(C) expelling populations

(D) the split of Czechoslovakia

**33.** What happened to the republics of the Soviet Union?

(A) They joined NATO.

(B) They became the CNS.

(C) They joined the Baltic states.

(D) They became sovereign nations.

**34.** What was one of the results of the end of the Cold War?

(A) more nuclear weapons

(B) no agreements between leaders

(C) an increase in U.S. troops

(D) cutbacks in U.S. troops

*Go on to next page*

> *Questions 35–39 refer to the following passage, which is excerpted from* CliffsQuickReview
> U.S. History I, *by P. Soifer and A. Hoffman (Wiley)*

### The Panic of 1873

During his second term, Grant was still unable to curb the graft in his administration, Secretary of War William Belknap was impeached by the House, and he resigned in disgrace for taking bribes from dishonest Indian agents. The president's personal secretary was involved with the Whiskey Ring, a group of distillers who evaded paying internal revenue taxes. A much more pressing concern though was the state of the economy.

In 1873, over-speculation in railroad stocks led to a major economic panic. The failure of Jay Cooke's investment bank was followed by the collapse of the stock market and the bankruptcy of thousands of businesses; crop prices plummeted and unemployment soared. Much of the problem was related to the use of greenbacks for currency. Hard-money advocates insisted that paper money had to be backed by gold to curb inflation and level price fluctuations, but farmers and manufacturers, who needed easy credit, wanted even more greenbacks put in circulation, a policy that Grant ultimately opposed. He recommended and the Congress enacted legislation in 1875 providing for the redemption of greenbacks in gold. Because the Treasury needed time to build up its gold reserves, redemption did not go into effect for another four years, by which time the longest depression in American history had come to an end.

35. What were the main problems President Grant had in his second term with his government?

(A) problems with his administration

(B) problems with whiskey

(C) problems with the IRS

(D) problems with personal bankruptcy

36. What type of money was used for investment?

(A) British pounds

(B) silver

(C) gold

(D) greenbacks

37. What was the cause of the Panic of 1873?

(A) investment failure

(B) bankruptcy

(C) over-speculation

(D) tax evasion

38. What followed the failure of Jay Cooke's bank?

(A) collapse of the stock market

(B) increase in market value

(C) business profitability

(D) rising crop prices

39. How did Congress end the depression?

(A) It provided easy credit.

(B) It leveled prices.

(C) It built up gold reserves.

(D) It hoarded greenbacks.

*Go on to next page*

Questions 40–42 refer to the following tables.

**Comparison of Gross Domestic Product**

Canada

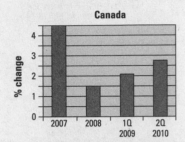

Mexico

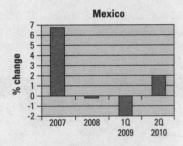

USA

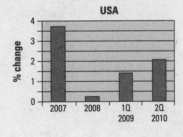

**Comparison of Major Indexes**

Canada

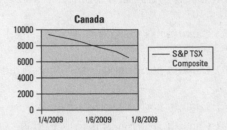

Mexico

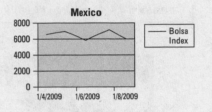

USA

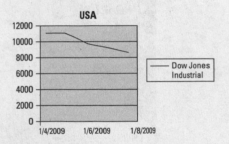

**Comparison of Value of Canadian Dollar and Mexican Peso in American Dollars**

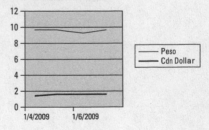

© John Wiley & Sons, Inc.

Go on to next page

40. By how much did the Mexican gross domestic product (GDP) outperform the U.S. GDP in the year 2007? [     ] percentage points

41. Why does Canada's GDP appear healthy as compared to that of the United States and Mexico?

    (A) Canada has consistently performed well.

    (B) Canada performed better than it did in 2Q.

    (C) Canada performed better in 1Q.

    (D) Canada performed better in 2008.

42. How did the Canadian dollar perform against the U.S. dollar, according to the graph?

    (A) moved higher

    (B) stayed the same

    (C) lost ground

    (D) finished even

---

*Questions 43–45 refer to the following political cartoon.*

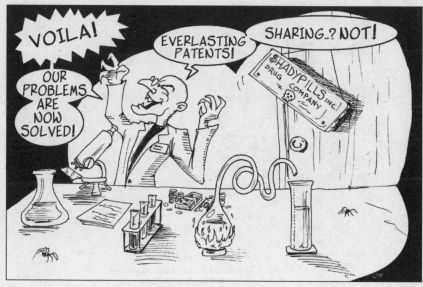

*Illustration by Ricardo Checa*

---

43. What is the setting for the cartoon?

    (A) living room

    (B) laboratory

    (C) playroom

    (D) library

44. What problem has the researcher been studying?

    (A) the common cold

    (B) a rare blood disease

    (C) hair loss

    (D) limited patents for medicines

45. What is the cartoon's implication?

    (A) Drug companies put caring for patients as their highest priority.

    (B) Natural remedies are better than medicine.

    (C) Drug companies place profits ahead of humanitarian concerns.

    (D) The scientist has found a miracle cure.

*Go on to next page*

# The Extended Response

**Time:** 25 minutes

**Your assignment:** The following information, the chart of U.S. Census Bureau data and the excerpt, come from a speech by President Obama (both extracted from a press release from the White House on December 4, 2013; www.whitehouse.gov). In this speech, President Obama addressed income inequality and changes to the distribution of wealth in American society. In your response, discuss this information and, with specific reference to the speech and chart and using your own life experience, explain why this is an enduring issue in American history. You have 25 minutes to plan, draft, and write your response in the space provided.

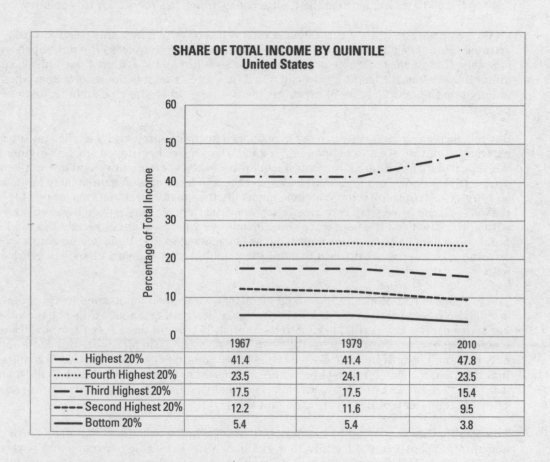

**SHARE OF TOTAL INCOME BY QUINTILE**
**United States**

|  | 1967 | 1979 | 2010 |
|---|---|---|---|
| — · Highest 20% | 41.4 | 41.4 | 47.8 |
| ········· Fourth Highest 20% | 23.5 | 24.1 | 23.5 |
| — — Third Highest 20% | 17.5 | 17.5 | 15.4 |
| - - - - Second Highest 20% | 12.2 | 11.6 | 9.5 |
| —— Bottom 20% | 5.4 | 5.4 | 3.8 |

Starting in the late '70s, this social compact began to unravel. Technology made it easier for companies to do more with less, eliminating certain job occupations. A more competitive world lets companies ship jobs anywhere. And as good manufacturing jobs automated or headed offshore, workers lost their leverage, jobs paid less and offered fewer benefits.

As values of community broke down, and competitive pressure increased, businesses lobbied Washington to weaken unions and the value of the minimum wage. As a trickle-down ideology became more prominent, taxes were slashed for the wealthiest, while investments in things that make us all richer, like schools and infrastructure, were allowed to wither. And for a certain period of time, we could ignore this weakening economic foundation, in part

*Go on to next page*

because more families were relying on two earners as women entered the workforce. We took on more debt financed by a juiced-up housing market. But when the music stopped, and the crisis hit, millions of families were stripped of whatever cushion they had left.

And the result is an economy that's become profoundly unequal, and families that are more insecure. I'll just give you a few statistics. Since 1979, when I graduated from high school, our productivity is up by more than 90 percent, but the income of the typical family has increased by less than eight percent. Since 1979, our economy has more than doubled in size, but most of that growth has flowed to a fortunate few.

The top 10 percent no longer takes in one-third of our income — it now takes half. Whereas in the past, the average CEO made about 20 to 30 times the income of the average worker, today's CEO now makes 273 times more. And meanwhile, a family in the top 1 percent has a net worth 288 times higher than the typical family, which is a record for this country.

So the basic bargain at the heart of our economy has frayed. In fact, this trend towards growing inequality is not unique to America's market economy. Across the developed world, inequality has increased. Some of you may have seen just last week, the Pope himself spoke about this at eloquent length. "How can it be," he wrote, "that it is not a news item when an elderly homeless person dies of exposure, but it is news when the stock market loses two points?"

But this increasing inequality is most pronounced in our country, and it challenges the very essence of who we are as a people. Understand we've never begrudged success in America. We aspire to it. We admire folks who start new businesses, create jobs, and invent the products that enrich our lives. And we expect them to be rewarded handsomely for it. In fact, we've often accepted more income inequality than many other nations for one big reason — because we were convinced that America is a place where even if you're born with nothing, with a little hard work you can improve your own situation over time and build something better to leave your kids. As Lincoln once said, "While we do not propose any war upon capital, we do wish to allow the humblest man an equal chance to get rich with everybody else."

The problem is that alongside increased inequality, we've seen diminished levels of upward mobility in recent years. A child born in the top 20 percent has about a 2-in-3 chance of staying at or near the top. A child born into the bottom 20 percent has a less than 1-in-20 shot at making it to the top. He's 10 times likelier to stay where he is. In fact, statistics show not only that our levels of income inequality rank near countries like Jamaica and Argentina, but that it is harder today for a child born here in America to improve her station in life than it is for children in most of our wealthy allies — countries like Canada or Germany or France. They have greater mobility than we do, not less.

The idea that so many children are born into poverty in the wealthiest nation on Earth is heartbreaking enough. But the idea that a child may never be able to escape that poverty because she lacks a decent education or health care, or a community that views her future as their own, that should offend all of us and it should compel us to action. We are a better country than this.

So let me repeat: The combined trends of increased inequality and decreasing mobility pose a fundamental threat to the American Dream, our way of life, and what we stand for around the globe. And it is not simply a moral claim that I'm making here. There are practical consequences to rising inequality and reduced mobility.

*Go on to next page*

*Go on to next page*

**STOP** DO NOT TURN THE PAGE UNTIL TOLD TO DO SO.
DO NOT RETURN TO A PREVIOUS TEST.

# Chapter 28

# Answers for Practice Test 2, Social Studies

· · · · · · · · · · · · · · · · · · · · · · · · · · · · · · · · · · · · · · · · · · · · · · · · · · · · · · · · · · · ·

This chapter has the answers and explanations for the Social Studies practice test in Chapter 27. We provide detailed answer explanations to help you review areas where you may need to do more work. Reading the explanations, even for the questions you got right, will help you understand about how these question-and-answer items are set up. If you're short on time and just want to check your answers, you can skip directly to the abbreviated answer key at the end of the chapter.

## Answers and Explanations

1. **B. Native American.** In the 1960s, after much debate, Native American was chosen as the name for the indigenous peoples. Other terms, such as *Indian, Amerindian,* and *indigenous peoples,* were discarded.

2. **B. He thought he'd reached the Indies.** Columbus thought he had reached the Indies when he landed in North America, so he called the natives "Indians." The other answers — the natives' being in the Western Hemisphere, the fact that the Americas hadn't been discovered yet, or the natives' being the hemisphere's first inhabitants — just don't make sense as reasons.

3. **D. anthropologists.** *Historians, activists,* or *Columbus* may also have used the term, but according to the passage, *anthropologists* is the correct answer.

4. **A. after an Italian explorer.** According to the passage, America was named after Italian explorer Amerigo Vespucci rather than Christopher Columbus, who discovered the lands.

5. **B. He thought Japan was much closer.** Columbus thought the circumference was a third less than it really was. As a result, he thought Japan was much closer than it turned out to be. The other answers are incorrect, according to the passage

6. **C. The war with the Muslims was over, and they could focus on other things.** Spain had been at war, trying to recapture Spain from Muslim conquerors. That done, the king and queen now had time and resources to focus on other ideas. The options of approaching France or England are wrong, based on the passage, and nothing in the passage indicates that the Spanish Crown was worried about competition from other countries.

7. **D. west.** According to the passage, Columbus sailed west to cross the Atlantic Ocean in search of Asia.

8. **A & B (he was arrogant; his demands were out of line).** Columbus was regarded as arrogant. He demanded the patrons cover all costs and award him the governorship of whatever colonies he established. Nothing in the text talks about learning Spanish, and Columbus's behavior is certainly not that of a shrewd politician.

9. **B. partial funding.** Columbus convinced Ferdinand and Isabella to partially fund the voyage. They certainly did not provide complete funding nor offer a commission on whatever he found.

10. **D. less than $25,000.** The labels on the lines on the graph indicate the income levels. The uppermost line is the one for household incomes less than $25,000.

11. **B. It has increased.** This is a somewhat tricky question because it reverses the way you'd normally answer. Fewer people were insured in the time period between 1999 and 2012, so the rate of uninsured households went up, or increased.

12. **C. around 2008 to 2009.** The sharpest change is an increase in uninsured households in the 2008 to 2009 period, probably because of higher unemployment during the recession. There was a similar change in the year following the 2001 recession, but it wasn't as broadly applied to all income groups as the later one.

13. **C. 1985.** The graph shows that in the period between 1975 and 1985, the position of males or females at college was intertwined. Only after 1985 is the number of women consistently higher than men.

14. **D. men 35+.** Where the graph indicates enrollment for men and women over 35, it's consistently the men whose enrollment is lower.

15. **D. that men have certain rights.** The passage lists two self-evident truths: that all men are created equal and that the Creator endowed men with certain rights. (*Self-evident* means evident without need of explanation or proof.)

16. **A. from the people.** According to the passage, governments were to get their power from the people. Getting power *from the Creator, among men,* and *from a new foundation* are incorrect answers, according to the passage.

17. **B & C (when government abuses and usurps people's rights; when government resorts to absolute despotism).** These two choices are correct. Prudence was a reason people shouldn't overthrow governments.

18. **C. He was an absolute tyrant.** George III had become an absolute tyrant. He was neither a kindly ruler nor a friend of the people. Causing injuries isn't the best answer.

19. **C. The people were suffering.** The people were suffering because of evils of the old government, which was the main reason they sought a new government. That means Choice (A) is completely wrong. The text states governments should not be changed lightly, so Choice (B) is wrong. The other answer may have some truth to it but isn't the main reason according to the passage.

20. **D. injurious to health.** Some researchers believe that cellphones are injurious to your health, particularly if they damage the brain or cause accidents while driving. The other answers — *wonderful invention, aid to communication,* and *useful appliance* — are all factors, but they aren't the ones depicted in the cartoon.

21. **A. foolhardy.** The cellphone user is foolhardy in that he's driving dangerously by not paying enough attention to the road. Other choices, such as *courageous,* are incorrect, And *talkative* and *cowardly* aren't the best answers, according to the cartoon.

22. **B. scientific research.** Some scientific research indicates that cellphones may represent a risk to health (radiation and brain tumors, for example). Movies, legends, and opinion aren't correct choices, according to the cartoon.

23. **D. They longed to be free.** Refusing to work was the main way slaves showed that they longed to be free. Illness, poorly done jobs, and destroyed equipment may have been other ways they showed their frustration, but, according to the passage, those answers aren't as important.

24. **A. It offered hope to all slaves of permanent escape.** The Underground Railroad actually succeeded in getting slaves to Canada, a permanent safe haven and a new life. The text doesn't support the idea that it was the most successful escape method nor that it supported slave rebellions. And there's no question that it actually existed.

25. **C. abolitionists.** The underground railroad was organized by the abolitionists. Other possible players, such as *Harriet Tubman, former slaves,* and *runaways,* may have been involved, but, according to the passage, they weren't the organizers.

26. **B. in the afternoon.** Pollution tends to be at its worst in the afternoon when exhausts and emissions are trapped. According to the passage, other times of day don't have as much pollution.

27. **C. exhausts and emissions.** Exhausts and emissions are the main sources of pollution. Other answers, such as record heat, air rising, and warmer air, are factors, but they aren't the most important ones.

28. **A & B (hot air trapping pollution; cars).** Pollution tends to be caused by emissions. In this case, the only available choice is cars. It is then made worse by the effect of hot air trapping the air pollution close to the ground. Although Congress may be a source of hot air and air pollution, it plays no role in this case. And *California* is just there to trip you up because it's mentioned in the passage as a place with poor air quality.

29. **B. Reduce emissions.** Pollution can best be prevented by reducing emissions. The other choices (changing the temperature, eliminating the hot air layer, and preventing air from rising) may contribute, but they aren't the best answers.

30. **C. Gorbachev.** Gorbachev ended the Cold War when he repudiated the Brezhnev Doctrine. Communist regimes, Brezhnev, and the Soviet Union are incorrect answers.

31. **The correct order is B, D, A, C (Brezhnev comes to power; Communism collapses in Poland; the fall of the Berlin Wall; Gorbachev resigns).** Although other events happened in between, this is the order of the events you have to choose from.

32. **C. expelling populations.** According to the passage, ethnic cleansing refers to the expulsion of minority ethnic populations. The other answers are incorrect because they don't refer specifically to how people were expelled.

33. **D. They became sovereign nations.** The former Soviet republics became sovereign nations. According to the passage, the Soviet republics weren't invited to join NATO and didn't become the Baltic States. The passage doesn't mention anything called CNS.

34. **D. cutbacks in U.S. troops.** All the factors except Choice (D) are the opposite of what the last sentence of the passage states, so Choice (D) is the only correct answer.

35. **A. problems with his administration.** The main problems President Grant faced involved grafts in his administration, which means that members of his administration faced all sorts of problems and left their jobs under pressure. The other answers are incorrect, based on the passage.

36. **D. greenbacks.** Greenbacks — not *British pounds, gold,* or *silver* — were used as a source of investment capital.

37. **C. over-speculation.** Over-speculation in railroad stocks led to the Panic of 1873. Other factors, such as *investment failure, bankruptcy,* and *tax evasion* may have also occurred, but they didn't directly cause the Panic of 1873.

38. **A. collapse of the stock market.** The failure of Cooke's bank was followed by a collapse of the stock market. The other answers are the opposite of what happened, according to the passage.

39. **C. It built up gold reserves.** The main way Congress ended the depression was to build up its gold reserves. Credit, prices, and greenbacks didn't have as much to do with the end of the depression.

40. **2.8** The Mexican GDP was 2.8 percentage points higher than the U.S. GDP. The other answers are simply incorrect, according to the graphs.

41. **A. Canada has consistently performed well.** According to the GDP graphs, Canada's economy has consistently performed well when compared to the economies of the United States and Mexico.

42. **B. stayed the same.** The value of the Canadian dollar is a straight line, which means its relative value stayed the same.

43. **B. laboratory.** The setting for the cartoon is a laboratory, not a living room, playroom, or library.

44. **D. limited patents for medicines.** The researcher has been studying limited patents for medicines. You can tell this from the phrase *everlasting patents*.

45. **C. Drug companies place profits ahead of humanitarian concerns.** The cartoon implies drug companies are greedy. Drug companies may also be caring or generous, but the cartoon doesn't suggest this.

### Sample Extended Response

The following sample essay would receive a reasonable mark. It isn't perfect, but it meets the criteria for an acceptable essay. It explains the issue, shows why it's an enduring issue, and links the essay directly back to the source material. It uses quotes from the source material and interprets the data. It (mostly) uses correct spelling and grammar and has topic sentences. It also shows that the writer had existing knowledge on the topic. (*Remember:* Your time is restricted. You're not expected to write a fabulous research paper in 25 minutes, only a good, draft-quality one.)

Compare the following sample to the response you wrote, and check out Chapter 7 for the scoring criteria and what evaluators look for in a response.

Inequality has been an enduring issue for America since the founding days. Our constitution is fiercely egalitarian. The structures of government were designed to limit the ability of any one group to dominate American life. At that time, the main concern was the development of a powerful elite. Today, that powerful elite exists, which we can measure by the degree to which the wealthy control the finances of the nation. Both the president's speech and the table show a clear trend: The age-old truth that "the rich get richer, and the poor get poorer" is certainly true. With that wealth comes power and the ability to control the American agenda. Further, the American Dream was all about equal opportunity and upward mobility for all. Both the president's speech and the statistical table show that this is no longer the case. That is certainly an enduring issue in America.

The table shows that the wealthiest 20 percent of the population have seen their share of the total income of the nation rise by some 8 percent since 1967. The second highest 20 percent of the population have seen their share of the wealth unchanged over the last 30-odd years. The bottom 60 percent of the population have seen a steady decline. This certainly shows the overall trend toward the concentration of wealth among the wealthiest portion of the population. Equally, it shows that those at the bottom are sinking further downward in their economic status.

President Obama's speech examines the results of this trend. This growing inequality of wealth has serious impacts on the lives of both the middle and working classes. He reminds us that corporations are shipping more and more jobs offshore. As a consequence, the remaining jobs are increasingly low-wage and low-skill employment. I know that repeated attacks by conservatives on the labor movement have made that situation even worse as well-paying union jobs continue to disappear. The president also reminds us that the infamous "trickle-down theory" first put forward by President Reagan is a sham. He reminds us that "investments in things that make us all richer, like schools and infrastructure, were allowed to wither."

The key comment in the president's statement is that this inequality "challenges the very essence of who we are as a people." It has become increasingly difficult for people at the low end of the income range to improve their position. He points out that people born into the bottom 20 percent of income range have less than a 1 in 20 chance of making it to the top. He points out that Americans face more challenges trying to improve their lot than citizens of many other wealthy nations of the world. Those countries now have greater upward mobility than America does.

From my own experience, I know that obtaining an education, the basic tool for upward mobility, is financially out of reach to many. This was not always the case. For some, the military was one way to move up in the world because it provided a degree of free education. Now the American military is cutting back. Those who depend on education loans are finding that they are graduating with an enormous debt. Worse, government inaction on interest rates for these loans is making that debt even worse. This may not be a problem for the top 20 percent of income earners, but it certainly is for the rest of us.

Based on the president's speech and the statistics, it is certainly safe to say that equal opportunity in America is under threat. It has been for many decades. Perhaps there is one glimmer of hope: the move to raise the federal minimum wage.

# Answer Key

| | | |
|---|---|---|
| 1. B | 2. B | 3. D |
| 4. A | 5. B | 6. C |
| 7. D | 8. A, B | 9. B |
| 10. D | 11. B | 12. C |
| 13. C | 14. D | 15. D |
| 16. A | 17. B, C | 18. C |
| 19. C | 20. D | 21. A |
| 22. D | 23. A | 24. C |
| 25. B | 26. C | 27. C |
| 28. A, B | 29. B | 30. C |
| 31. B, D, A, C | 32. C | 33. D |
| 34. D | 35. A | 36. D |
| 37. C | 38. A | 39. C |
| 40. **2.8** | 41. A | 42. B |
| 43. B | 44. D | 45. C |

# Chapter 29

# Practice Test 2: Science

• • • • • • • • • • • • • • • • • • • • • • • • • • • • • • • • • • • • • • • • • • • •

*T*he Science test includes multiple-choice, fill-in-the-blank, drop-down menu, drag-and-drop, and hot-spot items. They measure your reading comprehension of passages and visuals. You have 90 minutes to complete all the questions in this practice test, including two Short Answer items (which should take about 10 minutes each). Set a timer and watch the clock to help simulate the real test-taking experience. Do the easiest items first and remember the rules for guessing on multiple-choice if you can't find the answer.

The answers and explanations for this practice test are in Chapter 30. Be sure to review the explanations for all the questions, even for the ones you got right.

Unless you require accommodations, you'll be taking the GED test on a computer. Instead of marking your answers on a separate answer sheet, like you do for the practice tests in this book, you'll see clickable ovals and fill-in-the-blank text boxes, and you'll be able to click with your mouse and drag and drop items where indicated. We formatted the questions and answer choices in this book to make them appear as similar as possible to what you'll see on the computer-based test, but we had to retain some A, B, C, D choices for marking your answers, and we provide an answer sheet for you to do so.

# Answer Sheet for Practice Test 2, Science

| | |
|---|---|
| 1. _____ | 26. Ⓐ Ⓑ Ⓒ Ⓓ |
| 2. Ⓐ Ⓑ Ⓒ Ⓓ | 27. Ⓐ Ⓑ Ⓒ Ⓓ |
| 3. Ⓐ Ⓑ Ⓒ Ⓓ | 28. Ⓐ Ⓑ Ⓒ Ⓓ |
| 4. Ⓐ Ⓑ Ⓒ Ⓓ | 29. Ⓐ Ⓑ Ⓒ Ⓓ |
| 5. Ⓐ Ⓑ Ⓒ Ⓓ | 30. Ⓐ Ⓑ Ⓒ Ⓓ |
| 6. Ⓐ Ⓑ Ⓒ Ⓓ | 31. Ⓐ Ⓑ Ⓒ Ⓓ |
| 7. _____ | 32. _____ |
| 8. Ⓐ Ⓑ Ⓒ Ⓓ | 33. Ⓐ Ⓑ Ⓒ Ⓓ |
| 9. Ⓐ Ⓑ Ⓒ Ⓓ | 34. Ⓐ Ⓑ Ⓒ Ⓓ |
| 10. Ⓐ Ⓑ Ⓒ Ⓓ | 35. Ⓐ Ⓑ Ⓒ Ⓓ |
| 11. Ⓐ Ⓑ Ⓒ Ⓓ | 36. Ⓐ Ⓑ Ⓒ Ⓓ |
| 12. Ⓐ Ⓑ Ⓒ Ⓓ | 37. _____ |
| 13. Ⓐ Ⓑ Ⓒ Ⓓ | 38. Ⓐ Ⓑ Ⓒ Ⓓ |
| 14. Ⓐ Ⓑ Ⓒ Ⓓ | 39. Ⓐ Ⓑ Ⓒ Ⓓ |
| 15. Ⓐ Ⓑ Ⓒ Ⓓ | 40. Ⓐ Ⓑ Ⓒ Ⓓ |
| 16. Ⓐ Ⓑ Ⓒ Ⓓ | 41. Ⓐ Ⓑ Ⓒ Ⓓ |
| 17. _____ | 42. Ⓐ Ⓑ Ⓒ Ⓓ |
| 18. Ⓐ Ⓑ Ⓒ Ⓓ | 43. Ⓐ Ⓑ Ⓒ Ⓓ |
| 19. Ⓐ Ⓑ Ⓒ Ⓓ | 44. Ⓐ Ⓑ Ⓒ Ⓓ |
| 20. Ⓐ Ⓑ Ⓒ Ⓓ | 45. Ⓐ Ⓑ Ⓒ Ⓓ |
| 21. Ⓐ Ⓑ Ⓒ Ⓓ | 46. Ⓐ Ⓑ Ⓒ Ⓓ |
| 22. _____ | 47. Ⓐ Ⓑ Ⓒ Ⓓ |
| 23. Ⓐ Ⓑ Ⓒ Ⓓ | 48. Ⓐ Ⓑ Ⓒ Ⓓ |
| 24. Ⓐ Ⓑ Ⓒ Ⓓ | 49. Ⓐ Ⓑ Ⓒ Ⓓ |
| 25. Ⓐ Ⓑ Ⓒ Ⓓ | 50. Ⓐ Ⓑ Ⓒ Ⓓ |

# Science Test

**Time:** 90 minutes

**Directions:** Mark your answers on the answer sheet provided.

*Questions 1–2 refer to the following passage.*

### Hibernating Plants

We have many perennial plants in our gardens. Plants such as roses and irises grow and flower year after year. They hibernate through the winter and then come back to life at various times throughout the spring and early summer. Tulips are beautiful flowers that are among the earliest to come up every spring. They are fragile in appearance but manage to survive the uncertain weather of spring, blooming for a while and then sleeping for the rest of the year. The next year, they are ready to peek out of the earth and brighten your spring again.

Tulips survive because they grow from bulbs. Each bulb stores moisture and food during good weather. When the weather turns, the plant hibernates: The roots and leaves dry out and fall off, but the bulb develops a tough outer skin to protect itself. The bulb becomes dormant until the following spring, when the whole cycle begins again.

1. The [          ] of the tulip allows it to survive a rough winter.

2. Perennial plants

    (A) last one season

    (B) last many seasons

    (C) are difficult to grow

    (D) grow all winter

*Question 3 refers to the following passage.*

### Cells

Cells are the basic unit of all living things in the universe. Not only are flowers, weeds, and trees composed of cells, but you, your dog, and all other living things are also composed of cells. However, cells are different from organism to organism. That is why some plants produce roses and others produce dandelions and why some cells are in people and others in fish.

3. Which of the following is not composed of cells?

    (A) dogs

    (B) flowers

    (C) granite

    (D) forests

*Go on to next page*

---

*Questions 4–5 refer to the following passage.*

---

### Gunpowder

As you watch a Western on television, have you ever wondered how the bullet — also called a cartridge — is propelled out of the gun when the trigger is pulled?

Bullets are made of two parts, the jacket and the projectile. The jacket is filled with gunpowder and an ignition device, and when the ignition device is hit, the gunpowder explodes, hurling the projectile out of the barrel of the gun.

4. In the movies, guns with blank cartridges are used for effect. What part of the cartridge would be different from a cartridge used for target practice?

   (A) casing

   (B) barrel

   (C) gunpowder

   (D) projectile

5. If you wanted to reduce the force with which a projectile was hurled out of the barrel, you would

   (A) use a smaller jacket

   (B) use a smaller projectile

   (C) use a smaller gun

   (D) use less gunpowder in the jacket

---

*Questions 6–7 refer to the following passage.*

---

### Rocket Propulsion

Have you ever wondered how a rocket ship moves? Perhaps you have seen science-fiction movies in which a captain uses a blast of the rocket engines to save the ship and its crew from crashing into the surface of a distant planet.

Usually, a fuel, such as the gasoline in a car, needs an oxidizer, such as the oxygen in the air, to create combustion, which powers the engine. In space, there is no air and, thus, no oxidizer. The rocket ship, being a clever design, carries its own oxidizer. The fuel used may be a liquid or a solid, but the rocket ship always has fuel and an oxidizer to mix together. When the two are mixed and combustion takes place, a rapid expansion is directed out the back of the engine. The force pushing backward moves the rocket ship forward. In space, with no air, the rocket ship experiences no resistance to the movement. The rocket ship moves forward, avoids the crash, or does whatever the crew wants it to do.

6. Why is the rocket engine the perfect propulsion method for space travel?

   (A) It's very powerful.

   (B) It can operate without an external oxidizer.

   (C) It carries a lot of fuel.

   (D) It produces a forward thrust.

7. Fuel on a rocket ship may be [＿＿＿].

*Go on to next page* ⟶

> *Questions 8–16 refer to the following passage.*

### Where Does All the Garbage Go?

When we finish using something, we throw it away, but where is "away"? In our modern cities, "away" is usually an unsightly landfill site, piled high with all those things that we no longer want. A modern American city generates solid waste or garbage at an alarming rate. Every day, New York City produces 17,000 tons of garbage and ships it to Staten Island, where it is added to yesterday's 17,000 tons in a landfill site. We each produce enough garbage every five years to equal the volume of the Statue of Liberty. In spite of all the efforts to increase recycling, we go on our merry way producing garbage without thinking about where it goes.

In any landfill, gone is not forgotten by nature. By compacting the garbage to reduce its volume, we slow the rate of decomposition, which makes our garbage last longer. In a modern landfill, the process produces a garbage lasagna. There's a layer of compacted garbage covered by a layer of dirt, covered by a layer of compacted garbage and so on. By saving space for more garbage, we cut off the air and water needed to decompose the garbage and, thus, preserve it for future generations. If you could dig far enough, you might still be able to read 40-year-old newspapers. The paper may be preserved, but the news is history.

One of the answers to this problem is recycling. Any object that can be reused in one form or another is an object that shouldn't be found in a landfill. Most of us gladly recycle our paper, which saves energy and resources. Recycled paper can be used again and even turned into other products. Recycling old newspapers is not as valuable as hidden treasure, but when the cost of landfills and the environmental impact of producing more and more newsprint is considered, it can be a bargain. If plastic shopping bags can be recycled into a cloth-like substance that can be used to make reusable shopping bags, maybe American ingenuity can find ways to reduce all that garbage being stored in landfills before the landfills overtake the space for cities.

8. Why are the disposal methods used in modern landfills as much a part of the problem as a part of the solution?

(A) They look very ugly.

(B) They take up a lot of valuable land.

(C) The bacteria that aid decomposition do not thrive.

(D) Newspapers are readable after 50 years.

9. Why is recycling paper important?

(A) It saves money.

(B) It reduces the need for new landfill sites.

(C) Newspaper is not biodegradable.

(D) None of the above.

10. Why is solid waste compacted in a modern landfill?

(A) to reduce the odor

(B) to help the bacteria decompose the waste

(C) to make the landfill look better

(D) to reduce the amount of space it occupies

11. What is the modern landfill compared to?

(A) an efficient way of ridding cities of solid waste

(B) a garbage lasagna

(C) a place for bacteria to decompose solid waste

(D) a huge compost bin

*Go on to next page* ⟩

12. Why is it important for cities to establish recycling programs?

    (A) It's a positive activity for communities.

    (B) Recycling depots are less expensive to operate.

    (C) It's cheaper than the cost of new land-fill sites.

    (D) All of the above.

13. What can individual Americans do to reduce the amount of waste that is going into the landfills?

    (A) Eat less.

    (B) Reuse and recycle as much as possible.

    (C) Stop using paper.

    (D) Import more nitrogen.

14. Bacteria provide what helpful purpose in composting?

    (A) They help get rid of rodents.

    (B) They take part in chemical reactions.

    (C) They are part of the inorganic cycle.

    (D) They help decompose composting waste.

15. If municipalities lose money recycling paper, why do they continue?

    (A) The politicians don't know they are losing money.

    (B) Municipalities don't have to make money.

    (C) The public likes to recycle paper.

    (D) The cost is less than acquiring more landfill sites.

16. Why is garbage disposal a major urban problem?

    (A) Garbage trucks cause air pollution.

    (B) Ocean dumping is expensive.

    (C) Large landfill sites are expensive and could be used for other purposes.

    (D) All of the above.

---

*Questions 17–18 refer to the following passage.*

---

**Air Bags**

Most new cars are equipped with air bags. In a crash, the air bags quickly deploy, protecting the driver and front-seat passenger by inflating to absorb the initial force of the crash. Air bags deploy so quickly and with such force that they can injure a short adult sitting too close to the dashboard or a child in a car seat. This safety device has to be treated with respect. With the proper precautions, air bags save lives. In fact, a person in the front seat of a modern car equipped with air bags who also wears a seat belt stands a much better chance of surviving a crash than an unbelted person. The two safety devices work together to save lives but must be used properly.

17. In a front-end collision, air bags can be a <u>hazard, unless</u> occupants also use
    ⬚ .

18. Where is the safest place for an infant in a car seat in a car equipped with air bags?

    (A) in the rear seat

    (B) in the front seat

    (C) on the right side of the car

    (D) on the left side of the car

*Go on to next page* ⟹

*Questions 19–22 refer to the following diagram, which is excerpted from* The Sciences: An Integrated Approach, *3rd Edition, by James Trefil and Robert M. Hazen (Wiley).*

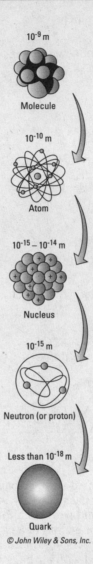

$10^{-9}$ m

Molecule

$10^{-10}$ m

Atom

$10^{-15} - 10^{-14}$ m

Nucleus

$10^{-15}$ m

Neutron (or proton)

Less than $10^{-18}$ m

Quark

© John Wiley & Sons, Inc.

19. According to this diagram, what is the building block upon which the other particles are made?

   (A) atom

   (B) molecule

   (C) neutron

   (D) quark

20. According to this diagram, how many times larger is a molecule than a quark?

   (A) 100

   (B) 1,000

   (C) 1,000,000

   (D) 1,000,000,000

*Go on to next page*

21. Scientists thought that the atom was the smallest particle that existed, but they were wrong. There are smaller particles than the atom, and the atom is not itself a solid. If people cannot see atoms, how can scientists know that there are smaller particles than atoms?

    (A) They guess.

    (B) They experiment.

    (C) They use powerful magnifying glasses.

    (D) They use logic.

22. The seat you are sitting on seems solid, but in reality, it is composed of atoms. Each of the atoms is composed of a nucleus, which is composed of neutrons and protons, but much of the space occupied by an atom is just empty space. This means that the chair you are sitting on is mostly empty space. It follows that when you stand on the floor of a building, you are ultimately being supported by ☐.

---

*Questions 23–24 refer to the following passage.*

---

### The Surface of the Moon

The surface of the moon is a hostile, barren landscape. Astronauts have found boulders as large as houses in huge fields of dust and rock. They've had no maps to guide them but have survived, thanks to their training for the mission.

23. The aspect of the lunar landscape that may make landing there dangerous is

    (A) Astronauts have to consider the possibility of hostile aliens.

    (B) The moon is full of large, uncharted spaces, some covered with very large boulders.

    (C) The moon has unlit landing fields with uncertain footings.

    (D) Not all maps of the moon are accurate.

24. What aspect of the moon makes the height of a boulder unimportant for the astronauts moving about?

    (A) Astronauts have training in flying.

    (B) There are special tools for flying over boulders.

    (C) Astronauts can drive around an obstruction.

    (D) Low gravity makes climbing easier, if it's necessary.

---

*Questions 25–26 refer to the following passage.*

---

### Pushing Aside the Water

If you fill a glass right to the brim with water, you have to drink it at its present temperature. If you decide that you want to add ice, the water spills over the brim. The ice has displaced an amount of water equal to the volume of the ice.

When you lower yourself into a luxurious bubble bath in your tub, the water rises. If you could measure the volume of that rise, you could figure out the volume of your body. Because you would displace a volume of water in the tub equal to the volume of your body, the new combined volume of you plus the water, minus the original volume of the water, equals the volume of your body. Next time you sink slowly into that hot bathwater, make sure that you leave room for the water to rise, or make sure that you are prepared to mop the floor.

*Go on to next page*

25. When you sink into a tub of water, you displace

    (A) your weight in water

    (B) a lot of water

    (C) bubbles

    (D) a volume equal to the volume of your body

26. If you wanted to find the volume of an irregularly shaped object, how could you do it?

    (A) Immerse the object in a pre-measured volume of water and measure the increase.

    (B) Measure the object and calculate the volume.

    (C) Weigh the object and calculate the volume.

    (D) Put the object in an oven and heat it.

---

*Questions 27–29 refer to the following passage.*

---

### Newton's First Law of Motion

In 1687, Isaac Newton proposed three laws of motion. These laws are not the types of laws that we are familiar with; they are statements of a truth in the field of physics. Newton's first law of motion states that a body at rest prefers to remain at rest, and a body in motion prefers to stay in motion unless acted upon by an external force. One example you may be familiar with is the game of billiards. Each of the balls will remain in its position unless hit by the cue ball. Once hit, the ball will continue to roll until the friction of the table's surface or an external force stops it.

Inertia is the tendency of any object to maintain a uniform motion or remain at rest. This law has been adopted in current language. When we say that businesses or people are being held back because of their inertia, we mean that they will either languish in their immobility or refuse to change direction in spite of all the input from employees and advisors. In 1687 when Newton was formulating his first law of motion, he was not aware of the profound effect it would have on the world of science and common language.

27. If your car becomes stuck in a snow bank, what must you do to free it?

    (A) Apply a force downward to increase the traction of the wheels.

    (B) Leave it at rest until it wants to move.

    (C) Apply a force in the direction you want it to move.

    (D) Sit on the hood to increase the weight on the front tires.

28. A company that refuses to change its ideas is said to suffer from

    (A) downturns

    (B) stability

    (C) manipulation

    (D) inertia

29. When you are driving at a steady speed on the highway, it takes great effort to stop suddenly because

    (A) the weight of the car is too light.

    (B) it takes too much power to start driving again.

    (C) brakes have a limited stopping potential.

    (D) your car tends to continue at the same rate.

*Go on to next page*

*Question 30 refers to the following passage.*

### Newton's Second Law of Motion

Newton's second law of motion states that when a body changes its velocity because an external force is applied to it, that change in velocity is directly proportional to the force and inversely proportional to the mass of the body. That is, the faster you want to stop your car, the harder you must brake. The brakes apply an external force that reduces the velocity of the car. The faster you want to accelerate the car, the more force you must apply. Increasing the horsepower of an engine allows it to apply greater force in accelerating. That is why drag racer cars seem to be all engine.

30. If you want a car that accelerates quickly, which attributes give you the best acceleration?

(A) light weight and two doors

(B) automatic transmission

(C) automatic transmission and two doors

(D) light weight and high horsepower

*Question 31 refers to the following passage.*

### Newton's Third Law of Motion

Newton's third law of motion states that for every action there is an equal and opposite reaction. If you stand on the floor, gravity pulls your body down with a certain force. The floor must exert an equal and opposite force upward on your feet, or you would fall through the floor.

31. A boxer is punching a punching bag. What is the punching bag doing to the boxer?

(A) bouncing away from the boxer

(B) reacting with a force equal and opposite to the force of his punch

(C) swinging with a velocity equal to that of the punch

(D) swinging back with a force greater than that of the punch

Questions 32–34 refer to the following passage.

**Why Don't Polar Bears Freeze?**

Watching a polar bear lumber through the frigid Arctic wilderness, you may wonder why it doesn't freeze. If you were there, you would likely freeze. In fact, you may feel cold just looking at photographs of polar bears.

Professor Stephan Steinlechner of Hanover Veterinary University in Germany set out to answer the question of why polar bears don't freeze. Polar bears have black skin. This means that, in effect, polar bears have a huge solar heat collector covering their bodies. Covering this black skin are white hollow hairs. These hairs act as insulation, keeping the heat inside the fur covering. This is like an insulated house. The heat stays in for a long period of time.

This is an interesting theory and does answer the question, except you may still wonder how they keep warm at night, when the sun isn't out!

**32.** The most important element in retaining the polar bear's body heat is its ☐.

**33.** What is the polar bear's solar heat collector?

(A) caves

(B) ice

(C) its furry coat

(D) its skin

**34.** If you had to live in the arctic, what sort of clothing would be most appropriate?

(A) insulated coats

(B) silk underwear

(C) black clothing with fur covering

(D) white clothing with fur covering

Questions 35–36 refer to the following diagram, which is excerpted from The Sciences: An Integrated Approach, *3rd Edition, by James Trefil and Robert M. Hazen (Wiley).*

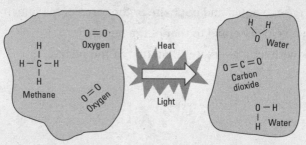

© John Wiley & Sons, Inc.

**35.** When methane burns, it produces light, heat, carbon dioxide, and water. Why would natural gas be a good choice for keeping your house warm in winter?

(A) The chemical reaction produces carbon dioxide.

(B) The chemical reaction produces light.

(C) The chemical reaction produces water.

(D) The chemical reaction produces heat.

**36.** If firefighters were faced with a methane fire, what would they want to eliminate to put out the fire?

(A) light

(B) water

(C) carbon dioxide

(D) oxygen

*Go on to next page*

---

*Questions 37–38 refer to the following passage.*

---

### Paternity Testing

DNA has become part of everyone's vocabulary, and several crime shows on television use it as a key plot element. DNA has put criminals in jail and freed others. It is used as proof in trials and is an important dramatic tool on many television dramas and talk shows.

Another use for DNA is not as dramatic. Because a child inherits the DNA of his or her parents, DNA testing can prove paternity. This is an example of a practical use for a scientific discovery.

37. Paternity testing compares the DNA of the child with the DNA of the ⬚⬚⬚⬚⬚.

38. Why is there generally no need for maternity testing when a child is born?

    (A) A mother's DNA is always the same as her children's.

    (B) Fathers are liable for support.

    (C) Mothers give birth to their own children.

    (D) It makes a better drama.

---

*Questions 39–44 refer to the following passage.*

---

### Space Stuff

Each space flight carries items authorized by NASA, but the quirky little items carried in astronauts' pockets are what catch the interest of collectors. Auction sales have been brisk for material carried aboard various space flights.

On the second manned Mercury flight, Gus Grissom carried two rolls of dimes. He was planning to give these to the children of his friends after he returned to Earth. If you carried two rolls of dimes worth ten dollars around Earth, they would still add up to ten dollars. When Gus Grissom returned to Earth, however, these dimes became space mementos, each worth many times its face value.

Although NASA does not permit the sale of items carried aboard space missions, many items have found their way to market. Eleven Apollo 16 stamps, autographed by the astronauts, sold for $27,000 at auction, but the corned beef sandwich that John Young offered to Gus Grissom never returned to Earth.

39. On which mission did Gus Grissom carry rolls of dimes?

    (A) first

    (B) second

    (C) third

    (D) fourth

40. What happened to John Young's corned beef sandwich?

    (A) It was sold.

    (B) It was left on the moon.

    (C) It was eaten.

    (D) Not enough information is given.

*Go on to next page* ▷

**41.** What is so special about items carried in an astronaut's pocket?

(A) Weightlessness changes their composition.

(B) They have been in space.

(C) Lunar radiation affects them.

(D) The pockets are made of a special material.

**42.** What would NASA authorize astronauts to carry into space?

(A) articles that might become valuable souvenirs

(B) extra oxygen

(C) documents

(D) tools for experiments

**43.** Why would autographed stamps be worth so much money?

(A) They are rare when personally autographed.

(B) Stamps always become valuable.

(C) People collect autographs.

(D) Astronauts don't give autographs.

**44.** What makes stamps a safer choice for an unauthorized space souvenir than coins?

(A) There are more stamp collectors than coin collectors.

(B) They are easier to autograph.

(C) They weigh less.

(D) All of the above.

---

*Questions 45–46 refer to the following passage.*

---

### Work

When we think of work, we think of people sitting at desks operating computers or building homes or making some other effort to earn money. When a physicist thinks of work, she probably thinks of a formula — force exerted over a distance. If you don't expend any energy — resulting in a force of zero — or if your force produces no movement, no work has been done. If you pick up your gigantic super-ordinary two-pound hamburger and lift it to your mouth to take a bite, you do work. If you want to resist temptation and just stare at your hamburger, you do no work. If your friend gets tired of you playing around and lifts your hamburger to feed you, you still do no work, but your friend does. In scientific terms, two elements are necessary for work to be done: A force must be exerted and the object to which the force has been exerted must move.

**45.** If the formula for work is Work = Force × Distance, how much more work would you do in lifting a 10-pound barbell 3 feet instead of 2 feet?

(A) half as much

(B) 3 times as much

(C) 1/3 as much

(D) 1½ times as much

**46.** Though you may see that you do work in climbing a flight of stairs, why do you also do work when you descend a flight of stairs?

(A) It is hard to climb down stairs.

(B) You have traveled a distance down the stairs.

(C) You feel tired after descending stairs.

(D) You have exerted a force over a distance.

*Go on to next page*

Questions 47–48 refer to the following figure and passages, which are excerpted from
*Physical Science: What the Technology Professional Needs to Know,* by C. Lon Enloe,
Elizabeth Garnett, Jonathan Miles, and Stephen Swanson (Wiley).

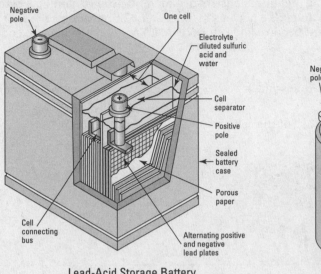

Lead-Acid Storage Battery

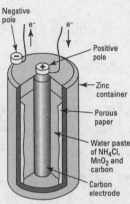

Dry-Cell Battery

© John Wiley & Sons, Inc.

### The Lead-Acid Storage Battery

One battery you rely on is the 12-volt lead-acid storage battery used in cars and trucks. This
battery is composed of six separate cells, each developing about 2 volts. By connecting the
six cells in series, the overall voltage becomes the sum, or 12 volts.

### The Dry-Cell Battery

The traditional dry-cell or flashlight battery is a zinc-carbon battery. It derives its name
from the fact that the liquid portion has been replaced by a moist paste of ammonium chlo-
ride, manganese dioxide, and carbon. These components are the anode portion of the cell,
and the zinc container serves as the cathode.

47. If you wanted a 48-volt lead-acid battery,
how many cells would it need?

(A) 24

(B) 26

(C) 28

(D) 36

48. What replaces the liquid-acid portion of the
lead-acid battery in a dry-cell battery?

(A) a moist paste

(B) a powder

(C) dry acid

(D) carbon and zinc

*Go on to next page*

---

*Questions 49–50 refer to the following passage.*

---

### The Cell and Heredity

Each cell in a living organism consists of a membrane surrounding a cytoplasm. The cytoplasm is like jelly and has a nucleus in its center. Chromosomes are part of the nucleus. They are important because they store DNA. DNA stores the genetic code that is the basis of heredity.

49. In a cell, why are the chromosomes important?

    (A) They determine the use of the cell.

    (B) They are proteins.

    (C) They are part of the nucleus.

    (D) They contain the DNA.

50. What part of the chromosome carries the genetic code?

    (A) membrane

    (B) cytoplasm

    (C) nucleus

    (D) DNA

## Short Answer #1

**Time:** 10 minutes

**Your assignment:** The world's climate is changing and is having an effect on each of us, whether or not we realize it. One of our major sources of protein is fish, and changes are occurring in the location and depth of fisheries. The changes we become aware of are those on the price stickers, but behind the sticker is a whole series of events that are impacting our food choice.

From your personal experiences and readings, explain how climate change has impacted your choice of fish as a main-course option. Write your answer on the following page. This task may require approximately ten minutes to complete.

*Go on to next page*

```
┌─────────────────────────────────────────────────────┐
│                                                       │
├─────────────────────────────────────────────────────┤
│                                                       │
├─────────────────────────────────────────────────────┤
│                                                       │
├─────────────────────────────────────────────────────┤
│                                                       │
├─────────────────────────────────────────────────────┤
│                                                       │
├─────────────────────────────────────────────────────┤
│                                                       │
└─────────────────────────────────────────────────────┘
```

# Short Answer #2

**Time:** 10 minutes

**Your assignment:** Read the excerpt from the U.S. Nuclear Regulatory Commission [NRC] website (www.nrc.gov) and write a short response to the following prompt in the space provided.

Radioisotopes have the ability to cure or destroy depending on how they are used. The development of nuclear medicine has created many advances in diagnosis and treatment that improve our quality of life. Explain how these developments are the wave of the future in medicine. This task should take about ten minutes to complete.

**Diagnostic and Therapeutic Uses of Radioisotopes**

Diagnostic procedures generally involve the use of relatively small amounts of radioactive materials to facilitate imaging of certain organs to help physicians locate and identify tumors, size anomalies, or other physiological or functional organ problems. Therapeutic uses of radioactive materials typically are intended to kill cancerous tissue, reduce the size of a tumor, or reduce pain.

**Common Nuclear Medicine Procedures**

Common nuclear medicine procedures that use radioisotopes regulated by the NRC and its Agreement States include the following examples:

- Brachytherapy
- Gamma knife
- Iodine treatment for hyperthyroidism
- Portable imaging devices in dentistry and podiatry
- Bone mineral analysis

**What Nuclear Medicine Isn't**

Other procedures may use radiation or perform functions similar to those of radioisotopes, but do not involve radioactive material and are not regulated by the NRC. Most of these are regulated by state health agencies, and include the following examples:

- X-ray
- Magnetic resonance imaging (MRI)
- Chemotherapy
- Mammogram

*Go on to next page* ⟹

**STOP**   **DO NOT TURN THE PAGE UNTIL TOLD TO DO SO.**
**DO NOT RETURN TO A PREVIOUS TEST.**

# Chapter 30

# Answers for Practice Test 2, Science

· · · · · · · · · · · · · · · · · · · · · · · · · · · · · · · · · · · · · · · · · · · · · · · · · · · · · · · · · · · ·

*I*n this chapter, you find the answers and explanations for the Science practice test in Chapter 29. Review the answer explanation for all the questions, even for the ones you got right, and keep track of areas where you need some additional studying. If you just want a quick look at the answers, check out the abbreviated answer key at the end of this chapter.

## Answers and Explanations

1. **bulb.** The passage describes how the bulb changes to allow the tulip to survive the winter. The complete explanation of how the bulb enables the tulip to survive is in the second paragraph.

2. **B. last many seasons.** Perennial plants grow year after year, so Choice (B) is the best answer according to the passage.

3. **C. granite.** All the answer choices except *granite* are living substances that are made up of cells. Granite is an igneous rock, not a living substance.

4. **D. projectile.** Because the projectile is the only part that leaves the gun and because movie producers and directors don't want to hurt anyone, the guns are altered so that the projectile does no harm. In most cases, there's no projectile, and the gun just makes a noise and a flash — nothing comes out of the barrel. The bullet still operates in a similar way with flash and noise, but the nonexistent projectile is harmless. The gunpowder is held in place by a paper stopper, which disintegrates when the gun is fired.

5. **D. use less gunpowder in the jacket.** The force that propels the projectile out of the barrel is the explosion of the gunpowder in the jacket. The force of the explosion is determined by the amount of powder in the jacket. If there's less powder in the jacket, there's less force propelling the projectile out of the barrel.

6. **B. It can operate without an external oxidizer.** In space, there's no oxidizer to take part in the chemical reaction needed for combustion. A rocket ship carries its own oxidizer and, thus, can travel through airless space. Rocket engines are also potentially very powerful, and produce forward thrust, but you must choose the most correct answer. Because the passage discusses oxidizers, Choice (B) is the best answer.

7. **a liquid or a solid.** The passage states in the second paragraph that "the fuel used may be a liquid or a solid."

8. **C. The bacteria that aid decomposition do not thrive.** The passage states that with the methodology used for burying solid waste in a modern landfill, the bacteria needed for decomposition can't survive. The reason for using landfills is that they require less space — not that they promote decomposition. Thus, the landfill and the processes used within it are as much a part of the problem as part of the solution. The other choices may be partially correct, but the key point in the text concerns the decomposition of wastes.

9. **B. It reduces the need for new landfill sites.** Newspapers do not readily decompose in landfill sites. Recycling newspapers, or many other items that would go to the landfill, reduces the need for new landfill sites. In large cities, land is expensive, and few people want to live next to a landfill site. Even if you remove the garbage by shipping it elsewhere, as New York City does, it still has to be dumped somewhere. This information, which the passage states, agrees with what you may have read in newspapers and seen on television. This passage is an example of a passage where previous knowledge blends in with the stated material.

Even though you may feel you know the answer, read the passage quickly to make sure. Sometimes your prior knowledge conflicts with what's stated in a passage.

10. **D. to reduce the amount of space it occupies.** Solid waste is compacted to reduce the amount of space it occupies, which also happens to make the landfill last longer. The waste is compacted in spite of the fact that doing so slows down decomposition and lengthens the life of the garbage.

11. **B. a garbage lasagna.** A modern landfill is compared to garbage lasagna because it's made up of alternating layers of compacted garbage and dirt. This method prevents timely decomposition.

12. **C. It's cheaper than the cost of new landfill sites.** The passage states that recycling is cheaper than continuing to acquire new landfill sites. The second option, It is cheaper to recycle, looks like a possible answer, but it isn't complete because it doesn't explain why recycling is cheaper. Be sure to read the answers carefully. Choice (C) encompasses points made in the passage and is the best answer.

13. **B. Reuse and recycle as much as possible.** As long as you dispose of waste through garbage collection or by taking it to the dump, there will be an excess amount of waste being disposed of. Every piece of waste that you can reuse or recycle lives on to be useful again and, thus, eliminates some of the waste in America.

14. **D. They help decompose composting waste.** The passage states that bacteria decompose waste. Though they may infect rodents and are part of the organic cycle, the most correct answer refers to decomposition. Unfortunately, modern methods of waste disposal in landfills reduce the effectiveness of the bacteria.

15. **D. The cost is less than acquiring more landfill sites.** Landfill sites are more expensive to acquire than the cost of recycling. In most cities, people hope to find new uses for recycled materials, which could increase the value of garbage.

16. **D. All of the above.** Choice (A) is possible, but it's a minor issue. Choice (B) isn't mentioned in the text, nor does it apply. That means Choice (D) is wrong. Thus Choice (C) is the best answer. Landfill sites are large and expensive for any city to buy, and the space could be put to better use. Needing fewer landfill sites (or smaller landfill sites) would save money.

You may notice a theme developing in these questions — something you may see as a pattern of answers. Be wary of looking for themes or patterns when answering questions on this test. If you think you've found one, be cautious because the theme or pattern may exist only in your head.

17. **seat belts.** The purpose of the air bag, according to the passage, is to absorb some of the forces in a front-end crash and prevent injury to the passenger. However, the rapid deployment of the bags may in itself injure the occupants of the car. The best solution is to also use seat belts.

18. **A. in the rear seat.** An infant is safest in the rear seat because, when deployed, the air bag is powerful enough to injure a small person (according to the third sentence of the first paragraph). The other four answer choices seem reasonable, but they're incorrect because the passage doesn't mention them.

19. **D. quark.** The diagram (going from bottom to top) indicates the process of building up a molecule. The quark is the smallest particle, and the molecule is the largest. Sometimes you have to read a diagram in an unfamiliar way to answer the question.

20. **D. 1,000,000,000.** According to the diagram, a quark is $10^{-18}$ meters across and a molecule is $10^{-9}$ meters across. The molecule would be $10^{-9}/10^{-18} = 1/10^{-9}$ or 1,000,000,000 times the size of a quark.

    A number with a negative exponent, like $10^{-9}$, equals 1/10 to the positive power of the negative exponent (for example, $10^{-9} = 1/10^9$).

21. **B. They experiment.** Scientists often develop experiments to test theories about items that are invisible to the naked eye. Curiosity drives scientists to try to find answers; experimentation proves that smaller particles than atoms exist. The other answers don't directly answer the question.

22. **atoms.** The passage states that everything is composed of atoms. As a result, the floor must be composed of atoms.

23. **B. The moon is full of large, uncharted spaces, some covered with very large boulders.** Landing a spaceship on large boulders is impossible, and the lack of charts makes accidentally meeting a boulder a possibility. A boulder as big as a house could do major damage to a spaceship. The passage states that there are such large boulders on the surface of the moon and that there are few accurate charts of the surface.

24. **D. Low gravity makes climbing easier, if it's necessary.** The moon has less gravity than Earth. Climbing requires lifting your weight against the force of gravity. It's easier to climb on the moon. With greatly reduced gravity, astronauts can jump fairly high. Whether or not they could jump over a house-sized boulder remains to be seen.

25. **D. a volume equal to the volume of your body.** The passage tells you that you would displace a volume equal to your own volume. Choice (A) looks like it may be correct, but the passage is about volume, not weight.

26. **A. Put the object in a pre-measured volume of water and measure the increase.** The object would displace a volume of water equal to its volume. Thus, putting an object in a pre-measured volume of water is one way to measure the volume of an irregularly shaped object.

27. **C. Apply a force in the direction you want it to move.** According to Newton, a force must be applied to move an object at rest. Newton, who never drove a car, said that you have to apply an external force on the object at rest (the car in this question) in the direction you want it to move. If you want your car to move deeper into the snow, you push it down. If you have a crane or a helicopter, which the passage doesn't mention, you apply a force upward to lift it out of the snow. Choice (C) is the best answer.

28. **D. inertia.** You find the answer to this question in the second paragraph of the passage.

29. **D. your car tends to continue at the same rate.** When driving at a uniform rate of speed, the car resists changes in speed. The car wants to continue to travel at the same speed. To change that speed suddenly, you must apply great effort to your brakes. While the weight, or mass, of the car plays a role in changing speed, that is only a partial answer.

30. **D. light weight and high horsepower.** Newton's second law of motion states that when a body changes its velocity because an external force is applied to it, that change in velocity is directly proportional to the force and inversely proportional to the mass of the body. If you decrease the weight of the body and increase the size of the external force, the acceleration increases.

31. **B. reacting with a force equal and opposite to the force of his punch.** Newton's third law of motion states that for every action there's an equal and opposite reaction. If the boxer is exerting a force on the punching bag, the bag is exerting an equal and opposite force on the boxer.

32. **hair.** The passage states that the hair acts as insulation, retaining the polar bear's body heat.

33. **D. its skin.** The passage states that the polar bear's dark skin collects heat from the sun.

34. **C. black clothing with fur covering.** If you were in the Arctic, you'd want to duplicate the experience of the polar bear. Black clothing with a fur covering is the best answer.

35. **D. The chemical reaction produces heat.** In cold weather, you need a source of heat to warm your house, and methane produces heat in the chemical reaction. The other answers are incorrect.

36. **D. oxygen.** Methane requires oxygen to produce light and heat. If there's no oxygen, the methane can't burn.

37. **father.** Paternity refers to the male half of a couple. If mothers were tested, it would be called maternity testing.

38. **C. Mothers give birth to their own children.** Under most circumstances, no one ever has any doubt on the day of the birth about who actually gave birth to a child. The mother is always obvious on that day. If the child were separated from the mother after birth, maternity testing could be an issue. But the question specifically asks about the day the baby is born.

39. **B. second.** According to the passage, Grissom carried the dimes on the second voyage. Anything that has traveled in space has added value as a collectible, which is why he carried this unusual item.

40. **D. Not enough information is given.** The passage tells you that the sandwich didn't return to Earth but nothing about what specifically happened to it. The other answer choices are speculation. On the test, you need to stick to the information you're given.

41. **B. They have been in space.** Because being in space is a rare occurrence, anything that has been there takes on a certain importance. Collectors want objects that are rare and about to get rarer.

42. **D. tools for experiments.** The purpose of space flights is scientific research, so you're looking for an item associated with carrying out experiments or performing the daily routines of space travel. None of the other choices fits the bill.

43. **A. They are rare when personally autographed.** Anything autographed by a famous person is valuable. When the object autographed is also available in limited quantities, it becomes more valuable still.

44. **C. They weigh less.** For safety, astronauts must account for every ounce of mass in the space capsule. Adding a lot of extra weight can be dangerous. Stamps take up less space and weigh less than coins so are a better choice for illicit souvenirs.

45. **D. 1½ times as much.** Because the force remains constant, the work done is proportional to the distance traveled, which means you would do 3/2 or 1½ times as much work.

46. **D. You have exerted a force over a distance.** Walking down the stairs, you have to exert a force against the force of gravity for a distance (the definition of work in physics). In real life, it seems easier to walk down a flight of stairs than walk up it, but, in both cases, work is being done.

47. **A. 24.** If you want a 48-volt lead-acid battery, and each cell produces 2 volts, you need 24 cells (48/2 = 24).

48. **A. a moist paste.** The moist paste replaces the acid in the battery.

49. **D. They contain the DNA.** The chromosomes contain the DNA that stores the genetic code, which determines heredity.

50. **D. DNA.** DNA in the chromosome stores the genetic code, which determines heredity. Choice (A) is mentioned as surrounding the cytoplasm, which isn't the answer to the question. Choice (B) is part of the organism, but the nucleus is part of it. Choice (C) is incomplete as the chromosomes. Choice (D) carries the genetic code.

## Sample Short Answer #1

The following is a sample response to the Short Answer #1 in Chapter 29. Your response should be a proper essay — that is, it should include an introduction, appropriate body content, and a conclusion. Compare your response to this sample, and check out Chapter 12 for more information about how these responses are scored.

Most of us are more than willing to change our food choices and menus when we go on a diet to gain or lose weight, but we are unhappy when we have to change our regular diet because our favorite food is unavailable or prohibitively expensive. Those of us who choose fish as a regular part of our diet have noticed a difference. What we don't often realize is the factors behind the changes.

Many fish and shellfish require a range of acceptable temperatures to survive. Cod, which live in the North Atlantic, can thrive at water temperatures below 54 degrees Fahrenheit and sea-bottom temperatures above 47 degrees Fahrenheit. At these temperatures, cod can go about their business of swimming around, getting caught in large nets, and reproducing. If the temperature rises above these temperatures, the young cod have a higher mortality rate, and the adult cod do not reproduce. This has a profound impact on us. We depend on plentiful young cod to restock the adult cod population and the adult cod population to supply cod and cod byproducts. As the ocean warms up, the cod population will decline, or the cod must move north to find colder water. In these new colder waters, new predators may reduce the cod population more than temperature could. In either case, the number of cod available for the production of cod liver oil or fish filets will be reduced if not eliminated.

Warmer water can produce a whole new set of dangers. Some diseases not met in colder waters become more prevalent in warmer waters. As fish stock move from one temperature area to another, they are faced with new dangers and new diseases. Temperature can also affect the reproductive cycle and migration of various species of fish. When these cycles are disrupted, the stocks can diminish, causing few fish to be available to the market and increasing the price charged for the product.

If these changes are caused by climate change, how do we mitigate the problem? We cannot change the temperature of the oceans, but we can become involved to mitigate the causes of climate change. It may seem like a monumental task, but it is up to each of us to decide what we are willing to do to help.

## Sample Short Answer #2

The following is a sample response to the Short Answer #2 in Chapter 29. Your response should be a proper essay — that is, it should include an introduction, appropriate body content, and a conclusion. Compare your response to this sample, and check out Chapter 12 for more information about how these responses are scored.

Radioisotopes are presently used to diagnose conditions and to "cure" others. Cancer is a contemporary plague but one of the means of controlling its spread is through the use of radioisotopes. The cancer cells can be destroyed through the bombardment of radioactivity. The destruction of these cancerous cells provides a "cure" for various forms of cancer and has the ability to prolong life for people afflicted with this disease.

Tumors can be located and identified through the use of small amounts of radioactive material. This form of diagnosis is fairly accurate and non-invasive. It allows doctors to diagnose abnormalities without surgery, saving lengthy recovery times.

In the field of dentistry and podiatry, imaging equipment can be reduced in size through the use of radioisotopes allowing for the practitioner to diagnose in their offices instead of admitting patients to hospital. This allows for speedier diagnosis at a lower cost, which is a benefit to all of us.

All is not perfect in the field of nuclear medicine. Regulations are required to ensure patient safety and specialized training is necessary to ensure accurate diagnosis. With the advances in nuclear medicine over the last generation, it is hard to predict what is coming next. As more and more is learned about the uses of this technique, we can look forward to new developments and procedures.

# Answer Key

| | | |
|---|---|---|
| 1. **bulb** | 2. **B** | 3. **C** |
| 4. **D** | 5. **D** | 6. **B** |
| 7. **a liquid or a solid** | 8. **C** | 9. **B** |
| 10. **D** | 11. **B.** | 12. **C** |
| 13. **B** | 14. **D** | 15. **D** |
| 16. **D** | 17. **seat belts** | 18. **A** |
| 19. **D** | 20. **D** | 21. **B** |
| 22. **atoms** | 23. **B** | 24. **D** |
| 25. **D** | 26. **A** | 27. **C** |
| 28. **D** | 29. **D** | 30. **D** |
| 31. **B** | 32. **hair** | 33. **D** |
| 34. **C** | 35. **D** | 36. **D** |
| 37. **father** | 38. **C** | 39. **B** |
| 40. **D** | 41. **B** | 42. **D** |
| 43. **A** | 44. **C** | 45. **D** |
| 46. **D** | 47. **A** | 48. **A** |
| 49. **D** | 50. **D** | |

# Chapter 31

# Practice Test 2: Mathematical Reasoning

· · · · · · · · · · · · · · · · · · · · · · · · · · · · · · · · · · · · · · · · · · · · · · · · · · · · · · ·

*I*n 115 minutes, you have to solve a series of questions involving general mathematical skills and problem solving. These questions may be based on short passages, graphs, charts, or figures. You must do the first five questions without a calculator, but after that, you can use a calculator for the rest of the test. You also have at your fingertips, a list of formulas to help you with some of the questions. Remember that the calculator and list of formulas aren't a magic solution. You have to know how to use them.

Memorizing the formulas and knowing how and when to use them will speed things up and can give you valuable time at the end to do any questions you had trouble with. Answer the easy question first to give yourself more time at the end for the more difficult questions.

Unless you require accommodations, you'll take the actual GED test on a computer, where you use the mouse and the keyboard to indicate your answer. We formatted the questions and answer choices in this book to make them appear as similar as possible to what you'll see on the computerized test, but we had to retain some A, B, C, D choices and provide an answer sheet for you to mark your answers.

# Answer Sheet for Practice Test 2, Mathematical Reasoning

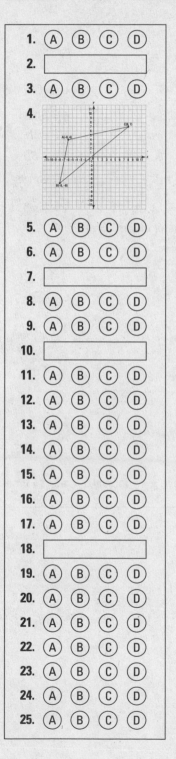

1. (A) (B) (C) (D)
2. [          ]
3. (A) (B) (C) (D)
4.
5. (A) (B) (C) (D)
6. (A) (B) (C) (D)
7. [          ]
8. (A) (B) (C) (D)
9. (A) (B) (C) (D)
10. [          ]
11. (A) (B) (C) (D)
12. (A) (B) (C) (D)
13. (A) (B) (C) (D)
14. (A) (B) (C) (D)
15. (A) (B) (C) (D)
16. (A) (B) (C) (D)
17. (A) (B) (C) (D)
18. [          ]
19. (A) (B) (C) (D)
20. (A) (B) (C) (D)
21. (A) (B) (C) (D)
22. (A) (B) (C) (D)
23. (A) (B) (C) (D)
24. (A) (B) (C) (D)
25. (A) (B) (C) (D)

26. (A) (B) (C) (D)
27. (A) (B) (C) (D)
28. (A) (B) (C) (D)
29. (A) (B) (C) (D)
30. (A) (B) (C) (D)
31. (A) (B) (C) (D)
32. [          ]
33. (A) (B) (C) (D)
34. (A) (B) (C) (D)
35. (A) (B) (C) (D)
36. (A) (B) (C) (D)
37. (A) (B) (C) (D)
38. (A) (B) (C) (D)
39. (A) (B) (C) (D)
40. [          ]
41. (A) (B) (C) (D)
42. (A) (B) (C) (D)
43. (A) (B) (C) (D)
44. (A) (B) (C) (D)
45. [          ]
46. (A) (B) (C) (D)
47. (A) (B) (C) (D)
48.
49. (A) (B) (C) (D)
50. (A) (B) (C) (D)

# Mathematics Formula Sheet

**Area of a:**

parallelogram $\qquad\qquad\qquad\qquad A = bh$

trapezoid $\qquad\qquad\qquad\qquad\quad A = \frac{1}{2}h\,(b_1 + b_2)$

**Surface Area and Volume of a:**

| | | |
|---|---|---|
| rectangular/right prism | $SA = ph + 2B$ | $V = Bh$ |
| cylinder | $SA = 2\pi rh + 2\pi r^2$ | $V = \pi r^2 h$ |
| pyramid | $SA = \frac{1}{2}ps + B$ | $V = \frac{1}{3}Bh$ |
| cone | $SA = \pi rs + \pi r^2$ | $V = \frac{1}{3}\pi r^2 h$ |
| sphere | $SA = 4\pi r^2$ | $V = \frac{4}{3}\pi r^3$ |

$(p = \text{perimeter of base } B;\ \pi \approx 3.14)$

**Algebra**

slope of a line $\qquad\qquad\qquad m = \dfrac{y_2 - y_1}{x_2 - x_1}$

slope-intercept form
of the equation of a line $\qquad y = mx + b$

point-slope form of the
equation of a line $\qquad\qquad y - y_1 = m\,(x - x_1)$

standard form of a
quadratic equation $\qquad\qquad y = ax^2 + bx + c$

quadratic formula $\qquad\qquad x = \dfrac{-b \pm \sqrt{b^2 - 4ac}}{2a}$

Pythagorean theorem $\qquad\quad a^2 + b^2 = c^2$

simple interest $\qquad\qquad\qquad I = prt$

$(I = \text{interest},\ p = \text{principal},\ r = \text{rate},\ t = \text{time})$

# Mathematical Reasoning Test

**Time:** 115 minutes

**Directions:** Mark your answers on the answer sheet provided.

1.  Yvonne is studying a map. She is 47 miles due south of where she wants to go, but the road goes 17 miles due west to an intersection that then goes northeast to her destination. Approximately how much farther must she travel because of the way the road goes?

    (A) 3 miles

    (B) 20 miles

    (C) 16 miles

    (D) 50 miles

2.  After asking for directions to a restaurant, Sarah was told it was 1,000 yards ahead, but her car's odometer reads distances in miles and tenths of miles. How many miles (to the nearest tenth) does she have to drive to find the restaurant? ☐ miles

3.  Arthur is making a circular carpet, using small pieces of cloth glued onto a backing. If he wants a carpet that is 7 feet 8 inches across, including a 2-inch fringe all around the carpet backing, how many square feet of backing does he need to cover, rounded to one decimal place?

    (A) 42.21

    (B) 46.14

    (C) 45.7

    (D) 42.2

4.  The vertices of a triangle are A (–6, 4), B (–8, –6), and C (8, 7). Using the figure on the answer sheet, circle the two ends of the longest side.

    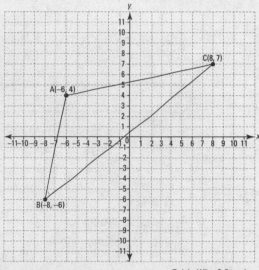

    © John Wiley & Sons, Inc.

*Question 5 refers to the following graph.*

**Results of Flipping Unbalanced Coins**

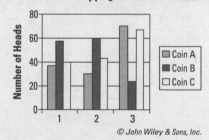

© John Wiley & Sons, Inc.

5.  As an experiment, a class flips three coins 100 times each and charts the results. The coins are not accurately balanced. From the chart, which coin during which series of tosses is closest to being balanced?

    (A) coin B, third set

    (B) coin C, third set

    (C) coin A, second set

    (D) coin B, first set

**Go on to next page**

6. Donna is very involved with speed walking. To keep from getting too bored, she has started counting how many breaths she takes for each of her steps. She figured that she takes three breaths for every 27-inch step. How many breaths does she take in a 1,000-yard walk?

(A) 5,332

(B) 2,126

(C) 4,767

(D) 4,000

7. Sam and Arnold were eating ice-cream cones. Arnold wondered what volume of ice cream his cone would hold if filled to the top. Sam measured the cone and found it to be 2½ inches across the top and 5½ inches high. The cone would hold [          ] cubic inches of ice cream, rounded to one decimal place, if it were filled to the top.

*Question 8 refers to the following table.*

### Room Level Dimensions

| Room | Measurement (In Feet) |
| --- | --- |
| Dining Room | 9.71 x 8.01 |
| Living Room | 19.49 x 10.00 |
| Kitchen | 13.78 x 7.09 |
| Solarium | 19.00 x 8.01 |
| Master Bedroom | 13.78 x 12.40 |
| Second Bedroom | 11.42 x 8.60 |

8. Singh has bought a new apartment and wants to carpet the living room, dining room, and master bedroom. If he budgets $35.00 per square yard for carpeting and installation, how much should he budget for these rooms?

(A) $1,674.08

(B) $1,457.08

(C) $1,724.91

(D) $1,500.08

*Go on to next page*

Questions 9–10 refers to the following information.

Carlos wants to buy a used car. He has been told that a car loses 4.3 cents from its book value for every mile over 100,000 that it has traveled. He sees just the car he wants, but it has 137,046 miles on the odometer. The book value of the car is $13,500.

9. Estimate the realistic value of the car to the nearest $10.

(A) $10,907

(B) $13,750

(C) $12,020

(D) $11,000

10. The realistic actual value of the car to the nearest dollar is $ _____ .

11. Elena wants to draw a mural on the wall of her house. The wall is 9 feet high and 17 feet long. To plan the mural, she draws a scale drawing of the area for the mural on a piece of paper 11 inches long. How high, in inches, should the drawing be to maintain scale?

(A) 6.2

(B) 5.8

(C) 8.5

(D) 9.0

12. If the slope of a line is 0.75, and $y_2 = 36$, $y_1 = 24$, and $x_1 = 12$, what is the value of $x_2$?

(A) 14

(B) –28

(C) 28

(D) –14

Questions 13–14 refer to the following table.

**Literacy Rates in Selected Countries**

| Country | Population | Literacy Rate (%) |
|---|---|---|
| China | 1,315,844,000 | 90.9 |
| Cuba | 11,269,000 | 99.8 |
| Ethiopia | 77,431,000 | 35.9 |
| Haiti | 8,895,000 | 54.8 |
| India | 1,103,371,000 | 61.0 |
| Israel | 6,725,000 | 97.1 |
| Russia | 143,202,000 | 99.4 |
| South Africa | 47,432,000 | 82.4 |
| United States | 298,213,000 | 99.0 |

*Go on to next page*

13. If the literacy rates of China, the United States, and Russia were compared, the greatest literacy rate would be how many times larger than the least?

    (A) 1.0

    (B) 1.1

    (C) 1.2

    (D) 1.3

14. How many more people (in millions) are literate in India than Israel?

    (A) 109

    (B) 666

    (C) 90

    (D) 100

15. The probability of an event taking place, P, is equal to the number of ways a particular event can occur, divided by the total number of ways, M, or P = N/M. To test this theory, a student removes all the picture cards from a deck. What is the probability that a card less than the number 6 will be drawn? (Aces are low in this case.)

    (A) 1 in 3

    (B) 1 in 5

    (C) 1 in 2

    (D) 1 in 4

    *Questions 16–17 refer to the following information.*

    Peter's grades in his final year of high school classes are 81, 76, 92, 87, 79, and 83.

16. To get a scholarship, Peter's median grade must be above the median grade for the school, which is 82. By how many points is he above or below that standard?

    (A) 2

    (B) 1

    (C) 0

    (D) 3

17. If Peter's goal is to graduate with a mean grade of 90 percent, by how many total points is he failing to achieve his goal?

    (A) 42

    (B) 43

    (C) 44

    (D) 45

18. Olga has a propane-powered car. She was told it was safe to fill her cylindrical propane tank at a rate of 1¾ cubic feet per minute. If the propane tank measures 4.8 feet long and 2.1 feet in diameter and is empty, it would require [          ] minutes to fill it.

19. The formula for compound interest on a loan is $M = P(1 + i)^n$, where $M$ is the final amount including the principal, $P$ is the principal amount, $i$ is the rate of interest per year, and $n$ is the number of years invested.

    If Amy invested the $1,574 she got as gifts for graduating from elementary school in a Guaranteed Investment Certificate, paying 3.75 percent compound interest calculated annually for the seven years until she graduates from college, how much money would she have?

    (A) $1,978.18

    (B) $462.67

    (C) $2,036.67

    (D) $1,878.18

20. Consider the equation $E = mc^2$. If the value of $m$ triples and the value of $c$ remains constant, the effect on $E$ would be how many times larger?

    (A) 9 times larger

    (B) 27 times larger

    (C) 3 times larger

    (D) the same

*Go on to next page*

21. An accident investigator calculates a car's speed during a skid by multiplying the following: the square root of the radius of the curve that the center of mass, *r*, follows times a constant, *k*, times the drag factor of the road, *m*. If the speed calculated was 47 miles per hour and the drag factor was 0.65, what was the radius of the curve that the car's center of mass followed?

    (A) 8.5

    (B) 5.8

    (C) 4.9

    (D) not enough information given

22. Vladimir is designing gas tanks for trucks. The length of the tanks is fixed, but the diameter can vary from 3 to 4 feet. How many more cubic feet of gas does the largest tank hold?

    (A) 3.00

    (B) 2.75

    (C) 4.75

    (D) you need to know the length of the tank

---

*Questions 23–25 are based on the following table.*

### Summary of Winning Numbers in Seven Consecutive Lottery Draws

| Draw Number | Winning Numbers |
| --- | --- |
| 1 | 8, 10, 12, 23, 25, 39 |
| 2 | 1, 29, 31, 34, 40, 44 |
| 3 | 1, 14, 26, 38, 40, 45 |
| 4 | 1, 6, 14, 39, 45, 46 |
| 5 | 10, 12, 22, 25, 37, 44 |
| 6 | 13, 16, 20, 35, 39, 45 |
| 7 | 10, 16, 17, 19, 37, 42 |

---

23. Based only on the results in the table and assuming that there are 49 possible numbers in the set to be drawn, what are your chances of drawing a 1 in your first draw?

    (A) 1 in 343

    (B) 3 in 343

    (C) 3 in 7

    (D) 1 in 49

24. If you had to pick one number in this lottery, what would be the odds based on these results that a number greater than 25 would appear in the winning numbers?

    (A) 26 in 49

    (B) 20 in 49

    (C) 17 in 49

    (D) 21 in 26

25. Louise had a theory that the median of the winning numbers in each draw in this lottery would be very close. Considering the winning numbers presented, is Louise's hypothesis accurate?

    (A) not at all

    (B) about half the time

    (C) occasionally

    (D) about a quarter of the time

*Go on to next page*

26. Jerry has started a business selling computers. He can buy a good used computer for $299 and sell it for $449. The only question he has is whether he will make money. If his overhead (rent, light, heating, and cooling) amounts to $48 per unit and his taxes amount to $3 per unit, how many computers will he have to sell to make $700 per week profit?

    (A) 6

    (B) 9

    (C) 7

    (D) 8

27. To be awarded a scholarship at Constant College, a student must score above the median of all the students in his or her year and have a mean mark of at least 90 percent. Georgio was hoping for a scholarship. Here are his marks:

    Mathematics: 94

    Applied Science: 92

    English: 87

    Spanish: 96

    Physics: 90

    The median mark for the graduating students is 86.5. How many percentage points above the required minimum mean score did Georgio score?

    (A) 3.2

    (B) 1.8

    (C) 86.5

    (D) 91.8

*Question 28 refers to the following table.*

### Geothermal-Electric Capacity in Selected Countries in 2004

| Country | Installed Capacity (Megawatts) |
| --- | --- |
| China | 6 |
| Italy | 502 |
| New Zealand | 248 |
| Russia | 26 |
| United States | 1,850 |

28. What is the approximate ratio of Installed Capacity of the largest to the smallest?

    (A) 274:2

    (B) 308:1

    (C) 5:4

    (D) 803:1

*Go on to next page*

29. Elayne wants to buy a new fuel-efficient car. She notices that a new car is advertised as getting 100 miles per gallon in city driving and 70 miles per gallon on the highway. After a week of record keeping, she produces the following table for her old car.

| Day | City Driving (Miles) | Highway Driving (Miles) |
|-----|----------------------|-------------------------|
| Monday | 30 | 5 |
| Tuesday | 35 | 25 |
| Wednesday | 25 | 10 |
| Thursday | 30 | 20 |
| Friday | 20 | 5 |
| Saturday | 5 | 70 |
| Sunday | 5 | 75 |

If Elayne's old car gets 18 miles per gallon in the city and 12 miles per gallon on the highway and gas costs $2.70 a gallon, how much would she save in a week by buying this new fuel-efficient car?

(A) $12.15

(B) $22.50

(C) $57.59

(D) $47.25

Question 30 refers to the following table.

## Interest Rates Offered by Different Car Dealerships

| Dealer | Interest Rate Offered |
|--------|------------------------|
| A | Prime + 2% |
| B | 7.5% |
| C | 1/2 of prime + 5% |
| D | Prime + 20% of prime for administrative costs |

30. Donald is confused. He is looking for a new car, but each dealership offers him a different interest rate. If the prime lending rate is 6 percent, which dealer is offering Donald the best terms to finance his car?

(A) Dealer D

(B) Dealer C

(C) Dealer B

(D) Dealer A

*Go on to next page*

31. The formula for average deviation in statistics is as follows:

    $$\text{Average deviation} = \frac{|x|}{n}$$

    where $x$ is the deviation, $|x|$ is the absolute value of $x$, and $n$ is the number of values.

    If the values for the deviation are −7, +6, +2, −13, −9, and +17, what is the average deviation?

    (A) 6

    (B) 7

    (C) 8

    (D) 9

32. Henry wanted to find out how many people watched *Four's a Mob*, the newest sitcom. He did a survey of 12 of his favorite friends and found that 10 of them had seen the last episode. Knowing that the population of the United States is more than 288,000,000, Henry calculated that 240,000,000 people watched his new favorite sitcom. The error in Henry's conclusion is that ⬚.

    ---

    *Questions 33–34 refer to the following information.*

    ---

    In September, Ken and Ben wanted to lose some weight by the following July. They figured that by supporting each other, eating a balanced diet with reduced calories and exercising, they could lose 0.5 pound per week.

33. What mathematical operation(s) would you use to calculate the amount of weight Ken and Ben could lose between the beginning of September and the end of June?

    (A) counting and adding

    (B) division and counting

    (C) counting and multiplication

    (D) subtraction

34. If Ken and Ben stick to their plans, approximately how much weight could they each lose between the beginning of September and the end of June?

    (A) 20 pounds

    (B) 30 pounds

    (C) 36 pounds

    (D) 48 pounds

35. Mary and Samantha are planning a 900-mile trip. Mary says that she can drive at an average speed of 45 miles per hour. Samantha says that she will fly, but it takes her 45 minutes to get to the airport and 1 hour and 15 minutes to get from the airport to her destination after she lands. If she has to be at the airport 3 hours before take-off and the airplane travels an average of 300 miles per hour, how many hours will Samantha have to wait for Mary?

    (A) 8

    (B) 9

    (C) 12

    (D) 16

*Go on to next page* ⟩

> *Question 36 refers to the following information and graph.*

The Queenly Hat Company of Lansing, Michigan, produces designer hats for women who feel that a hat completes an outfit. Their sales vary from quarter to quarter and factory to factory. The following chart reflects their sales for one year.

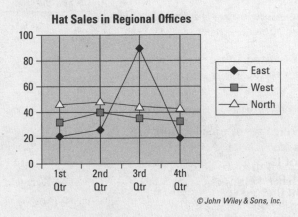

**Hat Sales in Regional Offices**

◆ East
■ West
△ North

© John Wiley & Sons, Inc.

36. Of the three factories, which factories and in which quarters are sales figures approximately in the ratio of 2:1?

    (A) east and west in 2nd quarter

    (B) west and north in 3rd quarter

    (C) east and north in 3rd quarter

    (D) west and east in 1st quarter

> *Questions 37–38 refer to the following table.*

## Life Expectancy for Urban Dwellers

| Age (In Years) | Males | Females |
|---|---|---|
| 10 | 61.4 | 67.3 |
| 20 | 50.3 | 55.1 |
| 30 | 40.4 | 45.1 |
| 40 | 32.8 | 36.5 |
| 50 | 22.1 | 26.4 |
| 60 | 15.2 | 17.8 |
| 70 | 9.9 | 10.7 |

*Go on to next page*

37. From the data presented in the table, what interpretation could be reached?

    (A) Women age better than men.

    (B) Men live longer than women in all age categories.

    (C) The number of years yet to live decreases with increasing age.

    (D) Urban dwellers live longer than rural dwellers in all age categories.

38. From the data presented, hypothesize why women live longer than men in an urban environment.

    (A) Women take better care of their health.

    (B) A greater percentage of men work in an urban setting.

    (C) Men are involved in more auto accidents in an urban setting.

    (D) Not enough information is given.

39. The cost of a finished item is equal to 2 times the production cost, plus 120 percent of the overhead costs at the retail level, plus profit. If three stores, A, B, and C, each sell the product, and Store B has a 50 percent raise in rent, how will this affect the selling price for the item?

    (A) The selling price would go down.

    (B) The selling price would remain the same.

    (C) The selling price would go up.

    (D) Every store would raise its prices.

40. Sol wanted to write the population of the United States in scientific notation for a project he was working on. If the population of the United States is 288,257,352 and he wrote it out as $2.8 \times 10x$, the value for $x$ is ☐.

41. Harry and Karry are preparing for the big race. They have been keeping track of their times in the following table.

| **Comparative Times** | |
| --- | --- |
| *Harry's Times (In Seconds)* | *Karry's Times (In Seconds)* |
| 15.6 | 15.9 |
| 14.9 | 16.1 |
| 16.0 | 15.8 |
| 15.8 | 16.2 |
| 16.1 | 14.8 |

    What conclusion can you reach from comparing their mean times?

    (A) Karry is slightly faster.

    (B) Harry is slightly slower.

    (C) They are about even.

    (D) Karry has a higher mean time.

42. Maria bought an apartment. The total floor area is 1,400 square feet. If the ceilings are 9 feet high and her air system withdraws and replaces 63 cubic feet of air each minute, how long, in minutes, does it take to withdraw and replace all the air in her apartment?

    (A) 180

    (B) 200

    (C) 220

    (D) 240

43. Peter is emptying his swimming pool. He can pump 9 cubic feet of water per minute. If his pool measures 45 feet by 12 feet with an average depth of 4 feet, when will his pool be empty if he starts pumping at noon on Tuesday?

    (A) 4 a.m. on Wednesday

    (B) 6 p.m. on Tuesday

    (C) 2 p.m. on Tuesday

    (D) 4 p.m. on Tuesday

*Go on to next page*

44. Mohammed works in sales. He compares his average paychecks for the last four weeks and finds that he has earned an average of $420.00 per week for the four-week month. If he earned $480.00 the first week, $400.00 the third week, and $550.00 the final week, how much did he earn the second week of the month?

    (A) $250.00

    (B) $280.00

    (C) $340.00

    (D) $190.00

45. Georgia started shopping with $500.00 in her purse. When she returned home after shopping, she had $126.00 in her purse and $83.00 in credit card receipts. How much did she spend shopping? $ _____

46. If you open a can flat along the seam and cut almost all the way around each end, what shape would you end up with?

    (A) a circle

    (B) a rectangle with a circle on each end

    (C) a rectangle

    (D) a circle with two rectangles on each end

47. Sonya's car uses gasoline in direct proportion to her speed. If she increases her average speed by 10 miles per hour to save time, the consequence is _____ .

    (A) she would save money

    (B) she would spend more money on fuel

    (C) she would spend the same amount as before

    (D) not enough information

48. A circle is drawn with its center at the origin and a diameter of 8 units. Where will the circumference intersect the negative *y*-axis? Circle this point on the graph.

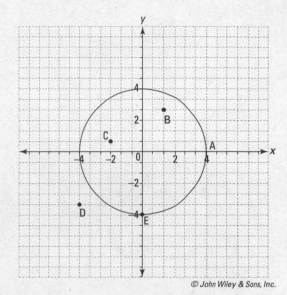

© John Wiley & Sons, Inc.

49. An accurate fuel gauge reads 1/8 full. If the fuel tank holds 24 gallons, how many gallons of fuel will fill it?

    (A) 18

    (B) 19

    (C) 20

    (D) 21

50. As part of a mathematics test, Ying was given the following equations to solve:

    $$4x + 2y = 20$$
    $$2x + 6y = 35$$

    What is the value of *y*?

    (A) 4

    (B) 5

    (C) 6

    (D) 7

**STOP** DO NOT TURN THE PAGE UNTIL TOLD TO DO SO.
DO NOT RETURN TO A PREVIOUS TEST.

# Chapter 32

# Answers for Practice Test 2, Mathematical Reasoning

● ● ● ● ● ● ● ● ● ● ● ● ● ● ● ● ● ● ● ● ● ● ● ● ● ● ● ● ● ● ● ● ● ● ● ● ● ● ● ● ● ● ● ● ● ● ● ● ● ● ● ● ● ● ● ● ● ● ●

*T*his chapter gives you the answers and explanations for the Mathematical Reasoning practice test in Chapter 31. The first question you may ask yourself is why you should bother with the explanations if you got the answers right. The simple answer is: The explanation walks you through the problem, from the question to the correct answer. If you made an error in the question and got it wrong, the explanation can save you from a lot of frustration. By following the steps, you can discover why and where you went wrong and figure out a way to not repeat the error on similar questions on the real test.

## *Answers and Explanations*

1. **B. 20 miles.** This problem is a test of your knowledge of how to use the Pythagorean theorem. Sketch out a map for this problem: Due south and due west are at right angles. So Yvonne's journey is a triangle, with the last part being the hypotenuse. Pythagoras (the guy who, as you may expect, came up with the Pythagorean theorem) said that the square of the hypotenuse of a right triangle is equal to the sum of the squares of the other two sides ($a^2 + b^2 = c^2$). Thus, the square of the last leg of Yvonne's journey equals 472 + 172 = 2,498. The square root of 2,498 is 49.98. Because none of the numbers in this problem has any numbers beyond the decimal point, you can round the answer to 50. However, the question asks how much further Yvonne must travel: She ended up traveling 17 + 50 = 67 miles and would have traveled 47 miles. Therefore, she traveled 67 – 47 = 20 miles farther.

2. **0.6.** To convert yards into miles, you have to divide the number of yards you want to convert into miles by 1,760 (because 1 mile equals 1,760 yards). One thousand yards is about 0.57 miles (1,000/1,760 = 0.568181818). Odometers usually read to one decimal point, so Sarah should drive about 0.6 miles, rounded up because the second decimal place is larger than 5, which would be just past the restaurant.

3. **D. 42.2.** The circular carpet has a diameter of 7 feet 8 inches, and it has a 2-inch fringe all the way around it. To calculate the diameter that will be covered by the backing, you have to subtract the width of the fringe (which you get by multiplying 2 inches by 2 because the fringe adds 2 inches to both sides of the circle):

   7 feet 8 inches – 4 inches = 7 feet 4 inches

   Because the units must be the same to calculate the area, you need to convert the diameter into inches: 7 feet 4 inches = 7 × 12 + 4 = 88 inches. The diameter is twice the radius, thus the radius of the covered area is 88/2 = 44 inches.

   Now you can use the formula for the area of a circle given on the formula page, $A = \pi \times r^2$, where $\pi$ is approximately 3.14. Thus, the area is 3.14 × 44 × 44 = 6,079.04 square inches.

   Because the question asks for an answer in square feet, you have to convert square inches to square feet by dividing by 144 (12 inches = 1 foot; 122 = 144): 6,079.04/144 = 42.215555 or 42.2, rounded to one decimal place.

Choice (B) is what you would've calculated if you forgot to subtract the fringe. Choice (A) is the result of not reading the question carefully; it's close, but it has two decimal places.

4. **BC.** This question tests your skills in geometry by asking you to calculate the lengths of sides of a triangle when given the vertices (corners of a triangle).

The length of the line joining the points $(x_1, y_1)$ and $(x_2, y_2)$ is $\sqrt{(x_2 - x_1)^2 + (y_2 - y_1)^2}$. Thus, when you substitute the three points of the triangle into this equation, you get the following lengths of *AB*, *BC*, and *CA* (or *AC*):

$$AB = \sqrt{(-8 - [-6])^2 + (-6 - 4)^2} = 10.198039 = 10.20$$

$$BC = \sqrt{(-8 - [-8])^2 + (-7 - [-6])^2} = 20.615528 = 20.62$$

$$CA = \sqrt{(-8 - [-6])^2 + (-7 - 4)^2} = 11.180339 = 11.18$$

From these lengths, you can see that the longest side of the triangle is *BC*.

If you sketch out on a graph and locate the points of this triangle, *BC* is obviously the longest side. Sketching could save you a lot of time calculating when the answer is this obvious, so try sketching first.

5. **D. coin B, first set.** This question asks you to draw an inference from a graph. Looking carefully at the graph, Coin B in the first set comes closest to 50 percent, which is the theoretical chance of a heads or tails landing when the coin is balanced.

6. **D. 4,000.** Here, you're asked to solve a problem using basic operations. If Donna takes three breaths for every 27-inch step and she walks 1,000 yards (which equal 36,000 inches because there are 36 inches in a yard), she takes 36,000/27 = 1,333.3 steps. If she takes three breaths per step, she takes 3 × 1,333.3 = 3,999.9 or 4,000 breaths during her 1,000-yard walk. An alternative method would be to solve this problem using unit conversions: (3 breaths/step) × (1 step/27 inches) × (36 inches/yard) × 1,000 yards = 4,000 breaths.

7. **9.0.** The shape of an ice-cream cone is a cone, and the volume of a cone is ⅓ × π × radius² × height, where π is approximately equal to 3.14 (this equation appears on the formula sheet).

To make the calculations simpler using the calculator, change the fractions to decimals:

2½ = 2.5, 5½ = 5.5, and ⅓ = 0.3333333

Now you have to insert the values from the question into the equation (remember that you find the radius by dividing the diameter by 2): Volume = 0.3333333 × 3.14 × (2.5/2)² × 5.5 = 8.9947896, or 9.0 cubic inches, rounded to one decimal place.

8. **C. $1,724.91.** In this question, you're given more information than you need. You're given the dimensions of every room in the apartment, but Singh doesn't want to carpet all of them. Because you can use the calculator in this part of the test, you can calculate an accurate answer. The first thing to do is calculate the area of each of the rooms Singh wants to carpet with the formula for area:

*Area = length × width*

(**Note:** The length and width must be in the same units.)

Substituting the numbers from the table for each room, here are the areas you come up with:

Living room: 19.49 × 10.00 = 194.90

Dining room: 9.71 × 8.01 = 77.7771

Master bedroom: 13.78 × 12.40 = 170.872

The calculator doesn't put a zero at the end of a number, so the area of the master bedroom has one fewer number to the right of the decimal point than the others, but that's okay.

Next, add the areas of the three rooms: 194.9 + 77.7771 + 170.872 = 443.5491.

Because the lengths and widths are in feet, the answer is in square feet, but the cost of the carpet is in square yards. To convert square feet into square yards, you divide by 9: 443.5491/9 = 49.283233, which is the area in square yards. You don't need all these decimal places, but because they're already entered into the calculator, you can keep them.

The carpet budget is $35.00 a square yard, so you have to multiply the total area Singh wants to carpet by the cost per square yard: 49.283233 × 35.00 = 1,724.9131.

You need an answer in dollars and cents, so you have to round to two decimal points. (The third decimal integer is 3, so you need to round down.) Therefore, the budget for the carpet is $1,724.91 — Choice (C).

9. **C. $12,020.** If you want to use approximate values in this problem, you can say that the car depreciates about 4 cents a mile over 100,000 miles. This car is about 37,000 miles over that milestone, which means it's depreciated about 4 × 37,000 cents. You want to solve this in terms of dollars, though, so to change cents into dollars, you divide by 100 (because each dollar has 100 cents): 37,000/100 = 370 dollars. Then multiply, 4 × $370 = $1,480.

You can then subtract this approximate value from the original price: $13,500 – $1,480 = $12,020.

10. **11,907.** Using the same calculation you use in Question 9 but using exact values, you get 13,500 – (4.3 × 37,046)/100 = 11,907.02 or $11,907, when rounded to the nearest dollar.

11. **B. 5.8.** This problem tests your skills in geometry and involves similarity of geometrical figures. To draw a scale drawing, the lengths and widths must be reduced in the same ratio. If the wall is 17 feet or (17 × 12 = 204 inches), and the paper is 11 inches long, the ratio of paper length to real length is 11:204. The width of the drawing must stay in the same ratio. If the height of the drawing is $H$, then 11:204 = $H$(9 × 12) or 11:204 = $H$(108). In other words, $\frac{11}{204} = \frac{H}{108}$. By cross-multiplying, you get $H$ = (11 × 108)/204 = 5.8. Note that the answer is rounded.

12. **C. 28.** This question tests your skills in algebra by asking you to evaluate a term in an equation. The equation for the slope, $m$, of a line is

$$m = \frac{y_2 - y_1}{x_2 - x_1}$$

Substituting the values into the equation, you get

$$0.75 = \frac{36 - 24}{x_2 - 12}$$

Then, because 0.75 is the same as 3/4, you can say the following:

$$\frac{3}{4} = \frac{12}{x_2 - 12}$$

Cross-multiplying, you get the following:

$$x_2 = \frac{84}{3} = 28$$

13. **1.1.** From the table, you can see that the highest literacy rate is Russia at 99.4 percent, and the lowest is China at 90.9 percent. The literacy rates for Russia and the United States are so close that, for all intents and purposes, they're equal, and, thus, there's no need to calculate the comparison.

If you consider the literacy rate for Russia divided by that for China, you get 99.4/90.9 = 1.093509351 or 1.1, rounded to one decimal place. The literacy rate of Russia is 1.1 times the literacy rate of China.

14. **B. 666.** The population of India is 1,103,371,000, of which 61.0 percent are literate. To calculate the number of literate people in India, calculate 61.0 percent of 1,103,371,000: 1,103,371,000 × 0.61 = 673,056,310. (Note that you have to change 61.0 percent to a decimal, 0.61, before you can do the calculation.)

The population of Israel is 6,725,000, of which 97.1 percent are literate. To calculate the number of literate people in Israel, calculate 97.1 percent of 6,725,000: 6,725,000 × 0.971 = 6,529,975.

To calculate how many more illiterate people there are in India, you have to subtract the number of illiterate people in Israel from the number in India: 673,056,310 − 6,529,975 = 666,526,335. Thus, there are 666,526,335 more illiterate people in India than in Israel, which really doesn't tell you anything except that the population of India is substantially larger than that of Israel. The answer is Choice (B), *666 million*.

Choice (A) is the number of illiterate people in India, which the question doesn't ask for directly. The other answers are just wrong.

In problems involving calculating big numbers, be careful reading the digits from the calculator and copying them to the page, and then recheck the numbers.

15. **C. 1 in 2.** This question tests your ability to calculate a probability. Use the formula given (P = N/M) to calculate the results. To draw a card less than 6, the possible cards to be drawn are 5 (less than 6) × 4 (the number of suits) = 20. The total possible number of cards is 52 (total cards in a deck) − the picture cards (4 jacks, 4 queens, and 4 kings), which is 52 − 12 = 40. Now, using the equation, the probability is 20/40 = 1/2, which is another way of writing 1 in 2.

16. **C. 0.** This question tests your skills in statistics by asking you to find the median of a group of numbers. You find Peter's median grade by putting his marks in ascending order — 76, 79, 81, 83, 87, 92 — and taking the grade that's right in the middle. If you had an odd number of grades, choosing the grade that's in the middle would be easy. Because you have an even number of grades, the median is the mean (or average) of the two middle numbers, or $\frac{81+83}{2}=82$. Because Peter's median grade is 82, the same as the school's, he is neither above nor below the target, and the correct answer is Choice (C), 0.

17. **A. 42.** This question is a test of your skills in data analysis. In this question, *mean* is used as a synonym for *average*. Peter's average grade is (81 + 76 + 92 + 87 + 79 + 83)/6 = 83. He's failing to meet his goal by 7 percent. Each percent is equivalent to one point per subject, or 7 × 6 = 42 points.

18. **9.5.** This question tests you on your skills in measurement involving uniform rates, such as miles per hour, gallons per minute, or, in this case, cubic feet per minute. The tank fills at a uniform rate, which means you can do the question without getting involved in a series of calculations. The volume of a cylinder = $\pi$ × radius$^2$ × height. Substitute the numbers from the question into this equation:

Volume of cylinder = 3.14 × (2.1/2)$^2$ × 4.8 = 16.61688 or 16.6

The safe fill rate is 1¾ or 1.75 cubic feet per minute. It would take 16.6/1.75 = 9.4857142 or 9.5 minutes (rounded to the nearest tenth) to fill the tank.

19. **C. 2,036.67.** Using the formula given on the formula sheet, you can calculate the total amount Amy would have at the end of seven years:

$$M = P(1+i)^n$$
$$M = \$1,574(1+0.0375)^7$$
$$M = \$1,574(1.0375)^7$$
$$M = \$2,036.67$$

20. **3 times larger.** This question tests your knowledge of equations by asking you to analyze how a change in one quantity in an exponential equation, $E = mc^2$, results in a change in another quantity. The variation between $E$ and $m$ in this function is linear and direct, which means that whatever happens to $m$ also happens to $E$. If $m$ is 3 times larger, so is $E$.

21. **D. not enough information given.** This question tests your ability to try to figure out an answer when you don't have enough information to complete a problem. Without the value of the constant, the answer can be anything.

22. **D. you need to know the length of the tank.** Without the length of the tank, you don't have enough information to answer the question.

23. **D. 1 in 49.** This question tests your skills in probability. If there are 49 possible numbers in a set, the probability of drawing any one number is 1 in 49.

24. **B. 20 in 49.** This problem tests your skills in data analysis by asking you to make inferences from data. If there are 49 numbers drawn in each draw, the odds of drawing a number greater than 25 is 20 in 49. If you count the numbers greater than 25 in the table, you find 20 of them.

    Although there's a lot of data in the table, lottery draws are discrete events (they aren't dependent on one another), and the results of one don't affect the results of another. Thus, you can consider only one draw for this question.

25. **C. occasionally.** This question tests your knowledge of statistics and measures of central tendency (in this case, the median). Consider the following adaptation of the given table. (The median is always the middle number when numbers are lined up from smallest to largest; when you have an even number of numbers, as you do here, take the two middle numbers, add them, and divide by 2 to get the median.)

### Summary of Winning Numbers in Seven Consecutive Lottery Draws

| Draw Number | Winning Numbers | Median |
|---|---|---|
| 1 | 8, 10, 12, 23, 25, 39 | 17.5 |
| 2 | 1, 29, 31, 34, 40, 44 | 32.5 |
| 3 | 1, 14, 26, 38, 40, 45 | 32.0 |
| 4 | 1, 6, 14, 39, 45, 46 | 26.5 |
| 5 | 10, 12, 22, 25, 37, 44 | 23.5 |
| 6 | 13, 16, 20, 35, 39, 45 | 27.5 |
| 7 | 10, 16, 17, 19, 37, 42 | 18.0 |

Louise's theory is a curious one in that she seems to have no basis for it. When considering the numbers presented, two of the medians are close, so the best answer is *occasionally*.

26. **D. 8.** To calculate the basic cost of the computer, you have to add the net cost plus the overhead (299 + 48 + 3 = 350). Because each computer costs Jerry $350 and he sells it for $449, he has a net profit of $99 (449 − 350 = 99) per computer.

    To calculate the number of computers Jerry would have to sell to make $700 a week, divide the amount of profit he wants to make ($700) by the profit on each computer ($99):
    $\frac{700}{99} = 7.070707071$.
    Because you can't sell less than one of a computer, you round up to 8.

27. **B. 1.8.** Georgio's mean mark is (94 + 92 + 87 + 96 + 90)/5, or 459/5 = 91.8. Because the minimum requirement is 90 percent, Georgio is 91.8 − 90 = 1.8 percent above the minimum, which is Choice (B). If you answered Choice (D), you forgot to subtract the minimum mark.

28. **B. 308:1.** The largest installed capacity is the United States with 1,850 megawatts, and the smallest is China with 6 megawatts. To calculate the ratio, you have to divide the largest by the smallest or divide 1,850 by 6 to get 308.3333333, which is approximately 308. The ratio is 308:1

29. **C. $57.59.** The simplest way to figure out this problem is to create a chart by figuring out the costs of the old car per day and the costs of the new car per day by dividing the miles driven by the mileage and multiplying by the cost per gallon. For example, on Monday, Elayne travels 30 miles in the city, so she spends 30 miles/18 mpg × $2.70 = $4.50 for her old car.

    After you find out how much Elayne spends on her old car and would spend on her new car per day, you have to add the costs for the seven days of the week together to get the costs per week for each car.

| Day | City Driving | Cost in Old Car | Cost in New Car | Highway Driving | Cost in Old Car | Cost in New Car |
|-----|------|------|------|------|------|------|
| Mon | 30 | $4.50 | $0.81 | 5 | $1.12 | $0.19 |
| Tues | 35 | $5.25 | $0.95 | 25 | $5.62 | $0.96 |
| Wed | 25 | $3.75 | $0.68 | 10 | $2.25 | $0.39 |
| Thurs | 30 | $4.50 | $0.81 | 20 | $4.50 | $0.77 |
| Fri | 20 | $3.00 | $0.54 | 5 | $1.13 | $0.19 |
| Sat | 5 | $0.75 | $0.14 | 70 | $15.75 | $2.70 |
| Sun | 5 | $0.75 | $0.14 | 75 | $16.88 | $2.89 |
| TOTAL | 150 | $22.50 | $4.07 | 210 | $47.25 | $8.09 |

    The savings are the difference between the old car's costs and the new car's costs: ($22.50 + $47.25) − ($4.07 + $8.09) = $57.59.

30. **Dealer D.** This question tests your ability to use number operations. If you adapt the table, it looks like this:

### Interest Rates Offered by Different Car Dealerships

| Dealer | Interest Rate Offered | Equivalent Rate |
|--------|----------------------|-----------------|
| A | Prime + 2% | 8% (6% + 2%) |
| B | 7.5% | 7.5% |
| C | 1/2 of prime + 5% | 8% (1/2 of 6% + 5% = 3% + 5%) |
| D | Prime + 20% of prime for administrative costs | 7.2% (6% + [20% of 6%] = 6% + 1.2%) |

    Dealer D is offering the best terms for financing the car.

31. **D. 9.** This question tests your skills in algebra because it asks you to use an equation to solve a problem.

    Using the formula given in the question, you can figure out that the average deviation is (7 + 6 + 2 + 13 + 9 + 17)/6 = 54/6 = 9. Because the absolute values are used, the numbers without the signs are used. You divide by 6 because there are six values to consider.

    The absolute value (what's inside the two vertical lines) of a number is its value without regard to its sign. So the absolute value of a negative number is always a positive number.

32. **his sample is too small.** In statistics, for results to be valid, samples must be large and random. In this question, the sample is too small to tell anyone anything of statistical significance, and the entire sample consists of friends, not randomly selected people. The best answer is that his sample is too small.

33. **C. counting and multiplication.** This question tests your skills in number operations by asking you to select the appropriate operations to solve this problem. To solve it, you count the number of weeks between September and the end of June and multiply by 0.5 (that is, 0.5 pound) to get the answer, so you use counting and multiplication.

34. **A. 20 pounds.** This question tests your skills in using estimation to solve a problem involving number operations. There are ten months between the beginning of September and the end of June. If you estimate that there are 4 weeks in each month (there are actually about 4.3 weeks per month), there are 40 weeks in this period of time. Each of them could lose about 20 pounds ($40 \times 0.5$).

35. **C. 12.** This question tests your skills in measurement to solve a problem involving uniform rates. If Mary can drive at an average speed of 45 miles per hour, it will take her $900/45 = 20$ hours to drive the 900 miles. Samantha, on the other hand, will travel at 300 miles per hour on a plane for a time of $900/300 = 3$ hours, but she will add $45 + 75$ (1 hour and 15 minutes is 75 minutes) + 180 (that's 3 hours in minutes) = 300 minutes, which is 5 hours ($300/60$). Her total trip would be 3 hours + 5 hours = 8 hours in duration, or 12 hours shorter than Mary's trip.

36. **C. east and north in 3rd quarter.** Looking at the graph, in the third quarter, the east plant seems to have produced twice (ratio of 2:1) as many hats as the north plant. This answer is considered an approximation because the graphs aren't perfectly accurate. It should be noted that the ratio of north to west in the fourth quarter also appears to have a 2:1 ratio. However, since that is not one of the choices, then the best answer is Choice (C).

37. **C. The number of years yet to live decreases with increasing age.** This question tests your ability to interpret data presented in a table. The data presented is the number of years left to live at different age levels. The only valid interpretation you can reach from this data is that the number of years yet to live decreases with increasing age, which is Choice (C).

Read the answers as carefully as you read the questions. Women may have a greater life expectancy, but that doesn't necessarily mean that they age better or worse than men. That's a topic for another question.

38. **D. Not enough information is given.** This question tests your skills in data analysis by asking you to evaluate arguments. You also have to discover whether you have enough information to decide on a reason women live longer than men. In this case, you don't have enough information in the table to develop any hypothesis, which means Choice (D) is correct. Always read questions carefully to make sure you have the information you need to answer the question before choosing an answer.

39. **C. The selling price would go up.** This question tests your skills in analysis by asking you to explain how a change in one quantity affects another quantity. The price of the article is set by a linear function involving the overhead (the costs of doing business that don't change with how many products you sell — things like rent, utility bills, salaries, and so on), the cost of acquiring the item, and the profit. If any of these numbers goes up, the selling price goes up, too, which is why the correct answer is Choice (C). In this equation, each of the terms affects the answer in a linear manner. If the rent goes up, either the selling price goes up or the profit goes down, but, in either situation, the raise in rent will have an effect on the basic cost of an item and, thus, the selling price.

40. **8.** This question tests your skills in number operations by asking you to write a large number in scientific notation. To write 288,257,352 in scientific notation, you start with an approximation — 288,000,000 is close enough. The number of zeroes defines the power of $x$. The population could be written as $28.8 \times 10^7$. Because Sol wants to write it more properly as $2.8 \times$ a power of ten, the power would have to be one higher than 7, or 8.

41. **D. Karry has a higher mean time.** This question tests your skills in statistics by asking you to compare measurements of central tendency (the means or averages). Harry's mean time is $(15.6 + 14.9 + 16.0 + 15.8 + 16.1)/5 = 15.68$. Karry's mean time is $(15.9 + 16.1 + 15.8 + 16.2 + 14.8)/5 = 15.76$. Karry has a higher mean time (which means that Harry is slightly faster).

42. **B. 200.** This question tests your skills in measurement by asking you to solve a problem involving volume. If the total floor area is 1,400 square feet and the ceilings are 9 feet high, the volume of the apartment is 1,400 × 9 = 12,600 cubic feet. If the air system can replace 63 cubic feet per minute, it requires 12,600/63 = 200 minutes to withdraw and replace all the air, which is Choice (B). The other answer choices are wrong, but Choices (A) and (C) are close enough that if you tried to do the question using approximations, you might become confused.

When some of the answers are close in value, it's worth the extra effort to do the calculations instead of estimating.

43. **D. 4 p.m. on Tuesday.** This question tests your skills in measurement and geometry. You have to solve a problem involving uniform rates. Peter's swimming pool holds 45 × 12 × 4 = 2,160 cubic feet of water. He can pump 9 cubic feet per minute. It would take him 2,160/9 = 240 minutes. To get from hours to minutes, divide by 60 (because every hour has 60 minutes). So it would take Peter 240/60 = 4 hours to empty his pool. If he started pumping at noon on Tuesday, Peter would finish four hours later, which is at 4 p.m. on Tuesday.

44. **A. $250.00.** This question tests your skills in algebra by asking you to analyze data used to calculate the mean of a set of numbers. If Mohammed earned an average of $420.00 for four weeks, he earned a total of 420 × 4 = $1,680.00. The other three weeks he earned $480.00 + $400.00 + $550.00 = $1,430.00. The remaining week he earned $1,680.00 – $1,430.00 = $250.00.

45. **457.** This question tests your skills in number operations. Georgia spent $500.00 – $126.00 = $374.00 plus $83.00 in credit card purchases, so she spent $374.00 + $83.00 = $457.00.

46. **B. a rectangle with a circle on each end.** This question tests your skills in geometry and spatial visualization. If you opened a can flat along the seam, you'd have a rectangle and two circles, one on each end. Questions of this type require the use of imagination. Imagine a can and cut it along the seam in your head, and then cut around the bottom and top to make it lay flat. The result would be a rectangle from the can itself and a circle on each end from the top and bottom.

47. **B. she would spend more money on fuel.** This question tests your skills by asking you to read carefully to answer a question. If Sonya's car uses gasoline in direct proportion to her speed, the faster she goes, the more gas she uses. The more gas she uses, the more it costs her to drive, which is an economic consequence — so she would spend more money on fuel.

48. **Point E (0, –4).** If the center is at the origin and the diameter (which is twice the radius) is 8 units, the circle will intersect each of the axes (that's the plural of axis) at a distance of 4 units from it. Therefore, it intersects the negative $y$-axis at (0, –4) or Point E.

49. **D. 21.** If the gauge reads 1/8 full, it has 24/8 = 3 gallons of fuel left in it. Because it holds 24 gallons, it needs 24 – 3 = 21 gallons to fill it.

50. **B. 5.** To solve these equations, you need to subtract one from the other and end up with just the $y$'s. To get rid of one of the variables using this method, you need to have the same coefficient in front of the variable you're planning to eliminate. You can multiply each term of an equation by a number and still maintain the equation. Here's how.

Multiply the second equation by 2 and leave the first equation as it is (or multiply by 1, which is the same thing):

$$1(4x + 2y = 20) = 4x + 2y = 20$$
$$2(2x + 6y = 35) = 4x + 12y = 70$$

Subtract, and you get $10y = 50$; $y = 5$.

Note that you can also multiply the second equation by –2 and add the two equations together. Either way gets you the same answer.

# Answer Key

1. B

2. **0.6**

3. D

4. **BC**

5. D

6. D

7. **9.0**

8. C

9. C

10. **11,907**

11. B

12. C

13. **1.1**

14. B

15. C

16. C

17. A

18. **9.5**

19. C

20. **3 times larger**

21. D

22. D

23. D

24. B

25. C

26. D

27. B

28. B

29. C

30. A

31. D

32. **his sample is too small**

33. C

34. A

35. C

36. C

37. C

38. D

39. C

40. **8**

41. D

42. B

43. D

44. A

45. **457**

46. B

47. B

48. **(0, −4)**

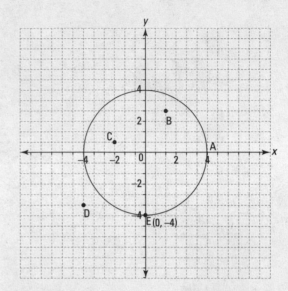

49. D

50. B

# Part VIII
# The Part of Tens

the
part of
tens

For a list of ten habits of highly successful GED test-takers, check out www.dummies.com/extras/gedtest.

# In this part . . .

✔ Check out ten tips for preparing for the GED test in the weeks, days, and hours leading up to the test.

✔ Plan your path to surviving on the day of the test and maximizing your scores.

✔ Discover all the things you can do with your GED diploma after you pass all the sections of the GED test, including using it as decoration in your home or office.

# Chapter 33

# Ten Surefire Ways to Prepare for the GED Test

*In This Chapter*

▶ Finding ways to improve your skills for each test

▶ Giving yourself time to study and sleep

▶ Preparing yourself for the big day

*O*f course you want to do well on the GED test — otherwise, you wouldn't be reading this book. But we also know that your time is limited, so this chapter gives you ten ideas and tips for preparing for the test, from selecting the right test-taking time for you to working through practice tests and getting familiar with the computer format, so you can do your very best on test day. These tips are all part of preparing for the big day. You want to be able to arrive at the test site with the least amount of worry and stress. Removing as many sources of stress before that day will make everything go much smoother.

## Selecting the Best-Possible Test Date

Why take time to prepare for the GED test when you have a million other things to do? Sure, you probably live a busy life all the time, but do your best to find a period in your busy schedule when you can concentrate on preparing for and passing the test. Because the test is administered in small test centers, you may be able to arrange a date and time that suit you. Choose the test date wisely. If you have enough time to prepare, you'll do well. It's just that simple. Select a date that gives you enough time to prepare but not one that's so far in the distance that you'll retire before you take the test. Check out Chapter 1 for information on scheduling the test.

## Taking Practice Tests

Taking practice tests before you take the actual test will help you get familiar with the test format, the types of questions you'll be asked, and what subject areas you may need to work on. Take as many practice tests as you can before test day, and take them under the same conditions as the actual test (and be sure to practice with the time limits, too).

You can find two complete practice tests for each section of the GED in this book (check out Parts VI and VII). Still want more practice? The GED Testing Service also provides some free practice tests at www.gedtestingservice.com/educators/freepracticetest. You also may want to try taking an Official GED Practice Test, available at testing centers, preparation classes, and online from the GED Testing Service. The official practice test in particular can help you predict your score, which allows you to see how close you are to passing the real GED test.

# Studying Subject-Matter Books

If you've taken all the practice tests in this book and reviewed the answer explanations (see Parts VI and VII), you may have identified key areas in which you're lacking skills. Although those practice tests can't help you predict your score on the real GED test, they can help prepare you for the actual test and give you a general idea of your strengths and weaknesses. If you didn't get at least 80 percent correct on any of the sample test sections, you need to work on your test-taking skills and the subject matter.

Visit your local bookstore or library (so you don't end up spending all your hard-earned money) for the many *For Dummies* books that are meant just for students. For example, consider the following fun, interesting, and easy-to-read books (all published by Wiley) that can either improve your skills or simply make you more familiar with (and, therefore, more comfortable with) certain subjects:

- *Algebra I For Dummies* and *Algebra II For Dummies,* by Mary Jane Sterling
- *Anatomy and Physiology For Dummies,* 2nd Edition, by Maggie Norris and Donna Rae Siegfried
- *Astronomy For Dummies,* 3rd Edition, by Stephen P. Maran
- *Biology For Dummies,* 2nd Edition, by Rene Fester Kratz and Donna Rae Siegfried
- *The Civil War For Dummies,* by Keith D. Dickson
- *Congress For Dummies,* by David Silverberg
- *English Grammar For Dummies,* 2nd Edition, by Geraldine Woods
- *Everyday Math For Dummies,* by Charles Seiter
- *Geometry For Dummies,* 2nd Edition, by Mark Ryan
- *Politics For Dummies,* 2nd Edition, by Ann DeLaney
- *U.S. History For Dummies,* 2nd Edition, by Steve Wiegand
- *World History For Dummies,* 2nd Edition, by Peter Haugen

To find other helpful *For Dummies* books, check out www.dummies.com.

Although the Reasoning through Language Arts section doesn't test your knowledge of literature, reading literature is a good way to help you prepare for that test. Consider reading one or two of Shakespeare's plays and other drama, novels from 1920 to the present, and recent short stories. If you're unsure about anything you read, simply do an online search for the book title and use keywords such as "analysis" and "content review." You can also check out old high-school English textbooks (from a used bookstore or the library) that deal with literature and writing skills, all of which are helpful.

You may also want to check out *SAT For Dummies,* 8th Edition, by Geraldine Woods with Peter Bonfanti and Kristin Josephson, and *ACT For Dummies,* 5th Edition, by Lisa Zimmer Hatch and Scott Hatch (both published by Wiley). Although these books are aimed at high-school juniors and seniors who are taking college-entrance exams, if you can master the review material and sample questions, you'll prepare yourself not only for the GED test but also for the next step, the college-entrance exams after you receive your diploma.

# Enrolling in a GED Test Preparation Class

If you like to interact with other people and prefer a teacher to guide you through your preparation, consider taking a *GED test preparation class* — a class designed to prepare you to take and pass the GED test. Costs for these classes vary widely, and some are offered free of charge. Consider whether you learn better on your own or in a group, and whether you have the time to take a class, and make your decision accordingly.

To find a class in your location, ask around. Talk to people you know who have taken the GED test, administrators and teachers at your local high school or college, or people at your local GED testing center. You may also be able to take distance-learning courses (where you do your assignments on your own and contact your instructor via the Internet), which may be a good choice for you.

You may also find that some subject areas, like math, require more help. Local high schools usually offer night-school courses for free or for minimal fees. Although these courses require more time, they also provide more direct help. Better yet, they're a lot less costly than private GED test-prep classes.

After deciding on a few potential classes, visit the class or instructor, if possible. Make sure that his or her teaching style matches your learning style. The preparation class will be a big investment of your time, so shop around wisely.

After finding a preparation class, consider joining or forming a study group with other GED test-takers. You can help each other study and ask each other questions about different aspects of the test. Be wary before committing to a group, though: If the other group members' idea of studying is to party for three hours to get ready for five minutes of study, and you want to study for three hours to get ready for five minutes of social activity, you won't be happy. Talk to the other members of the study group and find out what their goals are for the group. If you can find a suitable group, make a commitment and enjoy your new friends.

# Scheduling Time to Study

Whether you study on your own, with a group, or with an instructor, set aside time each day to study. Stick to your schedule as if your grade depends on it (and, by the way, it does!). Study regularly by doing the following:

1. **Take practice tests to find out in which subject area(s) you struggle.**

   Check each answer on the practice tests, and read all the answer explanations. Make sure you understand your mistakes.

2. **Focus your studies on the subject area(s) you're weakest in.**

3. **Take more practice tests.**

# Getting Familiar with the Computer

On the real GED test, you'll be typing on a keyboard, using a mouse to select or drag items, and reading and digesting information on the screen. The day of the test isn't the time to get familiar with the computer. Be sure to practice these skills before the test. If you don't have a computer, most public libraries offer access. Also consider taking a basic keyboarding class or computer literacy class at your local high school or community center. These classes are usually free, and they're useful if you're a novice.

# Preparing for the Test in Your Mind

To make yourself less anxious about the GED test, visualize yourself at the test center on test day. In your mind, see yourself enter the room, sit down at the computer, listen to the instructions, and reach out to the keyboard. Go through this routine in your mind until it begins to feel familiar. Then see yourself starting the test and scrolling through questions (questions that are likely familiar to you because you've taken many practice tests). See yourself noting the easy questions and beginning to answer them. By repeating this visual sequence over and over again in your mind, it becomes familiar — and what's familiar isn't nearly as stressful as what's unfamiliar. (This process is called *visualization* and really works at putting your mind at ease for the test.)

# Getting Good Rest the Week before the Test

As part of your plan for preparation, include some social time, some down time, and plenty of rest time because everyone performs better when well rested. In fact, your memory and ability to solve problems improve remarkably when you're properly rested.

Whatever you do, don't panic about your upcoming test and stay up all night (or every night for a week) right before the test. Last-minute cramming rarely works. Instead, plan your last week before the test so you get plenty of sleep and are mentally and physically prepared for the test.

# Making Sure You Have Proper Identification

To take the GED test, you need an acceptable picture ID. Because what's *acceptable* may vary from state to state, check with your state GED office or your local testing center (or check the information it sends you after you register) before the test.

The picture ID required is usually a driver's license or passport; at any rate, it's usually something common and easy to get. Just check in advance for what's required, and make sure you have it ready for test day.

# Practicing Your Route to the Test Site

On certain days and occasions, you just don't want to get lost or be late. These days include your wedding day, an important interview, and the day you're taking the GED test. Make sure you plan a route from your home or job, or wherever you'll be commuting from, to the testing site. Map it out and practice getting to the test center. If you're driving to the test center, make sure you know where to park. Arrive early enough that you can be sure to find a spot. Remember, you can't leave the car in the middle of the street if you expect to drive it home, too.

Leave extra time for surprises. You never know when your street could be declared the site for an elephant crossing or when a herd of oxen decides to meander across your road. The crowd, oxen, and elephants could make you late for the tests unless you allow yourself some extra time.

# Chapter 34

# Ten Ways to Survive Test Day

*In This Chapter*

▶ Avoiding common mistakes on test day

▶ Staying calm and focused so you can succeed

*B*esides all those hours of studying, to succeed on the GED test, you also need to know what to do on the day of the test and how to stay focused through each test section. In this chapter, we give you ten quick and easy ways to help you survive the GED test.

## Wear Comfortable Clothes

Consider the following situation. You're about to sit in front of a computer screen for at least 90 minutes (both the Mathematical Reasoning and Reasoning through Language Arts tests are longer). You'll be sitting on what will probably an uncomfortable chair. The room may be too warm or too cold.

Choosing from the following answers, what's the appropriate dress for the GED test?

(A) formal dress because this is an important occasion

(B) a parka over a bathing suit because one can never predict the weather

(C) something very comfortable so you can concentrate on the test

(D) your best clothes because you need to impress others

If you picked Choice (C), you have the right idea. Dress comfortably and in layers. All your concentration should be on the test, not your clothes, not on the people around you, and not on the conditions in the room.

## Arrive to the Test Site Early

Consider the following two characters, Paula Prepared and Peter Procrastinator. Both have prepared to take the GED test, but they have their own personality and individual quirks. On the day of the test:

✔ Peter arrives 15 seconds before the beginning of the test and feels nothing but panic. He barely arrives at the desk in time to begin the test and is so distracted that he takes 15 minutes to calm down, and by then, the test is well underway.

✔ Paula arrives 40 minutes early. She has time to get a drink, use the restroom, and relax before the test. Sitting calmly at the desk, Paula gets comfortable, listens to the instructions, and begins the test in a relaxed manner.

Who would you rather be?

Here's something else to consider: If you're late to the test site, you probably won't be allowed to enter, you'll likely have to reschedule the test for another time, and you'll probably have to pay again for the test. Who needs all this grief? All you have to do to prevent this tragedy is to arrive early for the test, which, contrary to popular belief, isn't as difficult as it may seem. You can plan ahead by checking out some route maps to the test site on the Internet. Or look into the schedules for your local public transportation services. If you decide to drive yourself, check the availability of parking and even practice your route to the test site (see Chapter 33). Do your research, leave extra time for unforeseen situations, and arrive early and ready for the test.

A couple of weeks before the test, confirm the time your test is supposed to begin and the testing center location in case it changed in the interim. You may receive a letter of confirmation before your testing date. If not, follow up with the testing center with a phone call.

# Keep Conversations Light and Short

A little bit of stress is normal when you walk into a test. So the last thing you want to do is increase your stress level by getting into a conversation with another test-taker and losing your focus.

Although it may seem antisocial, keep conversations to a minimum just before the test. If you want to exchange pleasantries about the weather, go ahead. If you want to arrange to go for coffee after the test, plan away. If you want to get into a serious conversation about how everything you've done to this point will only guarantee failure, run away as fast as you can and don't talk to anyone! If you've prepared, you're ready. Listen to the voice in your head that says you're ready, and don't let anyone at the testing center stress you out. If someone tries to corner you with conversation about how hard the test is or how they had to take out a mortgage to pay for repeated failures, pretend you only speak a rare dialect of Klingon, go to the restroom, or start coughing. Nobody wants to start up a conversation with a Klingon-speaking, contagious person with a weak bladder. Or you may want to try some more plausible excuses, but whatever you do, escape!

# Get Comfortable

You're going to be sitting in front of a computer screen for at least 90 minutes. Before starting the test, be sure to adjust the screen, the keyboard, and the chair to a comfortable position. The last person to use that computer may have been 6 feet 10 inches with arms like a gorilla. What was comfortable for him likely won't do for you. You want to get rid of any and all distractions, so taking a minute to adjust the computer station to suit you is well worth the effort. Also, after you start the test, you won't have the time to fuss around.

# Relax and Breathe

Feeling a bit of stress before taking the GED test is normal. Psychologists even say that a little bit of stress can help you function better. But it's a balancing act; you don't want to become so stressed that you can't think.

Here are some techniques that may help you relax before you take the GED test, or anytime you're feeling a bit stressed:

- **Think positively.** Instead of listing all the negative things that may happen, think about the positive things that can come of this situation. You *can* pass the GED test. You *can* go on to college. You *can* get a great job. You *can* win the lottery — well, maybe that's going too far. Don't be greedy. Just be positive!

- **Breathe deeply.** The first thing to remember during a stressful situation is to breathe. The second thing is to breathe deeply. Follow these steps:

   1. **Find your diaphragm.**

      No, not a *diagram* — although you could use a diagram to find your diaphragm. Your *diaphragm* is that flat muscle under your ribcage that fills your lungs with air. It's above your navel.

   2. **Breathe in and make your diaphragm rise as much as you can.**

   3. **Exhale slowly.**

   4. **Repeat, making your diaphragm rise higher each time.**

   After you see how this process relaxes you, try it before each test section.

- **Count backward from ten (in your head).** You can do this before any test, not just the math one. Start to count backward from ten with no thoughts in your mind. If a thought, even a teeny one, enters your mind, you have to start over. See how many times it takes to count from ten to one without a single thought entering your mind.

   Don't do this *during* the test, only *before* to help relax you. This exercise could eat up precious time if you tried it during one of the tests.

- **Clench and unclench your fists.** This simple relaxation technique involves your hands and reminds you to relax:

   1. **Sit with your hands in front of you.**

   2. **Inhale deeply as you slowly clench your fists.**

   3. **After your fists are clenched, slowly exhale as you unclench them.**

   You may have to repeat this process several times, but within a couple of repetitions, you'll begin to feel relaxed.

- **Stare out a window.** Stare out a window, far into the distance. Try to see a point beyond the horizon. As you do, feel your eyes relax. Let your eyes relax until the feeling spreads to every part of your body. Enjoy the feeling long enough to let go of all the stress that has built up. When you're calm and full of energy, return to the test.

   If your testing room doesn't have a window, stare at a blank wall and envision your favorite relaxing scene. Don't close your eyes, though. If you're the least bit tired or stressed, you may fall asleep and not wake up until the test is over.

- **Talk to yourself silently in the third person.** Tell yourself that you are prepared and can relax and do well. The third person allows you to detach your stress from yourself.

# Stay Focused on the Task at Hand

An archer who wants to hit the bull's-eye keeps all his mental faculties focused on the goal at hand. Nobody ever hit the center of the target daydreaming about the next social gathering. For this reason, put your mind on a leash; don't let it wander during the test. Letting your mind wander back to the greatest vacation you ever had can be very relaxing, but letting it wander during a test can be a disaster. You want your mind sharp, keen, and focused before and during the test, so concentrate on the task at hand — doing your best and passing the GED test.

Be sure to get plenty of sleep in the nights and weeks before the test. If you're well rested, you'll have an easier time focusing on each item and answering it correctly. Also, if you're planning to take the test in the morning, in the week before the test, set your alarm to awaken you at the same time you'll need on exam day.

# Look at Only Your Test

If there were a Biggest Mistake Award for test-takers, it'd go to someone who looks at his neighbor's computer screen during the test. This action is called cheating and is a very serious matter. Not only will you be asked to leave the testing center, but you may have to wait for several months to a year before you're allowed to schedule another test. So keep your eyes on your own test. More than likely, your neighbor will have a different test anyway.

 Don't even give the slightest hint that you may be looking at someone else's work. The test proctor probably won't care about what you were actually doing; what he'll see is you looking in the general direction of another person's computer, which is considered cheating.

# Start with the Easy Questions

As you begin the test, start with the easy questions — the ones you know you can do. As soon as the test questions come up on the computer screen, scroll through them quickly, identify the easy ones, and do those items first. Then you'll be ready to tackle the other questions in a relaxed, confident mood. Remember that the test is timed, so doing the easy questions first saves you time to use on the more difficult questions.

# Write Clearly and Carefully

You'll have a couple of essays and short-answer questions throughout the different sections of the GED test. Take time to prepare your ideas on the erasable tablet provided. Your essays will be evaluated on clarity as well as accuracy, so organization matters. Also, be sure to save some time to review your spelling and grammar. And, finally, make sure you stay on topic; anything else will count against you.

# Do Your Best, No Matter What

Not everyone passes the GED test the first time. If you've taken the test before and didn't pass, don't automatically think you're a failure — instead, see the situation as a learning experience. Use your last test as motivation to discover your academic weaknesses. Sometimes you can gain more from not succeeding than from succeeding. Whether you're taking the test for the first time or the third, focus on doing your best.

 You can retake any test section as required, generally up to three times a year. And you need to retake only the sections that you didn't pass. When you pass, you're done with that test section, no matter how you do on other sections. Each state has its own rules about retaking tests. You can find more information at www.gedtestingservice.com/testers/retake, or check with your local administrator.

# Chapter 35

# Ten Ways to Use Your GED after You Pass the Test

*In This Chapter*

▶ Getting the most out of your GED in your work life

▶ Reaping a few more personal benefits from your GED

*P*assing the GED test makes life more rewarding because it opens doors that you may not have even known were closed. You've probably already figured out why you want your GED; if not, this chapter shares ten great advantages the GED can give you.

## Getting a Job

Many employers want to see a high-school diploma or its equivalent before they even consider giving you a job. In fact, a high-school diploma is often used as a screening tool for interviews. A GED allows you to jump this hurdle. It shows potential employers that you've mastered skills equal to most high-school graduates. This accomplishment can help you get an interview, and, when the interviewer sees how brilliant you are, it can help you get a job. And to make that process easier for you, the GED Testing Service will automatically link your results to your transcript. After you send your results to an employer or college, it can link to a complete transcript and description of your achievements.

The U.S. government, one of the country's largest employers, accepts a GED as being equivalent to a high-school diploma. Who's going to argue with Uncle Sam?

## Being Promoted

If you're already working, you want to show your supervisor that you're ready for a promotion. The GED says, "I worked hard for this diploma and achieved something special!" Passing the GED test helps you show your employer that you're ready to do the same — that is, work hard — on the job. It also shows that you've taken responsibility for your life and are ready to take on additional responsibility at work. Earning a GED gives you certification that shows you've mastered skills and are ready to master some more.

## Showing Others What You Can Achieve

When you earn your GED, you show the world what you accomplished — on your own. You show that you're an independent learner. You caught up with all your old high-school friends, and you did it on your own. All you needed was a bit of help and direction. Be as proud of your accomplishment as those high-school friends are proud of their achievement.

Having completed your GED, now is the perfect time to visit old teachers and go to reunions to show your past acquaintances what you've accomplished. Sometimes we even think you should get to wear a badge that says, "GED — I Did It!" After all, being able to show others that you've accomplished something major, thanks to your own hard work and determination, is important — in both your personal and professional life.

# Including Your GED in Your College Portfolio

Your college portfolio lists all your skills and experiences in an organized manner. If you plan to pursue further education, many colleges have a particular format they want you to use for your portfolio; if yours doesn't, employment counselors can suggest generic formats. You can also make up a format. The important thing is to have a place where you list all your skills and experiences that you can take to college and job interviews.

Your GED is the centerpiece of your portfolio. The diploma is a stamp of approval on all your prior learning. It shows that you officially know what high-school graduates comprehend.

# Proving You're Ready for Further Education

After you master the skills required to earn your GED, you're ready to go on to the next step: college. Most colleges accept the GED as proof of the equivalency to high-school graduation. If your goal is further education, remind the registrars at the colleges you're interested in attending that you're a mature student who has worked hard to get where you are. Emphasize the real-world skills you've mastered by working in the real world, and explain how those skills make you a great candidate for college.

In his 2014 State of the Union address, President Obama reaffirmed the need to graduate more high-school students and to support their entrance into postsecondary institutions. Passing the GED test proves that you're ready to be one of these students.

# Setting an Example for Your Kids

If you're like most people, you want your kids (or grandkids) to be better educated and more successful than you were. As soon as you pass the GED test, you set the bar a little higher for them. Your accomplishment also reminds your kids that education is important — for you and, by your example, for them.

# Enhancing Your Wall Décor

You may already have interesting mementos of your life hanging on your wall, but what could be more exciting than your very own framed GED? A diploma looks great on your wall because it represents all the hard work you put in to passing the test — not to mention your accomplishment in doing so.

If you plan to frame your GED, make a couple of copies for prospective employers and colleges before you do so. Make copies of the transcript of your test results as well. That way, you're ready to include these copies with your job and college applications.

# Making You Feel like Part of a Select Group

Earning your GED means that you've outperformed 40 percent of high-school seniors, which in itself is impressive. It also places you among great company. Comedian Bill Cosby and the late founder of Wendy's, Dave Thomas, are GED graduates. Although no one can promise that passing the GED test will make you a show-business star or help you start a fast-food chain, it will make you feel very special. Who knows when you'll become famous enough to be listed in this section of a future edition?

# Motivating Yourself

One thing about taking challenging tests is that you have to face the challenges they throw at you on your own. You can use the fact that you overcame those challenges, thanks to your hard work and determination, to motivate yourself in your future endeavors. If you successfully passed the GED test through rigid preparation and planning, nothing can stop you. After all, you've accomplished something not everyone can do. Enjoy the feeling you get from passing the GED test, and use it as you go on to bigger and better pursuits.

# Improving Your Self-Esteem

When you pass the GED test, you're essentially a high-school graduate and can prove it (thanks to the handy diploma and transcript you receive upon passing the test). But the piece of paper is only concrete proof of your accomplishment. The real results are in your brain and in your own feelings about yourself. You need to remember that you passed the test by yourself — with a little help from preparation texts, perhaps — but the real work was yours. Remember the steps you took toward this accomplishment, and use that same approach to help you reach other goals. Remember that you were both the teacher and the learner. You deserve double credit for this major accomplishment. Let this accomplishment motivate you to your next challenge.

# Appendix

# Practicing Basic Computer Skills for the GED Test

● ● ● ● ● ● ● ● ● ● ● ● ● ● ● ● ● ● ● ● ● ● ● ● ● ● ● ● ● ● ● ● ● ● ● ● ● ● ● ● ● ● ● ●

**A**s of 2014, you no longer take the GED test using pencils and paper (unless you require a special accommodation), nor do you have to fill in the bubble answer sheets to mark your answers. Now you perform all the test activities on a computer. You use the mouse to select the correct answer, you use the keyboard to type up your Extended Response and Short Answer essays, and you even use the calculator and built-in formula sheet on-screen for the math and some science problems. Best of all, you get your results and a detailed breakdown of how you did within hours of completing the test.

Don't worry: Even if you're not familiar with using a computer, the test doesn't require you to be either an expert typist or an expert computer user. The GED Testing Service assures that even amateur users of computers won't be at any disadvantage in taking the test. However, it's to your advantage to practice your computer skills before test day so your unfamiliarity with the keyboard or mouse doesn't slow you down or frazzle you.

In this appendix, we walk you through the basic computer skills you need to know to take the computerized GED test. That includes using the mouse to click on the appropriate answer choice, to drag and drop items, or to manipulate text; getting familiar with the layout of the keyboard and some special keys you may need for typing in the basic word processor included on the test; and figuring out how to use the calculator, formulas menu, and symbols menu on-screen in the Mathematical Reasoning and Science test sections.

If you're unsure about how to do any of these skills, our advice is to practice, practice, practice. Working with any word processor on any computer will allow you to practice these skills. If you don't have a computer, check your local library, community college, or community center. These places often have computers available for public use, free of charge. They may even offer basic instructions. And if you find you need more computer keyboard practice, install one of the free or inexpensive typing tutors on your computer.

The computer isn't a magic box. You still have to prepare and prepare seriously to pass the test. The computer is an instrument; the real work goes on inside your head.

## Using a Mouse

The mouse skills you need to know when taking the GED test on a computer are pretty basic, and, no, they don't include figuring out how to put a tiny piece of cheese in a mousetrap without getting snapped yourself! We cover the basics of using a *computer* mouse in the following sections.

### Making selections

The most basic skill for using a computer mouse is just knowing how to select the correct answer. On the GED test, you do so in one of two ways: point and click or drag and drop.

### Point and click

In Figure A-1, you have a traditional multiple-choice question with four possible answers. To select an answer in this situation, you simply need to click on the correct choice. That means you need to move the mouse curser (the pointer) over the spot for the correct answer and then click the left mouse button. If you change your mind, simply click on another answer choice to override your first selection. You can click on the different answer choices as often as you want; just make sure the one you want is selected before you move on to the next question.

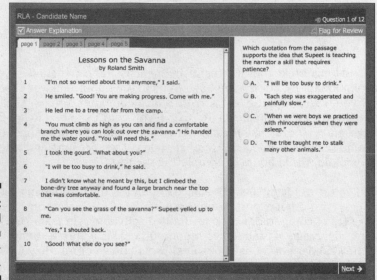

**Figure A-1:**
Standard split-screen multiple-choice item.

© 2014 GED Testing Service LLC

Math and science hot-spot questions also require you to use your mouse to select an answer. In these questions, the computer screen has a series of virtual "hot spots" or areas representing the correct answer. When you click on one of these hot spots with your mouse, it registers your answer. The remainder of the screen is wrong, so be sure of your answer when you click and where. In the example hot-spot question in Figure A-2, you simply click above the number on the plot line for the point to appear.

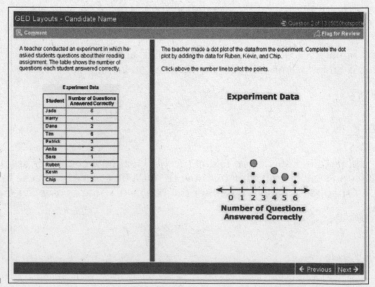

**Figure A-2:**
Hot-spot item with virtual live spots on the diagram.

© 2014 GED Testing Service LLC

### Drag and drop

When you encounter a question that tells you to "drag and drop," you simply pick up an object with your mouse (by clicking on the object and holding the left mouse button down), drag it to where you want it, and then drop it (release the mouse button) in that new location. If you've ever played Solitaire on a computer, you already know how to drag and drop. That's what you do every time you move a card from one pile to another. See Figure A-3 for the drag-and-drop feature the GED test employs.

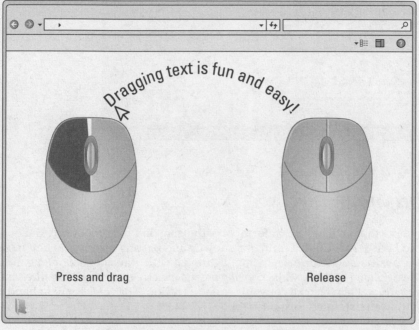

**Figure A-3:** Drag and drop objects by clicking and holding the left mouse button and then letting go to release it in the desired location.

© John Wiley & Sons, Inc.

## Moving around the page

The sample screen in Figure A-4 includes several tabs at the top of the text side of the screen. These tabs indicate that the text you're expected to read covers more than one screen page. Recognizing these tabs and what they represent is important because you need to read the additional material before you answer the question.

The second thing to note in Figure A-4 is a scroll bar on the right edge. It's the bar that runs up and down the right-hand side, with an arrow on either end and a darker section somewhere along its length. That bar tells you that you need to scroll up or down for more text (where there isn't enough content to create a new page or tab). To use your mouse to move the scroll bar up and down and make the screen move so you can see the additional text, simply click on the top or bottom of the bar. Alternatively, you can drag the light portion of the bar up or down for the same effect or use the scroll wheel on your mouse. When you're finished with the item, click on the Previous or Next buttons on the bottom right of the screen to go to a new or previous question.

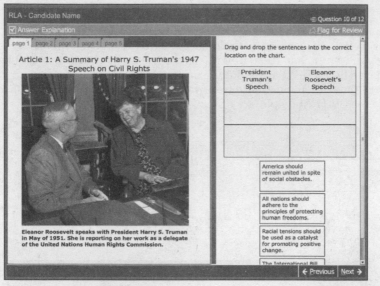

**Figure A-4:**
The tabs at the top left of the screen tell you that there's more text to read.

© 2014 GED Testing Service LLC

## Editing your text

Another important skill to be comfortable with using on the computer is the cut-and-paste or copy-and-paste functions. Cutting or copying and pasting means you can move some text to another position on your page by highlighting it with your mouse. *Cutting* means deleting it from the original position, while *copying* means exactly that: You leave the text in its original location as well as insert a copy into a new location. That can come in handy when you're writing an Extended Response on the GED test.

To cut or copy and paste, move the cursor to the beginning of the text you want, click on it with the left mouse button, and then continue holding down the button as you drag the mouse across the text to highlight the entire portion you want to copy or cut. Then click on the highlighted text with the right mouse button and select *cut,* which means delete, or *copy.* Holding the right mouse button down, you can move the text in its entirety to a new position. When the text is where you want it, simply release the mouse button. For you expert word processors, you can also use the customary keyboard shortcuts. You highlight the text you want, and then use the keyboard to activate the function: press Ctrl + C for copy, Ctrl + X to cut, or move the cursor to a new location and press Ctrl + V to paste.

You also need to be familiar with the concept of *do* and *undo* while you're writing and editing text. If you've used a word processor before, you know that those two little curved arrows at the top of the screen allow you to reverse an action. Those arrows are the Do and Undo buttons. You have the option to use these buttons on the Extended Response sections and on the Short Answer items of the test.

## Using the calculator

Even though you're not allowed to bring a calculator with you to the GED test, when you need to use a calculator, a digital image of a calculator appears on-screen. You interact with this calculator the same way you would with one in your hand. The only difference is that you push the buttons with the mouse by moving the cursor over the appropriate buttons and then clicking. If you're unsure how to use that calculator, the test offers a cheat sheet with instructions. However, to save yourself precious time while taking the exam, try to get some practice beforehand; the test uses a Texas Instrument 30XS calculator (see Figure A-5). You can try out the calculator or at least see a video on how it works at www.gedtestingservice.com/ged_calc_en_web. If you can afford it, you can buy the real thing for less than $30.

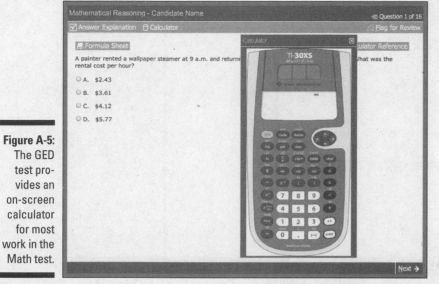

**Figure A-5:**
The GED test provides an on-screen calculator for most work in the Math test.

# Finding math formulas and symbols

In the Mathematical Reasoning and Science tests, you use formulas, and some questions require special symbols or signs. Don't worry — you don't need to memorize pages of formulas; the computerized GED test provides all the formulas you need in a handy, easy-to-access drop-down window (see Figure A-6).

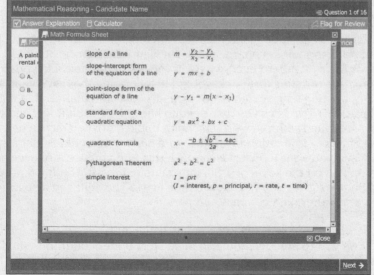

**Figure A-6:**
Clicking on the Formulas icon makes them appear.

You can also find the special symbols that aren't shown on your keyboard in a drop-down window by clicking on the Symbol button at the top of the screen, as you can see in Figure A-7, and then clicking on the Insert button. Microsoft Word has a similar drop-down window for special characters that you can use to practice. On the ribbon at the top of the Word screen, click on Insert and then click on the omega ($\Omega$) symbol to open a window with all sorts of letters and symbols. You can insert these symbols into the text just by clicking on them. The symbols drop-down window is similar on the GED test.

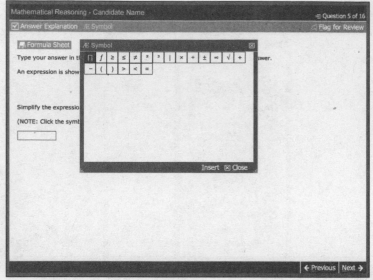

**Figure A-7:**
Click on
Insert to
make the
symbols
appear.

# Practicing Your Typing on a Keyboard

If you're more at home with a tablet or a touch screen or you still remember (or use) your old Selectric typewriter fondly, you'll want to sit down at a computer and practice typing on a keyboard before you take the GED test. You don't need to become a typing master; as long as you can hunt and peck with reasonable speed, you'll be fine. The only time when you need to do more than simply click with the mouse is on the Extended Response and Short Answer items, where you have to write either a short essay or a few paragraphs response.

Not being able to type may slow you down, so you should at least have a familiarity of where individual letters, punctuation, and numbers are located on the keyboard. For an example of a standard computer keyboard, check out Figure A-8. (**Note:** Standard North American keyboards aren't standard everywhere. If you learned to use a keyboard in a different language, practice with this form of keyboard before doing the test. Doing so will help you avoid typos and wasting time searching for symbols and punctuation that may not be in the accustomed location.) Two keys you also need to know are the Shift key and the Enter key. The Enter key, identified with the word *Enter* or a hooked arrow, starts a new paragraph or line of text. The Shift key is identified with the word *Shift* or sometimes just an up arrow. You hold it down when you want to insert a capital letter, and you use it to access the symbols found with numbers on the keyboard. So, for example, pressing Shift + 8 produces the asterisk. Pressing Shift + 1 gives you the exclamation mark. The Shift key also accesses various punctuation marks other than commas and periods.

The GED Testing Service (GED.com) offers an online half-length practice test for a fee (currently $6.00). It allows you to practice doing an online test under conditions similar to what you'll experience when taking the real test. It's worthwhile just to get familiar with the computer format alone. There's also a free quarter-length test, which isn't scored.

**Figure A-8:**
Standard
North
American
keyboard,
like what
you'll see on
the comput-
erized GED
test.

Reading and writing on a computer screen is very different from reading and writing on paper. Studies have shown that people tend not to read as deeply when reading from a screen and aren't able to organize their thoughts as easily when writing on-screen. However, you'll have an erasable tablet to jot down rough notes about key points in the on-screen text before starting your essay and to organize your thoughts before starting to write the actual essay. Practice reading and writing on-screen before you take the GED test, especially if you're not accustomed to working that way. It, too, is a skill that improves with practice.

# Index

# About the Authors

**Murray Shukyn, BA,** is a graduate of the University of Toronto with professional qualifications as a teacher at the elementary and secondary levels, including special education. He has taught at the elementary, secondary, and university levels and developed training programs for adult learners in the coffee and foodservice industries. During his extensive career, spanning more than 30 years, Murray has taught professional development programs for educators and is acknowledged as a Canadian leader in the field of alternative education. He was instrumental in the creation of such innovative programs for the Toronto Board of Education as SEED, Learnxs, Subway Academy, SOLE, and ACE. In 1995, Murray became Associate Director of the Training Renewal Foundation, which introduced the GED in the province of Ontario. As a consultant to government, media, and public relations companies, he has coauthored numerous textbooks and magazine and periodical articles with Achim Krull and coauthored several books to prepare adults to take the GED test with both Achim Krull and Dale Shuttleworth.

**Dale E. Shuttleworth's, PhD,** professional career as a community educator has included experience as a teacher, school-community worker, consultant, principal, coordinator, school superintendent, university course director, and executive director. He has been influential in policy development provincially, nationally, and internationally. Dale has been a speaker and resource leader throughout Canada and the United States and in Europe, Africa, and Asia. He has served as an expert/consultant to the Organization for Economic Cooperation and Development (OCED) in Paris. Dale is the author of more than 120 articles in books, journals, and periodicals. His publications include *Enterprise Learning in Action* (Routledge), *How to Prepare for the GED* (Barron's), *School Management in Transition* (Routledge), *The GED For Dummies* (Wiley), *Schooling for Life* (University of Toronto Press), *Playing Fast & Loose* (Campaign for Public Education), and *CliffsNotes GED Cram Plan* (Wiley).

**Achim K. Krull, BA, MAT,** is a graduate of the University of Toronto, with specialist qualifications in history and geography. He has taught at both the high-school and adult education level. Achim worked for many years in the academic alternative schools of the Toronto District School Board, as administrator/curriculum leader of Subway Academy One and cofounder of SOLE. He has written textbooks, teachers' guides, and a large variety of other learning materials with Murray Shukyn, including scripts for educational DVDs, as well as newspaper and magazine articles. Achim designed and currently teaches an academic upgrading program for young adults wanting to enter apprenticeships.

***Publisher's Acknowledgments***

**Acquisitions Editor:** Erin Calligan Mooney

**Senior Project Editor:** Alissa Schwipps

**Copy Editor:** Jennette ElNaggar

**Technical Editor:** Sonia Chaumette

**Art Coordinator:** Alicia B. South

**Project Coordinator:** Sheree Montgomery

**Cover Image:** ©iStock.com/jhuting

## Apple & Mac

iPad For Dummies, 6th Edition
978-1-118-72306-7

iPhone For Dummies, 7th Edition
978-1-118-69083-3

Macs All-in-One For Dummies,
4th Edition
978-1-118-82210-4

OS X Mavericks For Dummies
978-1-118-69188-5

## Blogging & Social Media

Facebook For Dummies, 5th Edition
978-1-118-63312-0

Social Media Engagement For Dummies
978-1-118-53019-1

WordPress For Dummies, 6th Edition
978-1-118-79161-5

## Business

Stock Investing For Dummies,
4th Edition
978-1-118-37678-2

Investing For Dummies, 6th Edition
978-0-470-90545-6

Personal Finance For Dummies,
7th Edition
978-1-118-11785-9

QuickBooks 2014 For Dummies
978-1-118-72005-9

Small Business Marketing Kit
For Dummies, 3rd Edition
978-1-118-31183-7

## Careers

Job Interviews For Dummies, 4th Edition
978-1-118-11290-8

Job Searching with Social Media
For Dummies, 2nd Edition
978-1-118-67856-5

Personal Branding For Dummies
978-1-118-11792-7

Resumes For Dummies, 6th Edition
978-0-470-87361-8

Starting an Etsy Business For Dummies,
2nd Edition
978-1-118-59024-9

## Diet & Nutrition

Belly Fat Diet For Dummies
978-1-118-34585-6

Mediterranean Diet For Dummies
978-1-118-71525-3

Nutrition For Dummies, 5th Edition
978-0-470-93231-5

## Digital Photography

Digital SLR Photography All-in-One
For Dummies, 2nd Edition
978-1-118-59082-9

Digital SLR Video & Filmmaking
For Dummies
978-1-118-36598-4

Photoshop Elements 12 For Dummies
978-1-118-72714-0

## Gardening

Herb Gardening For Dummies,
2nd Edition
978-0-470-61778-6

Gardening with Free-Range Chickens
For Dummies
978-1-118-54754-0

## Health

Boosting Your Immunity For Dummies
978-1-118-40200-9

Diabetes For Dummies, 4th Edition
978-1-118-29447-5

Living Paleo For Dummies
978-1-118-29405-5

## Big Data

Big Data For Dummies
978-1-118-50422-2

Data Visualization For Dummies
978-1-118-50289-1

Hadoop For Dummies
978-1-118-60755-8

## Language & Foreign Language

500 Spanish Verbs For Dummies
978-1-118-02382-2

English Grammar For Dummies,
2nd Edition
978-0-470-54664-2

French All-in-One For Dummies
978-1-118-22815-9

German Essentials For Dummies
978-1-118-18422-6

Italian For Dummies, 2nd Edition
978-1-118-00465-4

## Math & Science

Algebra I For Dummies, 2nd Edition
978-0-470-55964-2

 **Available in print and e-book formats.**

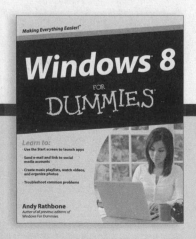

Available wherever books are sold. **For more information or to order direct visit www.dummies.com**

Anatomy and Physiology For Dummies, 2nd Edition
978-0-470-92326-9

Astronomy For Dummies, 3rd Edition
978-1-118-37697-3

Biology For Dummies, 2nd Edition
978-0-470-59875-7

Chemistry For Dummies, 2nd Edition
978-1-118-00730-3

1001 Algebra II Practice Problems
For Dummies
978-1-118-44662-1

## Microsoft Office

Excel 2013 For Dummies
978-1-118-51012-4

Office 2013 All-in-One For Dummies
978-1-118-51636-2

PowerPoint 2013 For Dummies
978-1-118-50253-2

Word 2013 For Dummies
978-1-118-49123-2

## Music

Blues Harmonica For Dummies
978-1-118-25269-7

Guitar For Dummies, 3rd Edition
978-1-118-11554-1

iPod & iTunes For Dummies, 10th Edition
978-1-118-50864-0

## Programming

Beginning Programming with C
For Dummies
978-1-118-73763-7

Excel VBA Programming For Dummies,
3rd Edition
978-1-118-49037-2

Java For Dummies, 6th Edition
978-1-118-40780-6

## Religion & Inspiration

The Bible For Dummies
978-0-7645-5296-0

Buddhism For Dummies, 2nd Edition
978-1-118-02379-2

Catholicism For Dummies, 2nd Edition
978-1-118-07778-8

## Self-Help & Relationships

Beating Sugar Addiction For Dummies
978-1-118-54645-1

Meditation For Dummies, 3rd Edition
978-1-118-29144-3

## Seniors

Laptops For Seniors For Dummies,
3rd Edition
978-1-118-71105-7

Computers For Seniors For Dummies,
3rd Edition
978-1-118-11553-4

iPad For Seniors For Dummies,
6th Edition
978-1-118-72826-0

Social Security For Dummies
978-1-118-20573-0

## Smartphones & Tablets

Android Phones For Dummies,
2nd Edition
978-1-118-72030-1

Nexus Tablets For Dummies
978-1-118-77243-0

Samsung Galaxy S 4 For Dummies
978-1-118-64222-1

Samsung Galaxy Tabs For Dummies
978-1-118-77294-2

## Test Prep

ACT For Dummies, 5th Edition
978-1-118-01259-8

ASVAB For Dummies, 3rd Edition
978-0-470-63760-9

GRE For Dummies, 7th Edition
978-0-470-88921-3

Officer Candidate Tests For Dummies
978-0-470-59876-4

Physician's Assistant Exam For Dummies
978-1-118-11556-5

Series 7 Exam For Dummies
978-0-470-09932-2

## Windows 8

Windows 8.1 All-in-One For Dummies
978-1-118-82087-2

Windows 8.1 For Dummies
978-1-118-82121-3

Windows 8.1 For Dummies, Book + DVD
Bundle
978-1-118-82107-7

**Available in print and e-book formats.**

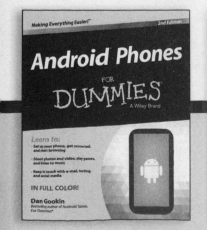

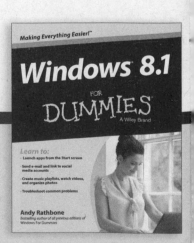

Available wherever books are sold. **For more information or to order direct visit www.dummies.com**